14.97
1900
N566j

D0786851

JOSEPH E. JOHNSTON AND THE DEFENSE OF RICHMOND

MODERN WAR STUDIES

Theodore A. Wilson
General Editor

Raymond A. Callahan
J. Garry Clifford
Jacob W. Kipp
Jay Luvaas
Allan R. Millett
Dennis Showalter
Series Editors

973.732
J72J
N566j

JOSEPH E. JOHNSTON AND THE DEFENSE OF RICHMOND

STEVEN H. NEWTON

UNIVERSITY PRESS OF KANSAS

**Christian Heritage
College Library**
2100 Greenfield Dr.
El Cajon, CA 92019

79990

© 1998 by the University Press of Kansas
All rights reserved

Published by the University Press of Kansas (Lawrence, Kansas 66049), which was organized by the Kansas Board of Regents and is operated and funded by Emporia State University, Fort Hays State University, Kansas State University, Pittsburg State University, the University of Kansas, and Wichita State University

Library of Congress Cataloging-in-Publication Data

Newton, Steven H.
    Joseph E. Johnston and the defense of Richmond / Stephen H. Newton.
        p.   cm. — (Modern war studies)
    Includes bibliographical references and index.
    ISBN 0-7006-0921-0 (alk. paper)
    1. Johnston, Joseph E. (Joseph Eggleston), 1807–1891—Military leadership.   2. Peninsular Campaign, 1862.   3. Generals—Confederate States of America—Biography.   4. Confederate States of America. Army—Biography.   I. Title.   II. Series.
    E467.1.J74N49   1998
    973.7'32—dc21   98-20557
                                                                        CIP

British Library Cataloguing in Publication Data is available.

Printed in the United States of America

10 9 8 7 6 5 4 3 2 1

The paper used in this publication meets the minimum requirements of the American National Standard for Permanence of Paper for Printed Library Materials Z39.48-1984.

To Faith,
without whom this would never have happened

CONTENTS

PREFACE

One of the most curious gaps in Confederate historiography is the lack of a detailed modern study of the Department of Northern Virginia under the leadership of Gen. Joseph E. Johnston. Certainly the earlier stages of the Peninsula campaign did not lack drama: Johnston's repeated confrontations with Jefferson Davis and Robert E. Lee, the sorties of the ironclad *Virginia,* the siege of Yorktown, the rearguard action at Williamsburg, the Valley sideshow, and the final confused fight at Seven Pines contain all the elements necessary for an interesting narrative. Nor did these operations lack significance. Had the Confederates lost Richmond in early summer 1862, that defeat, combined with the Federal capture of Memphis, Nashville, New Orleans, and Norfolk, probably would have ended the war and elevated George B. McClellan to the status of savior of the Union. Instead, following Johnston's wounding at Seven Pines, Lee took over the Army of Northern Virginia and drove the Yankees away from Richmond in short order, not only saving the capital for the moment but also beginning a period of Confederate resurgence in Virginia that kept the Union army at bay for nearly three years.

Only two book-length treatments written from a Confederate perspective have covered the Peninsula campaign: volume one of Douglas Southall Freeman's *Lee's Lieutenants* and Clifford Dowdey's *Seven Days: The Emergence of Lee*. Robert G. Tanner's *Stonewall in the Valley* (recently reissued in a revised edition) covers the Valley campaign and its relationship to events on the Peninsula. Craig Symonds gives substantial coverage to these operations in his biography of Johnston, and William J. Miller has edited the first three volumes of articles on the campaign, which are shedding some much needed light in a dark place. My own *Battle of Seven Pines* has dealt with the culminating battle of Johnston's tenure in some although admittedly not exhaustive detail, and Steven E. Woodworth's *Davis and Lee at War* attempts to place the campaign in the larger context of the war in Virginia. This is a surprisingly thin bookshelf for such a critical campaign.

To make matters worse, the three longest treatments are marred by serious flaws. Though Tanner deserves considerable praise for unearthing new material on the Shenandoah Valley, he has based his whole presentation of Johnston's and Lee's relationships with Thomas J. "Stonewall" Jackson on the interpretation originated by Freeman and extended by Dowdey. As a result, even in his revised edition he has failed to examine their basic assumptions, many of which upon close analysis turn out to be at best on shaky ground and at worst totally unfounded.

Dowdey's work has always been questionable in terms of evidentiary foundation, for although he wrote well he eschewed footnotes. Quite often the text made his sources apparent, but there were many occasions when Dowdey's strongest contentions (or in Johnston's case accusations) were erected entirely upon assertion rather than on documentation. This rather cavalier approach to scholarship was combined with outright hero-worship of Lee, whom Dowdey continually elevated through the literary device of contrasting his virtues with Johnston's supposed shortcomings. The theme of Dowdey's book can be summarized in a single sentence: Johnston's generalship was so inept that only the caution of McClellan, the Machiavellian maneuvers of Lee behind the scenes, and the fact that Johnston was wounded too badly to resume command of the army after Seven Pines allowed the Confederates to avoid the loss of Richmond.

Dowdey derived much of his interpretation from Freeman, though he extended it to the point of caricature. Freeman, though consistently more judicious and measured in his evaluations, also viewed Johnston through the prism of Lee. In *R. E. Lee* he made a point of trying to prove just how lax Johnston's administration of the army had been before Seven Pines, and he repeated the performance at greater length in *Lee's Lieutenants*. With prose more subtle and analysis much more penetrating than Dowdey's, Freeman nonetheless pursued the idea that the proper study of the Army of Northern Virginia always begins and ends with Robert E. Lee. Johnston, to Freeman, was a gallant man and a good soldier but only an adequate general at best. As Lee stepped on the stage as commander of the army in either of Freeman's works, the reader can almost feel the author's relief: the prologue is over, time for the main act.

Therein lies the problem. As long as the campaign leading up to Seven Pines is considered as merely a prologue and not as a separate entity, Johnston's operations remain hopelessly obscured in the long, deep shadow of Lee. The only way, I have come to believe, to understand the Confederate army in Virginia before Lee assumed command of the Army of Northern Virginia is to limit the scope of the inquiry to the tenure of Johnston's command. Thus this narrative, which commences after a short chapter to introduce Joseph

Johnston, begins with President Davis's mid-February summons of Johnston to Richmond to discuss withdrawing his army from the Potomac line and ends when the general topples from his horse on the evening of May 31, 1862. It is an unorthodox treatment for a military history, for none of the battles is decisive, more attention is paid to conferences in Richmond than to any single combat action, and when the book ends McClellan is still only a few miles outside Richmond. The fate of the city is still very much in doubt.

Yet focusing on the period between mid-February and late May allows time to deal with several key issues in far greater detail than did Freeman, Dowdey, or even Symonds. The conference in Richmond that decided that the army would pull back to the Rappahannock received a line from Dowdey, a page from Symonds, and two pages from Freeman; here it merits a chapter to explain it completely. The question of Johnston's administrative competence—often raised by his enemies and given great play by historians—is thoroughly investigated, as are his own strategic views, which turn out to have been much more complex and comprehensive than heretofore believed. I also take pains to relate the war in Virginia to operations in the western Confederacy. How did the fall of Fort Donelson lead not only to Shiloh but also to the withdrawal from the Potomac? How did P. G. T. Beauregard's defeat at Shiloh affect Davis's state of mind in the April 14, 1862, conference to determine whether or not Yorktown should be held? If one restricts the focus to Johnston's own portion of the Peninsula campaign, these issues and others can be addressed in depth.

It will become quickly obvious that the tenor of this work is pro-Johnston in terms of my assessment of the general's handling of his army. At one time such a position would hardly be considered controversial, but recent scholarship has been, if anything, less kind to the diminutive Virginian than were Freeman and Dowdey. A new generation of historians, with Richard M. McMurry in the vanguard, has so thoroughly assaulted his reputation with regard to Vicksburg and Atlanta that McMurry has proclaimed that "Johnston's reputation has all but collapsed." But as I have argued in other venues, the Johnston of 1861–1862 is not the Johnston of 1863–1864, and the general deserves an analysis of his campaign in Virginia on the basis of the facts underlying his defense of Richmond, not as a blind for arguments about Atlanta.*

*Richard M. McMurry, "A Policy So Disastrous: Gen. Joseph E. Johnston's Atlanta Campaign," in *The Campaign for Atlanta and Sherman's March to the Sea*, ed. Theodore P. Savas and David A. Woodbury, 2 vols. (Campbell, CA: Savas Woodbury, 1994): 2: 243; see also Richard M. McMurry, "'The Enemy at Richmond': Joseph E. Johnston and the Confederate Government," *Civil War History* 28 (March 1981): 5–31, and Steven H. Newton, "Johnston and Davis at Seven Pines: The Uncertainty Principle in Action," in *Campaign Chronicles, The Peninsula Campaign*, ed. William J. Miller, 3 vols. (Campbell, CA: Savas, 1997), 60–78.

What emerges is the portrait of a general who was much more complex in thought and action than even his advocates have tended to argue. One of the greatest difficulties in fairly assessing Joseph Johnston has been the haphazard manner in which his papers were preserved, compounded by his terse, often rigidly correct style of writing. The selection of his correspondence preserved in the *Official Records,* which has been too easily accepted as being nearly complete, turns out on closer examination to be fragmentary and grossly incomplete. Many of Johnston's letters written while on the Peninsula, for example, did not make it to publication, and when they are considered, the image of the general as refusing to communicate with his superiors requires substantial revision. Other letters and key meetings have been consistently dated incorrectly, or in some cases transcribed with major errors. Though Joseph Johnston could by no means have ever been characterized as developing the same sort of working relationship with his superiors in Richmond as did Robert E. Lee months later, the traditional picture of his being in diametric opposition to Jefferson Davis and company cannot accurately be pushed back into Virginia in 1862. Instead, I argue that Johnston and Davis were struggling dauntlessly to work in harness together, despite occasional misunderstandings.

None of the foregoing is to suggest that Johnston conducted a perfect campaign. By the end of the battle of Seven Pines it becomes evident to the historian (if not to his contemporaries) that Johnston lacked a firm tactical touch on the battlefield despite his skills in strategy, administration, and preparing an army for battle. On the other hand, Johnston's overall conduct of the campaign holds up quite well under scrutiny, and this evaluation is not based on what he *might* have done, as is so often the case of Vicksburg or Atlanta, but on the grounds of what he *did* accomplish. No recourse to special pleading is necessary to reach this conclusion, just an open mind and the willingness to look at new evidence.

ACKNOWLEDGMENTS

Among the many scholars who have taken the time to read (and often disagree with) this book in one of its many forms, and without whose perceptive comments and willingness to listen to a different interpretation it would never have reached publication, are Lesley J. Gordon, Ludwell H. Johnson II, Richard M. McMurry, Robert K. Krick, Craig L. Symonds, and Steven E. Woodworth. Many things with which they still disagree remain in these pages, but I hope that my arguments have been better honed because of their thorough reading and cogent comments. It is a tribute to the open nature of Civil War scholarship that I can find people of this caliber willing to help me attempt a revision of their own interpretations.

For his enthusiasm and gentle prodding to get on with it and get it published, I thank William J. Miller, editor of *Civil War*.

This book would not have been possible, at least not this year, without the support of my colleagues and the administration of Delaware State University, specifically William H. Flayhart, chair of the department of history and political science, and Johnny Tolliver, dean of the college of arts and sciences, who moved mountains to get me the sabbatical necessary to complete the final revisions.

Everyone at the University Press of Kansas has been exceptionally cooperative and supportive throughout the publication process, beginning with Editor-in-Chief Michael Briggs and extending through the entire organization. I have a special place in my heart for Claire Sutton, my freelance copy editor at UPK, whose meticulous work has much improved the clarity and accuracy of the manuscript and whose notes along the edges kept me smiling as I revised the next footnote.

Intangible debts are sometimes the deepest. Without my children, Marie, Alexis, and Michael, running rampant through the house for inspiration, or lacking the gentle (and sometimes not-so-gentle) prodding of my wife, Faith, this book would have arrived several years later and much poorer in spirit.

Joseph E. Johnston

1
THE GENERAL

The chance musket shot and the ricocheting shell fragment that wounded Gen. Joseph Eggleston Johnston in the early evening of May 31, 1862, effectively ended the Battle of Seven Pines. While worried aides dragged their commander to safety, the fighting that had raged between Richmond and the Chickahominy River for several hours degenerated into sporadic sniping. Rebels and Yankees alike collapsed in exhaustion. The conflict resumed in a desultory fashion the next morning, but neither the Confederate divisions defending the capital nor Maj. Gen. George B. McClellan's Army of the Potomac could muster the energy to strike a decisive blow. Each army had suffered about 5,000 casualties in a bloody stalemate. Later, the battle appeared significant chiefly because Robert E. Lee was appointed as Johnston's successor as a result of his wound.

Joseph Johnston always believed that his troops had been on the verge of victory when those unlucky shots knocked him from his horse. His attack had caught two corps of McClellan's army isolated from the main body by the rain-swollen Chickahominy. His right wing, under Maj. Gen. James Longstreet, had driven the enemy in disarray from three successive lines. The left, commanded by Maj. Gen. Gustavus W. Smith, was advancing under Johnston's eye to deliver the coup de grâce. "*Darkness only,*" Johnston insisted, prevented the complete defeat of the Federals that night. And on the following morning, he blamed the inaction of Smith, temporarily in command, for saving several Union divisions from destruction. Such an accomplishment would have silenced those critics who had begun to whisper that Johnston's only skill as a general lay in his ability to retreat. For the rest of his life, Johnston remained convinced that it had been his wounds that had prevented him from conclusively vindicating the strategy by which he had conducted the defense of Richmond.[1]

In retrospect, Johnston's tactical assessment was far from accurate. Unknown to him, by the time he was struck the entire senior command structure of his army had ceased to function. Smith had collapsed from a nervous ailment, leaving his deputy, Brig. Gen. W. H. C. Whiting, struggling to co-ordinate the movements of five disorganized brigades on a battlefield where undergrowth often limited vision to less than ten paces. On the right wing, Longstreet's failure to deploy along the correct road and a quarrel over senior-ity with Maj. Gen. Benjamin Huger had immobilized the majority of his troops all day. Those who did engage fought under Maj. Gen. D. H. Hill, the junior division commander involved in the attack. By dusk Hill's men had fought themselves out, and their general had become thoroughly disgusted with superiors who seemed content to sacrifice his soldiers while they bick-ered. Though Johnston's plan of attack had been sound enough, botched exe-cution produced a fiasco that resulted in a drawn battle only because conditions on McClellan's side of the line were equally confused.[2]

Later, Johnston's detractors argued that a mismanaged battle was the ap-propriate punctuation to conclude a mismanaged campaign. Since March his only major movements had been a pair of retreats that exposed all of Virginia north of the Rappahannock River and east of Richmond to the enemy. Fred-ericksburg, Yorktown, and Norfolk had fallen into Federal hands as the Army of the Potomac marched within five miles of Richmond. His most severe crit-ics suggested that the general had originally intended to surrender the Con-federate capital without a fight. These conclusions have been shared and so often reiterated by the majority of Civil War historians that they have gained nearly universal acceptance.[3]

Such an appraisal is grossly unfair to Johnston. It ignores the fact that one of his retreats was ordered by Jefferson Davis and that the other became nec-essary because Johnston was directed to place himself in a strategic cul de sac at Yorktown. Nor did Johnston exercise undisputed control over his own de-partment throughout most of the campaign. For long periods Gen. Robert E. Lee, commanding in Richmond, directed the operations of four of his eight divisions, usually without Johnston's knowledge, always without his consent, and often in a pattern completely at odds with Johnston's intentions. Between March and June 1862, Johnston spent almost as much time reacting to the actions of his superiors as he did to those of his opponent.

Nonetheless, Johnston's campaign in defense of Richmond must be rated as a strategic victory for the Confederacy. Primarily, it kept his army in being. Given the odds with which he had to contend, this was no mean feat. His withdrawal from Yorktown successfully extricated the Confederacy's major eastern field army from a carefully crafted double envelopment. Opposed by any commander less skillful than Johnston, McClellan might well have cap-tured the entire force. The Virginian's accomplishment stands out as even more remarkable, given the convulsions that racked the army as a result of the first conscription act; Johnston held his army together as a coherent fighting force despite the demoralizing and potentially destructive regimental elections. His operations also bought time, a commodity infinitely more valuable to the Confederacy than the territory for which he traded it. In the months Johnston delayed McClellan's advance, the arms production centers he defended stamped out thousands of new rifles and cast hundreds of cannon. Additional ordnance filtered into Southern ports through the Federal blockade. At the same time, a combination of Johnston's administrative efficiency, Lee's juggling of garrisons along the Atlantic Coast, and Rebel operations in the Shenandoah Valley and central Virginia allowed the South to neutralize the overwhelming numerical superiority with which McClellan had opened his campaign. Three weeks after Johnston fell, Lee opened the Battle of Mechanicsville with the largest Confederate army ever sent into combat and met McClellan with virtual parity of force. Johnston's defense of Richmond was the first and most critical Confederate success of 1862.[4]

Certainly no one had expected anything less than success from Joseph Johnston when the war began. Resigning his commission as brigadier general and quartermaster general of the U.S. Army after Virginia's secession in April 1861, the fifty-four-year-old Virginian seemed inevitably bound for glory. His military career had already spanned more than three decades, including command or staff service in every branch of the army. Nine wounds and four brevet promotions for gallantry attested to his coolness under fire. He was one of the most widely read soldiers in the army, an acknowledged scholar and expert in military history. Winfield Scott, the greatest American soldier between the Revolutionary and Civil Wars, had been his mentor. His closest contemporaries—at once both friends and rivals—were Albert Sidney Johnston and Robert E. Lee. "Johnston," concludes Jay Luvaas, "was one of the best prepared professional soldiers to enter Confederate service."[5]

Not a large man—"rather below middle height" according to British colonel Arthur Fremantle—Johnston stood about five-feet-eight-inches and weighed less than 140 pounds. Yet there was something in the way he moved that made him seem taller. A reporter for the *Southern Literary Messenger* overestimated his height by two inches and added that "he looks taller on account of his erect carriage." There was a quality about him that demanded attention but that also defied definition. It was more than the piercing gray eyes, the long straight nose, or the grizzled—though neatly trimmed—side-whiskers, mustache, and goatee. This was a quality that exceeded the sum of his individual parts: a sense of presence.[6]

He simply looked like a soldier. "Soldier-like," recorded Fremantle. "Every inch a soldier," said Henry Kyd Douglas. "The *beau ideal* of a soldier," recalled Richard Taylor. Benjamin S. Ewell, who served under the general for three years and knew him as well as any, told a group of veterans that Johnston "had more the appearance of a soldier than anyone I ever met in the Confederate, or subsequently in the Union Army."[7] Some of this martial quality still emanates from wartime photographs of Johnston. In them he is always posed in a position of not-quite-rigid attention, viewing the camera inquisitively, even suspiciously, as if it were a courier entering his headquarters in the middle of a battle, bearing what might be unpleasant news.

His personality ranged from bursts of spontaneous affection to guarded reserve. Major Robert Stiles remembered that he liked to greet close friends with a hug and a kiss. "He loved good cheer," recalled staff officer Archer Anderson, "he enjoyed a glass of wine, and his conversation at a dinner-table with congenial companions was often fascinating and memorable." Yet there was the colder side to Johnston's character; Bradley T. Johnson admitted him to be "quick-tempered and imperious." "Genial and confiding as he was to the friends he knew and trusted, he was reticent and ever aversive to those whom he did not like," observed Dabney Maury. Maury also remembered that Johnston "was quick to resent any freedom or liberty from those he did not like or know." "To me he was extremely affable," confided Fremantle to his diary, "but he certainly possesses the power of keeping people at a distance when he chooses."[8]

Fremantle also noted that Johnston's "officers stand in great awe of him. . . . Many of the officers told me that they did not consider him inferior as a general to Lee or anyone else." A considerable number of officers who served under both Johnston and Lee held the opinion that "Old Joe" was, at the very least, the equal of "Marse Robert." James Longstreet eulogized Johnston as "skilled in the art and science of war, [and] gifted in his quick, penetrating mind." After the war, Longstreet characterized Johnston rather than Lee as "the most accomplished and capable" of Confederate generals. He was praised by Richard Taylor for "great coolness, tact, and judgment," and Wade Hampton regarded him as a commander "in whose skill and generalship I have always entertained implicit confidence." Junior officers were even more effusive in their praise of Johnston. Though he entitled his memoirs *Four Years Under Marse Robert*, Robert Stiles opined of Johnston that "as a trained, professional soldier, I do not believe he had his superior, if indeed his equal, on this continent." Likewise, Henry Kyd Douglas concluded that "for clear military judgment and capacity to comprehend and take advantage of what is loosely termed 'the situation,' General Johnston was not surpassed by any general in either army."[9]

During summer 1861, Johnston seemed poised to fulfill the promise of his early career. In late July he slipped away from the Federals assigned to pin him in the Shenandoah Valley and rushed his small army to reinforce Brig. Gen. P. G. T. Beauregard at Manassas. Neither he nor anyone else had reason to suspect that July 21, 1861, represented the pinnacle of his career, the last moment in the war in which his reputation would be unstained by controversy or recriminations. At the time only the victorious general, the assured soldier, was visible. With a perspective that the participants lacked on that hot, dusty afternoon, Stephen Vincent Benet wrote wistfully of Johnston, "I'd like to have seen him that day."[10]

Superficially, Johnston's fortune continued in an upward spiral. He remained at Manassas after the battle and, ranking Beauregard, took permanent command of their combined armies. During October the War Department expanded his authority over what was styled the Department of Northern Virginia, extending his control over all Confederate forces in northwestern Virginia, the lower Shenandoah Valley, around Fredericksburg, and down the south bank of the Rappahannock to Urbana. When 1862 arrived, Johnston commanded the largest, best-equipped Confederate army in the entire South.[11]

Below the surface, all was not well. In August Johnston was stung by newspaper assertions that Beauregard, not he, had been primarily responsible for winning the Battle of Manassas. Questions arose about the army's failure to follow up the victory with an invasion across the Potomac. Ludicrous as the idea appeared to anyone privy to the actual strength of the army or the woeful inadequacy of its supplies, it nonetheless circulated quite freely throughout the Confederacy. Johnston could not respond to insinuations of inactivity without revealing his weakness and therefore had to suffer suspicions about his lack of offensive intentions in silence.[12]

In September he quarreled with President Davis over his rank. Historians have often cited this dispute as the main factor contributing to later discord between Johnston and Davis. The incident, asserts Douglas Southall Freeman, "aroused in Johnston a resentment that colored his views throughout the war." An examination of the evidence, however, suggests that the disagreement over rank may not have been the primary cause of the general and the president becoming, in the words of another biographer, "perfectly and entirely estranged and separated."[13]

The squabble began with Johnston's misreading of Confederate military law. On August 31 President Davis had submitted his list of nominations to the rank of general to Congress, which immediately confirmed them. The dates of the commissions were: Samuel Cooper, May 16, 1861; Albert Sidney Johnston, May 28, 1861; Robert E. Lee, June 14, 1861; Joseph E. Johnston, July 4, 1861; and P. G. T. Beauregard, July 21, 1861. Johnston read the list with "surprise and mortification" about two weeks later. His understanding of the appropriate statutes had led him to believe that he would rank first instead of fourth. Since he could not conceive of Davis, a former secretary of war, U.S. senator, and the preeminent constitutional lawyer alive, misreading the law, he presumed that his reduction was an intentional slight. He had to complain, "lest my silence be significant of acquiescence."[14]

In such temper when he sat down to write his letter, Johnston thought that events called for strong language. He baldly stated his belief that "this is a blow aimed at me alone," which resulted in "the benefit of persons neither of whom has yet struck a blow for the Confederacy." Contrary to what he later asserted, Johnston consulted with his brother Beverly on the phrasing of the letter and deleted 350 words so heated that, even when infuriated, he realized that he could not send to the president.[15] Stripped of invective, Johnston's argument seemed logical. Five brigadier generals had been created by Congress in the acts of March 6 and March 14, 1861. Section Five of the second act provided

> that in all cases of officers who have resigned, or who may within six months tender their resignations from the Army of the United States, and who may be appointed to original vacancies in the Army of the Confederate States, the commissions issued shall bear one and the same date, so that the relative rank of officers of each grade shall be determined by their former commissions in the U.S. Army, held anterior to the secession of these Confederate States from the United States.[16]

An amendatory act on May 16 allowed for the conversion of the title of "brigadier general" to "general," a change that Johnston contended could not affect the relative seniority of the officeholders. The determination of seniority would then be according to the precedence of the prewar commissions. "The order of rank established by *law*," as Johnston saw it, "was—first, J. E. Johnston (brigadier-general U.S.A.); second, S. Cooper (colonel, U.S.A.); third, A. S. Johnston (colonel, U.S.A.); fourth, R. E. Lee (lieutenant-colonel, U.S.A.)."[17]

Johnston correctly assumed that the Confederate Congress guaranteed former officers of the U.S. Army the same relative rank they had enjoyed before the war. What he missed was the fact that the act of March 6, 1861, changed the manner in which that rank was calculated. Section Twenty-nine wiped out any practical use for brevet rank beyond courts-martial and boards of inquiry. It also specified that an officer's seniority for purposes of command would be determined from his highest commission from the corps or arm in which he currently served. This provision accounted quite legally for Johnston's drop in the rankings. Samuel Cooper held a staff colonelcy as the U.S. Army adjutant general. He was assigned the same post in the Confederacy—with a specific prohibition against ever commanding troops—so his staff commission counted toward his seniority as a general. Johnston, on the other hand, had been transferred from the Quartermaster's Department and back to the line of the army. By Confederate law he then could claim only his highest *line* commission—lieutenant colonel of cavalry—in figuring seniority relative to Albert Sidney Johnston and Robert E. Lee. In those terms he was junior to both.[18]

Davis was ill when he received Johnston's letter of protest, and he knew that the general was aware of his condition. Had Johnston written more diplomatically, the president might have explained his interpretation of the statutes, no matter how sick he was. But stung by an attack on him in his sickbed, Davis fired back his famous bullet: "I have just received and read your letter of the 12th instant. Its language is, as you say, unusual; its arguments and statements utterly one-sided, and its insinuations as unfounded as they are unbecoming."[19]

There is a pervasive tendency to see this incident as the critical moment in which the Johnston-Davis relationship commenced an inevitable downward spiral, with disastrous consequences for the Confederacy's survival. Joseph Glathaar designates the exchange as having "ended the Davis-Johnston honeymoon." "The spat itself and the harsh tone of their 1861 correspondence," argues Richard McMurry, "combined with each man's hyperactive ego and fragile sense of self to undermine whatever possibility there might have been that the two would cooperate. Never, after mid-Spetember 1861, would either man find it possible to trust or confide in the other." As Craig Symonds puts it: "Davis and Johnston never again corresponded with one another about this issue, nor did they speak of it when they met. But it was always there."[20]

Although it is undeniable that the acrimony of the controversy over rank festered and developed into an unbridgeable rift between Johnston and Davis in the latter years of the war, contemporary evidence suggests that it did not immediately poison their working relationship. Despite the heat of their postal rhetoric, both men acted in such a way as to bury the conflict rather than escalate it. Davis did not retain Johnston's letter in the official files. Johnston neither threatened to resign nor intimated—then, or in the future—that he would not accept orders from any of the generals senior to him. Both men refrained from speaking of the issue to anyone besides their closest friends, and the conflict did not surface publicly until much later.[21] Each man seems only to have written one intemperate letter and then returned to his duties. Admittedly, their correspondence became more formal and less frequent. "My Dear General" and "Your Friend" disappeared from the headings and closings of their letters, but the reduction in the number of letters was not primarily the result of personal disharmony. The heated exchange had coincided closely with the appointment of Judah P. Benjamin as secretary of war. Because he trusted the former Louisiana senator so completely, Davis began delegating the routine details of the War Department to him, and the president's personal correspondence with his generals diminished during fall 1861.[22]

Johnston and Davis kept working together in harness, and only someone privy to their earlier letters would have detected the shift from their previous informality. In November, when Davis needed support for his contention that he had not prevented a pursuit of the defeated Federals after Manassas, Johnston promptly and unequivocally provided it. Johnston wrote flatteringly of Davis's personal popularity in February 1862: "Your presence here now or soon would secure to us thousands of excellent troops." This comment obviously pleased Davis, who replied, "I will visit the Army . . . as soon as other engagements will permit, although I cannot realize your complimentary assurance that great good to the army will result from it." Davis even defended Johnston's actions in March 1862 in a letter to W. M. Brooks of Alabama: "Though General Johnston was offended because of his relative rank, he certainly never thought of resigning."[23]

Publicly, the issue remained buried. No controversial articles appeared in the Richmond newspapers as they did when Davis and Beauregard differed over that general's report of the Battle of Manassas. Surprisingly, the ranks of the senior generals do not even seem to have been common knowledge. In January 1862, the *Richmond Enquirer* reprinted from the *Charleston Courier* what purported to be a definitive list of the relative ranks of Confederate generals. It is significant because it was inaccurate, citing the four top officers in order as Samuel Cooper, Albert Sidney Johnston, Joseph E. Johnston, and Robert E. Lee. No protests of corrections of the list ever ran, which surely would have been the case had the controversy over rank still been boiling. Five months later the same newspaper editorialized positively on the lack of any friction between Johnston and Lee: "With neither of the distinguished Generals, is there any mawkish punctilio about rank."[24] Though relations between the two men were considerably more strained at Seven Pines than this judgment suggested, the article nonetheless indicated that the question of seniority had not become fuel for public debate.

Yet throughout the campaign in defense of Richmond there was a noticeable and increasing tension between Johnston and Davis. If this developing rift was not primarily attributable to Johnston's disaffection over his rank, then what caused it? Johnston became more contentious with the president because he believed that Davis had condoned Secretary Benjamin and the rest of the military bureaucracy in Richmond in meddling with his legitimate prerogatives of command throughout the winter and spring. Davis, at the same time, was receiving reports from the War Department that Johnston could not be depended upon to carry out legitimate administrative directives. The president found the secretary's allegations easy to believe, as he had already experienced considerable personal frustration in unsuccessfully prodding Johnston to reorganize his brigades by states during the fall. Under the tremendous pressure of completely redirecting Confederate strategy in the wake of the Fort Donelson disaster, Davis failed to investigate these contradictory allegations as thoroughly as he should have. Instead, he believed Benjamin's accusations and rebuked Johnston for noncooperation.

Compared to the other decisions that Jefferson Davis faced in February 1862, the president's stance seemed a trivial matter. Yet the rebuke came near the beginning of the critical period in which the fate of Richmond would be decided, at a time when trust between the general and the president was becoming especially important. Unfortunately, it turned out to be a time when trust was increasingly being replaced by suspicion.

2

THE DEPARTMENT
OF NORTHERN VIRGINIA

Centreville, in northern Virginia, is eighty-one miles from Richmond. On February 13, 1862, when Jefferson Davis folded and sealed the letter he had just written to Joseph Johnston, he knew that it would not reach the general for at least two, probably three, and possibly as many as five days. A clerk collected it from his office and bundled it with the daily correspondence of the secretary of war and the adjutant and inspector general, which was also addressed to the Department of Northern Virginia. Sometime later the postman tossed that bundle into his sack and carried it several hundred yards to the Virginia Central Railroad depot on Broad Street. The presence of official mail in the bag would not have speeded his steps; the mail train to Centreville departed only once a day, early in the morning.[1] Besides, the carrier might have reflected, if the president had felt any particular urgency about his message, he could have sent a telegram.

When the train pulled out of Richmond in the morning, often as not two to three hours late and crowded with soldiers returning from furlough or a stay in the hospital, the locomotive struggled to keep up enough steam to maintain a speed of just under ten miles per hour. In 1860 the run would have been faster, but by the second year of the war Virginia railroads were already affected by the lack of spare parts produced in Northern factories. Couplings and bearings had to be used long after they should have been replaced because there were not—and never would be again—enough replacements. The engineers knew this and babied their machines, despite the fuming of generals and politicians.[2]

The route was both slow and circuitous. First, the Virginia Central swung northeast in a shallow arc that eventually curved back west to intersect the Richmond, Fredericksburg, and Potomac at Hanover Junction. The junction stood twelve miles north of the city, but the train meandered more than twice that distance before arriving there.[3] Following a brief stop, the train headed forty miles northwest, more nearly in a straight line, to Gordonsville. There some baggage handler or detailed soldier plucked the mailbag from the train and carried it across the freight ramp serving the Orange and Alexandria. In theory, the train from Richmond should have made a fairly close connection every afternoon with the one traveling north from Charlottesville to Manassas, but that was only theory. Most days the schedule ran so far out of kilter that the mail could sit for nearly twenty-four hours.[4] Once it was tossed aboard a northbound car, however, the process moved more quickly: eight miles to Orange Courthouse, sixteen more to Culpeper, and a further thirty-nine to Manassas Junction, most of it straight and well-graded. Manassas was only about six-and-one-half miles from Centreville.

Those six-and-one-half miles, however, were among the most difficult in the state. Winter storms had turned the roads of northern Virginia into muddy troughs that seemed to have no bottoms. A rider on a strong horse could manage only two miles an hour, and few of the horses hauling supplies—or mail—from the depot to Johnston's headquarters were strong or well fed. Overworked and undernourished, horses and mules simply fell down in the mud and died by the hundreds. Teamsters pushed their carcasses to the side of the road, where they stiffened and rotted, raising "a putrifaction that makes it quite unpleasant to go along there."[5]

Johnston, in an attempt to improve the flow of supplies to his army, had decided in December to extend a railroad spur from Manassas to Centreville. He was able to procure the track from Maj. Gen. Thomas J. "Stonewall" Jackson, who had made off with nearly a dozen miles of Yankee rails in a raid a few months earlier on the Baltimore and Ohio. Tredegar Iron Works in Richmond produced the spikes and nails to tie them together, and local landowners, albeit under duress, provided their slaves to grade the roadbed and lay the track. Johnston found former railroad engineer Stephen W. Presstman serving as a captain in the Seventeenth Virginia and detached him to supervise their labor.[6]

Johnston's railroad had just gone into barebones service when Davis's letter arrived at Manassas Depot. Only one dilapidated locomotive, impressed from the Orange and Alexandria, plied the line. The lack of a turnaround at the end forced the engineer to back cautiously over the bumpy road and the shaky bridge spanning Bull Run in order to make his return trip. No fueling stations existed along the route: if the train ran out of wood, the crew had to get off and cut down the nearest trees. Freight, baggage, soldiers, and official mail were unloaded unceremoniously into a muddy field near Centreville and left there for the army's staff to sort out as best they could.[7]

Eventually, when one aide or another recognized the mail sack among the flotsam, he would have taken it to Maj. Thomas G. Rhett, assistant adjutant general and Johnston's de facto chief of staff. Rhett sorted the mail every day, sifting through hundreds of reports; requests for furlough, appointment, or discharge; recruiting notices; and miscellaneous trivia, searching for official letters directed to his commander. When he was satisfied that he had found them all, he took them the final few feet to the next room: General Johnston's office.

A letter from the president demanded immediate attention. Unfortunately, Davis's February 13 letter does not seem to have survived, and only Johnston's indirect paraphrase years later, combined with the inferences that can be drawn from a telegram and letter he dispatched in response, suggest the content of the letter that set in motion Johnston's campaign to defend Richmond. "I was summoned to Richmond by the President," he recalled, "who wished to confer with me on a subject in which secrecy was so important that he could not venture, he said, to commit it to paper, and the mail."[8]

Despite the leisurely pace of its delivery, the summons must have contained some element of immediacy. At once, Johnston felt compelled to dash off a telegraphic answer, which requested a delay of one or two days while his second-in-command, Maj. Gen. Gustavus W. Smith, recovered from his most recent bout with a chronic nervous ailment. It must also have suggested to the general, despite his later recollection, the subject to be considered. Both men had been concerned for some time with the exposed state of Johnston's army, strung out along the Potomac frontier. The paragraph in Johnston's letter to Davis the same day, concerning the possible withdrawal of his forces deeper into Virginia, appears unmistakably to be the answer to a direct question, a question not contained in any of Davis's earlier letters.[9]

Johnston had good reason to be worried about the vulnerable disposition of his troops. The Department of Northern Virginia controlled the operations of all Confederate forces north of the Rappahannock River and in the Shenandoah Valley. To cover his front with even a thin crust of pickets and detached garrisons required Johnston to disperse his 47,617 effectives in a dangerous manner. Nearly half his strength was deployed in semi-independent columns, most of which were far too divided to march rapidly to reinforce each other in case of an attack. Jackson had 5,394 men in the Valley, isolated by a march of several days from Johnston's main position at Centreville. D. H. Hill held an exposed outpost at Leesburg with just 2,460 soldiers; his correspondence throughout the winter revealed his sensitivity to the possibility of being cut off by a quick Federal thrust across the Potomac. Along the Potomac south of Washington, D.C., W. H. C. Whiting's command of 7,596 protected ten miles of Johnston's exposed right flank from a surprise amphibious landing, but the troops were spread so thin that Whiting also lived in a continual state of anxiety about the security of his position. Likewise, Maj. Gen. Theophilus Holmes's

5,956 troops could maintain only a fragile screen of pickets from Aquia Creek down to Urbana on the Rappahannock. This deployment left Johnston at Centreville with a field army that—even if he counted his reserve artillery, cavalry, and the permanent garrison at Manassas—numbered only 26,211 men.[10]

North of the river, in an arc that paralleled Johnston's line from Harpers Ferry to the Eastern Shore, George McClellan's Army of the Potomac reported 185,420 present for duty—almost four Yankees to each Rebel. Not only numbers but also disparity of equipment favored the Federals; everything Johnston's troops lacked—rifles, cannon, horses, wagons, medicines, or rations—was available in abundance on the other side of the Potomac. A French observer with the Union army commented that "the volunteer is provided with everything, and is supplied so liberally with rations that he daily throws away a part of them," adding dryly that "one may imagine what such an army may cost." Even McClellan's most strident critics accredited him as the master organizer. Journalist and historian William Swinton wrote that "if other generals, the successors of McClellan, were able to achieve more decisive results than he, it was, again, in no small degree, because they had the perfect instrument he had fashioned to work withal."[11]

Despite the immensely greater handicaps under which he labored, neither his contemporaries nor historians have awarded similar accolades to Joseph Johnston. Brigadier General Robert Toombs complained in September 1861 that "I never knew as incompetent [an] executive officer." Secretary of War Judah P. Benjamin regularly accused Johnston of every administrative shortcoming from failure to file reports to neglecting to provide winter quarters for his troops. "Discipline had been lax under Johnston; drunkenness had been frequent; many things were at loose ends," concludes Douglas Southall Freeman, who takes pains to praise Lee, not Johnston, for nearly every positive step toward the organization of the Army of Northern Virginia. Clifford Dowdey has characterized Joseph Johnston as lacking energy and has contended that "while social life at headquarters was genial and relaxed, Johnston was a slovenly administrator and careless about details. He liked to be liked." More recently, Joseph Glathaar has criticized "Johnston's sloppy record-keeping and uninterested administration" of his command.[12]

Johnston's performance as an administrator that winter deserves more credit than he has been allowed. Few, if any, Confederate commanders ever organized an army facing such a disparity of numbers, had to contend with more serious shortages of munitions, or had to deal with such a high degree of bureaucratic interference from Richmond. If Johnston was not always completely successful in his efforts and if he sometimes became less than tactful in his communications, the difficulty of his circumstances must be considered as an extenuating factor.

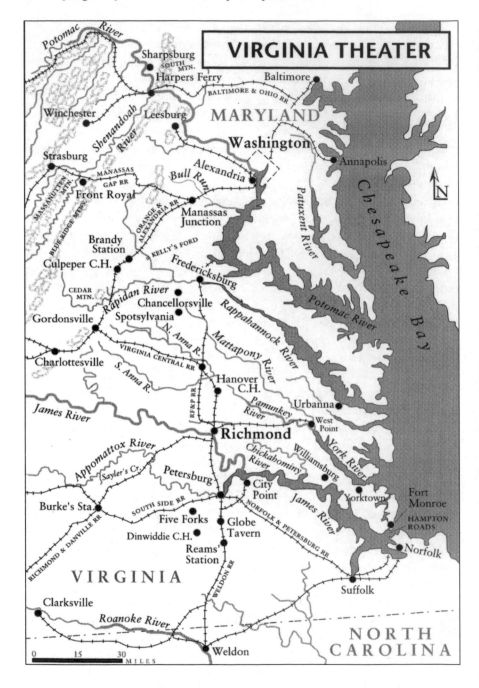

VIRGINIA THEATER

Johnston's soldiers were not merely outnumbered; man for man they were badly outgunned. The scarcity of firearms that plagued the Confederacy in the first year of the war was so severe that the weapons of hospitalized soldiers had to be consolidated to drill recruits in unarmed regiments. Those rifles and muskets actually on hand were a baffling mix of calibers, brands, and qualities. The best of them were issued to the infantry, and much of Brig. Gen. J. E. B. Stuart's cavalry made do with sabers, pistols, and shotguns. The state of the artillery was even more dismal. The fact that the army contained several men who would become the premier cannoneers of the war could not outweigh the scarcity of guns or the insufficiency of powder. Though the precise number is elusive, Johnston's entire department probably did not contain more than 175 pieces of field artillery; McClellan could deploy 465. Many of the cannon Johnston did possess were six-pounder smoothbores, too small to be effective on Civil War battlefields.[13]

The nationwide shortage of gunpowder prevented these batteries from conducting enough live-fire training to ensure their efficiency in combat. When the gunners did get to practice, the results were often demoralizing. In order to stretch its meager supply of powder, the Ordnance Department mixed in a proportion of less potent blasting powder. Brigadier General Samuel French, commanding the Confederate artillery blockading the lower Potomac, remembered that his ammunition "was very indifferent." "Sometimes," he recalled, "the Armstrong gun, at the same elevation, would not throw a shell more than halfway across the river; then again far over the river."[14] Such unpredictable differences in performance hardly instilled confidence in Johnston's cannoneers.

Aside from being outnumbered and inadequately armed, Johnston's troops also suffered from a high rate of sickness. Throughout the fall and winter, the number of soldiers confined to the hospitals, either near Centreville or farther back in Richmond or Charlottesville, varied between 13,000 to 16,000—the equivalent of two full-strength divisions. Hundreds died each month, and hundreds more were discharged by surgeons who pronounced them permanently unfit for military duty.[15]

Four circumstances beyond his control accounted for the high incidence of disease in Johnston's department. First, a significant proportion of his regiments had come straight to his army upon organization instead of remaining in camps of instruction for the first few weeks following their induction. Consequently, they experienced the normal run of "camp diseases" prevalent among new soldiers in both armies—miniepidemics of everything from typhus to influenza. This condition was exacerbated by the severity of winter in northern Virginia, which, to unprepared troops from the Deep South, seemed indistinguishable from the blizzards of the Arctic. Exposure to cold, wind, rain, and snow, combined with the inadequate shelter that the army could provide ("negro cabins," Toombs called them), increased the vulnerability of green troops to disease to such an extent that several whole regiments had to be withdrawn to Richmond because they were totally incapacitated. Medical care at the front ran from rudimentary to nonexistent, simply because there were neither enough doctors nor enough medicine. Many of the physicians available were apparently incompetent; D. H. Hill suggested that the health of the army would be vastly improved if "one half of our surgeons were hung." Finally, the diet of the soldiers was chronically low in vegetables and antiscorbutics but high in half-baked bread and sinewy pork or beef of questionable quality.[16]

Even if more plentiful supplies of weapons, ammunitions, accoutrements, medicines, and rations had existed, it is doubtful that the logistical situation of the Department of Northern Virginia that winter could have been significantly improved. The supply lines leading from Richmond to Manassas consisted of rickety, single-track railroads served by deteriorating equipment and administered so poorly that the government, the army, and the railroad companies sometimes lost sight of dozens of loaded freight cars for months at a time. Distribution at the receiving end was no more efficient, due to the inadequate number of draft animals that attempted to haul supplies over the muddy roads. Whiting's command on the Potomac provided a telling example of the consequences: though none of his troops were stationed farther than thirty miles from the railhead at Manassas Junction—and some as close as sixteen miles—he had to put his division on half-rations several times during the winter.[17] There were rations in the depots, but his dilapidated wagons could not bring them up fast enough to keep pace with daily consumption and certainly not quickly enough to build up a reserve stock.

The inevitable repercussion was a gradual erosion in the morale of Johnston's soldiers. Men who had sustained themselves through the fall on the flush of victory generated at Manassas found their will to continue slowly eaten away by months of inactivity and intolerable living conditions, neither of which showed any immediate prospect of improving. Regiments from Tennessee and Alabama petitioned the government to send them home. Hundreds of soldiers illegally extended their furloughs by skulking about Richmond instead of returning promptly to the army. Alcohol abuse, up to and including blatant drunkenness on duty by company and regimental officers, soared. The recruiters swarming over his camps found Johnston's men quite willing to sign up for almost any unit of any kind that could guarantee them that they would serve out their terms almost anywhere else. As the months of March, April, and May approached, when the enlistments of more than half the department's soldiers would expire, everyone from Jefferson Davis and the Confederate Congress down to Joseph Johnston and his subordinates feared the worst: the army threatened simply to melt away without ever fighting another battle.[18]

That an army in more than name existed in February 1862 was due primarily to the efforts of General Johnston. Contrary to the image saddling his memory, the general worked diligently to prepare his divisions to face the enemy and bent every resource he possessed toward maintaining their strength and propping up their sagging morale. Unlike the majority of his men, and many of his officers, Johnston allowed himself no vacations from the responsibilities of command: from the day he took charge at Manassas in July 1861 until he traveled to Richmond on Davis's direct orders in February 1862, Johnston remained with the army.[19]

Recognizing the dangers inherent in his army's dispersal, Johnston instituted a policy of quick response to enemy actions, designed to allow his widely separated columns to react without wasting time to refer to headquarters for specific orders. Jackson in the Valley and Hill at Leesburg were encouraged to communicate with each other directly and authorized to send reinforcements to any point of attack without contacting Centreville. In the same manner, Johnston instructed Whiting and Holmes to coordinate an immediate response to any Federal landing on the lower Potomac. He required Maj. Gen. Earl Van Dorn, who might have to march his troops on short notice to reinforce any of these positions, to have accurate maps of the roads on his flanks and to ensure that the bridges along his line of march were kept repaired. In this manner Johnston hoped that the speed of his reaction to any Union offensive might somewhat offset his inferiority in numbers. In the event that it would not, he ordered entrenchments built on the northern bank of the Rappahannock River to secure key bridges in case of a retreat.[20]

Johnston actively employed what would later be called counterintelligence procedures to deceive McClellan with regard to his weakness. He had logs painted black and discarded locomotive stovepipes mounted in the embrasures of his defenses at Centreville to conceal the fact that the few heavy guns deployed along the Potomac were the only ones that the army owned. Scarecrows were even erected to mimic gun crews. Until winter storms rendered major movements impractical, Johnston kept his brigades shuffling across his front as ostentatiously as possible, with the objective of convincing Yankee spies to count the same soldiers two or even three times. Likewise, French's field batteries on the Potomac stayed on the move all winter, digging in and firing a few rounds across the river, then limbering and deploying to a new location, so that Federal pickets could never get an accurate count of their numbers. A small passenger steamer, rechristened CSS *George Page*, was outfitted with one or two light cannon and "armored" with spare bits of iron. The vessel then ran back and forth between the Occoquan River and Chopawamsic Creek in a remarkably successful attempt to convince the enemy that the Confederates had managed to place a real ironclad warship on the Potomac. The combination of Johnston's efforts and McClellan's innate caution resulted in the Northern general's firm conviction that the Rebels in the Department of Northern Virginia numbered 150,000 instead of the 47,000 effectives actually present.[21]

Johnston could do little directly to improve the shortages of weapons, ammunition, equipment, rations, or medicines that plagued his army. He tried to augment his food supply locally, and an officer was sent to the capital to secure antiscorbutics. He also dispatched Brig. Gen. William Nelson Pendleton, chief of artillery, to Richmond, Staunton, and Lynchburg to scavenge for the harnesses, caissons, and forges necessary to make his field batteries tactically mobile. In the meantime the chief of ordnance, Maj. E. Porter Alexander, concentrated on keeping rigid control over the expenditure of every grain of powder that the army had been issued while carefully organizing his slender reserves into field trains to accompany each division when active operations commenced.[22]

Johnston reserved his primary efforts for improving the efficiency with which supplies were delivered from the railhead at Manassas to the troops in the field. In addition to the rail spur to cut down the hauling distance for the overworked teams, sawmills that had been erected to cut lumber for the army's winter quarters were kept running to produce planks in order to corduroy the worst roads. He appointed an inspector of transportation to initiate a systematic program of caring for the army's draft animals and maintaining its fleet of wagons. To assist the department's chief quartermaster, Johnston assigned another officer to take over specific responsibility for administering the stockpiles of materials at Manassas. Major Rhett, the army's chief of staff, constantly badgered division and brigade commanders, pursuant to Johnston's instructions, to submit accurate and timely strength reports so that only those supplies absolutely necessary would have to be carted forward to their positions.[23] Although the fundamental weakness of the entire Confederate war effort could not be offset by his program to increase the efficiency of his supply services, Johnston spared no energy in trying to get the most out of the little his country could provide him.

The general's other priority was to shore up the spirits of his soldiers. He believed firmly that his personal example and as rigorous a regimen of drill and discipline as the weather permitted were key ingredients to elevating morale. The sight of Johnston riding through the camps near Centreville was a daily occurrence. Like McClellan, Johnston held parades and reviews, personally complimenting those regiments that proved they had mastered the evolutions of the company and battalion. Moreover, he demanded that his commanders pay attention to tactical training. Exercises were conducted throughout the winter on both brigade and division levels. Idleness on days without formal drill was not tolerated; each morning, in every company, orderly sergeants called out the names of men detailed to improve the Centreville entrenchments, unload supplies from the freight cars, or upgrade the makeshift short line.[24]

Johnston also understood the importance of symbols to his soldiers. After General Beauregard designed a new Confederate battle flag, Johnston wrote to the governors of the states from which he drew his troops, requesting that each chief executive forward flags for his own regiments. Although only Gov. John Letcher of Virginia responded, Johnston used the occasion for as much ceremony as possible, holding a series of reviews for the governor to present the new banners. Later, he tried unsuccessfully to convince the president to ride up and address the army, hoping that an appeal from Davis would stimulate reenlistments. On his own, Johnston granted leaves and furloughs to as many soldiers as he considered could be safely spared at one time.[25]

Johnston also applied the rod. He attempted throughout the winter to crack down on the drunkenness of his officers, convinced that such a measure was a prerequisite for enforcing abstinence among the rank and file. Officers found intoxicated on duty were court-martialed and recommendations sent to Richmond that they be drummed out of the service. Resolutely, Johnston signed the first orders ever given in the Department of Northern Virginia for the execution of deserters and others found guilty of heinous crimes.[26] The scope and effectiveness of Johnston's program to support his soldiers' spirits and to improve the effectiveness of his army was unsurpassed by any other commander under similar conditions at any time during the war. It was rivaled only by his own efforts with the Army of Tennessee and by those of Lee with the Army of Northern Virginia in winter 1863–1864.[27]

Johnston's accomplishment stands out as even more remarkable because the entire civil-military bureaucracy in Richmond seemed consciously determined to undermine him. In nearly every area, Secretary Benjamin, Adjutant General Samuel Cooper, Quartermaster General Abraham Myers, or Commissary General Lucius Northrop directly opposed the field commander. Each official quarreled with Johnston in a manner revealing the petty vindictiveness of an administrator insistent on sustaining his own titular authority regardless of the consequences to the cause he served. Taken in sum, the counterproductive measures pursued by the Confederate administration threatened to undo Johnston's work.

He clashed constantly with the War Department over the question of weapons. Despite its lack of adequate armaments, Johnston's army was the strongest in the Confederacy. Thus Benjamin and Cooper pressured him incessantly to ship "surplus" muskets—which, in their minds, included those of hospitalized soldiers—to Richmond for distribution to new regiments. When Johnston demurred, arguing that "this deprives the different regiments of the means of arming their men who return from the hospitals," he found himself subject to a sudden surprise inspection by Cooper himself. Finally, in order to retain sufficient muskets to arm his own infantry, Johnston turned a blind eye while his subordinates illegally concealed guns from the Richmond authorities.[28]

Despite the well-known numerical and qualitative inferiority of Johnston's cannon, the Confederate War Department actually attempted, in September 1861, to halt the production of field guns at Tredegar Iron Works in favor of immobile coastal defense artillery. Johnston had to dispatch a special representative to Richmond to beg that the policy be changed. Even then, though the casting of field artillery was resumed, seacoast guns remained the government's priority.[29]

Both Myers and Benjamin inhibited Johnston's initiatives to improve the health of his troops. When Johnston requisitioned additional blankets for his men, Myers peevishly demanded that the general first provide the names of the troops who needed them; he completely ignored the request for antiscorbutics. The War Department failed to require the hospitals in the rear areas to notify commanders when their patients died or received discharges, which left Johnston completely ignorant of their fate until they happened to reappear in camp. The few hospital administrators conscientious enough to try on their own to communicate this information to the army found themselves blocked by the reluctance of Cooper's office to provide them with the correct forms.[30]

Johnston's effort to improve the efficiency of his supply system was stymied at every turn by Meyers and Northrop—often with Cooper's complicity. By way of answering Johnston's desperate pleas for more forage for his horses, Myers observed that "considerable savings would be affected [*sic*]," if "the animals could be subsisted without hay." He suggested that Johnston substitute a mixture of "corn shucks, wheat straw and wheat chaff, cut into and mixed with corn meal, or corn meal and bran." Myers stood on the letter of an obscure technicality to prevent Johnston's subordinates at outlying posts from naming their own chief quartermasters, a response echoed by Northrop with respect to commissaries. When William L. Cabell, Johnston's chief quartermaster, was transferred, Myers opposed Johnston's choice for a successor and allowed the eventual nominee to become embroiled in a distracting fight over relative seniority.[31]

Northrop contested Johnston's plan to supplement his troops' diet by local purchase, sticking to a centralized system of acquisition that sometimes required food bought in northern Virginia to travel to Richmond on the overtaxed railroad before turning around to return to Johnston's department. When the commissary general finally did locate a meatpacking plant in Johnston's area, it was over Johnston's vociferous protests; the site of the plant at Thoroughfare Gap was a tactically vulnerable location. Cooper meanwhile refused to sanction Johnston's appointment of an inspector of transportation and delayed action on many other requests from Johnston and his subordinates to increase their logistical staffs. As Longstreet acidly observed in early 1862, it represented a sorry state of affairs when the government reduced a division commander personally to inspecting wagon axles for enough grease instead of appointing a captain to do the job.[32]

Possibly the most egregious outrage confronting Johnston was the unceasing campaign by Secretary Benjamin to undermine the general's command authority. The Louisianian ruled the War Department as if it were a personal fiefdom. He sent orders directly to Johnston's subordinates without consulting or even informing the general. He first acknowledged, then arbitrarily repudiated Johnston's organization of the army into two corps. Benjamin fostered a climate in the War Office that made it acceptable for everyone, from the lowest private to a general officer, to send him requests without channeling them through the department commander. More often than not, even when official papers passed through Johnston's hands, Benjamin would overrule his decision in an apparent matter of course. Much of Johnston's trouble eradicating alcoholism among his officers could be traced to Benjamin's refusal to implement the recommendations of Johnston's courts-martial. The general remonstrated unsuccessfully with the secretary, complaining that "the rules of military correspondence require that letters addressed to you by members of this army should pass through my office." As he wrote, Johnston grew both angrier and more ascerbic: "Let me ask, for the sake of discipline, that you have this rule enforced. It will save much time and trouble, and create the belief in the army that I am its commander."[33]

At the same time, Benjamin undercut Johnston's furlough and reenlistment program by granting authorization to dozens of recruiters to move among Johnston's camps to try to entice unhappy infantrymen into signing up for new companies of artillery and cavalry. These recruiters arrived armed with furloughs approved by the secretary of war, which Johnston possessed no power to contravene. Johnston also confronted Benjamin on this issue, pointing out: "You will readily perceive that while you are granting furloughs on such a scale at Richmond I cannot safely grant them at all." There should be a system, Johnston insisted. "If the War Department continues to grant these furloughs without reference to the plans determined on here, confusion and disorganizing collisions must result."[34]

Benjamin denied that he had ever acted so improperly, even though the most superficial glance at the letterbooks of the War Department would have proven him a liar.[35] Following this exchange, D. H. Hill forwarded a sheaf of authorizations signed by Benjamin to General Cooper, with the sarcastic request: "Will you be kind enough, General[,] to forward this note to the Hon. J. P. Benjamin that he may be advised that there is a forger in his office."[36] In order to keep his army from evaporating, Johnston directed his commanders to stop granting any furloughs in addition to those demanded by Benjamin and looked the other way when some of his subordinates tossed the ubiquitous recruiters into the guardhouse. As Maj. Gen. Richard S. Ewell fumed in a letter to his fiancée, "Had the Secretary of War's orders and permits been carried out by General Johnston as regards Artillery and Cavalry, the whole army would have been broken up except those two branches."[37] Eventually, Johnston brought his complaints to the attention of Jefferson Davis. Instead of inspecting the evidence, Davis simply asked Benjamin for an explanation. The secretary's response was a collection of misleading—if technically correct—statements, facile half-truths, and outright falsehoods, tied together by his lawyer's charisma into a rationalization that a close friend could find acceptable. Johnston, in fact, came out of the exchange with a mild rebuke, Davis observing that Benjamin "has complained that his orders are not executed, and I regret that he was able to present to me . . . many instances to justify that complaint."[38]

That Jefferson Davis was predisposed to find against Johnston in an administrative matter by spring 1862 should not have surprised the general, for he had unwittingly contributed to the president's attitude in an exchange that had far more significant immediate consequences than the question of Johnston's rank. The army assembled during and after Manassas had virtually been thrown together without any regard for the consistent organization of its brigades. Such an arrangement was tolerated in the emergency and for a time ignored in the warm glow of victory. Both Confederate law and the politics of state pride, however, looked forward to the moment in which the soldiers from each state could be gathered into homogenous brigades, which would, as Judah Benjamin argued, "gratify the natural State pride of the men, and keep up that healthful and valuable emulation which forms so important an element in military affairs."[39]

As president, politician, and proud Mississippian, Jefferson Davis considered this issue very important, but following Manassas he admitted that "I would not, for slight cause, change the relation of troops and commanders, especially where it has been long continued and endeared by the trials of battle." Nonetheless, he reminded his generals as gently as possible that "the authority to organize regiments into brigades and the latter into divisions is by law conferred only on the President, and I must be able to assume responsibility of the action taken by whomsoever act for me in that regard." The legislation, he explained, was "designed, as far as should be found consistent, to keep up the State relation of troops and generals." So strongly did Davis feel about the issue that he pressed for it when he visited the army; lobbied Johnston, Beauregard, and Smith incessantly through October 1861 to make the changes; and failing to achieve his end through persuasion had Cooper issue orders mandating the reorganization.[40]

Johnston resisted the process, both actively and passively, at every step. He cited the farflung nature of his dispositions, the difficulties imposed by the muddy roads, and imminent expectations of a Federal attack. Each of these rationalizations could be defended, but none reflected his true reason for opposing and delaying the change. The truth was that Johnston's key subordinates—Beauregard, Smith, Whiting, and others—pressured him to do so. For Beauregard and Smith the change would have involved considerable shifting of units back and forth between their de facto army corps and would have erased the last distinctions between the original Armies of the Potomac and the Shenandoah. Irrelevant as this fine point may have seemed in Richmond, it was an important consideration in internal army politics. Other officers, like Whiting, were proud of their mixed brigades and did not wish to relinquish any of their regiments: "They are used to me, and I to them, and accustomed to act together." Whiting felt that the whole issue had been raised at the behest of ambitious Mississippi politicians and categorized the president's desire for state brigades to be "a policy as suicidal as [it] is foolish."[41]

Unfortunately, in deciding to listen to his subordinates and to procrastinate in implementing a reorganization, Johnston failed to gauge just how intensely Davis felt about the matter. It became abundantly clear to anyone reading the president's correspondence that his chief concern was that of the troops from his home state and of finding appropriate commands for Brigadier Generals Charles Clark and Richard Griffith, longtime political allies from Mississippi. In the organization of the army's brigades, Davis complained on October 10, 1861, "Mississippi troops were scattered, as if the State was unknown. Brigadier-General Clark was sent to remove a growing dissatisfaction; but, though the State had nine regiments there, he (C.) was put in command of a post and depot of supplies." Although Davis initially addressed the issue in terms of the entire army, it was evident by early December that he would be satisfied if Johnston would give him some help only with the troops from his own state. Benjamin wrote that "the President now finds the Mississippi regiments scattered as far apart as it is possible to scatter them." "He does not desire to control your discretion" in controlling the army's operations, Benjamin told Johnston; "he confines himself to directing that his repeatedly expressed wishes and orders about the Mississippi regiments be carried into effect."[42] This was the crux of the issue, as baldly as it could be stated in an official communication: Davis would for all practical purposes drop the whole question if Johnston would give him what he needed with the Mississippi brigades.

In one of his poorest decisions, Johnston stood by Whiting and temporized again ("I only ask for an authority rarely withheld from a general commanding an army"), forwarding to Richmond an insubordinate letter from Whiting refusing to accept an all-Mississippi command. In the explosive response to that missive, which very nearly cost Whiting his career, Johnston missed not only the point of what Davis had been requesting but also failed to divine how this exchange might affect the president's opinion of his administrative capacity.[43] With myopic obtuseness, Johnston never made the connection between this incident and Davis's instant willingness two months later to accept the secretary of war's allegations on faith. Instead, the general perceived the president as arbitrarily supporting an old friend, even at the expense of sound military policy.

From Johnston's perspective, Davis's refusal to consider his case only increased a feeling of alienation that had been growing for months. His letters to Whiting revealed this mood as early as November 1861. On November 9 he predicted darkly that "the Secretary of War will probably establish his headquarters within this department soon." Three days later, Johnston advised Whiting that "General Cooper replied today that the guns you asked for should be sent without delay. This does not encourage me much as to time. In Richmond their ideas of promptitude are very different from ours." Concerned in January that the government was seeking a pretext on which to replace him, Johnston joined Beauregard and G. W. Smith in an effort to begin saving papers and drafting memorandums to prove that they had been doing all they could, despite Richmond's interference, to strengthen the army.[44]

By the time he started to the capital in answer to the president's summons, the gulf between Joseph Johnston and Jefferson Davis was, like the distance between Centreville and Richmond, much greater than it first appeared.

3
DECISION IN RICHMOND

Lead-gray clouds invaded the sky over Richmond on February 19, 1862. Steady rain suited the mood of the city. Despite Jefferson Davis's pending inauguration as the Confederacy's permanent president, few Richmonders felt either festive or optimistic. In little more than a month an unbroken string of defeats had destroyed the confidence of the city on the James River. The gloomy atmosphere deepened as the list of catastrophes lengthened: a rout at Fishing Creek; the fall of Fort Henry and Roanoke Island; and now some dire, although still unspecified, disaster at Fort Donelson. An aide to the governor observed that depression paralyzed the city. Businesses closed, and in the streets, hotels, and bars, "people did nothing but collect together in groups and discuss our disasters."[1]

The uneasy crowds wandering the city grew larger every day. The influx of people associated with the Confederate administration, expanded industries, and the armies defending Virginia had swollen the population of Richmond to more than twice the prewar total of 38,000. Camps of instruction and military hospitals had been established throughout the city. Hundreds (possibly thousands, no one kept an accurate tally) of soldiers on furlough loitered in the streets, searching for a place to spend the night. Makeshift prisons housed several thousand Federal prisoners, and Yankee officers who had filed paroles with the provost marshal walked around freely. Refugees from occupied portions of the state migrated to the capital. Their numbers, too, were impossible to estimate. The inauguration, scheduled to occur in three days, had attracted an additional horde of visitors, creating even more overcrowded conditions.[2]

These invasions had predictable results. Already inflated prices for food and lodging kept climbing. "Groceries are very high without any fixed price," complained one Richmond newspaper, adding that "it is very difficult to give correct quotations as prices are changing every day." Renters bitterly attacked landlords who "run up miserable wooden shells, or . . . lease crazy brick tenements, in convenient locations, and ask the most enormous rents for uncomfortable rooms."[3]

Visitors who could afford it paid to stay in private homes. Hotels sold space on cots spread around their lobbies at exorbitant prices, but even this expedient could not meet the demand for temporary housing. Those who found no other place to stay frequented the bars and gambling "hells" as late in the evening as possible and then slept wherever they could.[4] The crime rate soared: murder (especially strangling) and highway robbery were particularly prominent, and "disorderly houses" proliferated. The *Richmond Examiner* observed that "a glance at the police report . . . must convince everyone that this city is not a safe place to 'thrash' about in at night." The *Dispatch* pointedly recalled that the English had solved their crime problem only by resorting to liberal use of the death penalty.[5]

The gross overcrowding of the city created an atmosphere in which rumors multiplied like mosquitoes on a stagnant pond. Real intelligence about the war was conspicuous by its absence, and the most improbable tales circulated with full credence. Richmond newspapers printed every report and hoped for the best. On February 19 the fate of Fort Donelson was still the subject of wild speculation. Neither the president nor the War Department had released any firm news.[6]

At 8:00 A.M. Davis and his cabinet secretaries had sequestered themselves on the second floor of the Customs House, which had been donated by Virginia to the national government. The meeting continued for hours, the participants apparently oblivious of the curious bystanders in the street below while clerks and assistants transacted the routine business of government. Questions of grand strategy, it was assumed, were under consideration, and speculations about potential decisions started circulating.[7]

Into this climate of depression, uncertainty, and misinformation, the morning train from Centreville, late as usual, wheezed slowly along the Shockoe bottom into Richmond, bearing new grist for the rumor mills. At the Virginia Central Railroad on Broad Street, passengers began the struggle to exit the ramshackle cars. Couriers carrying official dispatches, soldiers on furlough, commissary officers, recruiting agents, newspaper reporters, and the few private citizens who still held passes to ride the densely packed train bumped against each other as they pressed toward the street. The one exception, the man who would have waited until the crowd passed, or for whom it would have instinctively parted, was Joseph Johnston.[8]

Johnston had not visited the capital since June 1861, and his arrival raised new and much more direct fears for the safety of the city. Why had Johnston come to Richmond? As he walked up Broad Street and turned past Capitol Square, the questions no doubt followed him. Had he come in response to a presidential summons or traveled on his own initiative? Revealing nothing of his purpose, the general strode straight into the Customs House; Davis's secretary immediately interrupted the meeting to inform the president of his caller.[9] Could disaster be imminent in northern Virginia, or were the recent Union advances about to be answered by a counterinvasion across the Potomac? In the hotels and bars the questions flowed along with the drinks. Why had Johnston come to Richmond?

Most members of the cabinet were equally mystified by the general's sudden appearance. The meeting's expressed purpose had been to edit a draft of Davis's inaugural address. Though he certainly did not consider his advisers to be "a cabinet of dummies," as did the *Richmond Whig,* the president limited his confidence in dealing with the military crisis to Secretary of War Judah P. Benjamin.[10] The remaining five officers—Secretary of the Treasury Christopher Memminger, Secretary of the Navy Stephen Mallory, Attorney General Thomas Bragg, Postmaster General John Reagan, and acting Secretary of State William Browne—had no inkling that Davis had chosen this particular day to announce a major shift in Confederate strategy.

To appreciate the significance of Davis's pronouncement, it is necessary to understand his grand strategy for the first year of the war. In fall 1861, the president had coolly accepted a desperate but calculated gamble on behalf of his new nation. Without sufficient rifles, cannon, powder, or shot to conduct decisive military operations, he boldly authorized his generals to push their poorly equipped, severely outnumbered armies as far forward as possible.[11] If audacity could disguise abject weakness long enough, he hoped that a combination of home production and imports through the blockade would provide the weapons to launch real offensives.

It was an outrageous bluff, extending far beyond the Department of Northern Virginia. While part of Gen. Albert Sidney Johnston's army attempted to blockade the Mississippi River from Columbus, Kentucky, the remainder had invaded the central part of the state and rattled sabers loudly at Bowling Green. "Create an impression that this force is only an advance guard," Johnston instructed Maj. Gen. William J. Hardee. Making noise was the best Hardee could do: most of his troops were either sick or unarmed.[12] From southern Missouri, Maj. Gen. Sterling Price and his ragtag regiments, many of whom had not even been sworn into Confederate service, tried their best to maintain a threatening posture, and in west Texas Brig. Gen. Henry H. Sibley marched his motley 3,700-man Army of New Mexico toward Arizona. The rest of the Confederate army guarded the Atlantic or Gulf coasts against amphibious descent by the U.S. Navy.[13]

For months following the Confederate victory at Manassas the strategy worked. George McClellan believed the intelligence estimates that attributed to Johnston's army more than twice its actual strength. In Kentucky, Maj. Gen. William T. Sherman insisted in November 1861 that Confederate troops at Bowling Green "far outnumber us." His successor, Maj. Gen. Don Carlos Buell, was skeptical about Rebel numbers but still counted almost every Rebel soldier twice.[14] Partly as a result of an aggressive Southern military policy, the major Union armies remained inactive through the fall and into the winter. When 1861 ended, Jefferson Davis could look out over a national defensive perimeter that was essentially intact.

The inherent weakness of the president's strategy was that by committing his available troops to the frontiers he could not maintain a substantial reserve. His expectation that sufficient arms could be obtained to create such a reserve was not realized: only 15,000 rifles had slipped through the blockade since September 1861, nearly half of which arrived on a single vessel. These weapons had to be rushed to the front as soon as they were unloaded at the docks. Internal production was gearing up, but when the crisis struck, Col. Josiah Gorgas's Ordnance Department required an entire month's production of rifles to outfit a single regiment. The situation with regard to powder was equally dismal. Of the 400,000 pounds that Gorgas required, so little had arrived in Southern ports that in late January there were fewer than twenty-five charges per gun available to the batteries defending the coasts. Thus, when Federal offensives cracked open the eggshell in Kentucky, Tennessee, and North Carolina, almost nothing stood between the Northern armies and the heartland of the Confederacy.[15]

Like many gamblers, Davis had refused to fold his hand and start a new game until his losses were enormous. By February 17, when he learned that Fort Donelson had surrendered, the overall military situation was grave. Brigadier General Ulysses Grant's army, supported by gunboats, stood between the two wings of Sidney Johnston's department, in perfect position to strike the communications of either. Buell meanwhile advanced slowly but inexorably through central Kentucky toward Nashville. The success of Maj. Gen. Ambrose Burnside's amphibious expedition into Albemarle Sound proved the ability of the Federal navy to land troops along almost any stretch of coastline and also directly menaced Norfolk and the crucial railroad line between Richmond and Wilmington. Only the front in northern and eastern Virginia remained quiet, and it was apparent that this represented the calm before the hurricane. Johnston had pointed out to Davis in his February 16 letter that McClellan "controls the water, however, and can move on the Potomac as easily now as in midsummer." Furthermore, the general cautioned that "we cannot retreat from this point without heavy loss. If we are beaten, this army will be broken up, and Virginia, at least, lost."[16]

The president later admitted his miscalculation, though even in his eulogy for the failed strategy Davis did not repent having accepted the risks. "I acknowledge the error," he wrote on March 15, 1862, "of my attempt to defend all of the frontier, seaboard, and inland; but will say in justification that if we had received the arms and munitions which we had good reason to expect, the attempt would have been successful and the battle-fields would have been on the enemy's soil."[17] Belying his reputation for inflexibility, as soon as the surrender of Donelson was confirmed, Davis completely reoriented Confederate grand strategy in less than forty-eight hours.

His decisions were certainly influenced by the opinions of his senior generals, many of whom had recently written concerning ominous increases in Federal strength, often including specific strategic suggestions. General Robert E. Lee, whose judgment Davis implicitly trusted, had advised from South Carolina on January 8 that

> the forces of the enemy are accumulating, and apparently increase faster than ours. I have feared, if handled with proportionate ability with his means of speedy transportation and concentration, it would be impossible to gather troops necessarily posted over a long line in sufficient strength to oppose sudden movements.
>
> Wherever his fleet can be brought, no opposition to his landing can be made except within range of our fixed batteries. We have nothing to oppose to its heavy guns. . . . The farther he can be withdrawn from his floating batteries the weaker he will become.

Lee reiterated this warning on February 10, admitting that although "I exceedingly dislike to yield an inch of territory to our enemies they are, however, able to bring such large and powerful batteries to whatever point they please, that it becomes necessary for us to concentrate our strength."[18]

On February 13, Maj. Gen. Braxton Bragg, another officer whose views the president valued, had addressed Secretary Benjamin with his own suggestions: "Our means and resources are too much scattered. The protection of persons and property, as such, should be abandoned, and all our means applied to the Government and the cause. Important strategic points only should be held." Bragg advised the removal of troops from all but the largest ports and the complete military evacuation of Texas, Florida, and Kentucky. "A small loss of property would result from their occupation by the enemy; but our military strength would not be lessened thereby, whilst the enemy would be weakened by the dispersion."[19]

Nor did the president lack the opinions of the two Generals Johnston. Joseph Johnston had alerted Davis on February 16 of the vulnerability of his own extended line. Though Sidney Johnston remained out of contact on February 16 and 17, almost a month earlier he had posted to Richmond a similar warning of imminent calamity. Given the Federal potential for using the Ohio, Cumberland, and Tennessee Rivers to launch amphibious assaults, he argued that to believe "that they will suspend them in Tennessee and Kentucky during the winter months is a delusion. All the resources of the Confederacy are now needed for the defense of Tennessee."[20] Thus the consensus among the generals in whom Davis placed the greatest trust was that the survival of the Confederacy depended on a concentration of its limited resources in defense of a few critical points, even at the risk of losing large sections of territory with less military value. Yet ultimately Davis had to face the situation by himself, directly assisted only by an inexperienced secretary of war.

He acted both resolutely and quickly. By February 18 letters drafted by Benjamin at the president's direction had been dispatched to the department commanders. Union numerical and naval superiority, combined with the arms shortage and the arguments of his generals, had convinced Davis that "it may not be possible, with our limited means, to protect every point which the enemy can attack by means of his fleets." Benjamin's orders to Bragg stated the case even more frankly: "The heavy blow which has been inflicted on us by the recent operations in Kentucky and Tennessee renders necessary a change in our whole plan of campaign." The new strategy subordinated considerations of local defense to a national effort concentrated on preserving the economic vitals of the Confederacy. Garrisons would be ruthlessly stripped away from less important points and transferred to more critical theaters of war. The emphasis of military operations was to change from static, linear defense to the more active "offensive-defensive" of field armies maneuvering and counterpunching the enemy. "We must dismiss all ideas of scattering our forces in defense of unimportant points and concentrate them at vital lines," Benjamin told Maj. Gen. Mansfield Lovell.[21]

Davis contemplated a reduced but still viable defensive perimeter. His first priority was to seal off Federal penetrations in Tennessee, safeguarding the material resources of Mississippi, Alabama, Georgia, western Tennessee, and the only direct rail connection between Virginia and the Mississippi River. "No effort will be spared," Benjamin assured Maj. Gen. Leonidas K. Polk on February 18, "to save the line of communication between Memphis and Bristol, so vital to our defense."[22] To provide Sidney Johnston with the means to defend his department, troops were dispatched from almost all quarters of the country. Eastern Florida and parts of eastern North Carolina were abandoned outright, as were the small islands off the coast of South Carolina and Georgia. The only Atlantic ports to be held in strength were Wilmington, Charleston, and Savannah. In the Gulf, the Confederates quit Pensacola, removed all but heavy artillerymen from Mobile and the small Texas ports, and reduced the forces defending New Orleans. Troops from Missouri were ordered east of the Mississippi, and the garrison at Columbus, Kentucky, evacuated its fixed positions to join the army in the field.

Despite the resistance that Davis knew he would meet from both Congress and the state governments, he saw his decision as a purely military one and as such above the bounds of factional politics. He believed, as he had written to Polk in September 1861, that "it is true that the solution of the problem requires the consideration of other than the military elements involved in it; but we cannot permit the indeterminate qualities, the political elements, to control our action in cases of military necessity."[23] By January, after months of bickering with governors who seemed to balk at every war measure, no matter how essential, Davis expressed himself far more bluntly. Attorney General Bragg recorded in his diary that Davis exploded in a cabinet meeting: "If such was to be the course of the States towards the Gov't the carrying [on] of the war was an impossibility—that we had better make terms as soon as we could, and those of us who had halters around our necks had better get out of the Country as speedily as possible."[24] Nor was Davis mistaken in his belief that any strategic withdrawal would provoke public outcries from his opponents. Even as he convened his advisers to inform them of his decisions, the House of Representatives was counting electoral votes to certify his election as president under the permanent Constitution. No sooner had the results been confirmed than Tennessee congressman Henry S. Foote rose and demanded "that a committee be appointed to enquire into the cause of the recent disasters which have befallen our arms."[25]

The cabinet was the first group of civilian politicians, albeit a friendly one, to whom Davis announced his radical shift in policy. Explaining in detail the dismal state of military affairs, "the Pres't said the time had come for diminishing the extent of our lines—that we had not men in the field to hold them and must fall back."[26] The news astounded his audience, and in some way it directly affected each of them. Both Postmaster General Reagan of Texas and Navy Secretary Mallory hailed from states that Davis had already ordered to be denuded of troops. The weakening of garrisons at key ports was of special concern to Mallory, whose department had ironclads under construction at

Norfolk and New Orleans. He was already contemplating deploying the completed *Virginia* into the Chesapeake to "make a dashing cruise on the Potomac as far as Washington" and dreamed of using the armored frigate to attack New York.[27] Davis's bombshell suggested that his bases of construction might no longer be secure. Treasury Secretary Memminger had to calculate the impact of the withdrawals on an already faltering economy and the credibility of $130 million worth of Confederate bonds soon to be issued, and Secretary of State Browne had to find ways to minimize the negative diplomatic consequences of surrendering large tracts of territory without a contest. For Attorney General Bragg the president's revelations sparked a more personal response. This was the first he had heard of his brother, Maj. Gen. Braxton Bragg, being ordered from the quiet Gulf to the crumbling front in Tennessee. Already pessimistic about the Confederacy's chances, he found that Davis's news left him too distracted to concentrate.[28]

The president, however, had not finished explaining his new strategy. His second priority, after solidifying a line in Tennessee, was the defense of Richmond. Johnston's army, and those of Major Generals John B. Magruder and Benjamin Huger guarding the coastal approaches to the city at Yorktown and Norfolk, had been among the few organizations not drained of troops in the concentration on Tennessee.[29] Catastrophes in the west and the more immediate defeat at Roanoke Island had convinced Davis that the extended line of defense in Virginia was equally vulnerable to dismemberment by Federal naval power. "The President was farther [*sic*] of the opinion," recorded Bragg, "that we must fall back from Manassas and in the Valley of Va. as far as Stanton [*sic*]."[30]

Davis's concern for the capital's safety was not the result of some unbalanced, monophobic refusal to acknowledge threats to other theaters of war. He was quite aware of the resources and industrial potential of the Mississippi Valley and the interior of Georgia. Those regions held his nation's future—if it were to have one—because only by retaining them and developing their productive capacity could the Confederacy hope to sustain a long war. Davis also recognized, however, that the loss of Richmond in early 1862 would almost immediately end the war. If the western heartland represented the Confederacy's future, the eastern capital was the rebellion's present. "Richmond," Peter Parish has observed, "was in effect the economic as well as the political capital of the Confederacy." The city's four largest banks had combined assets exceeding $10 million, a figure especially significant to a capital-poor nation. Richmond was the major flour-milling center for the southeast and an important transportation terminus for the region. Five railroad lines radiated from the city like spokes from a wheel and heavy barge traffic plied the upper James

River canal system, and oceangoing vessels could dock just below the city. The only arsenal in the South currently capable of mass-producing small arms was located in Richmond.[31]

Yet as important to the survival of the Confederacy as those attributes were, they were secondary to the city's capability for heavy manufacturing. "Iron was the key to Richmond's greatest economic advantage to the Confederacy," concludes Emory Thomas. "The city was the center of industry south of the Potomac. In 1860 she claimed four rolling mills, fourteen foundries and machine shops, a nail works, six works for manufacturing iron railing, two circular-saw works, and fifty iron and metal works."[32] But rather than the breadth of Richmond's iron industry what made it a critical asset was the concentration of production capacity in a single firm: Joseph R. Anderson's Tredegar Iron Works.

Tredegar carried the South through the first year of the war. Even though there were eighty-one establishments turning out bar, sheet, or railroad iron in the Confederacy, Tredegar alone accounted for better than 37 percent of the total production. By the end of February 1862, Anderson's firm had delivered 68 field guns and 197 pieces of heavy artillery; most of the other establishments were either still in the process of tooling up to cast cannon or had defaulted on their contracts. Mallory's ironclads would have been impossible without Tredegar: the plant cast the metal plates that covered the *Virginia* as well as her rifled guns and was forging the main shaft for the *Mississippi*.[33]

Beyond supplying the armed forces, Tredegar possessed the unique capacity, given enough time, to bring other industrial plants up to its own level. Though there were ten rolling mills in the South after secession, only Anderson's company owned the steam hammer necessary for sustained mass production. Tredegar thus had the capability not only to manufacture ordnance materials but also to create new manufacturing establishments and to supplement existing ones. Tredegar repaired the rifling machinery captured at Harpers Ferry that sent 500 new weapons a month from the Fayetteville arsenal to the front. Even as Davis and his cabinet met, the firm had just completed the twelve rolls, six bed circles, and ten shafts necessary to put the huge Augusta Powder Mill into operation. A second steam hammer cast in Richmond eventually allowed the foundry at Selma, Alabama, to begin producing heavy guns. None of the munitions plants or navy yards that sustained the Confederate military economy despite the blockade could have been built without the support of the Tredegar Iron Works.[34] Later diversification of ordnance production somewhat diminished Tredegar's critical importance, but in February 1862 and for some six months thereafter, Anderson's firm represented the single resource without which the Confederacy could not survive.

As politically important as defending northern Virginia might be, and as agriculturally significant as was the Shenandoah Valley, Davis correctly subordinated both to the defense of Richmond.

With a flourish of real-life dramatic timing, the president had just mentioned his intention to withdraw from the frontiers of Virginia when Johnston's arrival was announced. Most of the cabinet was unaware of Davis's February 13 letter to the general, and because Johnston had been forced to delay his trip due to G. W. Smith's illness, even the president had not known exactly when to expect him. Davis left the room to confer with Johnston for a few minutes before bringing him into the meeting. He first assured the general that rumors of an impending transfer of G. W. Smith to east Tennessee were false and then brought him up to date on the latest intelligence from the west, explaining his concentration in Tennessee and telling him that he was just in time to help decide the question of withdrawing his own army.[35]

Johnston readily admitted that from a purely military perspective, withdrawal from northern Virginia to a more defensible position behind the Rappahannock was desirable. But he emphasized the difficulties of such a maneuver while winter lingered, calling them "almost insurmountable." According to Attorney General Bragg, the general described

> the present condition of the roads, the want of means by the Rail Road Road [*sic*] to do it expeditiously, and the great sacrafices [*sic*] we would have to make, as any movement of the kind would be very soon known to the enemy. He seemed to think that the enemy could and would advance by coming down to Aquia Creek and getting to Fredericksburg. Our heavy guns could not be well moved or got away from Evansport.[36]

This last comment provoked a lively discussion about the ways and means of retiring Whiting's heavy artillery from the Potomac. After explaining the practical difficulties of such a removal, Johnston finally ended the debate by pointing out that new Federal positions on the Maryland shore made it impossible to perform any such maneuver in secret. At that, Davis tabled the matter and asked Johnston to consider the issue more fully and to return the next day to continue the debate.[37]

Before the cabinet resumed editing the president's inaugural address, Davis made several more important comments on his strategy in Virginia. Bragg wrote that Davis said "that unless something of the kind was done"—referring to a withdrawal by Johnston—"Richmond would be taken, that we must have troops in supporting distance to repel an attack from North or South by Burnside, who he thought would endeavor to advance to Suffolk, isolate Norfolk which must fall & then advance upon Richmond." He believed that Federal strategists would also divert Commodore David D. Porter's mortar fleet to assist Burnside. Recognizing that the forces deployed in a broad defensive arc around the capital were commanded by five independent generals, the president admitted that he had been considering Lee's recall from Georgia to orchestrate their operations. But Lee, Davis revealed, believed that Savannah was in immediate danger of attack and did not think he could safely depart the area for at least a week, perhaps more. "It was left undecided," recorded Bragg.[38]

Exactly when Johnston left the meeting is not clear. Bragg's diary can be read as implying that he was dismissed prior to Davis's comments about recalling Lee to Virginia, but the entry is too ambiguous to be offered as definitive evidence. Johnston never stated, then or later, whether he had heard the remarks, although his correspondence with Lee during the next month can also be read in such a manner as to indicate that he had. That question notwithstanding, Bragg's notes clearly settle two key issues. First, the idea for withdrawing Johnston's army originated with Davis: it was indeed under discussion before Johnston ever entered the room. Second, the journal also confirms explicitly that Davis was considering Lee's transfer to Virginia to exercise a specific coordinating command function. The context also suggests, though again stopping short of outright assertion, that the president had no intention of turning complete control of the defense of Richmond to Joseph Johnston.

For his part, Johnston, regardless of when he left the Customs House, probably had other matters on his mind. Immediately, he wanted to see his wife, who was residing in a Richmond hotel. Though she had visited him frequently—his critics said excessively—during the winter at Centreville, he had not seen her in some weeks. On his way to the hotel his natural reserve and his sense of military security no doubt served to deflect the inquiries of curious civilians as to his business in the capital. But in the hotel lobby, General Johnston met a man whose questions he could not so easily avoid.

Twenty-eight-year-old Col. Dorsey Pender of the Sixth North Carolina had just finished a thirty-day leave to see his wife; he had signed into the hotel overnight to await the morning train back to Centreville. From the moment he arrived in Richmond that morning, Pender had been hearing rumors that the cabinet was in session to discuss the withdrawal of the army from Centreville and Manassas. The dozens of details such a move would entail for a regimental commander must already have been running through his mind when he saw his commander enter the hotel. Without hesitation, Pender approached Johnston and put the question directly: Was the army being withdrawn? Johnston, horrified at this breach of security, politely brushed off the colonel's inquiry with a negative answer but one that did not totally convince the younger officer.[39] The exchange also placed Johnston in an even more defensive frame of mind with reference to the administration. Davis had ordered him to Richmond with a secret summons, but the general found the subject being bantered about openly in the streets. How far could he trust civilian politicians with military secrets?

According to Bragg, the general never broached that subject at the cabinet meeting on the following morning. Johnston did say that he considered a withdrawal from Manassas "advisable, but every means of doing it and saving our artillery & stores, especially the heavy guns on the Potomac, seemed to be wanting—it was next to impossible." This comment was followed by another "prolonged discussion," as Johnston somewhat derisively labeled it, over more schemes to save Whiting's exposed cannon. Nothing in this conversation would have improved the professional soldier's view of his civilian superiors.[40] The meeting "terminated without the giving of orders," recalled Johnston, "but with the understanding on my part that the army was to fall back as soon as practicable." Bragg's diary supports this statement and notes with reference to the selection of a new position that Johnston "was directed however to have a reconaissance [*sic*] of the country in his rear with reference to another line, and it is probable that the Rappahannock will be selected."[41]

Three years later, Davis asserted that a reconnaissance had been necessary because Johnston did not have any idea of the country behind him:

> On enquiry into the character of his position at Centreville, he stated that his lines there were untenable; but, when asked what new position he proposed to occupy, declared himself ignorant of the country in his rear. This confession was a great shock to my confidence in him. That a General should have been for many months in command of an Army, should have selected a line which he himself considered untenable, and should not have ascertained the topography of the country in his rear, was inexplicable on any other theory than that he had neglected the primary duty of a commander.[42]

The charge reflected the antipathies of 1865 instead of the realities of 1862. Johnston was hardly ignorant of the land behind him; he had already ordered a survey of the Rappahannock line when his engineers fortified the bridge crossings.[43]

The question of exactly where Johnston's retreat would cease was left undecided. This ambiguity was understandable, given that the objective of the withdrawal was to move Johnston's troops into closer supporting distance of

Richmond, should either McClellan or Burnside launch an amphibious attack on the city. Such a movement would also entail a retrograde by Stonewall Jackson in the Shenandoah, who would otherwise have been left in an exposed position. Neither Johnston nor Davis wanted to yield an inch of soil unnecessarily, and so each would have favored a position for Johnston's main army close enough to defend Richmond but far enough north to support Jackson as far down the Valley as possible. The Rappahannock looked like the natural choice for such a deployment, but both men knew that the final decision was a future judgment to be based largely on the Federal reaction to Johnston's movement. Further, Johnston was aware that the defense of Richmond was the administration's stated priority, and only someone in Richmond, receiving daily intelligence reports from all parts of Virginia and North Carolina, could decide exactly how near to the capital he should withdraw. So his destination, though provisionally the Rappahannock River, had not been determined with finality.

Leaving the meeting, probably sometime in the early afternoon, Johnston spent the remainder of the day transacting minor administrative affairs with Adj. Gen. Samuel Cooper.[44] He planned to return to Centreville the following morning and did not, of course, mention the outcome of the cabinet meeting to anyone not already privy to the decision. Yet that evening, if the memoirs of an ardent congressional foe of the administration are to be believed, the general may have committed an indiscretion of another sort.

Just a few days earlier, Henry Stuart Foote had arrived in Richmond, newly elected to Congress from Nashville, Tennessee. Originally a Mississippi politician who had defeated Davis in a particularly acrimonious gubernatorial race in 1853, Foote was an avowed opponent both of secession and the current administration. "That Confederate Tennesseans elected pro-Union Foote to the Southern Congress," observes Patricia Faust, "is almost as puzzling as their representative's willingness to serve." Not so much love of the Confederacy as hatred for Davis convinced Foote to accept his election, and he wasted no time in beginning to pillory the president's war policies. Even as Johnston prepared to leave the cabinet meeting on February 20, Foote, "an orator of the fist-pounding Bible-spouting variety," on his first day in Congress attacked Davis so bitterly that he missed fighting a duel with Albert Gallatin Jenkins of Virginia by the narrowest of margins.[45]

That night, according to Foote's 1866 memoirs, "I chanced to be invited to a dinner-party, where some twenty of the most prominent members of the two houses of the Confederate Congress were congregated, including the Speaker of the House of Representatives, Mr. Orr of South Carolina, and others of equal rank." Johnston, Foote asserted, had also been invited but took little part in the conversation until the subject turned to Judah Benjamin. While discussing the war secretary's "gross acts of official misconduct," Foote recorded,

> one of the company turned to General Johnston, and inquired whether he thought it even *possible* that the Confederate cause could succeed with Mr. Benjamin as War Minister. To this inquiry, General Johnston, after a little pause, emphatically responded in the *negative*. This high authority was immediately cited in both houses of Congress against Mr. Benjamin, and was in the end fatal to his hopes of remaining in the Department of War.[46]

No specific corroboration for Foote's anecdote has been found beyond the fact that Arkansas congressman Thomas B. Hanly called for Johnston's appearance before the House on February 25 to testify during the confirmation debates. Considerable circumstantial evidence suggests that such a response would not have been out of character for Johnston. James Orr, the only other individual mentioned by name in the story, had been colonel of the First South Carolina Rifles before he had resigned to enter Congress; it is not unlikely that he would have invited Johnston to the dinner. Johnston's alleged comments were certainly consistent with his personal opinions, as both his own memoirs and contemporary correspondence testify. The early postwar date by which Foote wrote also gives his account more credibility since most of the controversies over Johnston's defense of Richmond that might have colored the congressman's memory had not yet surfaced.[47]

If Foote's account is accurate, Davis's friends in Congress could hardly have avoided telling him that Johnston's opinions were being quoted in debates to discredit Benjamin. Such an indiscretion by the general at the expense of the president's friend would have only increased Davis's distrust of his field commander. Even if the anecdote was fabricated or exaggerated, it indicates the climate of suspicion already existing between the two men at a time when the need for mutual confidence was paramount.

That level of trust declined again, in Johnston's mind, the following day. Riding the slow-moving train back to Centreville, he made profitable use of the hours by discussing details of the upcoming withdrawal with one of his commissary officers, Maj. B. P. Noland, who chanced to be riding in the same car. They were interrupted by a friend of Johnston's, "an acquaintance from the county of Faquier, too deaf to hear conversation not intended for his ear," who told Johnston that he, like Dorsey Pender, had heard that the army was being withdrawn from Manassas. Aghast, the general asked him for the source of his information. It had come, Johnston said later, "from the wife of a member of the Cabinet."[48]

4
WITHDRAWAL FROM THE FRONTIER

The rain came down in sheets on Inauguration Day. The deluge "fell in torrents, and the streams and gutters were like the flowing of little rivers." Jefferson Davis and his Negro footmen, attired in somber black, approached the wooden platform beside the statue of George Washington. "This ma'am, is the way we always does in Richmond at funerals and such like," one coachman told an inquisitive spectator. The tall Mississippian bent to kiss the Bible and then stood bareheaded in the rain and delivered his speech. It was vintage Davis, logical and concise if not inspiring. Attorney General Thomas Bragg remarked that, after all the in camera editing, "it is the best seasoned document surely that ever was issued." Bragg also said that February 22 was "one of the worst days I ever saw." "Very few heard the inaugural address" over the drumming of the rain, recalled one observer, and in the depression gripping the crowd there was a common feeling that the war had passed the point where the words of politicians mattered much.[1]

In Centreville it was also raining, but General Joseph E. Johnston met his staff indoors, where they could hear him. Back from the capital for less than twenty-four hours, he was determined to waste no time in executing the directive to withdraw his army. He hoped in about two weeks to remove enough supplies and heavy guns to allow himself freedom of maneuver. It was an overly optimistic timetable, considering the difficulties Johnston faced. His subordinates had no experience in planning the movement of an entire army on so much as a route march, much less a retreat with all baggage over muddy roads. His troops, though tolerably well drilled in tactical evolutions, were equally innocent of real marching experience. Mountains of supplies—from 2.7 million pounds of meat at Thoroughfare Gap to the excess trunks of his gentlemen officers—had to be removed down the inadequate railroad line. Something had to be done with W. H. C. Whiting's cannon along the Potomac. Worse, everything had to be accomplished in complete secrecy, lest

George McClellan sense that something was afoot and attack one of the outlying garrisons just as the withdrawal began.

Johnston knew that the command structure of his army was dangerously weak. In little more than three months Generals P. G. T. Beauregard, Edmund Kirby Smith, Earl Van Dorn, and seven brigadiers had left the army for causes ranging from transfer to election to Congress, aggrieved resignation to suicide. The result, as Johnston wrote Davis, was that "the army is crippled and its discipline greatly impaired by the want of general officers." He noted that one brigade was being commanded by a lieutenant colonel and that one entire division had no general: "At least half the field officers are absent—generally sick."[2]

Nor could Johnston feel absolutely confident in the abilities of the officers left with him. His senior major general, Gustavus W. Smith, was a forty-one-year-old Kentuckian and personal friend from prewar days who had received his commission based primarily on his reputation as an engineer and on Johnston's own recommendation: "Smith is a man of high ability, fit to command in chief." Smith had "gone South" only after Manassas, and he had thus far had little chance to prove Johnston correct or to live up to his own aura of self-assurance. He had been impressive as an administrator during the winter—even the irascible Robert Toombs admitted that "the army has been a great gainer by his appointment." But Smith suffered from some mysterious nervous malady that could send him to bed for days at a time without warning. Such an attack had already delayed Johnston's trip to Richmond for three days; would the stress of active operations make his condition worse?[3]

A year older and physically Smith's opposite, James Longstreet had the robust constitution of a draft horse. A fighter rather than a thinker by nature, Longstreet actually benefited from being slightly deaf. As one officer remembered: "He impressed me then as a man of limited capacity who acquired reputation for wisdom by never saying anything—the old story of the owl. I do not remember ever hearing him say half a dozen words beyond 'yes' and 'no,' in a consecutive sentence." He owed an early commission as a brigadier general to an accident of timing but justified it and his next promotion with his performance at Manassas. Like Smith, he proved his worth as an administrator, reputedly paying more attention to drilling his division than any other officer.[4] Yet as Johnston began to consider the evacuation he had reason to worry about Longstreet's state of mind. Throughout the winter Longstreet had joined in the convivial atmosphere around headquarters, enlarging on prewar notoriety as a skilled poker player. In early February, however, not long before Davis summoned Johnston to Richmond, tragedy had struck the Georgian. In a single week three of his children died of a fever in Richmond; by

February 25, Longstreet had only just returned from an emergency leave to bury his dead. Now his silence appeared to be the silence of brooding and depression.[5] How would this affect him as a division commander?

The third major general with Johnston's field army had just received his second star: Richard Stoddert Ewell advanced to division command on January 24, 1862, two weeks before his forty-fifth birthday. "Bald as an eagle," recalled one staff officer, Ewell "looked like one; had a piercing eye and a lisping speech." He was a hypochondriac, sometimes an insomniac, and when he grew excited, he swore until "he made the air blue." In an army of eccentrics, "Dick" Ewell stood out as a genuine character. But what of his military ability? Richard Taylor remembered that more than once Ewell turned to him and asked, "What do you suppose President Davis made me a major-general for?" His deployment on the right flank had kept him from winning any acclaim at Manassas, and the bleak fall and winter had not given him any chance to demonstrate potential for greater responsibility. Perhaps the fact that Ewell was a Virginian had helped. Virginia had contributed sufficient troops to the army to fill one of its four divisions, but after Stonewall Jackson's transfer to the Shenandoah there had been no major generals from the Old Dominion and only three brigadiers. Maintaining a careful political balance between the number of regiments and the number of generals from each state had always concerned Jefferson Davis, and as the senior Virginian under Johnston's immediate command, Ewell quite possibly benefited as much from his state affiliation as from a military reputation.[6] Though neither Longstreet nor Smith had proven his ability to handle a division in combat, both must have represented less of a question mark in Johnston's mind than Ewell, who had not had enough time to prove himself competent even at the administrative level.

The other two major generals assigned to the Department of Northern Virginia held detached commands. Fifty-seven-year-old Theophilus H. Holmes, the North Carolinian in charge of the Aquia District, had been a friend of Davis and a classmate of Johnston at West Point (though at far ends of the class—Johnston finished thirteenth and Holmes forty-fourth of forty-six). He had advanced to the rank of major in the infantry by 1861 due more to tenacity and the inexorability of army seniority than to any spark of talent; nonetheless, that Holmes was one of only fifteen active, field-grade officers to resign his commission guaranteed him early promotion in the Confederate army. From his relatively quiet headquarters at Fredericksburg, Holmes had faced no opportunity to prove himself competent or otherwise, though Johnston had already had at least one occasion to criticize him for dilatory performance of his duties.[7] The question of Holmes's ability would not have weighed too heavily on Johnston's mind, because the withdrawal would affect the Aquia command the least.

Thomas J. "Stonewall" Jackson, however, held a much more critical and dangerous post. Wintering his troops at Winchester, the thirty-eight-year-old Virginian already faced growing Federal threats from the north and west; when Johnston withdrew the main army from Centreville, a quick thrust by McClellan from the east could trap Jackson in a very tight sack. Yet political and military realities demanded that Jackson not relinquish a foot more of Valley soil than absolutely necessary. It was an assignment demanding equal portions of boldness, judgment, and skill—talents that the next few months would reveal Jackson possessed in abundance. In February 1862, however, no one suspected Jackson of harboring seeds of genius. Davis had characterized him in a January 31 cabinet meeting as "utterly incompetent." Both the president and Secretary of War Judah P. Benjamin thought him a poor administrator who played favorites with his troops when assigning the best quarters. His subordinates verged on outright mutiny during the winter, complaining to Richmond of mistreatment at the hands of their general. His personality before his rise to fame tended to be seen as arbitrary and querulous rather than eccentric and endearing, and his appearance did not improve his image. "Above the average height, with a frame angular, muscular, and fleshless," wrote Henry Kyd Douglas, Jackson "was, in all his movements from riding a horse to handling a pen, the most awkward man in the army." Even after he had become a lieutenant general, Jackson's peers respected him more than they loved him. A. P. Hill characterized his commander in November 1862 as "that crazy old Presbyterian fool" and suggested that "the Almighty will get tired of helping Jackson after a while [*sic*], and then he'll get the d——ndest thrashing."[8]

Johnston, who had been Jackson's superior since May 1861, at Harpers Ferry, had his own opinion of the dour Virginian, one that seems to have been more favorable than the consensus. Unlike many other officers, Jackson always filed his reports on time, kept Johnston apprised of his position and intentions, and appeared capable of evaluating intelligence about enemy numbers and intentions. Johnston did believe that Jackson tended to be overly aggressive. Commenting on Jackson's plan for a winter campaign the previous year, Johnston observed: "It seems to me that he proposes more than can well be accomplished." But once the government had committed to the operation, Johnston wholeheartedly supported Jackson against all his critics; after an embarrassing directive from Benjamin countermanded his own orders, Jackson attempted to resign, and Johnston felt strongly enough about him to delay his letter and press for a reconsideration. To the secretary of war, Johnston wrote: "I don't know how the loss of this officer can be supplied."[9] After the war Johnston implied—as did almost everyone else—that he had seen early signs of the talent for independent command that Jackson later demonstrated, but the evidence does not support this assertion. Still, it is clear that Johnston rated Jackson much higher in February 1862 than did almost anyone else.

Among Johnston's brigadiers, four figured significantly in his plans for maneuvering the army: Jubal A. Early, D. H. Hill, J. E. B. Stuart, and W. H. C. Whiting. All were West Point graduates, and Johnston considered them as candidates for promotion. In the absence of government action, the general had decided to advance them unilaterally to higher levels of responsibility in fact if not in title.

Early was a forty-five-year-old Virginian who had resigned from the army in 1838 to pursue a legal and political career in his home state, interrupted only by volunteer service in the Mexican War. He had opposed secession but quickly devoted himself to the Confederacy, accepting the colonelcy of the Twenty-fourth Virginia. His conduct at Manassas won him a general's star, and by February 1862 Johnston had begun using him as a division commander. Stoop-shouldered, addicted to chewing tobacco, argumentative, ambitious, and profane, Early elicited extreme responses from his peers: they either liked him or hated him. Longstreet in particular found him distasteful and distrusted his capabilities, but Johnston disagreed and consistently handed Early critical assignments.[10]

Daniel Harvey Hill commanded the detached garrison at Leesburg, which was stronger than a brigade though not quite as large as a division. A forty-one-year-old North Carolinian, Hill had resigned from the army in 1849 to become a professional educator. An ardent Southern nationalist who eagerly embraced secession and had been elected colonel of the First North Carolina, he won the first land engagement in Virginia at Big Bethel, securing his promotion to brigadier general. Hill's coolness under fire was already well known. When he wanted to know the range and caliber of enemy guns across the river, Hill paraded up and down the banks with an escort until the Federals fired on them. Some rounds fell short and others flew overhead. Before the barrage ended, Hill casually took a pick and began digging up shells embedded in the ground to measure their size. Notoriously moody, his letters and reports read more like newspaper editorials than military correspondence. Referring to the constant barrage of furlough requests among his soldiers, he complained that "it was my hopes [*sic*] to have been a soldier in this war, but I have only been a passport clerk."[11] Hill's competence and nerve were essential components in any withdrawal plans, because for at least two days after the movement began, the Leesburg garrison would be outside its fortifications and too far away from the army to be reinforced if attacked.

Covering the withdrawal would be the responsibility of the army's cavalry brigade, commanded by James Ewell Brown "Jeb" Stuart, a Virginian just turned twenty-nine. Stuart had been a protégé and special favorite of Johnston's when the two served together in the First Cavalry on the Kansas border in the 1850s. They were reunited in 1861 when Stuart commanded the cavalry rearguard action that screened Johnston's movement from the Valley to Manassas so successfully that the Federal commander did not know for several days that the Confederates had departed. Naturally flamboyant, he seemed at times not to take the war any more seriously than a jousting tournament; his headquarters tent rang with music and laughter throughout the evening and was decorated in front with a captured Blakely rifled cannon, next to which was chained a trained raccoon. On duty, however, even his critics admitted that Stuart was the consummate professional. Johnston described his cavalry commander to Davis as "a rare man, wonderfully endowed by nature with the qualities necessary for an officer of light cavalry. Calm, firm, acute, active, and enterprising, I know no one more competent than he to estimate the occurrences before him at their true value."[12]

William Henry Chase Whiting commanded the de facto division of three brigades blockading the lower Potomac and guarding Johnston's right flank. The thirty-seven-year-old Mississippian had a well-deserved reputation as one of the best engineers in the army. He had graduated first in his West Point class of 1845, achieving the highest grades ever recorded. Assigned to Johnston's staff in early 1861, he had planned the rail movement to Manassas. Johnston and Whiting had been friends long before the war, and both that acquaintance and Johnston's professional evaluation of Whiting's skills led to a promotion to brigadier general on July 21, 1861. Whiting supervised the defenses along the Potomac with energy and imagination. He had multiple firing positions constructed for each of his few heavy guns and periodically rotated them, successfully disguising his weakness from the Federals across the river. These positions were fortified only from the front and left in the direct line of sight of concealed field batteries placed farther back from the river, so that if a Union raiding party ever seized one of his forward batteries he could drive them off quickly.[13]

Despite his technical competence Whiting often was a management problem for his commander. Personally popular with the troops, who dubbed him "Little Billy," he was excessively pessimistic; Longstreet recalled of Whiting that "though of brilliant, highly cultivated mind, the dark side of the picture was always more imposing with him." This trait was aggravated by intermittent bouts of severe depression and impulsive outbursts. Johnston occasionally chided him gently about the former and repeatedly had to protect him from the consequences of the latter. In January 1862, Whiting's intemperate letter refusing command of a brigade of Mississippians had so aroused the president's ire that he demanded Whiting be demoted to major of engineers. Only some uncharacteristically diplomatic letter writing by Johnston and an abject apology he forced out of Whiting sufficed to save his commission.[14] Johnston was aware that Whiting had grown despondent over the fall of Fort Donelson and that the Mississippian's state of mind would figure prominently in his calculations.

Thus the senior command structure of the Department of Northern Virginia in late February 1862 was hardly a cause for optimism. The leadership in Johnston's department looked almost like that of an army recently defeated instead of one about to conduct a major movement. Nor could Johnston lean too heavily on his staff. He had written Davis on February 16 that he had "no competent staff," a condition that existed for three reasons. First, neither West Point nor the prewar U.S. Army had emphasized staff training. Second, those officers who had somehow acquired staff experience, with few exceptions, preferred field command to a supporting role, which meant that most staff billets were filled either with untrained civilians, political appointments, or officers of such mediocre talent that they could not manage a higher commission. Third, Confederate law followed U.S. precedent and parsimoniously restricted the number of staff officers that even an army commander could appoint to ridiculously inadequate figures: Johnston's staff for the Department of Northern Virginia numbered only eleven officers, supplemented by about a half-dozen aides-de-camp.[15]

As Civil War staffs went, Johnston's was about average. The two men at the top of the organization, Col. George W. Lay, acting inspector general, and Maj. Thomas G. Rhett, assistant adjutant general, were West Point graduates; they were also examples of that peculiar nepotism that often infected the Confederate military. Lay was the son-in-law of Supreme Court Justice and Assistant Secretary of War John Archibald Campbell and was the former aide of Lt. Gen. Winfield Scott. He had the dubious distinction of being one of the very few officers to resign from the U.S. Army as lieutenant colonel without ever receiving a general's star during the war. Though experienced, Lay lacked energy: War Department staffer Robert G. H. Kean thought he possessed "sound principles of administration but . . . little *vim* in the head." He was also, by some reports, an alcoholic.[16]

Thomas Rhett had both lineal and marital ties to the top of Confederate society: his uncle was South Carolina fire-eater Robert Barnwell Rhett; his father-in-law, Virginia politician Thomas F. Mason; and his wife's uncle, diplomat James M. Mason. In April 1861 Rhett had been a major and an army paymaster, and when he entered Confederate service, he did so at his old rank. Rhett, like Lay, never became a general, and his failure to advance seemed to center on his personality; he was good-natured company and a fine poker player but hated paperwork and accepted a staff appointment only as a personal favor to Johnston. There were persistent (and unfounded) rumors that Davis discriminated against him because of his uncle's unyielding antiadministration stance.[17]

Among the rest of the professionals there were men from whom more might be hoped. Captain Edwin J. Harvie, one of Rhett's assistants, was competent as a junior staff officer, possibly because he had more or less the same job that he had held as a lieutenant in the Ninth U.S. Infantry. The chief commissary, Lt. Col. Robert G. Cole, had managed the food supplies at Manassas with reasonable efficiency, but his authority did not extend to the government meatpacking plant at Thoroughfare Gap. Arguably the most talented army surgeon to enter the Confederate army was Maj. A. J. Foard, Johnston's chief surgeon; but Foard's authority was severely constrained by the Richmond bureaucracy. Colonel William N. Pendleton, chief of artillery, would prove himself to be a fumbling tactician, though he was more than adequate for the administrative demands that had so far been placed upon him. The chief of ordnance, however, Maj. E. Porter Alexander, was one of the most talented artillerymen to serve in either army throughout the war.[18]

The four nonprofessionals on the staff were Maj. Archibald H. Cole, inspector of transportation; Maj. A. Pendleton Mason, assistant adjutant general; Maj. Alfred W. Barbour, chief quartermaster; and Maj. B. P. Noland, the commissary of subsistence at Thoroughfare Gap. Cole, a loyal Johnston partisan, was energetic, outspoken, and assertive in carrying out his duties, regardless of any lack of training. Mason had almost certainly acquired his commission as a result of family influence; he was the brother-in-law both of Rhett and Lay and Judge Campbell's son-in-law. He seems to have adapted well, but his assignment was primarily clerical. Johnston is on record as having doubts about the competence both of Barbour and Noland, an ominous sign since the Quartermaster and Commissary Departments were primarily responsible for evacuating the goods stored near Centreville, Manassas, and Thoroughfare Gap. Neither man had any formal training for his post nor evidenced any native talent, but under Confederate law Johnston had no authority to replace them.[19] Thus, Johnston's staff represented that uneven mixture of talent and mediocrity peculiar to most Civil War–era headquarters.

Even if the staff could plan the army's movements and the subordinate generals could direct them, just how well the troops could execute them was another critical question. The Rebel soldiers inhabiting the camps in northern Virginia in February 1862 were not yet the lean, fast-marching infantry-men who would outpace the Federal army time and again over the next three years. Instead, Johnston's brigades were composed of men who had fought no more than a single, short battle (and only about half of them had done that) and then spent a winter drilling in the muddy fields beside their camps. They naively believed that this experience made them seasoned veterans. "A trunk had come with each volunteer," Johnston later bemoaned, recalling the extent of his soldiers' baggage. After detailing the long list of items that Confederate soldiers thought essential in the first year of the war, Carlton McCarthy of the Richmond Howitzers recalled that the soldiers in 1861 and 1862 "were so heavily clad, and so burdened with all manner of things, that a march was tortured." Confirming Johnston's recollections, he observed that "subordinate officers thought themselves entitled to transportation for trunks, mattresses, and folding bedsteads, and the privates were as ridiculous in their demands."[20]

When Johnston issued orders to reduce the troops' impediments to "light marching order," reluctance to part with the luxuries of camp life combined with an ignorance of military terminology to create tremendous confusion. What exactly was "light marching order"? Captain James Conner recorded that in the Hampton Legion the term meant "nothing but blankets and over-coats, and one day's rations, cooked, in their haversacks. The wagons followed with two days' rations and the cooking utensils." Brigadier General Richard Taylor allowed his men a blanket, an extra shirt, an extra pair of drawers, two pairs of socks, and an extra pair of shoes; officers were allowed to strap a tent "fly" to their saddles. The most tragicomical description of "light marching order" came from Col. Thomas W. Thomas of the Fifteenth Georgia. "We were ordered to put ourselves in 'light marching order'—what that was I had to figure out," he wrote. "Cooking utensils was the most vexed question before me—my ten company commanders were at all points about it. . . . Why Sir a treaty can be made with England and France, yea with the North itself, with less diplomatic skill and talent than it required to settle the question of skillets." He complained that "I have had to decide how much a frying pan weighed, how much a skillet, how much a tin pail, how much a coffee pot—even if a credit was to [be] allowed because the handle was off."[21]

Besides troops, the sheer bulk of supplies and equipment possessed by the Department of Northern Virginia represented an almost insurmountable obstacle to rapid movement. In Richmond, Johnston had emphasized that "saving our artillery & stores, especially the heavy guns on the Potomac" would be "next to impossible." From Aquia to Evansport, Whiting deployed at least forty-five heavy cannon, ranging in size from 8-inch rifled guns to 42-pounder naval smoothbores. Some of these guns had limited mobility, and these were the ones that Whiting constantly maneuvered from point to point, but most of the heavy cannon were firmly planted on siege carriages, rendering them immovable. Not only did Whiting lack draft animals to haul the guns off if field carriages could be improvised, but the horses and mules he did possess were among the weakest in the department.[22] Plainly, some other method of removing the guns had to be found.

As a logistical conundrum, saving Whiting's guns paled in comparison to salvaging the mounds of supplies in the army's rear. These had increased all winter because Johnston did not have the wagons to distribute the goods. Considering every category of supply—from food and uniforms to ammunition and blankets—3,240,354 pounds of stores had accumulated at Manassas Junction, despite Johnston's attempts in January and February to have deliveries from Richmond halted. On the army's left flank at Thoroughfare Gap stood the meatpacking plant, erected over Johnston's objections. On the train back from his Richmond conference, the general found in his discussions with Major Noland that the meat surplus was far greater than he had imagined. Piled up in warehouses or sitting in open fields were 1,510,819 pounds of pork and 1,195,914 pounds of beef to be evacuated out of Union reach.[23] Without even considering the supplies on hand at the division or brigade level, Johnston's staff had to plan on employing inadequate trains and a dilapidated railroad effectively enough to spirit away nearly 6 million pounds of material.

Johnston's final problem was secrecy. Outnumbered nearly four to one, he could not afford to let McClellan divine his intentions and attack his columns during the vulnerable days after leaving their old entrenchments and before arriving at new positions. A variety of threats existed. The Federals might combine an attack from the Allegheny Mountains with an advance against Winchester to trap Jackson's division. Likewise, a thrust northwest from Alexandria, simultaneous with one southeast from Harpers Ferry, could potentially pick off D. H. Hill as he retired from Leesburg. Nor was the least of Johnston's fears a sudden amphibious landing on the lower Potomac within hours of the time Whiting deserted his batteries on the river. This move would put Brig. Gen. Joseph Hooker's division in among Whiting's trains before his own men had struggled more than a few miles down the muddy roads.

Only an impenetrable cloak of deception could cover the army through its first, critical hours of retreat, and as Johnston reviewed his position it must have been obvious that such secrecy would be difficult, if not impossible, to achieve. He had just experienced the incredible security leaks that prevailed in the Confederate capital; no details confided to the government could be considered safe. Quite probably, the suspiciously natured Johnston would have assumed, McClellan already knew that a retreat was being discussed. If not, the Federal commander would become aware almost as soon as the railroads began hauling supplies away from Manassas; the lines were simply too porous to keep such an operation secret. Worse still, Hooker's men on the Maryland side of the Potomac had been busily erecting new observation towers that might spot any withdrawal the moment it began. Once the army began to move, its only protection would be the screen provided by Stuart's cavalry brigade—1,300 horsemen organized into five-and-one-half regiments—that might find itself opposed by more than 8,000 blue troopers. To make matters worse, both in reality and in Johnston's mind, Gen. Samuel Cooper was attempting to strip him of one of his best regiments, the First North Carolina Cavalry.[24] If removing the army from the frontiers of Virginia appeared to be a monumental task, removing it secretly must have seemed impossible.

Johnston handled the challenge of mobilizing his department for a withdrawal in the same manner as he might have when serving as the quartermaster general of the U.S. Army. He delegated the responsibility for each category of goods to a particular staff member and then left that officer almost entirely to his own initiative. Given the uneven quality of his staff, this approach might well have been a recipe for disaster, but assisted by a healthy dose of McClellan's usual timidity, it resulted instead in a reasonably well-executed maneuver—unmolested by the Federals and accompanied by a much smaller loss of critical supplies than Johnston's detractors, past and present, have often claimed.

Major Noland received responsibility for the meat at Thoroughfare Gap. Johnston directed him to proceed immediately to the meatpacking plant and shut down the operation. Noland was then to begin removing the bulk of the meat from the storehouses to the loading platforms by the railroad while shipping off directly what he could to Warrenton in his own wagons. The empty buildings were to be burnt or disassembled. Agents were to be appointed and dispatched to Mount Jackson and Orange Courthouse to arrange for the reception and storage of the meat. Meanwhile, Johnston delegated to Major Cole the responsibility for arranging special trains to pick up the tons of beef and pork. Noland assured Johnston that if enough trains ran to Thoroughfare, he could empty the facility in little more than a week.[25]

To Lieutenant Colonels Cole and Barbour fell the task of emptying the depots at Manassas and Centreville. Instead of continuing the system of assigning labor details on a rotating basis from nearby brigades, they received a permanent working party from Ewell's division to remain under their exclusive control during the evacuation. Johnston distrusted Barbour's competence, so he limited the quartermaster to preparing stocks on hand for removal while delegating coordination of transportation to the two Coles and Brig. Gen.

Isaac Trimble. The Coles were to supervise the wagon trains, and Trimble was to use his own brigade to load the trains. Johnston seems to have chosen Trimble for this assignment because he had been a railroad engineer and an administrator for thirty years and might be expected to know how to handle any crisis that arose. Pendleton and Alexander each received responsibility for preparing their commands—the reserve artillery and the ordnance train—for the move. Johnston informed them, however, that when the time came they would each be subordinated to one of the division commanders for purposes of security and marching orders.[26]

Johnston handled the army's remote detachments differently, since his staff could not be expected to supervise them closely. In Jackson's case he relied on the Valley District commander's proven administrative competence, entrusting him with the general outlines of the operation and leaving him the details to work out by himself. Jackson received orders on March 1 to prepare his command to move in case the main army had to fall back. The letter of instruction has not been found, but Jackson's response two days later made it clear that he understood his assignment to be "keeping between you and the enemy and at the same time opposing his advance along the valley." The logistics of preparing Jackson's division for eventual retreat were far simpler than those facing Johnston, both because of its smaller size and the useful—if uncomfortable—experience in rapid movements that Stonewall's officers had gained in the Romney operation. Without any fuss, Jackson had his sick and wounded shipped to Staunton and Charlottesville, relocated his main depot to Mount Jackson, and had the movable supplies of the army loaded onto wagons. Major John A. Harman, the profane chief quartermaster in the Valley, had the wagon trains ready to move several days before Jackson ordered the evacuation of Winchester. No question of wasted supplies was ever raised when the Army of the Valley retreated.[27]

Holmes's task in the Aquia District was even simpler. His depot at Fredericksburg would remain within his lines after the retreat, and the only evacuation of men or supplies he would have to accomplish was the withdrawal of Brig. Gen. John G. Walker's brigade from Aquia and Potomac Creeks and the destruction of a few miles of railroad. His most pressing task would be to safeguard Johnston's right flank—specifically Whiting's division—from a sudden Federal landing. Since Holmes had little more to do than react to direct orders, Johnston decided to keep communication to him down to an absolute minimum. This stance was more than justified in Johnston's mind because, with no direct telegraphic link between Centreville and Fredericksburg, any messages to Holmes would have to pass through Richmond, with all the potential breaches of security therein implied.[28]

The main question facing D. H. Hill's Leesburg garrison was more strategic than logistical: to what point should his troops march? Jackson clearly believed that Hill should withdraw into the Valley and join his division and kept trying to bring Johnston around to this view, even after the retreat had begun. He wrote the army commander on March 8 that "if you can spare Hill and let him move here at once, you will never have any occasion to regret it. The very idea of reenforcements coming to Winchester would, I think, be a damper to the enemy." Besides, Jackson argued, "I greatly need such an officer; one who can be sent off as occasion may offer against an exposed detachment of the enemy."[29] Though there was compelling logic underlying Jackson's request, Johnston decided that to dispatch Hill into the Shenandoah would run contrary to Davis's general strategy of bringing as many troops as possible into supporting distance of Richmond. Hill rejoined the main army.

In the meantime, Hill's primary concern was security. The Confederates at Leesburg were too few to quit their post without the advantage of surprise. Johnston advised Hill not to burn any supplies or facilities he might have to abandon because he could not manage a thorough job of destruction without attracting enemy attention. The retreating column was, however, to set fire to every railroad bridge along its line of march. So that Hill's soldiers could concentrate on swift movement instead of on protecting bulky trains, Johnston had provisions for 3,000 men stationed along his route. Hill kept his own counsel about the impending retreat to the last possible moment. He even kept the patriotic ladies of Leesburg sewing flannel cloth into powder bags for the cannon until the very day of the evacuation, though one sharp artilleryman noticed that the ladies had been instructed to concentrate on producing smaller bags for field guns instead of the larger items required for the siege guns Hill planned to abandon on the banks of the Potomac.[30]

Besides the supplies at Thoroughfare and Manassas, Whiting's heavy artillery along the Potomac was Johnston's other major concern. The understrength teams that had not been able to transport rations efficiently during the winter clearly could not be expected to evacuate forty-five guns weighing between 8,000 to 17,000 pounds each and the stores of an entire division. The only practical option seemed to be to build rafts and to attempt to float the heavy artillery down the Potomac to the railhead at Aquia under the noses of Federal lookouts. Whiting had been ordered to investigate that possibility when Johnston returned from Richmond. He consulted his chief of artillery, Gen. Samuel French, as well as Capt. Frederick Chatard of the Confederate navy and Col. J. Johnston Pettigrew, commander of the North Carolina regiment supporting many of the guns. Pettigrew believed that it might be possible to build rafts that could carry the guns, but French and Chatard were adamant that the operation was not safe. "I deem the attempt to get them there [Aquia Creek] by water with our means, in the face of the enemy, impracticable and hazardous," French reported on February 24. "The steamers guard the river closely and the enemy from the opposite shore see everything at the batteries, and you may rest assured that by the time two-thirds of the guns were dismounted it will be discovered and an attack be made by the steamers and from the guns opposite." Johnston passed on this information to Davis the next day, taking responsibility for the decision not to try to haul away the guns overland: "The land transportation would, it seems to me, require too much time and labor, even were the roads tolerable. They are not now practicable for our field artillery with their teams of four horses." The best that could be done was to destroy the guns in place so that the enemy would not benefit from their capture.[31]

Meanwhile, as Johnston dealt with each of the peripheral issues of evacuation, the major impediment to tactical mobility—the 6 million pounds of supplies at Thoroughfare and Manassas—stubbornly refused to cooperate with his timetable. The main reasons were the inefficiency of the Virginia railroads on which the army depended, the failure of the Confederacy to assert formal control over those lines, and Johnston's own reluctance to become involved in the day-to-day details of the evacuation. Johnston's original conception of the operation had been sound enough, but as his plans began to go awry he did not intervene as immediately or as actively as necessary to keep it on schedule.

Transporting 6 million pounds of cargo, based on an average carrying capacity of 16,000 pounds per freight car, required at least 375 cars. The Orange and Alexandria Railroad, which had the primary responsibility for evacuating everything as far as Gordonsville, had begun the war with only 140 boxcars and flatcars. A significant number of these had been seized by the Federals in Alexandria, and since then, the steady drain of wartime service without replacement parts had whittled the fleet down even further. Because the run from Manassas to Gordonsville passed over a single line of track with short and infrequent turnouts for passing trains, scheduling was of paramount importance. Still, the evacuation should have been possible. With the average locomotive pulling fifteen cars, the entire stockpile of the Department of Northern Virginia should have required slightly more than two trains a day during the period Johnston allowed for preparing the withdrawal.[32]

Unfortunately, the government's reluctance to assume control of the railroads, even in an active military theater, left Johnston and his officers compelled to negotiate with civilian superintendents, such as Orange and Alexandria president John S. Barbour Jr., instead of simply requisitioning what they needed. This arrangement proved to be an exercise in frustration. Barbour promised trains to Noland for transporting the meat from Thoroughfare without informing the supply officers at Manassas. When those officers cried foul and began seizing trains, they unknowingly intercepted the cars heading for the meatpacking plant.[33]

Noland had begun disassembling the plant on February 22; tons of meat were "taken from the houses and placed on platforms for convenience of loading the cars. The force of hands was increased, and every possible arrangement on our part was made for sending off the property." But no trains came. By early March only forty-five freight cars had been loaded. Noland frantically commenced loading as much of the meat—now beginning to spoil—as possible into his inadequate fleet of wagons, "although," he reported angrily, "many trains passed the point and several of them were entirely empty." The process of removing the meat actually delayed Johnston's withdrawal by several days and continued even after the infantry had marched south. It ended only when Lt. Col. Thomas T. Munford of the Second Virginia Cavalry, commanding the rear guard of Stuart's cavalry screen, ordered the remains of the stockpile burned at noon on March 12 as the last Confederate troops quit northern Virginia.[34]

Though the aroma of burning meat certainly pervaded the district for many hours, the scale of the waste and destruction has been distorted by participants and historians out of proportion to reality. Jubal Early contended after the war that so much meat was lost that it "embarrassed us for the rest of the war, as it put us on a running stock." Johnston himself is often cited for his comment to Jefferson Davis on March 13, 1862, that "more than half of the salt meat at Thoroughfare was left there for want of the means of bringing it away." Comparing this ration to the total amount of meat reported at the plant, Douglas Southall Freeman has concluded that "more than 1,000,000 pounds were destroyed or given to farmers in the neighborhood." This has become the standard account of the affair, further expanded and exaggerated by later writers until it reached the hyperbolic proportions exemplified by Robert Tanner's description in *Stonewall in the Valley:* "Unable to empty an army packing plant, Johnston consigned a million pounds of beef to the flames, and his ill-fed retreating columns were tormented by the aroma of sizzling steak." Jeffrey Lash's recent study of Johnston's use of the railroads, undertaken in part to support the thesis of "the overall inferiority of Confederate commanders," indicts the general, who "almost willfully failed to use

the Virginia railroads to save irreplaceable resources." Joseph Glathaar casti-
gates the general for "abandoning or destroying fabulous quantities of equipment, foodstuffs, and personal baggage," and Steven Woodworth characterizes
the retreat as "a logistical disaster."[35]

Indeed, nothing close to 1 million pounds of meat burned. According to
Noland's official report (filed two weeks after Johnston made his off-the-cuff
estimate), of the 2,706,733 pounds of pork and beef at Thoroughfare on February 22, 86.3 percent of it was successfully evacuated, leaving only 369,819
pounds beside the railway. In the last two days before the burning, Noland
estimated that at least 200,000 pounds more were given away to neighborhood farmers, leaving only 169, 819 pounds to be incinerated—a far cry from
1 million pounds. Yet even a loss of 369,000 pounds of meat seems at first
like a sizable one. How important was it? The original stockpile had represented 2,971,156 daily rations of meat, figured at the often optimistic standard of three-quarters of a pound of pork or one-and-one-quarter pounds of
beef for one soldier for one day. Against the "Aggregate Present" (ration
strength) of 42,860 officers and men for the Potomac District at the end of
February, this amount constituted a reserve of only 69.3 days. The total
poundage either given away or burned amounted to no more than a 9.8 days'
meat ration for Johnston's army. The supposed towering mountain of food
condemned to the flames represented between three and five days' rations for
the withdrawing soldiers. This amount was hardly enough to have seriously
"embarrassed" the Confederacy for the rest of the month, much less for the
rest of the war.[36]

The situation at Manassas Junction was equally troublesome. Trimble,
Johnston's designee to handle the loading of supplies on the trains running
south, became embroiled in controversies with railroad officials, Quartermaster
Gen. Abraham Myers, and other officers from Johnston's army. Johnston,
who could conceivably have stepped in and asserted his authority as the commander on the spot, did not, primarily because he seems to have been far more
engrossed with the orders for the retreat of his divisions. This stance left Trimble, Barbour, and the two Coles struggling to meet their commander's schedule for the withdrawal, and in this effort they were draconian. Any damaged
equipment or spoiled rations were shoved to the side. What could not be
loaded was passed out to the troops retreating through the town or
destroyed.[37]

It is difficult to document what fraction of the total they abandoned
because no report as thorough as Noland's was ever filed regarding the evacuation of Manassas Junction. Only Lt. Col. R. G. Cole's 1871 letter, cited by
Johnston in his *Narrative*, provides any quantification of the total number of

supplies in the depot, and his account is questionable on two grounds. The first is the normal vagary of hindsight, combined with Cole's status as a passionate Johnston partisan in postwar debates. The second problem is that Cole's language is ambiguous, and it is impossible to be certain that his figure of 1,434,316 pounds of supplies left behind does not include the 369,817 pounds of meat at Thoroughfare. Cole's account does clearly claim that at least 443,000 pounds of bread, flour, and vinegar were abandoned because they had already spoiled.[38]

Without specific statistics, the best information on just what Johnston's army left behind can be found in Federal reports. Two days after Johnston evacuated Manassas, J. S. Potter entered the town with the first Union cavalry. On March 12 he testified before the Joint Congressional Committee on the Conduct of the War concerning his observations:

> Several hundred barrels of flour, that they had attempted to destroy by burning lay there in a pile partly consumed. There was also a part of a train of cars there, partially destroyed. Among other things, I found a very complete printing office, army blanks, &c., and I should think a little paper had been printed there. The place was generally in a ruin. The depot was burned, some cars and a locomotive or two destroyed, a bridge blown up, several buildings destroyed, and [was] altogether the most desolate scene, it seemed to me, that the human eye could rest upon.[39]

More dispassionately, McClellan, who had the best of motives to exaggerate the booty found in Confederate camps, reported that he had found "many wagons" but only "*some* caissons, clothing, ammunition, personal baggage, &c." He closed his description by noting that he found "the country entirely stripped of forage and provisions."[40] The context of Federal accounts, supported by numerous Rebel reminiscences, strongly suggests that most of the supplies abandoned at Manassas fell into one of three categories: spoiled rations, excess personal gear, or broken-down transport. From a logistical standpoint, therefore, Johnston's evacuation of Thoroughfare Gap and Manassas Junction, though no textbook masterpiece of supply management, did not merit the scorn it has often received.

The withdrawal has also been censured on operational grounds. In *Lee's Lieutenants,* Freeman has described Johnston's movement orders as having been "wretchedly drawn," with "marches not precisely timed in relation to one another." Further, Johnston is criticized because Holmes "was not informed of the withdrawal or told what to do with the troops or heavy guns on his sector. Neither the President nor the Secretary of War was advised when the movement would begin or what the lines of retreat would be."⁴¹ Again, Freeman's assessment has become the standard, even though he neglects many key points, and his account rests on slender evidence.

Moving several columns simultaneously over roads that one South Carolinian characterized as "awful; stiff clay, mud, and water; we stalled about every hundred yards," could not have been organized on a precise minute-by-minute timetable. Instead, Johnston followed the principal of decentralized authority that he had instituted during the winter. Early's division marched first, followed by Smith and Longstreet on parallel roads. Smith was assigned to direct William Pendleton's reserve artillery and the Leesburg garrison, and Longstreet supervised Col. J. B. Walton's Washington Artillery Battalion. Ewell's division formed the infantry rear guard, with the dual assignment of supporting Stuart's cavalry and scouring the country one last time for provisions and forage.⁴²

Attention had in fact been paid to many small details of the retreat. Extra tents had been ordered to shelter the troops turned out of winter cabins. Small parties of pioneers were dispatched to improvise temporary crossings over rain-swollen streams. Each division had a bridge on the Rappahannock assigned to it, and when the troops arrived at the river they discovered that the railroad bridges had already been planked over to accommodate wagons. They also found Johnston's previously prepared entrenchments and stacks of incendiary material piled neatly beside the right of way, just in case Federal pursuit might be quicker than anyone imagined. The entire maneuver, recalled Richard Taylor, "was executed with the quiet precision characteristic of General Johnston, unrivaled as a master of logistics." Of course, the march was muddy and uncomfortable for soldiers unaccustomed to long marches and not as yet resigned to giving up the luxuries of camp life, but this result was unavoidable and, in Johnston's eyes, probably not a bad thing.⁴³

Whiting's withdrawal from the Potomac was not conducted under Johnston's direct eye, but Whiting and French both received considerable supervision from the army commander in terms of the manner in which he wanted the evacuation conducted. Johnston spoke at length with each man at least once during the planning phase and dispatched five letters of instruction to Whiting and three to French during the two weeks prior to the move. Those letters spelled out Johnston's intentions clearly. Heavy guns to be abandoned were to be destroyed in place as quickly and quietly as possible. Whiting was to phase his withdrawal from north to south: "If I telegraph 'It is time,' give your orders and move. Hampton should have a start of some hours. How would it do for him to start after dark, leaving pickets, and march to the road leading from Bacon Rice to your camp, bivouac, and march at your hour next morning?" Johnston later admonished Whiting that since his would be the first brigade in the department to withdraw, "Hampton must move off as cunningly as possible." Whiting would supervise the movement until he reached Fredericksburg, where his force would automatically come under the authority of Holmes.[44]

Holmes had been intentionally left in the dark until March 8, the day the evacuation began. The decision to do so, while possibly defensible on the grounds of security, understandably infuriated Holmes, who felt he had been misused and complained immediately to Cooper. But his very complaint indicated how thorough Johnston's orders had been when Holmes finally received them. When Whiting's brigades arrived, Holmes was to "place these troops beyond the Rappahannock and only to hold the Potomac with strong outposts, breaking up the wharf at Aquia and being ready to destroy the railroad from thence to Fredericksburg."[45] This letter, which is the mainstay of Freeman's contention that Holmes was ill-informed, actually indicates that he received reasonably complete operational instructions in a timely fashion, although he was never made privy to the underlying strategy. Johnston can be criticized primarily for not having taken a few more pains to assuage his subordinate's ego.

Holmes's aggrieved letter to General Cooper may have been the first formal notice that Richmond received of the beginning of the movement. Johnston had been purposefully vague about his starting date in his communications with Davis because he worried that to be specific might result in further leaks, which might in turn cost him the several hours of secrecy he needed to extricate Whiting's and Hill's commands from their exposed positions. Aside from that consideration, since Johnston believed he had been given positive authorization to conduct the withdrawal, he reckoned that setting the exact date was a decision completely within an army commander's purview.

Johnston always acknowledged that he did not communicate with Richmond until the movement was well under way: "The withdrawal from Centreville was not known in Richmond until after the army had taken its position on the Rappahannock." He sent his first official notice of the move two days after it began, on March 12, by which time Smith's, Longstreet's, and Early's divisions had crossed the river, and both Whiting and Hill had reached safe havens. In a purely military sense, Johnston could defend his actions. Despite his attempts at secrecy, the operation became known to the Federals all too rapidly. Hooker reported Whiting's evacuation within less than a day, and Col. John Geary discerned Hill's retreat from Leesburg in about twelve hours. Federal cavalry tentatively probed Stuart's cavalry screen in the Manassas area on March 8 and 9. The *Richmond Examiner* published complete reports of the movement on March 11, correctly inferring that the intent of the operation was to place Johnston's army in better position to participate in the defense of the capital. Bragg's diary indicates that the withdrawal may already have been common knowledge in Richmond when that edition was printed.[46]

The consequence that Johnston overlooked, underestimated, or ignored was the quite predictable result that his reticence had on his relationship with Jefferson Davis.

5
ENTER LEE

Even as Confederate rear guards at Leesburg and Dumfries spiked the heavy guns and laid powder trails into their magazines, and as Maj. B. P. Noland waited impatiently for trains to cart away his mountains of beef and pork, two events occurred that had distinct implications for the defense of Richmond. The first was the return of Gen. Robert E. Lee to the capital city after an absence of several months; the second was the sortie of the ironclad *Virginia* into Hampton Roads. The combination of the two served to confuse an already strained relationship between Joseph Johnston and Jefferson Davis.

General Lee rode the Richmond and Petersburg Railroad into the city, accompanied by a single aide, twenty-four-year-old Capt. Walter H. Taylor. Lee's arrival was so unheralded that it is still impossible to determine with absolute certainty whether he entered the capital on March 6 or 7. What is clear is that as the train lumbered over the James River bridge below the smokestacks of the Tredegar Iron Works, Lee himself had no idea why Jefferson Davis had abruptly summoned him to Richmond.[1]

Lee was the son of Revolutionary War hero and Virginia governor "Light Horse" Henry Lee. He had served on Winfield Scott's personal staff in Mexico, earning three brevet promotions for gallantry; he twice held the prestigious position of superintendent of the U.S. Military Academy. Thus when Lee had resigned his commission as colonel of the First Cavalry and turned down an offer to command the Union army in April 1861, he went South to great expectations. Virginia immediately conferred upon him command of the state's forces, Gov. John Letcher citing his "talent, experience, and devotion to the interests of Virginia." "Whether we have the right of secession or revolution," said Jubal Early on the floor of the Virginia State Convention, "I want to see my State triumphant. I do believe that it will be triumphant under the lead of Major-General Lee." When Virginia formally entered the Confederacy, Davis appointed Lee as the third-ranking general in the army, behind only Samuel Cooper and Albert Sidney Johnston.[2]

For Lee, who turned fifty-five in January 1862, the first ten months of the war were filled with personal frustration and public criticism. "There is no place I can expect to be but in the field," he wrote his wife on May 2, 1861, anticipating that his administrative assignment to coordinate the defense of Virginia from Richmond would end with the establishment of the Confederate government.[3] He was mistaken; Davis retained him at his desk throughout the summer. Much to Lee's disappointment, his only contribution to the victory at Manassas was the necessary but personally unsatisfying task of forwarding troops and supplies to Joseph E. Johnston and P. G. T. Beauregard.

In August the president allowed Lee into the field with an ill-defined supervisory command in western Virginia. At first he was ebullient at the prospect of active duty and sent his wife optimistic letters filled with descriptions of the country: "The mountains are beautiful, fertile to the tops, covered with the richest sward of blue grass & white clover. The inclosed fields waving with the natural growth of timothy. . . . This is magnificent grazing country." But within a month the realities of his position eroded his confidence and depressed his buoyant spirits. His outnumbered troops had few supplies, and measles raged through their camps. His subordinates, political generals untutored in military operations, feuded with each other and ignored his instructions. Even nature seemed to have turned against him: "Rain, rain, rain, there has been nothing but rain," he complained to his son. "So it has appeared to my anxious mind since I approached these mountains."[4]

Lee first discovered the biting criticism of the Southern press when the incompetence of Brigadier Generals John Floyd and Henry Wise combined with his own tactical inexperience and resulted in an inglorious failure to drive the enemy off Cheat Mountain in mid-September. Beauregard might be hailed as the Confederacy's Napoleon and Jackson nicknamed Stonewall, but the sobriquets reserved for Lee were Granny and Evacuating Lee. At first he was stoic: "Everybody is slandered, even the good. How should I escape?" But by October the harshness of the Richmond papers had become so unrelenting that even the reserved Lee could not keep himself from reacting, at least to family and close friends. "I am sorry," he wrote in October, "that the movements of the armies cannot keep pace with the expectations of the editors of the papers. I know they can regulate matters satisfactorily to themselves on paper. I wish they could do so in the field." Referring bitterly to his most recalcitrant subordinate, Lee remarked, "Genl Floyd has the benefit of three editors on his staff, I hope something will be done to please them."[5]

Jefferson Davis, however, had been fully aware of the handicaps under which Lee had attempted to operate and never allowed public opinion to shake his faith in those he trusted. In November he recalled Lee from the rain-soaked mountains and dispatched him to oversee the coastal defenses of South Carolina, Georgia, and Florida. The assignment did not bring a respite from either politicians or publishers but did carry the unequivocal authority of departmental command. Lee inherited the same dismal conditions Johnston had found in northern Virginia: "The volunteers dislike work & there is much sickness among them besides. Guns too are required, ammunition, & more men." Faced with defending hundreds of miles of coast with fewer than 30,000 soldiers and inadequate artillery, he instituted a policy of defense in depth at critical points and abandonment of isolated or insignificant islands, maintaining a mobile reserve along the coastal rail line. The key to his defensive system was to avoid direct confrontation with the "enemy's big boats"; "I am in favor of abandoning all exposed points as far as possible within reach of the enemy's fleet of gunboats & of taking interior positions, where we can meet on more equal terms." This difficult decision earned him the enmity of the planters, whose holdings were then exposed to Yankee depredations— "Low-country gentlemen curse Lee," recorded one observer. Lee was unmoved by the criticism; several letters that he posted to Richmond during this period were instrumental in providing the president with his rationale for shortening the lines of the Confederacy on a much larger scale.[6]

Lee's state of mind by this point was gloomy, although hardly desperate. The same day he received Davis's telegram summoning him to Richmond, he wrote to his daughter Annie that the times "look dark at present, & it is plain we have not suffered enough, labored enough, repented enough, to deserve success." He was pessimistic about the South's commitment to the war: "Our people have not been earnest enough, have thought too much of themselves & their ease, & instead of turning out to a man, have been content to nurse themselves & their dimes, & leave the protection of themselves & families to others." Though he could not dismiss the numerical superiority of the Federals—"against ordinary numbers we are pretty strong, but against the hosts our enemies seem to be able to bring everywhere, there is no calculation"—he was still combative: "If our men will stand to their work, we shall give them trouble & damage yet."[7]

By the end of February, Lee's scanty resources had been seriously depleted by Davis's strategic redeployment of several of his regiments to Tennessee. Unhappily, and in the face of great local opposition, Lee completed his almost total withdrawal of Confederate forces from eastern Florida while cutting his garrisons along the Georgia and South Carolina coasts to the bone. Certain that the Federals would assault Savannah when they learned of his reduction in force, Lee went to that city in order to direct its defense personally. He was there on March 2 when the abrupt and unrevealing telegram from the president arrived: "If circumstances will, in your judgment, warrant your leaving, I wish to see you here with the least delay."[8] Lee delayed his departure just long enough to write out detailed instructions for Brig. Gen. A. R. Lawton, commanding in Georgia, and to turn over the department to his deputy, Maj. Gen. John C. Pemberton. Leaving Savannah on March 3, he arrived in Charleston the next day and took the train north for Richmond on March 5. Whatever speculation the Virginian made on the nature of Davis's orders, it is almost certain that he did not anticipate that the president wanted to appoint him commanding general of the Confederate army.[9]

Even had Lee been publicly expected in Richmond, the events of March 8 would have immediately overshadowed his entrance. Shortly after noon, the Confederacy's first ironclad, the converted frigate *Merrimac,* rechristened the *Virginia,* steamed slowly out of the Norfolk Navy Yard, down the Elizabeth River, and into Hampton Roads. The *Virginia,* recalled Capt. John Taylor Wood, who commanded her aft gun, "was an experiment in naval architecture, differing in every respect from any then afloat." Her officers and crew "were strangers to the ship and to each other. Up to the hour of her sailing she was crowded with workmen. Not a gun had been fired, hardly a revolution of the engines had been made, when we cast off." The vessel could make only five knots and had such a large turning radius that it required nearly forty minutes to bring her about. "She was as unmanageable as a water-logged vessel," Wood commented.[10]

She was also nearly invulnerable. In an action lasting four hours, Adm. Franklin Buchanan's ship rammed and sank the thirty-gun sloop *Cumberland,* pounded the fifty-gun *Congress* into surrender with her rifled cannon, and ran the frigate *Minnesota* aground. Shot after shot ricocheted harmlessly off her angled iron plating. Watching the unequal fight from Ragged Island on the south bank of the James River, Brig. Gen. Raleigh Colston found that a freak acoustical effect imparted an air of eerie unreality to the conflict: "To our amazement, not a sound was heard by us from the beginning of the battle. A strong March wind was blowing directly from us toward Newport News. We could see every flash of the guns and the clouds of white smoke, but not a single report was audible."[11]

The repercussions of the engagement, however, rang loud and clear. The *Virginia* "made obsolete the navies of the world," observed Shelby Foote, "between noon and sunset of that one day." The clash, editorialized the *Richmond Examiner,* "opens a new chapter in naval warfare, and marks a new era in the struggle which the South is engaged in." The effect of the news on the Confederate capital, recalled one Richmonder, "was electrifying. . . . For days, this glorious engagement filled all hearts and minds. Nothing else was talked of." The "gunboat fever" that had haunted the city on the James evaporated in hours; one newspaper commented wryly about residents who claimed to have been able to hear the sound of the battle. Even the appearance of an opposing ironclad, the *Monitor,* the next day could not keep optimistic citizens from visualizing a fleet of *Virginias* smashing the blockade and securing Southern independence.[12]

Commanders on the spot predicted far less grand results. Naval officers knew that "at no time did the *Virginia* attain the power and capacity of a seagoing vessel or exceed the measure of usefulness originally designed for her—that of harbor defense." Major General Benjamin Huger, commanding at Norfolk, did not want to keep risking the ironclad in Hampton Roads and suggested that she be limited to operating inside Norfolk Harbor. Writing from Yorktown, Maj. Gen. John B. Magruder predicted that "the *Merrimac* [*sic*] will make no impression on Newport News, in my opinion, and if she succeeds in sinking the ships lying there it would do us little or no good."[13]

Despite these cautions, the first genuinely good news in months introduced an atmosphere of near-euphoria into the Confederate high command. War Secretary Judah P. Benjamin admonished Huger that "none of us are of the opinion that it would be proper to lose the vast advantage resulting from the enemy's fright at the bare idea of the *Virginia* reappearing among the wooden ships." Naval Secretary Stephen Mallory, who fervently believed in the ironclad's ability to "make a dashing cruise on the Potomac as far as Washington" or even New York, where "she would shell and burn the city and the shipping," was reluctant to give up his dreams. He pressed the ship's commander for the next month to make "a dash in York River, or even further." Lee himself was never optimistic enough to plan raids on Northern cities, but he also subscribed to the idea that the vessel could cruise into the York River and disrupt Federal shipping there. An inflated idea of the *Virginia*'s capabilities probably influenced Davis to believe that the ship could so effectively protect Norfolk and Yorktown that he could afford to transfer a substantial number of troops from eastern to northern Virginia. He telegraphed Johnston on March 10 that "further assurances [have been] given to me this day that you shall be promptly and adequately reinforced, so as to enable you to maintain your position."[14]

Johnston, of course, had already begun the withdrawal before Davis sent the message, although the president would not know that for at least another twenty-four hours. Unfortunately, the chance juxtaposition of Johnston's decision not to inform the authorities in Richmond of the start of the operation with Lee's appearance there and the brief elation at the early exploits of the

Virginia led to a further deterioration of their relations. It also put Lee in a position to begin modifying Davis's plans for the defense of Richmond.

Exactly when Davis knew Johnston had evacuated his position is difficult to determine. He told Johnston that he had received his "first information of your retrograde movement" on March 15, although he later admitted that "I have had many and alarming reports of great destruction of ammunition, camp equipage, and provisions, indicating precipitate retreat; but, having heard no cause for such a sudden movement I was at a loss to believe it." The Speaker of the Virginia House of Representatives, Thomas Babcock, apparently delivered first news of Johnston's movements to Davis on the afternoon of March 10, and Thomas Bragg's diary suggests that the entire cabinet immediately fell to discussing the retreat: "Our Army of the Potomac [*sic*] is moving everything back. I fear it will be a bad business." Nor could the president—even in a strictly official sense—have portrayed himself as unaware of the operation after March 11, when the Richmond newspapers began reporting the story.[15]

The most thorough coverage in the newspapers came from the antiadministration *Richmond Examiner,* which perhaps not coincidentally had close ties to Johnston.[16] Characterizing the operations as "the judicious movements of our army," the *Examiner* detailed not only the extent of the retreat but correctly named Johnston's new line, and even analyzed the strategic thinking behind Davis's decision to pull back:

> The grand movement of the army on the Potomac, in withdrawing from its offensive line on the river of that name, and assuming a defensive one on the line of the Rappahannock and Rapidan, places a new complexion on the entire war in Virginia.
>
> The policy of this change of position with reference to the intended attack of the enemy is obvious. The Potomac was the proper base for offensive operations against Maryland and Washington city; but as a line of defense for Richmond, or for general resistance, it is the most dangerous that could be held.[17]

The paper further asserted that "General Johnston is understood to have the confidence of the administration to such an extent that, as a singular exception, he has the control and direction of military movements in his department entirely in his own discretion." Though the paper's antagonistic stance certainly alienated the president, Bragg's diary indicates that topics covered in the *Examiner* were often discussed in cabinet meetings. It stretches coincidence to the breaking point to believe that no one in the cabinet or in

Davis's own entourage would have brought such an important story to his attention. There were other indicators that the move had commenced. Theophilus Holmes's letter of complaint was posted to Samuel Cooper on March 9, and Lee's response, dated March 14, reveals that he already knew that the march was under way. Johnston himself mailed a letter announcing the change of base to Davis on March 12, although the president never acknowledged receiving it.[18]

Given the evidence that Davis must have been aware of Johnston's actions well before March 15, why did he deny any such knowledge? One possibility is that the president had convinced himself that he never issued positive orders for the retreat, that it was only discussed as a contingency plan, and that Johnston had not been authorized to initiate it without further consultation. The preserved correspondence between the two men from February 23 through March 6 is unfortunately quite ambiguous. Davis later cited it to prove he had never ordered or authorized the move, and Johnston quoted many of the same letters to argue the opposite case.[19]

Davis's first significant letter of the period, dated February 28, began by admitting that Johnston's appreciations of George McClellan's intention to advance very soon "clearly indicate prompt effort to disencumber yourself of everything which would interfere with your rapid movement when necessary." Following a discussion of potential defensive lines and the likelihood of reinforcing Johnston's army, the president returned to the topic of retreat:

> In the mean time, and with your present force, you cannot secure your communication from the enemy, and may at any time, when he can pass to your rear, be compelled to retreat at the sacrifice of your siege train and army stores, and without any preparation on a second line to receive your army as it retired. As heretofore stated in conversation with you, it is needful that the armies on the north, the east, and the proximate south of this capital should be so disposed as to support each other. With their present strength and position the armies under your command are entirely separated from the others.
>
> Threatened as we are by a large force on the southeast, you must see the hazard of your position, by its liability to isolation and attack in rear, should we be beaten on the lines south and east of Richmond; and that reflection is connected with consideration of the fatal effect which the disaster contemplated would have upon the cause of the Confederacy.

Davis then commented on the need to save supplies and presented his analysis of Jackson's position in the Valley. To this point the letter resembled a strategic appreciation, but in the last few lines the president included three sentences rife with the potential to be interpreted in different ways: "As has been my custom, I have only sought to present general purposes and view. I rely on your special knowledge and high ability to effect whatever is practicable in this our hour of need. . . . Let me hear from you often and fully."[20]

Honorable men could disagree concerning Davis's intentions in crafting those sentences and be so sure of their reading that they never realized the ambiguity inherent therein. Johnston clearly had been given authority to maneuver his army as he saw fit if directly attacked, but could he order a retreat without enemy action? He firmly believed that he had already been given instructions to conduct the withdrawal and would have read those sentences as confirmation that the president had left the timing up to him. To Davis the phrase "let me hear from you often and fully" may well have betokened a desire to be consulted prior to any nonemergency action. Incredibly, each man seems to have been so sure of his own interpretation of the words that after February 28 neither bothered to make sure of the other's intentions.

Certainly the letter that Davis dispatched to Johnston on March 4 showed that the president by then hoped that events would render the evacuation unnecessary: "I am making diligent effort to re-enforce your columns. It may still be that you will have the power to meet and repel the enemy." Yet Davis still sounded a note of pessimism, observing that "it is not to be disguised that your defective position and proximity to the enemy's base of operations do not permit us to be sanguine in that result. It is therefore necessary to make all due preparations for the opposite course of events." Though Davis ended the letter with the usual admonition to "please keep me fully informed and frequently advised of your condition," he coupled this with a reiteration of the army commander's latitude of action. "You will be assured that in my instructions to you I did not intend to diminish the discretionary power which is essential to successful operations in the field, and that I fully rely upon your zeal and capacity." The letter, which probably arrived after the withdrawal had commenced, would not have decisively cleared up potential misunderstandings even had it arrived two days earlier.[21]

Thus it is possible that Davis did not credit the early reports of Johnston's withdrawal because he could not believe that Johnston would disobey what he evidently considered to have been direct orders. It is also possible that Davis's response to the retrograde may have been colored by Lee's arrival in Richmond. Lee, to Davis's great surprise, did not agree with his plans to reduce the length of Confederate lines in Virginia.

As soon as the president had developed his strategic concept of subordinating all operations in Virginia to the defense of Richmond, he had realized that a major command problem existed. The city itself was the logical central point from which to coordinate the movements of Johnston's department with those of John Magruder, Huger, and the Richmond defenses; and although Davis undoubtedly believed himself competent to direct those armies, he was realistic enough to understand that he could not do so while serving as the country's chief executive. As much as the president personally admired Judah Benjamin and supported his tenure at the War Office, he also recognized the folly of entrusting an untrained, if brilliant, civilian with what amounted to an operational command. General Samuel Cooper had evidenced neither the talent nor the inclination to handle such an assignment. Johnston himself, as the ranking commander in the area, would naturally command any combined army; but for several reasons he was a poor choice for the overall responsibility. Probably most important to Davis was his belief that Johnston's presence was essential to the morale of the Department of Northern Virginia. "I had no wish," Davis remarked later, and in a slightly different context, "to separate him from the troops with whom he was so intimately acquainted, and whose confidence I believed he deservedly possessed."[22] Less significant, but still a consideration, was the friction that Davis recognized not only between himself and Johnston but also between the general and the bureau chiefs in Richmond. These facts argued against bringing Johnston to Richmond, especially when combined with the general's apparent willingness to consort with the administration's political enemies.

In order for Johnston to be retained in command of his own army yet subordinated to the orders of a supervising commander, Confederate law required that the new officer outrank him. Eliminating Cooper, only Sidney Johnston and Robert E. Lee met that qualification. The other Johnston, deeply involved in the campaign to redeem the disasters in Tennessee, was obviously not a candidate for the post. Almost by default, as soon as Davis settled on his new concept for defending Richmond by organizing a theater command, the choice fell on Lee. None of these circumstances, however, should be construed to suggest in any way that to Davis Lee represented a Hobson's choice. The president had unwavering faith in Lee's capacity as a commander, despite his superficially disappointing Confederate career. Moreover, Lee had been the original architect of Virginia's defenses, had planned most of the fortifications then under construction, and had a thorough knowledge of the terrain in northern and eastern Virginia.[23] Davis may also have believed that the rank-sensitive Johnston might be more amenable to accepting direction from an old friend.

The position that Davis planned for Lee was originally to be entitled commanding general of the Armies of the Confederate States, following the U.S.

practice of depositing that title on the senior general officer in service in the nation's capital. This appointment would allow Lee not only to control operations in Virginia but also to deal with a variety of military matters throughout the Confederacy—matters that were not readily resolved by civilians, as had been proved by the experience of having Leroy P. Walker and Benjamin in the War Office. Davis's friends in Congress introduced a bill to allow the appointment. Even the president's opponents supported the measure because they believed that it would take much of the management of the war out of his hands; but when Davis received the bill, he balked at the wording of the legislation. The commanding general could be appointed only by the president "with the advice and consent of the Senate," and he was empowered "when he shall deem it advisable, [to] take command in person of our army or armies in the field." Both of these provisions gave Davis pause, the first because he did not admit that Congress had the right to place restrictions on his appointive powers as commander in chief, and the second because it put the assumption of field command at the general's discretion, not the president's. Douglas Southall Freeman has suggested that these questions of constitutional authority represented the foundation of Davis's objections: "Strict construction of the organic law was a matter of political conscience, for which he would do battle even if the enemy's divisions were at the doors of the capitol."[24]

Compelling as this argument seems, Davis's veto message contained a second line of reasoning, which may have come to him from consultation with Lee or after reflection on the personality of Johnston. "No general would be content to prepare troops for battle, conduct their movements, and share their privations during a whole campaign if he expected to find himself superseded at the very moment of action." Impatient to install Lee officially, Davis resolved his dilemma by using his own executive power on March 13 to order Lee "assigned to duty at the seat of government" and "under the direction of the President . . . charged with the conduct of military operations in the armies of the Confederacy."[25]

Lee did not welcome another desk assignment—"I cannot see either advantage or pleasure in my duties"—and the newspapers denigrated it as a reduction "from a commanding general to an orderly sergeant." Historians have tended to interpret Lee's distaste and the public derision toward the position as supporting the view that Davis had placed him in an essentially powerless advisory post. Freeman has described the assignment: "Davis entrusted to him the minor vexious matters of detail. . . . On the larger strategic issues the President usually consulted him and was often guided by his advice," yet never "was Lee given a free hand to initiate and direct to full completion any plan of magnitude. He had to work by suggestion rather than by command." "The grandiose official designation was almost meaningless," contends Clifford Dowdey, "and he was advisor in name only. From the beginning, Davis apparently regarded Lee as something of an executive assistant." More recently, Hermann Hattaway and Archer Jones have argued that "Davis created informally through Lee's appointment a modern chief of staff," an interpretation that credits Lee with more power than previously assumed but that still characterizes him as having no command authority.[26]

Such was not the case. From March 14 until June 1, 1862, Lee styled himself and functioned as the Confederacy's commanding general. Davis referred to him as the "commanding general," as did the secretary of war. Walter Taylor described his duties as "military advisor to the President and as commanding general of all the armies in the field." Colonel T. A. Washington and Maj. A. L. Long, both of whom soon joined Lee's staff, habitually referred to him as the commanding general and phrased letters in his behalf as definitive orders and not requests. Lee acted directly and not at all as if he believed his title to be purely nominal. On his own authority he issued General Orders to the army, transferred troops between departments, and directed the Adjutant and Inspector General's Office to settle organizational questions to his specifications. He signed the majority of his letters to commanders of departments as "Robert E. Lee, General, Commanding."[27]

Following U.S. Army precedent, Lee did not seek to control the activities of Sidney Johnston because Johnston's commission predated his own, but in his dealings with other generals there is ample evidence that Lee's command authority was acknowledged throughout the army. General Cooper immediately began to forward all operational inquiries from field commanders to "General Lee, Commanding." The list of general officers who directly addressed Lee as the commanding general included P. O. Hebert in Texas, Henry Heth and Humphrey Marshall in western Virginia, Benjamin Huger in Norfolk, John B. Magruder in Yorktown, John Pemberton in South Carolina, and even Joseph Johnston himself.[28] Clearly Davis did not recall Lee from the Atlantic Coast to serve as a figurehead. Though Lee commanded "under the direction of the President," this qualification existed in both Davis's appointment orders and in the vetoed legislation. Indeed, the only diminution of power intended by the president was the prohibition against Lee's assuming a field command without positive orders. To have emasculated the post would have defeated Davis's intent in making Lee the direct supervising commander for the defense of Richmond.

The problem that developed in the triangular relationship among Davis, Johnston, and Lee was not, therefore, one of any ambiguity in Lee's authority. It was one of strategic conception: Lee did not agree with the premise upon which Davis and Johnston had agreed to conduct operations. Though necessity had required him to retire inland to oppose the Federals along the coast, Lee consistently disapproved of intentionally relinquishing territory in anticipation of an enemy offensive. He outlined his rationale for retaining positions as far forward as possible in a letter to Maj. Gen. John C. Breckinridge in March 1864:

> The enemy generally, in his advances in the country, threatens several sections and rapidly advances against one, and concentration of our troops can only be made on a retired line. The longer, however, he can be held on an advanced line the more certainly can concentration be made to oppose him in retired positions.[29]

There was an emotional as well as an intellectual component to Lee's disinclination to yield Virginia soil to the Yankees. Much of his personality was tied up with his identification as a Virginian; during the secession crisis, Freeman represents Lee as "determined from the outset that he would adhere to Virginia and defend her from any foe." Though it is probably incorrect to extend this argument as far as have Thomas Connelly and Archer Jones and to assert that "one might infer that Lee was fighting for Virginia and not the South," there is little room to doubt that Lee felt a special obligation to contest the Federals grudgingly for every piece of the Old Dominion's territory.[30]

Lee had even more personal reasons to reject strategic withdrawals. He had already lost his ancestral home in Arlington to Union occupation in 1861, which concerned Lee for financial as well as for emotional reasons: "Everything at Arlington will I fear be lost," he had written G. W. C. Lee in January 1862, "& it will take all the land at the White House & Romancoke to pay the legacies to the girls with interest." A Federal advance up the York River would threaten White House directly, endangering not only the family's financial stability but also the safety of Lee's invalid wife.[31] These were, however, secondary considerations. Lee, like many other Southerners, was willing to risk personal ruin and family disaster to achieve independence. To Lee, Davis's plan to withdraw Johnston's army—and Jackson's detachment in the Valley—simply made little, if any, military sense, especially given the *Virginia*'s apparent ability to defend the mouth of the James River. After the war, he confided to Col. John S. Mosby that he believed Johnston's withdrawal had been a great mistake. Attorney General Thomas Bragg noticed on March 10 that, with respect to Johnston's withdrawal, Lee "had not been informed of it, I suppose, and to me it seemed he did not approve of the movement."[32]

Lee's letter to Theophilus Holmes on March 16 is also significant with regard to his appreciation of the military situation in Virginia. After observing that the muddy condition of the roads would probably prevent a general advance by McClellan, he continued:

> But that he will advance upon our line as soon as he can, I have no doubt. To retard his movements, cut him up in detail if possible, attack him at disadvantage, and, if practicable, drive him back, will of course be your effort and study. *It is not the plan of the Government to abandon any country that can be held,* and it is only the necessity of the case, I presume, that has caused the withdrawal of the troops to the Rappahannock. I trust there will be no necessity of retrograding farther. The position of the main body of the Army of the Potomac seems to have been taken in reference to the reported advance of the enemy up the Shenandoah Valley. A report from General Johnston of his plans and intentions has not yet been received. His movements are doubtless regulated by those of the enemy.[33]

For Lee, ten days after arriving in Richmond and three days after his appointment to the army's senior post, to say that "it is not the plan of the Government to abandon any country that can be held," represented a complete reversal of Jefferson Davis's pronouncement to an astonished cabinet on February 19 that "the time had come for diminishing the extent of our lines." Thus, Davis's hard line in response to Johnston's withdrawal may well have been a reaction to Lee's strongly held opinion that strategic retreats were not only unnecessary but positively dangerous.

If such were the case, then it would explain the next immediate controversy between Davis and Johnston: where to position his army. At the February 20 cabinet meeting, Davis ordered Johnston "to have a reconnaissance of the country in his rear with reference to another line, and it is probable the Rappahannock will be selected." Johnston had trouble securing sufficient engineers to perform such a survey.[34] Besides, Davis's February 28 letter led him to think that the position of his forces was a strategic, rather than a tactical, question; he would locate his army however close the president thought it should be to Richmond and fortify that position as best he could.

Accordingly, on March 13 Johnston informed Davis that as soon as he had emptied the reserve depot at Culpeper Courthouse, "I shall cross the Rapidan and take such a position as you may think best in connection with those of other troops." The president asserted in 1865 that he took this as a declaration that Johnston was "ignorant of the topography of the country in his rear." Yet Johnston's letter itself contains strong evidence that such was not the case, for it included a well-conceived suggestion for the positioning of the army. "By proper management of the railroad it seems to me that, from the neighborhood of Gordonsville 20,000, or even 30,000, men might be thrown into Richmond in a single day." Centering his divisions on Gordonsville would also leave Johnston ready to dispatch troops quickly to support Jackson in the Shenandoah.[35]

The president chose to interpret Johnston's letter in the narrowest possible terms and essentially to repudiate his own strategic design of the previous month. Instead of acknowledging his intent to bring Johnston's army within supporting distance of the capital, Davis wrote to the general:

> I have not the requisite topographical knowledge for the selection of your new position. I had intended that you should determine that question. . . . The question of throwing troops into Richmond is contingent upon reverses in the West and Southeast. The immediate necessity for such a movement is not anticipated.[36]

"To further inquiry from General Johnston as to where he should take position," Davis said in his memoirs, "I replied that I would go to his headquarters in the field, and found him on the south bank of the river, to which he had retired, in a position possessing great natural advantages." The narrative of this visit is extremely confusing, and many of the specifics are contradicted by other evidence. Davis implied that the visit began at Rapidan Station and continued to Fredericksburg only when Johnston expressed ignorance of the defensive potential of the lower part of the Rappahannock River. Johnston and his staff consistently denied throughout the decades following the war that the president had ever visited the main body of the army. The dates and locations of the correspondence of Davis and Johnston, as well as casual references to the trip by Lee and Bragg, suggest that the president took the train to Fredericksburg on March 21 and returned to Richmond in the evening of March 22. He did, however, travel to Fredericksburg via Gordonsville, though there is no direct evidence that he visited Johnston's lines there. Even when he was collecting evidence for his memoirs, the statements submitted to Davis in 1885 mentioned only a visit to Fredericksburg, not to the Rapidan.[37]

Specific itinerary aside, why did Jefferson Davis visit Joseph Johnston? Davis claimed that he did so to help Johnston select a satisfactory defensive position, a task made necessary because Johnston "had neglected the primary duty of a commander" in determining a safe line of retreat. If this were the case, it is difficult to explain why the president waited a week to act after receiving

Johnston's inquiry. By the time Davis met Johnston, the army had already taken a permanent line on the south bank of the Rappahannock, complete with artillery emplacements on commanding hills and entrenchments around the bridges. Nor did it make sense for the chief executive of the Confederate states to spend two days surveying a defensive line forty miles north of the capital when he had just appointed a commanding general to supervise the operations of the armies in the field.

Contemporary letters and telegrams suggest that Davis visited Johnston for another reason entirely. Federal advances in North Carolina and the first landing of troops from the Army of the Potomac at Fortress Monroe had convinced Davis—and Lee—that the main Union effort was to be made against either Richmond or Norfolk from the southeast. The president went to see Johnston in order to gauge personally the feasibility of withdrawing some infantry and artillery from the Department of Northern Virginia to reinforce the other departments defending Richmond. He also needed to find a senior commander to accompany the troops.[38] Fully aware of Johnston's sensitivity to having his army raided for general officers, Davis probably decided that it would be better to confront him on the issue in person. Davis planned to have two brigades of infantry, each supported by an artillery battery, sent to the capital, from which they could be deployed with about a day's notice to North Carolina, Norfolk, Yorktown, or even back to the Rappahannock.[39] Loath as he was to part with any of his soldiers, Johnston recognized that this sort of maneuver was precisely why he had been withdrawn closer to Richmond, and he could not have argued against the logic of establishing a centrally located reserve, no matter how small.

Davis's plan allowed Johnston to rid himself of one general in whom he had little confidence and to advance another for whom he had great plans. Theophilus Holmes had never been a favorite with his commander, and his loud fits of pique at being kept in the dark during the withdrawal had greatly embarrassed Johnston. Since then, even though reinforced by W. H. C. Whiting's 7,000 men, Holmes maintained an incessant barrage on Richmond over the untenability of his position. Unfortunately, his date of rank made him senior to every other major general in the Department of Northern Virginia except G. W. Smith. As a native North Carolinian, Holmes was a politically acceptable choice if a senior officer had to be sent to oppose Ambrose Burnside. Johnston, therefore, was hardly unhappy about agreeing to let him go. Holmes's departure paved the way to advance Smith from division commander to the semi-independent command of the Aquia District.[40]

Johnston and Davis seem to have only one prolonged private conversation during the president's stay in Fredericksburg. It occurred around midday on

March 22, when the two men rode north across the Rappahannock onto Stafford Heights, accompanied only by a few aides, who discreetly fell back out of earshot. What they discussed remains a subject for conjecture; neither man ever alluded to the conversation in letters or memoirs. At the end of the ride, President Davis did agree with General Johnston that the north bank of the river, and even the city of Fredericksburg, could not be held against a determined enemy attack. To one of Holmes's aides Davis quipped, "To use a slang phraze [*sic*], your town of Fredericksburg is right in the wrong place." Following this excursion, the president met with several delegations of towns-people; drafted the orders detaching Holmes, two brigades, and two batteries from Johnston's army; and caught the afternoon mail train back to Richmond.[41]

Those two weeks, from March 7 to March 22, 1862, represented a definite, if undramatic, turning point in the Confederate defense of Richmond. Davis, once committed to a close defense of that city, was vacillating between his own concept and that of Lee, who envisioned keeping the Federals at arm's length for the longest practical time. Eventually, by mid-April, Davis subscribed totally to Lee's idea of defending as much of Virginia as possible instead of concentrating on the defense of the capital. Between March 22 and April 17, 1862, however, neither Davis nor Lee had complete control of Confederate strategy. From Johnston's perspective, the result was a series of mixed messages from his high command. First, the president seemed to authorize his withdrawal from the frontier, and then he essentially repudiated it. Next, Davis told Johnston on March 15 that there was no immediate need to consider shuttling troops into the capital but reversed himself a week later. In his *Narrative* Johnston represented the president during this visit as "uncertain," and his correspondence over the next few weeks indicated that he often wondered just who was in charge of operations in Virginia—Davis or Lee.[42]

6

SHOULD YORKTOWN
BE DEFENDED?

Sixty miles south of Norfolk, on March 20, 1862, the Federal transport *Delaware* deposited two companies of Col. Thomas G. Stevenson's Twenty-fourth Massachusetts on the undefended wharves in Washington, North Carolina. The cannon had been removed from the batteries designed to protect the town, and the pilings, sunk to obstruct the Tar River, were too far underwater to keep back a shallow-draft transport. A drillmaster of some repute in the prewar Massachusetts militia, Stevenson formed his men up and marched them smartly into the center of the town. At the courthouse, "We nailed the Stars and Stripes to a flag pole" while "the band played national airs and men cheered." The Bay State soldiers then reshouldered arms, marched to their boats, and steamed back down to Pamlico Sound. The astonished residents of Washington had been "occupied" for about an hour, but the message was clear: the U.S. Navy could land troops almost anywhere along the unprotected Confederate coast.[1]

As disquieting as was the news from North Carolina, a more ominous storm was finally breaking; while Joseph Johnston and Jefferson Davis conferred in Fredericksburg, George McClellan had already begun his much-delayed grand offensive. *New York Times* reporter William Swinton watched in awe as the Army of the Potomac struck its camps around Washington and marched to the docks in Alexandria and Annapolis. Four hundred assorted steamers and schooners, escorted by the North Atlantic Blockading Squadron, had been contracted to shift the army to Fortress Monroe as the prelude to McClellan's advance on Richmond. Swinton watched, day after day, as the troops tramped across the wharves and jammed themselves into the transports. The figures went down in his notebook as the Yankee soldiers boarded the boats: "one hundred and twenty-one thousand five hundred men, fourteen thousand five hundred and ninety-two animals, forty-four batteries, and the wagons and ambulances, ponton-trains [*sic*], telegraph materials, and enormous equipage required for an army of such magnitude."[2]

The movement of such a considerable host, spread out over several weeks, could not be concealed. Confederate pickets near Gloucester Point on the York River reported "twenty-eight steamers, four floating batteries, [and] twenty-six sails of different kinds" heading for Fortress Monroe on March 20. From Norfolk the same afternoon, a signal officer observed "nineteen steamers loaded with troops and nine schooners" in Hampton Roads. The flotilla seemed endless: "Sometimes I counted several hundred vessels at the anchorage, and among them twenty or twenty-five large steam transports waiting for their turn to come up to the quay and land the fifteen or twenty thousand men whom they brought," recalled Prince Henrí de Joinville. A civilian reported to John Magruder's pickets on March 24 that "the re-enforcements of the enemy that arrived at Old Point yesterday . . . extend as far as the eye can observe toward Hampton. The force is immense—entirely out of my power to estimate." From Yorktown, Magruder had no such qualms about guessing: he placed Federal numbers between Fortress Monroe and Newport News that day at 35,000. "Should he advance now he would carry all the strong points, and re-enforcements would be too late," Magruder warned the secretary of war.[3]

The problem for the Confederates was that McClellan's intentions were far from clear. That the Union commander might be moving his entire army down the Chesapeake Bay was only one of a number of options that Davis and Robert E. Lee had to consider. McClellan could be planning to deploy one or two corps to Fortress Monroe to attack Yorktown or Norfolk to draw Confederate reserves away from a projected advance from Manassas or Aquia Creek. Hampton Roads might also be just a temporary stopping place for divisions reinforcing Maj. Gen. Ambrose Burnside's operations in Pamlico Sound, which threatened Norfolk from the south. Nor could a similar transfer of troops to augment the long-anticipated attack on Savannah be ruled out.

Lee had no choice but to entrain Theophilus Holmes and his two brigades for North Carolina as soon as they arrived in Richmond, to prop up the sagging defenses and morale of the state. Thus, Davis's central reserve had been committed at the very start of the campaign. The remaining troops around Richmond were dispatched to Magruder, but the number amounted to no more than two Alabama infantry regiments, which had been kept at the capital because they suffered from a high degree of sickness, and the cavalry battalion of the shattered Henry Wise Legion. Lee also alerted Magruder and Benjamin Huger to be prepared to reinforce each other in an emergency.[4] Once these moves had been made, Confederate forces in the long arc from the lower Shenandoah Valley, extending along the line of the Rappahannock to Fredericksburg, down the York River to Gloucester and Yorktown, across the James to Norfolk, along the line of the Wilmington and Weldon Railroad through North Carolina, and down the South Carolina and Georgia coasts, had been fully deployed. No point could be materially strengthened without creating a corresponding weakness at another, and no substantial field army could be collected without denuding some vital position almost completely.

Such dispersal bothered the president, in part because it seemed like a return to the fully extended lines that had failed so miserably in Tennessee and in part because he had become a believer in concentrating larger field armies for offensive blows. Lee, on the other hand, had a distinct propensity for conducting operations with separate columns and never seems to have doubted his own ability to delay the enemy long enough with detachments to force him to reveal his objective. Once that happened, Lee would marshal his own forces to fight it out on ground of his own choosing.[5] In this case, as soon as Lee was convinced that McClellan was intent on advancing up the York-James Peninsula, he commenced shuffling reinforcements to the Yorktown line. Douglas Southall Freeman has described Lee's policy as "a most interesting example of provisional reconcentration to meet an undeveloped offensive" and a "daring, piecemeal reconcentration" accomplished with the full support of Jefferson Davis. Freeman also has asserted that Lee's concept had to be implemented in spite of the resistance from Johnston: "Several days' exchange of correspondence . . . convinced Lee that his old friend would not willingly fall in with his plan."[6] This interpretation overstates the concord between Lee and Davis and exaggerates the apparent friction between Lee and Johnston out of all proportion.

Davis indeed favored a proposal made by Magruder as early as March 21 that, given 30,000 reinforcements from Johnston's army, he would attempt to "crush the enemy, and perhaps with the assistance of the *Virginia* take Fort Monroe." The president directed Lee to sound out Johnston on the feasibility of the plan, which the commanding general did on March 25, but in language that carefully disowned responsibility for the idea: "*The President desires to know* with what force you could march to re-enforce the Army of the Peninsula or Norfolk. . . . From the accounts received nothing less than 20,000 or 30,000 men will be sufficient, with the troops already in position, successfully to oppose them." Lee knew that such a number of troops represented the majority of Johnston's force and that for him "to organize a part of your troops to hold your present line, and to prepare the remainder to move to this city, to be thrown on the point attacked," would be tantamount to exposing central Virginia to the Federals. Later correspondence indicated that he had expected Johnston to object to such a proposition, which may have accounted for his repeated emphasis that the plan had been originated by Davis: "*The*

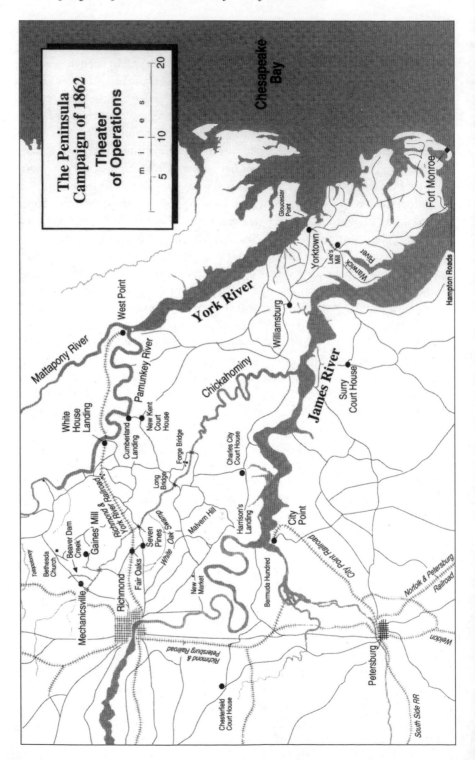

The Peninsula Campaign of 1862
Theater of Operations

object of the President is to prepare you for a movement which now appears imperative, as no troops are available but those of your army to meet the enemy concentrating on the coast."[7]

Lee wrote to Johnston concerning a wholesale shift of his army because Davis instructed him to do so, but a subsequent letter to Magruder clearly indicated that he did not think it yet time to begin decisively concentrating the Confederacy's forces. That letter, dated March 26, revealed that his own thinking ran along different lines. He began by observing that it was still impossible to tell whether the Union army intended to attack Norfolk or to advance on Richmond. Thus, he concluded, "*until some conclusion can be drawn as to his point of attack it would be manifestly improper to accumulate at either the army to oppose him.*"[8]

Johnston had no reason to suspect that Lee and Davis did not completely agree on proper strategy. Besides, Lee's March 25 letter accorded perfectly with what Johnston had understood to be Davis's original strategy for protecting Richmond: using interior lines to transfer troops from one threatened point to another. After the departure of Holmes's two brigades, the Department of Northern Virginia deployed about 35,000 men between Fredericksburg and the Rapidan. Johnston, in a response that seems to have confounded Lee, quickly agreed to the premise of a massive transfer of his divisions: "If summoned to Richmond, I shall leave on this frontier only such a force as is now employed on outpost duty, for the mere purpose of masking the movement. This will enable me to take to Richmond at least 25,000 men."[9] The next day, in support of his belief that a movement away from his line could be successfully covered by a screening force with little risk, Johnston forwarded to Richmond an intelligence report from Richard Ewell's division. The letter contained several observations indicating that the Federal forces around Manassas had no intention of advancing: "Soldiers are in good spirits, saying they do not expect another battle will be fought. . . . They are working very slowly at Bull Run Ridge, apparently for effect. No other repairs are going on. . . . All the soldiers now at Manassas look to be removed to another point."[10]

Much to Johnston's surprise, a telegram arrived from Lee on March 27, ordering him not to move his army to Richmond as previously suggested but to detach and forward 10,000 men to the Confederate capital. The decision made no sense to Johnston: "The division of the troops of this department made by the telegram of this afternoon leaves on this line a force too weak to oppose an invasion, and furnishes to the threatened point a re-enforcement too small to command success." Nonetheless he obediently ordered 7,500 men from the main body and a brigade of 2,500 from G. W. Smith's district entrained for Richmond. Johnston's only remonstrance against the order was a request that the authorities in Richmond reconsider their original plan: "I beg leave, with all deference, to suggest to the President the expediency of transferring to the point about to be attacked the whole available force of this department."[11] Again he forwarded intelligence reports suggesting that the Federals had no offensive intentions in northern Virginia or in the Valley, beyond movements designed to distract Confederate attention from the true point of attack. There was activity among the Yankees around Manassas, but Johnston's pickets were quite skeptical about any possibility of a Federal attack. General J. E. B. Stuart concluded from the reports of his cavalry outposts that Maj. Gen. Edwin V. Sumner's Second Corps "made a great to-do crossing and recrossing Cedar Run, firing artillery at a few vedettes, and the like. . . . I begin to think this is a mere demonstration." Jackson reported that, after his abortive attack at Kernstown, "the enemy are still at Strasburg, and I see no indication of an advance."[12]

Lee responded on March 28 with two very confusing letters. The first indicated that, when the dispatch ordering Johnston to detach 10,000 troops had been sent, Johnston's own letter agreeing to bring 25,000 had not yet been received in Richmond. The letter then placed upon Johnston the responsibility of deciding how many troops to send but without giving him any indication of whether northern or eastern Virginia was considered to be the most threatened point. "It is inferred that you apprehend no attack upon your line. If this inference is correct, you can commence the movement of your troops to this place." Next, Lee informed Johnston that President Davis had been responsible for reducing the number of troops to be transferred from 25,000 to 10,000 because he desired "to have a portion in position here to throw where required, while the balance might follow if necessary." Reiterating that it was still impossible to determine the ultimate objective of the Army of the Potomac, Lee ended by leaving the decision completely up to Johnston: "You can therefore, with this understanding of the case, proceed to forward the desired re-enforcements in part or whole, as in your judgement they can be spared from the defense of your line."[13]

This letter left more questions unresolved than it answered. Having sent Holmes and two brigades to North Carolina, was it the intent of Davis and Lee to reestablish a central reserve in Richmond and attempt to hold everywhere? If so, the idea seemed to contradict the earlier precept of throwing the entire army against one Federal advance. Nor did Lee ever explain why it would not be preferable to have a large force in Richmond, regardless of whether McClellan planned to attack Yorktown or Norfolk. "With this understanding of the case," Lee had said, Johnston could use his discretion in deciding whether to send 10,000 men or himself bring 25,000 to Richmond. There was no such "understanding" to be derived from the letter—it included no hint of just how high a priority Johnston should assign to the Rappahannock line.

Lee's second letter only deepened Johnston's confusion. In it, Lee suggested that the greatest disaster that could happen would be the loss of the upper Shenandoah Valley, which he believed would follow if Johnston were forced off his present line. The decision as to whether to detach 10,000 or march with 25,000 men was still to be Johnston's, but Lee had added an entirely new constraint: protecting the rail line between Richmond and Staunton. "As a mode of expressing to you the limit which it is intended to affix I will cite the remark of the President, that the loss of the Central road and communication with the valley at Staunton would be more injurious than the withdrawal from the Peninsula and the evacuation of Norfolk."[14] This sentence would have stood out in Johnston's view as distinctly as if it had been written in red letters a foot high because it represented yet another reversal by Davis. Just a month earlier, the president had informed Johnston and his cabinet that he planned to withdraw up the Shenandoah Valley as far as Staunton as an integral part of his strategy to subordinate the defense of Virginia to the defense of Richmond. Yet Johnston was being told that the loss of Norfolk, which entailed the loss of the shipbuilding capacity at the Navy Yard and the probable scuttling of the *Virginia,* and a retreat up the Peninsula, which would allow a Federal advance within a dozen miles of Richmond, were both preferable to the loss of his line on the Rappahannock. It almost seemed as if Lee intended to provide Johnston with reasons *not* to move his army to Richmond.

In the wake of these letters, Johnston declined to send any more of his brigades to Richmond without specific orders; he was unwilling to take the responsibility for denuding a line suddenly declared critical by his commanding general.[15] He possessed no estimates of the strength of the enemy on the Peninsula, or, for that matter, any information concerning the numbers of Magruder's army or the reliability of his defensive line. Nor did he feel that such a decision would be his to make—was not the coordination of the several armies defending Richmond why Lee had returned to Virginia? He could only speculate about the reasons for the hesitations and vacillations of his superiors, and their inconsistencies did not relieve him from the responsibility to defend his own lines until directed elsewhere.

Thus, Johnston spent the next few days consolidating his own defenses. Jackson's abortive attack on a Federal division at Kernstown on March 23 revealed the strength of Maj. Gen. Nathaniel Banks's Union forces in the lower Shenandoah. Johnston ordered Jackson to avoid further combat unless he could lure the enemy far enough south to make rapid reinforcement from the main army and a surprise attack with superior numbers feasible.[16] Ewell's division and Stuart's cavalry brigade, the army's only units north of the Rapidan River, had been left to picket as actively as possible, in order to prevent the Federals launching a surprise attack on their own. It became daily more evident that no Union advance from Manassas was contemplated and that the center of Johnston's line—four divisions under James Longstreet, D. H. Hill, Jubal Early, and D. R. Jones—was by far the most secure portion.

Accordingly, Johnston delegated temporary command of the main body to Longstreet and rode to G. W. Smith's headquarters at Fredericksburg. Smith's post seemed the most exposed in the Department of Northern Virginia. Though his six brigades contained twice as many men as Jackson's division in the Valley, his location was susceptible to an amphibious flanking movement from several angles. Union transports could ascend the Rappahannock as far as Fort Lowry, and if McClellan gained access to the York River he could place a force on Smith's supply line. Combined with what was, at the time, the universally admitted indefensibility of the city of Fredericksburg from a frontal assault, Smith's men were in a precarious situation. Making matters worse, no direct telegraph line existed between Fredericksburg and Rapidan Station, which meant that any emergency communication had to pass through the hands of the telegraph operators in Richmond; those operators did not work at night.[17]

Johnston seems to have arrived in Fredericksburg about March 30 and remained there until April 5. He and Smith certainly spent a good deal of time discussing their ideas of the correct approach to Confederate strategy. The army commander conducted several reviews of the troops in order to bolster morale. Yet the entire visit was pervaded by a sense that Johnston was simply marking time, waiting for Lee and Davis to decide how to use his army.[18] Curiously, between March 29 and April 2, Johnston neither sent any communications to Richmond nor received any from Lee. None appears in the *Official Records,* though that is hardly conclusive evidence; a great many of Johnston's letters and telegrams do not appear there. More significantly, both of Johnston's letterbooks and his telegraph register are devoid of any messages to Richmond. Likewise, Lee's letterbook contains no missives directed to Johnston. Neither the files of the War Department nor those of the adjutant and inspector general reveal any attempt to converse with the commander of the Department of Northern Virginia. The next communication to Johnston from Lee was dated April 3, 1862.[19] What explains these five days of silence while every hour saw more Federal transports disgorge troops onto the docks at the tip of the Peninsula?

From Johnston's perspective, the answer is relatively simple: always economical with words, he often went days without writing to Richmond if he had no new information. Meanwhile, Lee, confident that Johnston would report any significant developments, concentrated his attention entirely on the Peninsula. McClellan's deliberate caution in refusing to advance from Newport News until more than 50,000 troops had been landed actually kept Lee from figuring out his intent until early April. On April 1, he wrote to Holmes in North Carolina that "while making demonstrations . . . on the Peninsula against General Magruder, his real object is to attack Norfolk." Until April 4, Lee's correspondence indicated that he still leaned toward believing Norfolk to be McClellan's primary target. Unsure, he waited and watched, delaying the orders that would send a significant number of troops to reinforce Magruder.[20]

He almost waited too long. McClellan himself arrived at Fortress Monroe on April 2. Five divisions of the Army of the Potomac—about 58,000 men— had preceded him. On the morning of April 3, two columns of Federal troops marched toward Yorktown. Magruder deployed only about 10,000 Confederate soldiers to resist him, immediately withdrew his most exposed outposts, and retired into his lines at Yorktown.[21] It was a strong, but not impregnable, position. The Peninsula narrowed there to a width of a little more than six miles, two-thirds of which was blocked by the Warwick River. The upper end of the river had been improved as an obstacle by opening several dams and flooding a few dozen acres of farmland. Heavy cannon at Yorktown and at Gloucester Point across the river kept Federal gunboats at bay. Yorktown proper was enclosed in a large earthwork, designed more to protect the batteries erected to blockade the York River than to hold the town against a frontal assault. Between the fort and the flooded area were two partially completed redoubts connected by a line of hastily dug rifle pits. Outnumbered nearly six to one, with the trenches between the redoubts and the fort still incomplete and many of the gun embrasures at Yorktown gaping empty, Magruder could not have held the line for more than a day against a determined attack.[22]

Yet McClellan did not even probe his lines until April 5. By that time, Lee had satisfied himself as to Federal intent and began rushing reinforcements to the Peninsula. Cadmus Wilcox's Alabama brigade (one of the two sent to North Carolina with Holmes) and Raleigh Colston's Virginia–North Carolina brigade from Norfolk were immediately ordered to the Yorktown line. And on April 3 Lee telegraphed Johnston to send 10,000 more troops to Richmond.[23]

This order put Johnston back onto the horns of a dilemma. On April 2 and 3, the enemy division at Aquia had begun demonstrating against G. W. Smith's outposts, conceivably as a prelude to an assault on Fredericksburg.

Lee's message neither confirmed nor abrogated Johnston's previous grant of discretion with regard to detaching the troops and did nothing to cancel the earlier injunction about the necessity of holding the Rappahannock. Johnston decided that his position needed clarification, so he immediately wired Richmond with the latest reports of enemy activity around Fredericksburg and requested definitive orders. In the meantime, he directed Longstreet to prepare the divisions of Hill, Early, and D. R. Jones for transfer to Richmond but only authorized the Georgian to load Early's division on the trains without specific orders.[24]

The orders to Longstreet, delivered by courier, arrived promptly. The telegram to Richmond did not; the office there had been shut down for the evening. Frustrated, Johnston dispatched an aide with a letter for Lee on the morning train to Richmond. By this time, he also knew that Jackson had reported the enemy advancing in the Valley and had called on Longstreet for reinforcements. Johnston desperately needed an answer: Did the Rappahannock or the Peninsula have priority in the eyes of his superiors? If communications with the Shenandoah Valley were still the paramount consideration, Johnston wanted Lee to know that the loss of 10,000 more troops "will make us too weak to hold this line if pressed in front and on the left flank at the same time." Johnston emphasized that this decision needed to be made in Richmond, not in northern Virginia: "The President, however, will always have the means of judging where those troops are most needed."[25]

Lee's reply represented the first unequivocal order that Johnston had received in weeks: "The movement of the troops from your line must immediately be made to this place. Enemy advancing in force from Old Point." The transfer of troops instantly resumed, and Johnston telegraphed Lee on April 5 with confirmation and, very likely, a repeated suggestion that all of his troops, except a screening force, be employed on the Peninsula. Lee responded by again asking Johnston whether he thought his own line safe from attack, ignoring Johnston's consistent concern over the relative priority of the defense of northern and eastern Virginia. Johnston saw the situation as one that required the Confederates to risk defeat in one area to ensure a reasonable chance of victory in the other. "The invading army could not be defeated without the concentration of the Confederate forces; but they were always more divided than the much more numerous army of the enemy," he remarked years later in specific reference to another campaign. Yet the generalization reflected his thinking on the defense of Richmond as well.[26] Lee, it seemed to Johnston, was the man in position to calculate the odds and weigh the risks; therefore Lee should make the critical decision of where to concentrate and resist the Federals.

As diplomatically as he could, Johnston tried to prod his friend to a decision. He reported on April 6 that most of Sumner's Second Corps seemed to have been withdrawn from Manassas and that Banks was exerting no pressure on Jackson. He pointed out that the trains carried troops to Richmond so slowly that there remained abundant time for Lee to consider a full redeployment of his army. He included a gentle reminder that the responsibility for such a major strategic decision had to come from Lee: "I cannot here compare the state of affairs in my front with those of others, and cannot, therefore, decide understandingly whether troops are less needed here than elsewhere, which seems to me to be the question. He who directs military operations from information from every department can."[27]

McClellan probed the Yorktown line with two divisions on April 5. Magruder fired every gun he could train on the advancing Yankees and paraded his outnumbered soldiers as ostentatiously as possible, hoping to bluff the Union commander into believing that he had far more than 11,000 men in his defenses. His imposture succeeded more effectively than he could have dreamed; within two days, McClellan had concluded that Yorktown was so "strongly fortified, armed, and garrisoned, and connected with the defenses of the Warwick by forts and entrenchments, the ground in front of which was swept by the guns of Yorktown," that the Army of the Potomac would have to take it by siege rather than by assault.[28]

Magruder, of course, was not privy to his opponent's decision and expected hour by hour that McClellan would punch through his thinly held line. His correspondence with Lee revealed nerves strained to the breaking point. "I have made my arrangements to fight with my small force," he informed Lee on April 5, "but without the slightest hope of success." He required a minimum of 10,000 more troops to hold his line. By the evening of April 6, after two days of Federal probing, he reported gloomily that "they discovered a weak point, where numbers must prevail. . . . Re-enforcements come very slowly, and will probably be too late." As the succeeding days passed, however, McClellan showed no signs of aggressive intent. Howell Cobb's brigade from Norfolk arrived, as did those of Jubal Early, Richard Griffith, and Robert Rodes from the Department of Northern Virginia. Newly promoted to major general, D. H. Hill appeared and took over supervision of the Yorktown fortifications, freeing Magruder to concentrate on the remainder of his line. Magruder had recovered his composure by April 8 and ceased to predict calamity. If he received enough field guns to secure Mulberry Island on the Warwick, he informed Lee, "and if the Warwick line can be successfully defended . . . McClellan is defeated, at least until the iron-clad vessels of the enemy shall be in such numbers as to make forts useless."[29]

Magruder's days as an independent commander were numbered. Davis, Lee, and George Wythe Randolph—Judah P. Benjamin's replacement as secretary of war—agreed that the concentration of Confederate forces on the Peninsula required a more senior and less mercurial commander. Lee directed Johnston on April 8 to report to Richmond, bringing with him all the troops from the Department of Northern Virginia except for a force to mask the maneuver.[30] Fourteen days had passed since the idea of transferring Johnston's army to oppose McClellan had first been proposed. During this time, there had been no aggressive enemy movement of any consequence in northern Virginia, but there had been a continuous Federal buildup on the Peninsula. Instead of decisively reinforcing Magruder to withstand the Army of the Potomac, the Confederate high command had preferred to augment him in driblets: a regiment here, a brigade there. What saved the Confederates was not Lee's "provisional reconcentration," for that came far too late to be effective, but the timidity of the Federal commander. Had McClellan been able to nerve himself for an attack even as late as April 7, he probably would have crashed through the Yorktown line, captured or dispersed the Army of the Peninsula, and begun his march on Richmond.

By the time he received the latest instructions from Lee, Johnston had only two divisions left that could be deployed to the capital, those of Smith and Longstreet, plus Stuart's cavalry brigade and William Pendleton's reserve artillery. Given discretion when called upon to send off earlier detachments, he had purposely withheld his most trusted subordinates and their troops so that wherever he might be eventually deployed he would have them at hand. Now he instructed each to move his unit to Richmond, by foot as well as by rail in order to save time.[31]

Meanwhile, Johnston spent a day or two arranging the forces that would maintain at least the crust of a defense in northern Virginia and the Shenandoah Valley. There was no question of weakening Jackson's three brigades in the Valley; although recruits and soldiers returning from their reenlistment furloughs had raised his strength to about 8,500, his division was still not much more than a corps of observation. The same applied to Richard Ewell's division of roughly 7,500 men in three brigades on the middle Rappahannock. Brigadier General Charles W. Field remained at Fredericksburg with about 2,300 men when the other five brigades of G. W. Smith's division retired, leaving only about 18,000 infantry between that city and the Valley.[32] It was obviously an insufficient number of troops to contest a full-scale invasion, yet Johnston did not plan for these three officers to conduct an entirely passive defense. His observations of Federal movements in northern Virginia convinced him that there was no coordinated plan of attack among the various Union commanders. Though in the aggregate much stronger than his own divisions, the Yankees often marched and countermarched in such haphazard fashion that on more than one occasion it might have been possible to concentrate equal or possibly superior Confederate numbers against a single Federal unit.[33] Such a strategy was risky, but if it worked it promised to confuse and delay any Union advance much more effectively than could 18,000 infantry waiting passively in their rifle pits, strung out over more than 200 miles.

Accordingly, Johnston instructed Jackson to retreat toward Swift Run Gap if the Federals approached so that he would then be close enough to Ewell's position to call on that division for reinforcements and attack. He ordered Ewell to be ready to march to Jackson's assistance and to reconnoiter the roads leading from the Rappahannock to the Shenandoah. In the meantime, Johnston also authorized Ewell to make any local attacks on isolated Union forces in his own front that he thought might be successful. Johnston knew that this sort of defense required that his subordinates have the maximum amount of latitude to make their own decisions without wasting the time to request permission for every proposed movement. "The question of attacking the enemy in front of you is one which must be decided on the ground," he told Ewell. "It would be well to drive him away; you would be freer to aid Jackson, and it might make, perhaps, a diversion in his favor." Again he emphasized that each division commander was free to make his own tactical decisions within the overall framework in which Johnston had left him to work: in committing to an offensive move "you have to consider relative forces, the enemy's position, and the facilities for crossing the river. If these are favorable, counted with our confidence in the superiority of our troops—if you feel confident after considering these things, attack." Accurate intelligence was essential to the success of an attack and would determine the ability to retain central Virginia and the middle Shenandoah Valley as well as the survival of his two outnumbered divisions. Thus Johnston left more than half his cavalry and some of his finest outpost commanders in northern Virginia.[34]

Johnston probably received his orders from Lee sometime in the evening of April 8. Organizing the transfer of two divisions and the cavalry brigade and arranging the defense of Jackson, Ewell, and Field took him about two days. He arrived in Richmond either late on April 11 or early on April 12. Davis, Randolph, and Lee brought him up to date on McClellan's inactivity and the strength of Magruder and Huger. Magruder's newfound confidence in his ability to hold his lines was stressed while Huger's pessimism concerning his defenses at Norfolk was discounted. The ability of the *Virginia* to keep the James River closed to Federal transports was highlighted. The president then informed Johnston that his command would be extended over the Peninsula and Norfolk, where a concerted attempt to resist or even to defeat the Army of the Potomac would be made.[35]

Johnston may have been skeptical; none of the information presented by his superiors had been gathered firsthand. Davis had never been to the Peninsula. Lee had helped plan Magruder's second line of defenses at Williamsburg and had been the one who suggested the flooding of the Warwick River, but he had not set foot on the Peninsula since summer 1861. Randolph had served as Magruder's chief of artillery before his appointment to the War Office, but even his observations were weeks out of date; he could not have known, for instance, how near to completion were the redoubts connecting Yorktown to the inundations at the head of the Warwick. With Yorktown less than a day's travel from Richmond, it seemed to Johnston somewhat risky to make major strategic judgments without any officer more senior than Magruder or Huger having personally examined the ground. Davis concurred and proposed that since Longstreet's and Smith's divisions were still a day or two from the capital, Johnston should use the time to conduct an inspection of his expanded department before making any final decisions about the placement of his troops. Johnston quickly agreed.[36]

The following morning, Johnston rode the Richmond and York River Railroad to White House and from there boarded one of the contract steamers ferrying troops and supplies down the river. Whiting, who had arrived in Richmond that morning, accompanied him, both as a close friend and as an engineering officer. Probably about midmorning, the two arrived at the dock in Yorktown. The river at that point was only about one mile wide, and Johnston could have seen the Confederate batteries on Gloucester Point on the north shore through the mist. The Federal gunboats swarming just out of range at the river's mouth must have seemed much closer.[37]

The fortification around Yorktown consisted of an earthwork seven to ten feet high and fifteen to twenty feet thick, fronted by a ditch that averaged ten feet deep. In many places Magruder's engineers had followed the outlines of Gen. Charles Cornwallis's 1781 ramparts, which resulted in a fort that hugged the perimeter of the town. The work had been originally designed to protect the water batteries commanding the river and to hold the town against a siege, not to block the Peninsula to an enemy marching west. Johnston and Whiting thus noted several peculiarities that diminished the fortification's capacity to withstand McClellan's advance. As many of the land batteries faced away from the Federals as toward them. Virtually all the heaviest rifled cannon had been emplaced to cover the river and could not be brought to bear on the Union army. The walls of the fort that directly confronted McClellan were actually the weakest: three to five feet narrower than those in the rear. Few of the batteries or the traversing trenches back to the powder magazines had overhead cover. Most of the bombproof shelters that should have kept the gun crews safe when McClellan's artillery opened up were unfinished.[38]

These deficiencies Johnston and Whiting could see for themselves. It remained for D. H. Hill to present his commander with more depressing news. He pointed out that labor in the protective works around the batteries proceeded slowly because he did not have tents, and sleeping on the open ground in a period of heavy rains had rendered many of his troops too ill to work. There were not enough sandbags on hand to build up protective walls around the open embrasures, and he had only sixty-five rounds per gun—just sixteen rounds each for his best rifled pieces. With so little ammunition he could neither respond to the harassment of the gunboats nor prevent McClellan's men from digging siege parallels. Even if he had sufficient ammunition, Hill told Johnston bitterly, it would not have improved matters much. The rifled cannon produced at the Tredegar Iron Works were so undependable that they were equally as likely to explode and kill their own crews as to harm the enemy. Standing upon the parapet of his works, Hill delivered the coup de grâce with a gesture toward the enemy lines. About 800 yards in front of the wall lay a band of trees that broke his gunners' line of sight, behind which the Yankees could hide and construct their own batteries. He had known about those trees since he had been at Yorktown in 1861, but no axes had ever come from Richmond to cut them down.[39]

Johnston listened to most of Hill's information in silence. When the North Carolinian had completed his list of the position's inadequacies, Johnston asked him how long he thought he could hold his post after McClellan opened fire.

"About two days," Hill said.

Johnston looked surprised and replied, "I supposed about two hours."[40]

What did Hill think should be done? D. H. Hill was never slow to express his opinions, and it is certain that he told Johnston exactly what he wrote to the secretary of war the following day: "Would it not be better to let our railroads in North Carolina be cut, our cities in South Carolina and Georgia captured, and have the whole Southern army thrown here and crush McClellan?" The policy of shifting brigades and divisions piecemeal from threatened point to threatened point angered him: "By attempting to hold so many points we have been beaten in detail, and are losing all that we have been trying to hold." Though the Confederates could not match the weight of Union ordnance, Hill had confidence in Southern élan. "We must fight on the field and trust to the bayonet. If we had 100,000 men here we could march out of the trenches and capture McClellan, unless he had a swift-footed horse."[41]

Much of what Hill said appealed to Johnston—he had long been an advocate of concentrating a large Confederate army even if doing so risked capture of the areas stripped of troops. Yet he had to ask himself: Where to employ it? He did not yet know if there was a place anywhere along Magruder's line from which he might profitably take the offensive.

After instructing Hill to begin moving some of his heavy guns from the water batteries to places where they could bear on the Union army, Johnston left to examine the remainder of the defenses. Four hundred yards of trenches, fairly well covered by abatis, extended south from the front corner of the Yorktown works. Though adequate as an extension of the main work, this row of rifle pits suffered from two major defects. The line dead-ended in a swamp instead of connecting with the entrenchments around Magruder's secondary redoubts between Yorktown and the Warwick River. As a result, infantry stationed there could neither reinforce the positions to their right nor be quickly withdrawn if threatened with overwhelming numbers. The second deficiency was the lack of a drainage system; soldiers fighting from those trenches would have to do so in water that varied from ankle- to knee-deep.[42]

Carefully picking their way across the boggy ground that separated those trenches from the lesser redoubts—an open, if swampy, expanse about 300 yards wide—Johnston and Whiting arrived at the larger of the two subordinate fortifications, Fort Magruder. This redoubt had front walls as high and thick as those at Yorktown and mounted three heavy cannon that could fire toward the Union lines. However, it had been originally designed to confront an enemy approaching from the south, not from the east. Thus, as the two generals stood within the fort, they could easily see at least one hill within McClellan's lines from which cannon could rain shells directly down into the gun emplacements.[43]

The second redoubt sat about 300 yards farther south and was both smaller and unnamed. Its square shape provided adequate protection for gun crews, but the same Yankee-occupied hill overlooked it as well as Fort Magruder. The cannon in this work were not long-range guns, only smoothbore field pieces. They would be absolutely useless until faced with a direct assault by the Union infantry. The trenches extending from Fort Magruder to the smaller redoubts were extensive and somewhat better drained than those immediately around Yorktown, although their layout seemed haphazard, almost as if dug by troops interested in protecting their own camps rather than having been laid out by engineers seeking to establish an effective line of fire. The entire system spanned about 800 yards of the front but did not join the works at Yorktown on the left or the Warwick defenses on the right. Only a broken line of rifle pits, crowned with varying heights of parapets and filled to varying depths with water, connected the redoubts to Magruder's next defensive point at Wynn's Mill. This arrangement did not appear too dangerous from a defensive point of view, because the two generals could see that the area in front of these irregular entrenchments had been flooded by closing the Warwick River dams. Nonetheless, a question remained: How quickly could a brigade be moved laterally from the redoubts across nearly 3,000 yards of broken ground to support Wynn's Mill in case of an emergency?[44]

At Wynn's Mill, Johnston met Jubal Early, who had assumed command of that part of the line a few days earlier. After his own inspection of the York-town-Warwick defenses, Early had predicted to Magruder that the line "must be inevitably broken, sooner or later, and in that event our whole force gobbled up." He preferred an immediate retreat to the Chickahominy River. Showing Johnston and Whiting around his sector, which consisted of nothing more than rifle pits and hastily dug-in field batteries, Early attempted to press this idea on his commander. Johnston had seen too much already and had grown increasingly taciturn: "He did not seem disposed to discuss the matter, and I desisted."[45]

Whether Johnston and Whiting traveled any farther down the Warwick than Wynn's Mill is questionable. It is also uncertain when Magruder joined his new commander; he had not been informed of Johnston's visit in advance.[46] Magruder did not attempt to hide or rationalize the deficiencies of his line, for he had never claimed it to be anything more than a hasty expedient occupied as a last resort. Eventually, thinking perhaps of Hill's plan to gather an army of 100,000 men and seize McClellan, Johnston asked Magruder just how an army on this line could ever attack the Federals, since Magruder himself had flooded the only likely lines of approach to the enemy's positions.

The question would have astounded Magruder, who had never intended the line for anything other than a hasty defense. His suggestion to be reinforced by Johnston's army to conduct an offensive had been made three weeks earlier on March 21, at a time when McClellan's forces had not advanced beyond Big Bethel. Since being invested at Yorktown, he had given up any idea of attacking the enemy. Of 31,500 men, once he subtracted the garrisons at York-town, Gloucester Point, Williamsburg, Jamestown Island, and Mulberry Island, barely 23,000 remained to hold a line seventeen miles long. Far from planning to attack McClellan, his most recent strategic suggestion to Richmond had been to evacuate Norfolk and the entire Peninsula except for a small garrison at Yorktown and to combine his and Huger's armies with Johnston's for a counterinvasion across the Potomac. Nor did Magruder have any illusions about the position of his army once McClellan managed to open either the York or James Rivers; he lived with the threat of a flotilla of gunboats and transports steaming up one or the other to land Federal divisions in his rear.[47]

Johnston had seen enough. He had intended to tour Magruder's second line of works at Williamsburg, then cross the James, examine the *Virginia* personally, and inspect the harbor defenses of Norfolk. The information provided by Magruder and Hill, combined with the evidence before his own eyes, convinced him, however, that although Magruder had performed a miracle of improvisation, no rational general would commit an army to defend such a place. The 31,500 men already there were at grave risk. A week later Johnston put on paper what he must have been thinking on April 14: "No one but McClellan could have hesitated to attack. The defensive line is far better for him than for us."[48]

As he boarded the steamer for the return trip to Richmond, Johnston realized that he faced an even larger problem at the capital. His superiors believed that Yorktown was defensible and were resolved to send his entire army into a cul de sac. How was he to convince them that such a course represented sheer lunacy?

7

DECISION IN RICHMOND II

One week before Joseph Johnston left Richmond on his inspection tour of the Peninsula, Sidney Johnston attempted to redeem his own reputation and Confederate fortunes in the west with a surprise attack on Maj. Gen. Ulysses S. Grant's army at Shiloh, Tennessee. Since the surrender of Fort Donelson, Johnston had been retreating before the Federal gunboats that roamed freely up the Tennessee and Cumberland Rivers and avoiding contact with the Yankee armies that followed in their wake. Nashville and Columbus had been evacuated. Desperately, Johnston, assisted by P. G. T. Beauregard, struggled to assemble an army to resist the Union offensive. They gathered together the remnants of their demoralized garrisons, to which were added thousands of troops that Jefferson Davis stripped from coastal fortifications. One brigade came at the cost of uncovering New Orleans, another left Pensacola defenseless, and a third thinned Southern lines on the Georgia coast. In early April, fate finally seemed to smile on Sidney Johnston: Grant's army had encamped without entrenchments on the banks of the Tennessee River, separated by a long day's march from the nearest supporting column.

"I hope you will be able to close with the enemy before his two columns unite," Davis telegraphed his friend on April 5; "I anticipate victory." Johnston, attempting to forge a motley collection of garrison troops and nearly untrained recruits into something resembling an army, tried to inspire his men with what he hoped would be a prophetic line: "Tonight we will water our horses in the Tennessee River." On the morning of April 6, he sent his divisions into a battle that became the largest and bloodiest yet fought on American soil. The next message Davis received was a wire from Beauregard that evening: "We this morning attacked the enemy . . . and after a severe battle of ten hours, thanks be to the Almighty, gained a complete victory." Beauregard signed himself "General, Commanding," for his telegram also included the news that "General A. S. Johnston . . . fell gallantly leading his troops into the thickest of the fight." Beauregard's assurance of victory wilted quickly.

Within a few days, having withdrawn to Corinth, he claimed only a partial defeat of the Union army, admitting that "next day, finding Buell's forces arriving on the field to re-enforce Grant, I withdrew." Ominous rumors reached Richmond that Beauregard had canceled the orders for one last charge at dusk, which might have completely annihilated Grant's force. By April 9, he was expecting that the enemy would attack him "with over-whelming force" and was predicting the loss of "the Mississippi Valley, [and] probably our cause," if he were not immediately reinforced.[1]

The argument that Beauregard made for receiving massive reinforcements paralleled almost exactly the one that Joseph Johnston presented on his return to Richmond. Beauregard reasoned that "we could even afford to lose for a while Charleston and Savannah for the purpose of defeating Buell's army, which would not only insure us the valley of the Mississippi, but our inde-pendence."[2] Implicit in Beauregard's letter—at least from Davis's point of view—was a criticism that the president remained unwilling to make tough choices, to take the chance of losing in one region to secure victory in another. Had they been on better terms, Davis might have asked the Louisiana gen-eral whether he realized that just to give him the *chance* to defeat Grant, the president had already risked Fort Pulaski, New Orleans, and Pensacola. By April 14 Davis was uncertain that those places would fall, one after the other, during the next month, but he surely knew that such was a likely consequence of having fought, much less having failed to win, at Shiloh. Henceforth, the president would be a great deal more careful before he authorized another massive troop redeployment on the basis of a general's confidence in victory. Davis had already bet once on the man he considered the Confederacy's great-est general and lost.

Johnston, of course, lacked this insight into the president's mind. Having rushed back from the Peninsula, he confronted Davis the moment the presi-dent entered his office. He immediately launched into a criticism of John Magruder's dispositions, concluding that "although they were the most judi-cious that that officer could have adopted when he devised them, they would not enable us to defeat McClellan." The best that could be achieved was to delay the Army of the Potomac for a few weeks. Eventually though, Johnston argued with uncharacteristic loquacity, George McClellan's heavier guns would dismount the Confederate cannon, and "that being done, we could not pre-vent him from turning our position, by transporting his army up the river and landing in our rear, or by going on to Richmond and taking possession there."[3]

Johnston insisted that an alternative plan be instituted, and on the trip back up the York River he had devised one. It was a combination of his own inclinations with ideas borrowed both from Magruder and D. H. Hill, and he proposed it with every certainty that it represented an original and irrefutable vision:

> Instead of only delaying the Federal Army in its approach, I proposed that it should be encountered in front of Richmond by one quite as numerous, formed by uniting there *all the available forces of the Confederacy in North Carolina, South Carolina, and Georgia,* with those at Norfolk, on the Peninsula, and then near Richmond, including Smith's and Longstreet's divisions, which had arrived. The great army thus formed, surprising that of the United States by an attack when it was expecting to besiege Richmond, would be almost certain to win; and the enemy, defeated a hundred miles from Fort Monroe, their place of refuge, could scarcely escape destruction. *Such a victory would decide not only the campaign, but the war.*[4]

It never occurred to Johnston that not only was his concept unoriginal but that the president had already tried it in another theater of the war. That Beauregard had also suggested it during the past week probably only served to make Davis even more cautious.

Yet Johnston had brought firsthand information from the Peninsula that could not be discounted. If he was correct, and McClellan's eventual penetration of Magruder's line was a foregone conclusion, then the implications of that situation had to be considered. Could Norfolk be held without Yorktown? On what line could the Federal advance be resisted if the Union navy controlled the York and James Rivers? Tactfully, Davis told Johnston "that the question was so important that he would hear it fully discussed before making his decision," suggesting that the general return at 11:00 A.M. to meet with him and with Secretary of War George Randolph and Gen. Robert E. Lee. Feeling somewhat outnumbered, Johnston asked if he could invite G. W. Smith and James Longstreet to join the conference. Davis agreed.[5]

Johnston spent most of the time before the meeting tracking down his two division commanders. Longstreet he probably found in his camps; Smith, he finally located at the Spottswood Hotel only thirty minutes before the appointed time. There, his second-in-command had nearly collapsed from the exertions of the previous few days and his chronic nervous malady. Smith told Johnston that he felt entirely too ill to participate in such an important conference. Johnston was insistent and rapidly acquainted the Kentuckian with the dangers inherent in allowing the remainder of the army to be deployed to Yorktown. Convinced by Johnston's arguments, Smith said that he would attend. An inveterate writer of memorandums, he rose from his sickbed to put Johnston's position on paper.[6]

The six men gathered first in the president's office but later adjourned for dinner and reconvened at Davis's house, a site selected because the continuation of the meeting there was unlikely to be noticed or disturbed. Davis allowed Johnston, as the person whose concerns had required the conference, to speak first. Johnston was uncomfortable speaking in front of groups—even when he knew everyone present he often had trouble finding the right words—so he began by handing the president Smith's memorandum. The paper called attention to the deficiencies of Magruder's defenses and proposed essentially the same plan that Johnston had earlier given the president, except that Smith's version specified that a concentrated army at Richmond should also include Confederate troops from the Shenandoah Valley. This strategy formed the centerpiece of the debate that followed.[7]

Both Smith and Longstreet had some preference for an alternative that involved using the army thus formed for a counterinvasion across the Potomac, but neither man actually mentioned this option. Longstreet, due to his deafness, had a difficult time following the conversation. The first time he did open his mouth, to speculate on just how long McClellan might delay the opening of his siege batteries, Davis cut him off abruptly. "From the hasty interruption," the Georgian recalled, "I concluded that my opinion had only been asked through polite recognition of my presence, not that it was wanted, and said no more."[8] Smith had been active in the hour immediately after his memorandum had been read, speaking more to the wisdom of a Confederate concentration than to conditions on the Peninsula, which he had not seen. As the discussion eventually grew more spirited, Smith's stamina waned. He became pale and ceased speaking. At length he felt so faint that he had to ask Davis if he might lie down on a couch in the adjoining room. Within a few minutes, he fell asleep and did not rouse until the very end of the meeting, when the key decisions had already been made.[9]

The lack of participation by his two subordinates left Johnston, as he had feared, arguing his case alone. Longstreet's silence he could understand and forgive. The Georgian was never talkative at the best of times, and the depression caused by the deaths of his children still hung over him. Johnston moreover had never included him among the circle of his intimates with whom he discussed strategy and politics. As far as military opinions went, Johnston would have preferred to bring Whiting, who had seen Magruder's line and was one of the army's most respected military engineers, but Johnston knew that Whiting was still persona non grata with the president for his refusal to accept command of the Mississippi brigade in December. Longstreet's assessment was correct: he had been brought to the meeting because of the solidity of his physical presence more than because of any intellectual contribution he was expected to make.[10]

Smith's withdrawal, however, angered Johnston. The Kentuckian had secured his commission on the strength of Johnston's recommendation and had always been privy to the most secret counsels of the army. After the transfers of Earl Van Dorn and Beauregard, Smith became Johnston's primary confidant. Then "on the most important occasion of the kind in my life," Johnston had almost been forced to beg his second-in-command to attend. In his urgency, Johnston perhaps underestimated the extent of his subordinate's illness and interpreted Smith's later silence as reticence, his departure from the room as desertion. Rumors floating around the upper levels of the army during the next week confirmed just how upset Johnston had been: it was reputed that he told Whiting not long after the meeting that if Smith had not fallen asleep the army would never have been sent to Yorktown.[11]

For his part, Jefferson Davis did not take an active role in the discussion either. He had convened the group to explore the consequences of Johnston's revelations about Confederate weakness on the Peninsula. Though his immediate reaction to Johnston's strategy was negative, he wanted to consider the general's arguments thoroughly. He respected Johnston's opinions even when he did not agree with them, and if he had to decide against the general he wanted Johnston to believe that his ideas had received a fair hearing. Circumstantial evidence suggests, however, that Davis did not come to the meeting with his mind already made up. Johnston's proposal did not differ in theory from the strategy that the president himself had initiated prior to Shiloh; he remained willing to risk territory if he could be convinced that the potential gains were commensurate with the probable losses. He saw his proper part as the ultimate decision maker, not as an active participant.[12]

Thus the debate was left to Johnston, Randolph, and Lee. Randolph, like Longstreet, came to the conference still relatively new to such critical policy deliberations. The gaunt, forty-four-year-old Virginian, however, had a personal assurance that Longstreet lacked. In a society where family ties assisted access to power and augmented personal credibility, Randolph's pedigree was as good, if not better, than that of anyone else in the room. Johnston and Lee might be descended from Revolutionary War heroes and Virginia politicians, but the secretary of war was the grandson of Thomas Jefferson. Though participation in such a meeting was still a novelty, Randolph, unlike Longstreet, never doubted his right to be there, and he brought with him three areas of personal expertise that had particular bearing on the questions at hand. He was the only man in the room with any significant naval experience, having served six years at sea before his nineteenth birthday and an additional two in land assignments before ill health forced him to resign his midshipman's commission. He qualified, in general, as an artillery expert, having raised the Richmond Howitzers, and specifically, as being knowledgeable about John Magruder's guns, having been the chief of artillery on the Peninsula until mid-February. Along with Lee, he was thoroughly acquainted with the disorganization of the army caused by the Bounty and Furlough Act and the tricky, behind-the-scenes negotiation under way to write the Confederacy's first conscription act. Naturally reserved in his demeanor, Randolph, like Smith, also suffered from a chronic illness—in his case, pulmonary tuberculosis. The disease had necessitated his resignation from field service, and active debate would have tired him almost as quickly as it did the Kentuckian. He would have measured his responses, conserved his energy, and attempted to contribute to the conversation as dispassionately as possible.[13]

Thus, the meeting included three men—Longstreet, Smith, and Davis—who said very little for differing reasons, and Randolph, who participated, but did so in a restrained and intellectual manner, leaving the brunt of the disagreement between Joseph Johnston and Robert E. Lee. Smith remembered that the debate became, even before he left, "very heated."[14] Yet Johnston and Lee were not only old friends since their cadet days at West Point but men of great emotional restraint, at least in public display. What explains a meeting at which, with the fate of their country at stake, tempers flared, and neither man was willing to budge an inch from his position?

First, it must be understood that their relationship of nearly forty years contained as many elements of rivalry as of camaraderie. Tension and competitiveness had existed between the Johnstons and the Lees since their fathers' day. Peter Johnston and Henry Lee had fought together in the Revolution, but in the following decades their paths had diverged. Johnston became a Republican, Lee a Federalist; in the General Assembly they argued opposing views on the Alien and Sedition Acts. Both men were politically successful—Peter Johnston becoming a circuit judge, Henry Lee attaining the governor's chair—but their two families represented one of the basic political divisions within Virginia. The Lees came from the old Tidewater tobacco elite, connected by blood and marriage to the Byrds, Randolphs, and Carters. The Johnstons hailed from the rougher southwestern portion of the state, and their ties were to a newer, more widespread breed of Southern aristocrats: the Floyds of Abingdon, the Breckinridges of Kentucky, and the Prestons of South Carolina. In the middle decades of the nineteenth century, the political and financial fortunes of families like the Johnstons were on the rise, those of the Arlington-Tidewater clans to which the Lees belonged in decline.[15]

When Joseph Johnston first met Robert E. Lee at the U.S. Military Academy, the two did not become instant best friends. Academic attrition among the other Virginians in their class, however, slowly brought them together. Their personalities seemed agreeably matched. Both were serious about their studies, although Johnston concerned himself perhaps a fraction less with his grades to the exclusion of all else than did Lee. He occasionally slipped off to go ice skating, infrequently visited the infamous Benny Havens tavern, and was rumored to have embroiled himself in at least one fistfight over the charms of a barmaid. Yet the seeds of a lifelong friendship were certainly sown. It was Lee who comforted Johnston when he received the news that his mother had died. Years later, Johnston recalled Cadet Lee as "full of sympathy and kindness, genial and fond of gay conversation, and even of fun, that made him the most agreeable of companions." In the first few years after receiving their commissions, the young lieutenants were often stationed together, and their friendship deepened. It was Lee who laughed at Johnston's romantic escapades, and Lee who crossed a battlefield in Mexico to bring personally to Johnston the news that his nephew Preston had been killed. For the rest of his life, Joseph Johnston always remembered that when he broke the news, Lee had tears in his eyes.[16]

They were both young officers on the rise in an essentially peacetime army, where promotions came so slowly that they often involved waiting for a senior officer to die of old age so that everyone below could step up. In this race for advancement a basic difference emerged between the personalities of the two Virginians. Lee had aspirations to higher rank, but overt ambition drove Johnston almost relentlessly. He resigned from the army in 1837, he told his brother Beverly, "principally because, from the rules of our Service, of promotion by regiments, many of my juniors who had the luck to be assigned to regiments in which promotion was less slow than in that to which I belonged had got before me." Johnston accepted a new commission when the Corps of Topographical Engineers was formed, promising better chances for promotion, only after being assured that his break in service would not be counted against his seniority.[17]

Johnston never saw rising in rank as anything but a contest, for there were too many junior officers and too few senior positions. A series of letters he wrote to his nephew while Preston was a cadet are particularly revealing of this facet of Johnston's personality. "Determine to beat your competitors & you will never fail to do it," he admonished the younger man. "Endeavor . . . to be foremost—& remember that such efforts are never thrown away; for tho' your competitor should be before you, the benefits of your very exertions in the contest will be felt thro' life." At another point he advised Preston to avoid some of the mistakes he had made: "In selecting your regt. or corps you must consider which is worth most—agreeable *present* position, in a staff corps, or better promotion in the infantry, rifles, or arty. I am inclined to the rifles." Promotion, Joseph Johnston admitted to his brother Edward in 1851, was "a thing I desire more than any man in the army."[18]

He pursued it with a vengeance, assiduously cultivating the good opinion of any senior officer who might help him advance his cause, from Brig. Gen. William J. Worth to Lt. Gen. Winfield Scott. In the Mexican War, Johnston accepted the lieutenant colonelcy of a temporary regiment in the hopes that his two-rank promotion might become permanent. His rank expired with the regiment, but Johnston carried on an eight-year fight with the War Department and three successive secretaries of war to gain legal recognition for a brevet promotion based on his temporary rank. Twice he applied directly for commissions in newly forming regiments, and in 1860 Johnston transferred from the cavalry to staff duty to receive a promotion to brigadier general as quartermaster general of the army.[19]

"No other officer of the United States Army of equal rank, that of brigadier-general, relinquished his position in it to join the Southern Confederacy," he proclaimed in his *Narrative*. This distinction was important to Joseph Johnston because his two major rivals for advancement had always been Lee and Sidney Johnston. Lee had graduated ahead of Johnston at West Point, outranked him as a captain on entering Mexico, and had been placed by then–Secretary of War Jefferson Davis one notch above him in the corps of cavalry when it was organized in 1855. Sidney Johnston had been a colonel of volunteers in Mexico when Joseph Johnston was a temporary lieutenant colonel, also ranked above him in the cavalry, and received a brevet promotion to brigadier general in 1858 for commanding the Utah Expedition. Thus the matter of relative seniority among the three was a critical issue to Joseph Johnston, explaining his angry reaction to Davis's decision to rank him behind the other two among the generals of the Confederate army. Still unconvinced of the legality of that ranking, Johnston found himself once again in a position where Lee was superior. Friends or not, Johnston resented Lee's seniority.[20]

For the most part, Lee had always managed to be detached and philosophical about Johnston's passion for advancement—but he could afford to be, since he had always remained one step ahead of his friend until Johnston's appointment as quartermaster general. His 1846 comment on Johnston's maneuvering to gain a staff post is typical of Lee's attitude toward the issue: "Joe Johnston is playing A[d]j[utant] Gen'l in Florida to his heart's content. His plan is good, he is working for promotion. I hope he will succeed." In 1860, when Johnston, not Lee, received the promotion from lieutenant colonel to brigadier general, Lee did not manage to remain quite so detached. He did write his old friend a letter of hearty congratulations, opening with "My dear General: I am delighted at accosting you by your present title, and feel my heart exult within me at your high position." Three months earlier, however, his heart had not exulted so strenuously when he wrote his son Custis of Johnston that "in proportion to his services he has been advanced beyond anyone in the army and has thrown more discredit than ever on the system of favoritism and making brevets."[21]

Even though both Virginia and the Confederacy had promoted him above Johnston again, from Lee's perspective his old friend had so far enjoyed a much better war. To this point the war for Lee had primarily been a desk job; his only true field service in western Virginia had brought him nothing but public criticism and personal frustration. Johnston shared the laurels for winning at Manassas and had spent the intervening months in command of the South's largest and best-equipped field army. Lee's own military secretary, Armistead Long, admitted years later that "at this time General J. E. Johnston bore the highest reputation in the Confederacy, since by his manoeuvring [*sic*] with Patterson in the Valley, his splendid success at Manassas, and his masterly retreat from Centreville he had acquired a world-wide renown."[22] Though outranking his friend and invested with the position of commanding general, Lee saw Johnston as having achieved the two goals that he desired in war: reputation and a field command.

These tensions were submerged beneath the masks of friendship and professional courtesy that existed between the two Virginia generals on April 14, 1862. Each man would have denied that his objectivity or his decisions could be swayed by such personal resentments, and each undoubtedly would have thought he was telling the truth. But each man also eventually discovered that the stress of conducting a war at long odds could produce extreme emotional responses, decades of professional soldiering notwithstanding. The chances of judgment being affected increased when those tensions underlay profound intellectual disagreements.

Four questions dominated the dispute, and a fifth critical one never seems to have been asked by anyone at the meeting. Could Norfolk be held if McClellan gained the Peninsula? How long could the Yorktown-Warwick line be maintained against the Federals? Did the loss of that line necessarily equate with the loss of the entire Peninsula and a retreat to the environs of Richmond? Was the concentration of troops from Georgia and the Carolinas that Johnston proposed desirable or even possible? The unasked question was whether or not any possible compromise existed between the strategic stances of Johnston and Lee.

"I don't think there was any difference of opinion as to the necessity of evacuating Norfolk if the Peninsula was evacuated," Randolph testified before a Congressional committee ten months later. Even with the *Virginia* blocking direct approaches to the harbor, McClellan only had to march far enough up the Peninsula to reach a point on the James River at which the channels were too shallow for the ironclad to operate effectively. A pontoon bridge thrown across the river would then allow him to land on Benjamin Huger's supply lines, link up with Ambrose Burnside's force in North Carolina, and completely isolate the Norfolk garrison. Retaining Norfolk—or more precisely the Gosport Naval Yard—was a key strategic issue for the Confederates. Randolph, representing the interests of the navy, pointed out that its capture would entail the loss of "our best if not our only opportunity to construct in any short time gunboats for coastwise and harbor defense." He did not overestimate the importance of the facility. Nearly 1,200 heavy guns had been seized there in the first days of the war, providing the scaffolding upon which most of the Confederacy's coastal defenses had been erected; several hundred still remained, protecting the harbor. Removing them quickly would be no more practical than saving W. H. C. Whiting's cannon on the Potomac had been.[23]

Even irreplaceable heavy ordnance was secondary to the significance of the Gosport Navy Yard. Though the last Union garrison had attempted to burn it to the water's edge, the shipyard was the best facility of its kind available to the South. The conversion of the *Merrimac* into the *Virginia* had been its most heralded project so far, but not its only one. Workers had begun construction in March on the *Richmond*, a second ironclad designed along the same lines as her predecessor. The presence of two such vessels in Hampton Roads would secure the mouth of the James River beyond any doubt. During 1861 the navy yard had also partly armored the converted merchant steamer *Patrick Henry*, which, with her ten guns, was the second most powerful Confederate warship operating in the James River. Two sailing sloops of war, the *Plymouth* and the *Nansemond*, had been completed in the first months of 1862; two more were under construction, and Naval Secretary Stephen Mallory envisioned a fleet of the pesky little vessels with which to harass Federal blockaders. Not only the ships currently under construction would be lost if Norfolk fell, but also the capability to produce many more would be sacrificed.[24]

Johnston, who had cut his inspection trip short before visiting Norfolk, found himself hard-pressed to refute any of these arguments. Had he traveled to the port, an interview with Huger might have provided him with a counterargument. Norfolk's strategic importance could not be disputed, but McClellan's army on the Peninsula hardly represented the only threat to its safety. In mid-February the "mosquito fleet" of gunboats protecting Elizabeth City, North Carolina, had been destroyed by the Federal vessels attached to Burnside's expedition. Elizabeth City guarded the southern entrance to the Dismal Swamp Canal, a waterway that could be traversed by light-draft gunboats all the way to Suffolk. Although the Union troops had then turned their attention farther south to New Berne, the right flank of Huger's position lay wide open. Only a thin screen of wretchedly armed Confederates stood between Burnside and the one railroad connecting Norfolk to the rest of Virginia. Even if the Peninsula might be held indefinitely, Johnston could have argued, that alone would not guarantee the long-term safety of Norfolk; but he did not know that, and so Randolph's point stood unassailed.[25]

Johnston scored heavily in return on the question of Yorktown's ultimate defensibility. He admitted that, although Magruder's line could not stand a heavy bombardment, it could probably hold out against a frontal assault by McClellan's army, even if his 31,500 men received no further reinforcements. However, he maintained that the cautious Federal commander would never order such an attack; if he had ever had such an inclination, McClellan would have tried to force the line weeks earlier when Magruder could field fewer than 10,000 soldiers to oppose him. Johnston probably used words similar to those that he wrote to Lee two weeks later: "It is plain that General McClellan will adhere to the system adopted by him last summer, and depend for success upon artillery and engineering. We can compete with him in neither."[26] The argument made sense to everyone. Randolph recalled that there was unanimity of opinion "that if the enemy assaulted our army at the Warwick River line we should defeat them." Johnston also successfully convinced them—possibly with Randolph's help—that if "they made regular approaches . . . and took advantage of their great superiority of heavy artillery, the probability would be that one flank, or both, of the army would be uncovered." Randolph concluded that "thus the enemy, ascending York and James Rivers in transports, could turn the flank of the army and compel it to retreat."[27]

Sensing his advantage, Johnston pressed two more points that he thought argued effectively against deploying more troops onto the Peninsula. First, he portrayed the climate as being so unhealthy that many of Magruder's men had already become too ill to be of any use; should Smith's and Longstreet's divisions be sent there, a similar depletion of their strength could be expected. Even if this did not occur, the increased number of troops to support on the Peninsula could bring the Confederacy no material benefit. The two divisions would not give Johnston numbers close enough to McClellan's to justify an attack on the open field, and Magruder's flooding had ensured that no matter how numerous an army was transferred to the Peninsula, it could not reach the Army of the Potomac to attack it.[28]

This indictment of the policy of damming and flooding the Warwick River probably stung Lee, who had at least approved it and may actually have suggested it. Instead of responding directly to Johnston's assertion that the Yorktown line was inevitably untenable, he raised a new objection. The loss of that line did not necessarily mean the loss of the entire Peninsula. Davis remembered that Lee "insisted that the Peninsula offered great advantages to a smaller force in resisting a numerically superior assailant." Specifically, Lee argued that where the Peninsula narrowed to a four-mile width at Williamsburg as well as along the banks of the Chickahominy River there were secondary positions from which Johnston's army might delay the enemy or even inflict defeat upon him. He recalled that the previous year he had devised the plans for a continuous line of works at Williamsburg from which to rally against the Federals. This line should be much easier to hold than the Yorktown line. Magruder had several times reported progress in constructing the fortifications. Cannon in place on Jamestown Island could probably blockade the James River.[29]

If that line had to be evacuated, the few bridges over the Chickahominy and the tangled swamps around its banks would provide Johnston yet another chance to confront McClellan from a favorable position. Forced to fight for one or more of the crossings, the Army of the Potomac would have a difficult time bringing its superior numbers to bear, and the marshy ground would not be favorable to heavy artillery. Lee apparently envisioned a protracted fight before the Yankees could force the river. The Federals could be deterred from any attempt to land behind Johnston's line by burning all the wharves on the York and the James and by making "such display of force in front of the landings which the enemy may approach as will retard their advance from the rivers to the interior of the country."[30]

The image of a deliberate, step-by-step retreat, with the possibility of inflicting a series of sharp repulses—or even a major defeat—on the Union army appealed to the president, especially given the state of Richmond's defenses: the city was in no way prepared to stand a siege. Excavation had begun on only four of the eighteen batteries in the ring of fortifications around the capital, and those that had been constructed did not inspire confidence. Most of the powder magazines contained two or three feet of standing water, and large tracts of woods obscured the field of fire from many of the batteries. These problems were not even the worst defects of the positions. Colonel Charles Dimmock, chief of ordnance for the state of Virginia, had reported at the end of February that the batteries had been sited too near the city: "So near can the enemy come that the city can be shelled and burned before our works are captured." Of course, Dimmock admitted that his protest was somewhat academic, since only 25 of the 218 cannon needed to arm the batteries had been mounted. Dimmock, like Lee, felt that "the line of defense should be near the banks of the Chickahominy."[31]

Again the brevity of Johnston's tour of the Peninsula prevented him from countering Lee's arguments. He did not know that the line of fortifications at Williamsburg had not been completed to Lee's specifications. Instead, they had been modified into a series of detached forts without Lee's knowledge or consent. Alfred Rives, chief of the Confederate Engineer Bureau, had supervised this change, and even he recognized that they were fatally flawed. "I would take occasion here to condemn, as a general system, small detached redoubts, although you might infer from what you see near Williamsburg that I am in favor of them," Rives told Magruder's chief engineer on March 20. "I was, when they were commenced, completely inexperienced. . . . I now know and have known for some months past that the system is most defective, making a line equally strong it is true, but equally weak at the same time." Nor did Johnston know that the James River was more than a mile and a half wide at Jamestown Island and that it was questionable whether the thirteen poorly entrenched guns there could keep the river closed. Beyond the island, the next and only point below Richmond from which the James River could be effectively blocked was Drewry's Bluff, a point where construction of entrenched batteries had barely been begun.[32]

No one in the room really knew much about the practicality of defending behind the Chickahominy River. The necessity of sending out most of the Engineer Bureau's officers either to Johnston or to Magruder had delayed a survey of the river. Even Lee, who advocated the river as a third line of defense, did not know the condition or even the number of bridges spanning the stream. Most of the arguments seem to have been made by examining a blue line on some map. Yet even such a cursory examination should have revealed that a Union army that drew its supplies from the York River rather than from the James could sidestep uncomfortably close to Richmond without ever contesting the river crossings. This possibility would force Johnston to keep more than twenty miles of the winding river under observation—a line significantly longer than Magruder's at Yorktown. No entrenchments or batteries had ever been erected along the Chickahominy, and the river was navigable to Federal gunboats more than a dozen miles inland. Nor did any Confederate batteries exist to keep the Union navy from landing troops west of the river's mouth. Finally, the climate around the swamps was, if possible, even more malarial than that in the vicinity of Yorktown.[33]

Johnston's shock at seeing the condition of the Yorktown-Warwick River defenses, and the understandable urgency he felt in returning to explain their defects to the president, had again deprived him of vital details. Lee's contentions about the practicality of defending the Peninsula even after Magruder's line was evacuated won the day in Davis's mind. At this moment in the debate then, Lee was far ahead on points. The ultimate fall of Yorktown had been the only particular he had conceded. Against this, he had successfully argued that its defense should be protracted as long as possible to preserve Norfolk and that the remainder of the Peninsula was defensible. He then attacked Johnston's suggestion to bring troops from the Carolinas and Georgia to Virginia.

The numbers themselves seem to support Johnston. His two divisions in Richmond, plus Magruder's army, were thought to total in excess of 55,000 men. Even discounting the cavalry screen and Charles Field's tiny command, Stonewall Jackson and Richard Ewell could contribute 16,000 infantry. Despite reinforcing the Peninsula, Huger still retained 12,000 troops at Norfolk. In the Department of North Carolina there were 20,000 Confederate soldiers and another 29,000 in the Department of South Carolina and Georgia. Most of these troop strengths had been underreported by their commanders, and more regiments were in the process of organization. With at least 83,000 men already present in the Old Dominion, Johnston presented a convincing numerical argument that reducing the coastal defenses to minimal garrisons at Wilmington, Charleston, and Savannah could raise his numbers to parity with the Army of the Potomac, which was accurately believed to have between 100,000 to 120,000 soldiers.[34]

There were practical objections to Johnston's plan, and Lee made the most of each one. He objected to Johnston's premise that risking the loss of Charleston and Savannah against the chance to defeat McClellan was an acceptable gamble. The Atlantic ports currently represented the major pipeline through which the South was receiving weapons from abroad. These weapons were particularly critical at just that moment because most of the new regiments in Confederate camps of instruction had none. Lee was well aware that he could not yet arm all the troops that had volunteered for the war within the last month.[35]

Yet even if losing Charleston and Savannah represented a fair trade for McClellan's army in purely military terms, the same was not true in a political sense. As Davis was well aware, the ardor of most governors and many Confederate soldiers was limited to the defense of their home states. Governors had already grudgingly resisted every transfer of troops from their coasts, and regiments serving far from home continually petitioned the government to send them back. With the army undergoing the reorganization of all the one-year troops, Lee, Randolph, and Davis feared that thousands of soldiers would allow their enlistments to expire if they thought that the government had no commitment to protecting their homes while they served elsewhere.[36]

Severe logistical problems also existed. Just how rapidly the rickety network of Confederate railroads could deliver tens of thousands of soldiers to Virginia was more than questionable, and the inability to do so might well be critical. It the massive redeployments Johnston suggested—unprecedented in scale even by the pre-Shiloh concentration—were set in motion, a slow performance by the railroads could spell disaster. A moment of vulnerability would exist while the troops were in transit. During this time, neither the Atlantic ports nor Johnston's army would be at full strength; if the trains rolled too slowly, this moment of weakness might stretch out for several weeks. A coordinated Federal attack on Charleston and Savannah simultaneous with a penetration of Magruder's line might rapidly end the war, it was true—with a Confederate surrender. Celerity of motion, even willing cooperation, was something that everyone in the room knew the railroads could not be depended upon to provide. It is unlikely that Davis or Lee could have resisted the urge to point out to Johnston that he had blamed the difficulties in his withdrawal from northern Virginia on the railroads. The maneuver that Johnston proposed would require a far greater level of coordination between a minimum of six different railroad companies.[37] How did Johnston expect this to be accomplished?

The general's answer would have been the response that any number of Confederate officers suggested at various critical points in the war: government control of the rails. This was a proposition to which Davis and Randolph were not hostile, but the Confederate Congress disagreed. Even as the president, the secretary, and the four generals met, the House Committee on Military Affairs was in the process of first emasculating and then killing a bill to provide for emergency military control of the railroads. In just three days, Augustus R. Wright of Georgia and Thomas J. Foster of Alabama successfully attacked any such idea as "subversive of, and in direct contravention to, the great and fundamental principle of State sovereignty." Even had he agreed with Johnston, Davis did not possess the power necessary to implement the general's plan.[38]

Again, there were counterarguments to most of these objections, but Johnston did not—in fact could not—have known them. Confederate intelligence on the coast was so bad that the conferees did not know that their army in the Carolinas and Georgia substantially outnumbered the Union forces there. Theophilus Holmes deployed 20,000 men in North Carolina; Burnside opposed him with 14,000. John Pemberton reported 29,000 "present for duty" along the lower coast, and Federal Maj. Gen. David Hunter listed only 17,000 soldiers in the same category. Johnston was more correct than he knew. By attempting to defend everything, the Confederacy had dispersed a larger number of men so widely that the Union navy could almost always deliver enough Yankees to any given point to guarantee local superiority. Careful concentration at critical points would have allowed the Southern army to defend the coastline with no more than the number of troops the Federals were using to attack it. This strategy would have freed at least 18,000 men to reinforce Virginia, which could have given Johnston more than 100,000 men, the minimum number he needed to confront McClellan on the open field.[39]

Removing just over one-third of the soldiers on the coasts would have been politically touchy but not impossible for the Davis administration. The transportation objections could have been overcome by using a concept that Gen. Braxton Bragg proved to be effective in a few months: that of operating the railroad as if it were a strategic pipeline, shuttling a few troops from each garrison a few miles north to "bump" the next garrison farther along the route. Confederate experience in moving troops in this manner suggests that 18,000 troops could have been brought to Virginia in less than three weeks without unduly exposing any critical point on the coast.[40] As to the question of reorganization, Johnston could have argued that he intended to use those troops for an offensive, thus offsetting any decline in morale resulting from a partial evacuation of the coast. An opportunity to strike a blow at the invading Federals had to be more satisfying to the minds of Confederate soldiers than meekly sitting and waiting for the fearsome gunboats to appear.

Johnston, however, could make most of these contentions in theory only, without citing specific details. He did not *know* the realities of Confederate and Union troop strengths on the coast—he had only the assertions of Lee and Randolph that the Yankees deployed far more men. He had never been thoroughly informed of the extent of the scarcity of weapons. Nor had he researched the technical details of actually moving thousands of Confederate soldiers to Virginia. Lee, on the other hand, seemed to possess every answer necessary to support his case, and those answers, even if incorrect, stood unchallenged by the end of the evening.

By midnight, in Davis's mind, the debate had narrowed down to a choice between two radically different options. Johnston proposed an almost immediate withdrawal from the Peninsula, Norfolk, and much of the coast, luring McClellan inland where he could be assaulted by an army of at least equal, if not superior, numbers. Lee advocated committing as many troops as were currently available—Johnston's two divisions—to resist McClellan's advance inch by inch, preserving Norfolk for as long as possible and hoping that an opportunity to strike a blow might present itself even to an outnumbered army. Johnston's plan required immediate massive risks, offering an eventual chance for a strategic victory. Lee's plan deferred the risks in the hope that time might provide a better solution. To Davis, leery of repeating the mistakes of the past few months, Johnston's proposal entailed an unacceptable level of risk. He finally announced his decision: he would follow Lee's line of reasoning. Johnston's army would be committed to the defense of the Peninsula.[41]

Before examining Johnston's reaction to the president's declaration, it is important to realize that the chief failure of Davis's advisers was in allowing the question to be narrowed down to two mutually exclusive choices. The Confederacy's two senior field generals had an obligation, in a council called for the purpose of determining grand strategy, to lay out for their chief executive all the possible solutions to the problem facing him. But Johnston and Lee became so enmeshed in their own arguments that they did not present their president with a full range of options. A third, possibly much more sound strategy for defending Richmond existed.

Assuming the correctness of Johnston's view that Magruder, with 31,500 men, could hold out just as long at Yorktown against McClellan as could Johnston with an army of 55,000, the question actually boiled down to the most effective use that could be made of the 23,500 men in Smith's and Longstreet's divisions, Stuart's cavalry brigade, and the fifty-six guns of Pendleton's artillery reserve. Sending them to the Peninsula was one option, but so was retaining them in Richmond as the nucleus of Johnston's *Grande Armée*. Even discarding the more or less fantastical schemes of Smith and Longstreet to join Jackson and Ewell to cross the Potomac, there was another option.

The remainder of Johnston's army could have been kept in the immediate Richmond area to facilitate the very delaying strategy that Lee advocated. Those 23,500 men represented a labor force capable of completing the Richmond defenses and of erecting the vital batteries at Drewry's Bluff. Obstructions and delaying positions could have been prepared at the Chickahominy bridges. White House and Eltham's Landing on the upper York River and those below Harrison's Landing on the James could have been strongly enough garrisoned to discourage Federal landing even after the Yorktown-Warwick line crumpled. His flanks secure, Magruder could have dropped back from Yorktown to Williamsburg where, despite the shortcomings of the fortifications, he would have been able to stall McClellan on a line not seventeen but four miles long.

In many ways, such a plan would have satisfied the wishes of both Lee and Johnston. Two divisions holding the retired flanks of the Peninsula would have maximized the time to be gained in a delaying action and would have increased materially the chances of successfully combating the enemy at the Chicka-hominy. The time gained, even as much as two or three months, would mean more rifle-muskets produced in the factories and landed in the ports, leading to a substantial reinforcement of Johnston's army. If he could not have met the Army of the Potomac with exact numerical parity, he certainly could have fielded 85,000 to 90,000 men—no worse a disadvantage than he had faced at Manassas.[42] Furthermore, his army would have the advantage of awaiting the Yankees behind a third or fourth successive defensive line, the final one of which would necessarily have drawn McClellan away from his naval support.

Although such a plan might well have been workable, it could never arise while Johnston and Lee discussed the problem as adversaries because it would have required each man to compromise on at least one of his most dearly held strategic precepts. Johnston would have had to accept an operational concept that seemed at odds with his own belief in the need to concentrate the Con-federacy's outnumbered troops. Maneuvering with detached—even isolated—columns never bothered Lee, but he always advised meeting the enemy as far forward as practical with as many troops as possible. Keeping better than two divisions in the Richmond area violated his natural urge to close with the Fed-erals and strike a blow. The two men could have arrived at such a plan only in a spirit of collaboration, a feeling sadly lacking between good friends that night.

Davis, choosing from the plate set before him, decided to follow the argu-ments and instinct of Robert E. Lee. He told Johnston that the next morn-ing the general should start his army for the Peninsula. The president acknowledged years later that he had known that Johnston "did not agree with this decision" but that "he did not ask to be relieved," which Davis evi-dently interpreted as acquiescence in his verdict. Johnston's own postwar com-ment in the *Narrative* has often been cited as evidence that he secretly planned to disobey Davis's orders and pursue his own strategy of withdrawal without reference to the wishes of the government: "The belief that events on the Peninsula would soon compel the Confederate government to adopt my method of opposing the Federal army, reconciled me somewhat to the necessity of obeying the President's order." Douglas Southall Freeman has contended that this ex post facto admission "curiously and not creditably revealed the man," and Clifford Dowdy has taken it as evidence that "when Johnston left the meeting to return to Yorktown, he had no intention of obey-ing the intent of the order."[43]

It cannot be inferred from his later statement that Johnston engaged in willful deception of the government, unless he kept this view to himself; the only evidence of that fact is Johnston's own words. The published phrasing is ambiguous and does not conclusively settle the question of whether the general voiced this opinion—this prediction, actually—or whether he left the meeting in a taciturn, sulky mood. The original draft of Johnston's memoirs is, however, much more definitive. After receiving Davis's instruction, Johnston wrote, "*I replied* that nothing reconciled me to obedience to this order but confidence that the cautious character of the Federal General would permit me to extricate my troops, after their flank was uncovered by the destruction of Yorktown."[44] He had not been at all reticent about arguing his case with vehemence for several hours; there was no reason for him to stop giving the president his opinions just because he had lost the debate.

Discouraged, but determined to follow his orders and buy as much time as he could and still save the army from a trap of his own government's creation, Johnston, with Longstreet in tow, left the room. In the parlor, he roused the sleeping Smith and informed him of the outcome of the discussion.[45] There was quiet talk of the next day's preparations, and the three men departed to begin their campaign.

8
ISOLATED ON THE PENINSULA

Major Robert Anderson had formally surrendered Fort Sumter in Charleston Harbor on April 14, 1861. The next week Abraham Lincoln called for 75,000 volunteers, and Virginia seceded. Tents arose on the fringes of Richmond as Gen. Robert E. Lee struggled to organize the state's volunteers. In a short time, regiments from the rest of the Confederacy began to arrive, some of the earliest being the First and Second South Carolina, veterans of the bombardment of Fort Sumter. A crowd gathered at the railroad station to meet them; and, as Richmonder Sally Putnam recalled, "they bore the appearance of guests at a holiday festival, rather than the stern features of the soldier." Hundreds of Richmond's citizens flocked to the camps to hear the story of the war there had thus far been: "The evening dress-parade attracted admiring crowds of ladies, to whom every soldier seemed a hero."[1]

By April 15, 1862, however, both the city and the soldiers knew a great deal more about war. When Thomas Bragg looked out his window at the troops marching through Richmond to the Peninsula, he thought that they appeared "rough but hardy . . . very muddy & . . . anything but neat and trim." The horses pulling field pieces and caissons down Broad Street he thought "much reduced in flesh and all looked woebegone."[2] These were not the polished young dandies who had marched so gaily off to battle a year ago; these were gaunt men who had spent a winter under canvas, subsisting on short rations, and pulling guard duty in the mud. Some of them were veterans in the true sense, having seen combat at Manassas, Ball's Bluff, Dranesville, or in a dozen other nameless skirmishes.

In many cases, the trip to Richmond had not been easy or even safe. The train conveying Col. John B. Gordon's Sixth Alabama suffered a head-on collision with a locomotive returning up the same track. "Nearly every car on the densely packed train," Gordon remembered, "was telescoped and torn into pieces; and men, knapsacks, arms, and shivered seats were hurled to the front and piled in horrid mass against the crushed timbers and ironwork." Several soldiers died in the wreck, and dozens more were seriously injured. Even walking to Richmond did not guarantee a safe trip. The Hampton (South Carolina) Legion marched to the capital from Fredericksburg through rain, hail, and sleet. In makeshift shanties of poles and pine brush, the men in Capt. James Conner's company slept wet and shivering cold, their blankets lagging behind on supply wagons. Fires would only reluctantly ignite to cook their biscuits or their bacon. Conner sourly described the latter as having just "one streak of lean and five inches of fat." Of sixteen new recruits his company had received in the previous month, three died of exposure on the march.[3]

Wet and bedraggled as Joseph Johnston's regiments were, to the citizens of the city they represented the army that would hold George McClellan at bay, so Richmonders turned out en masse to welcome them. Bands played, women waved handkerchiefs from second-floor windows, and the streets were lined with families, friends, and well-wishers. The day broke bright and clear for a change, and soon after dawn the streets filled with the sound of the tramping feet of James Longstreet's division. They had walked from Centreville to the Rapidan; and when the call came to pull back to Richmond, Longstreet's men marched, while other troops took the trains. Sarcastically, the soldiers dubbed themselves "Longstreet's Walking Division," and opined that if Jefferson Davis ever planned for them to reinforce New Orleans, he would probably tell them to foot it.[4]

They made a show of their passage through Richmond, nonetheless. At the division's head rode its phlegmatic commander, James Longstreet, whose mulelike stamina allowed his appearance to belie the fact that, since the meeting the previous evening, he could not have had any sleep. Most of the band music was lost on the nearly deaf Georgian, but his staff cantered about on their best mounts, raised their hats, and saluted the crowds. Behind them came the infantry, in columns of half-companies "with music, banners, mounted officers, artillery, etc.," one soldier recalled. "Soldiers left the ranks to grasp the hands of friends in passing," wrote one Richmonder, "to receive some grateful refreshment, a small bouquet, or a whispered congratulations." Ten thousand troops took a long time to march past a given point, and the cheering went on for hours before the last Confederate soldier passed down to the wharf at Rocketts to board the boats for Yorktown. Some were heartened by the turnout; others barely noticed. A private in Brig. Gen. George Pickett's Virginia brigade ignored the demonstration and "sadly gazed at the shop windows where loaf-bread, and clean clothing, and books, and other needed articles so tantalized my eyes, and empty pockets."[5]

Jeb Stuart's cavalry paralleled Longstreet's division, flowing down the side streets to equally enthusiastic applause. "They swept through our streets on that beautiful morning, with their horses in good order, their own spirits buoyant and cheerfull [*sic*], many of them wearing in their caps bouquets of the golden daffodils of early spring," said Sally Putnam. Stuart camped his brigade just outside the city limits and allowed his men one last night on the town before trotting toward Yorktown. Yet for all the showmanship and pageantry of the horse soldiers, Longstreet's assistant adjutant general, Moxley Sorrel, believed that the finest spectacle of the day had been staged by Brig. Gen. Robert Toombs. Always more politician than general, Toombs led his troops "past the crowds at Spottswood Hotel, with childlike delight." His brigade was composed of one Virginia and four Georgia regiments. Toombs "put himself at the head of one regiment and moved it out of sight amid hurrahs, then galloping back he brought on another, ready himself for cheers, until the brigade was down the street."[6]

The procession through the Richmond streets was to be the last moment of glory for some time to come. Gustavus W. Smith's division, which had marched directly to White House on the York River, boarded a motley collection of schooners and small steamers for the trip to Yorktown. Longstreet's men crowded on flatboats at Rocketts, which lurched slowly down the James River toward Jamestown. Conditions on the boats were horrible: there was no food, no water, no provision for sanitation, and in most cases, no place either covered or ventilated to sleep. Brigadier General Joseph Kershaw's South Carolinians had found themselves forced, on an earlier trip, to rotate between the holds of their small sailboats and the deck: it was a choice between freezing or suffocating. Pickett's men used the hours that the tug pulling their flatboat needed to clear the obstructions at Drewry's Bluff to cut tethers to keep sleeping soldiers from being washed overboard. It was a miserable experience for the infantry, and the cavalry and artillery saw little more comfort as they trooped down the muddy roads that crossed the Chickahominy.[7]

Nor did the conditions that Johnston's men found around Yorktown make up for the poor conditions on the trip. The trenches in the lines were flooded, the ground for the camps boggy, the rain unceasing, the food bad, and the Federal artillery and sharpshooters annoying—sometimes fatally so. Soldiers assigned to the redoubts or the rifle pits spent their days digging in deeper, often in direct sight of the enemy. Pickett's men erected one earthwork only by the expedient of posting a lookout to shout "Lie down!" when he saw the smoke issue from the mouths of distant Yankee cannon. Kershaw's troops scoured the area for scraps of wood to maintain bonfires around the clock. During the day, soldiers not on duty huddled around them; at night they competed for sleeping positions near the flames. Porter Alexander echoed the sentiments of most Confederate soldiers when he claimed that "in the whole course of the war there was little service as trying as that in the Yorktown lines."[8]

Johnston did not immediately accompany his soldiers to Yorktown on April 15. Instead, he spent the day working out administrative details with Lee and Samuel Cooper. He had two major worries: the forces left in northern Virginia and his wagon trains. Johnston's primary concern about Stonewall Jackson, Richard Ewell, and Charles Field was not that they might be overwhelmed, for he believed each of the Confederate columns to be much more mobile than the Yankees who opposed them. He worried more about any coordinated actions. With the department commander on the Peninsula, the time lag for correspondence between Johnston and Jackson could easily exceed a week. Johnston reiterated to Ewell that all questions of attack and retreat "must be decided on the ground"—in the time necessary for letters and telegrams to find him, precious opportunities might be lost.[9] He instructed Jackson and Ewell to forward their correspondence to him through Cooper's office. This was proper military procedure in the strictest sense, but it is difficult to escape the suspicion that Johnston may have preferred to keep internal departmental letters out of Lee's hands. The April 14 meeting marked a low point in the friendship of the two men. Not only did Johnston know that Lee differed from him on strategy, but he also may have suspected that the other Virginian planned to use his power as commanding general to put some of his concepts into practice while Johnston was isolated on the Peninsula.

The question of the Department of Northern Virginia's wagon trains was one of disposition and security. While the Confederates held the James and York Rivers, sufficient, if not overly ample, supplies could reach Yorktown by water, saving the necessity of committing the rickety wagons and worn-out horses to the muddy Tidewater roads and malarial atmosphere. In the event of a retreat, however, the threat of Federal gunboats prowling up the rivers would close that route of supply. Within a few days Johnston's army would need to be met by wagon trains of food and ammunition, or else disaster might result. The solution to this problem was to keep Johnston's wagons in Richmond, loaded and ready to meet the army with only a few hours' notice. Hundreds of wagons could not be left in the capital without a guard. Eventually, the decision was reached that, until Johnston called for them, the wagon trains would become the security responsibility of Brig. Gen. John H. Winder, provost marshal of Richmond and commander of the newly expanded Department of Henrico.[10]

Johnston was pleased to be relieved of the necessity of guarding the wagons but hardly happy about the status of Winder's department. The Department of Henrico had been established in December 1861 to put Richmond under military control. Winder, a Marylander, was willing to suffer personal unpopularity to ride herd on Union prisoners, guard various military facilities, discipline soldiers on furlough, and smell out anti-Confederate conspiracies. He never had enough men assigned to him to do more than a minimally adequate job, and his enemies periodically accused him of favoritism, terrorism, and even treason. Winder, with Davis's full support, persevered at his task, nonetheless. On March 26, Davis and Lee extended Winder's authority to include Petersburg and all the territory within ten miles of both cities. Ostensibly, the president and commanding general made this decision in order to organize better the rail transfer points that would have to be used to shift troops in an emergency. It would also place responsibility for the completion of the Richmond fortifications and the batteries at Drewry's and Chaffin's Bluffs in the hands of a single officer. From Johnston's perspective, however, Winder's appointment created a dangerous pocket of another's authority at the central point among the wings of his widespread army. Messages, troops, and supplies had to pass back and forth through a bottleneck that he did not control; Johnston could not even send his own provost marshals into the city to round up stragglers. Johnston protested this state of affairs, but Davis and Lee refused to give him authority over Winder.[11] Disheartened at this outcome, Johnston boarded a steamer on the York River the morning of April 17 and arrived at Yorktown again that evening, just four days after his inspection tour. The next morning he officially assumed command of the army.

McClellan had been uncharacteristically aggressive in the past few days. On April 16, concerned that Confederate cannon at Dam no. 1 could harass the construction of some of his siege batteries, the Union commander ordered Brig. Gen. William F. "Baldy" Smith to "reconnoiter" the Rebel position. Smith moved up a Vermont brigade and a pair of field batteries and opened fire across the creek separating the two lines. The Confederate counterfire, from a single cannon, was silenced in about an hour, with the crew driven from their gun. Smith ordered the Third Vermont, along with several companies of the Fourth, to wade the creek and probe the now-quiet rifle pits in front of his position. The ease with which the Confederate artillery had been silenced encouraged McClellan, who had ridden to Smith's headquarters sometime after the beginning of the action. He told Smith to move up his other two brigades. If circumstances permitted, he should attempt to take and hold the dam, not just examine it.[12]

The only forces from the Army of the Peninsula that had actually been in the trenches to oppose the Federal probe were a single six-pounder from a Georgia battery and a company of pickets from the Fifteenth North Carolina of Brig. Gen. Howell Cobb's brigade. The rest of the outwork was filled with "Quaker guns"—blackened logs between wagon wheels—and most of the North Carolinians were several hundred yards to the rear, draining and improving their camps. Colonel Robert McKinney, a Virginia Military Institute graduate, ordered his men to arms as soon as word came back that the enemy had crossed the creek. McKinney did not wait for reinforcements, a proper military but personally fatal decision. He could see more Yankees gathering across the water and knew that if he did not clear the Vermonters out of his rifle pits quickly, Smith's division would soon wade the creek in force. McKinney double-timed his Tarheels toward the enemy, who opened fire as soon as the North Carolinians came into range. Out in front of his men, the colonel lined them up to return fire, and the two sides traded volleys until a Federal minié ball caught McKinney in the forehead and killed him instantly. Though his lieutenant colonel later denied it, the Fifteenth North Carolina fell back in some confusion amid cries from the ranks that it had been ordered to retreat.[13]

McKinney's prompt response had brought other Confederate units to the field. A second regiment from Cobb's brigade, the Sixteenth Georgia, and two companies of a third, the Second Louisiana, rushed without orders to the sound of the firing, where they met the Seventh and Eighth Georgia of Brig. Gen. D. R. Jones's brigade marching up from the other direction. These regiments joined the rallied Fifteenth North Carolina to form a force the size of a brigade, probably numbering over 2,000 men. Less than half an hour had passed since the Third Vermont had first occupied the rifle pits, and the regiment's position was growing precarious. Reinforcements did not appear to be moving up as ordered, and after the first skirmish with the North Carolinians, Col. Breed N. Hyde discovered that few of his men had any dry ammunition left. He dispatched a runner to Smith's headquarters with this information and settled in to hold the rifle pits as long as he could.[14]

No Confederate general had yet arrived to coordinate the activities of the North Carolinians, Georgians, and Louisianians who had converged at the point of attack. Precious minutes ticked by until Col. George T. Anderson, commander of the Eleventh Georgia and senior field officer of Jones's brigade, rode up and assumed command. Quickly, he deployed the troops into line and gave the order to fix bayonets. Unlike McKinney, he did not intend to halt and return the fire of the Vermonters; he would accept initial casualties in order to close with superior numbers and regain the trenches before any more Yankees could cross the creek. Hyde, finding himself greatly outnumbered and having received neither reinforcements nor dry powder, shouted for a retreat, losing about ninety-five men killed, wounded, or captured, before he got his regiment back across the dam. Both sides concentrated more troops on opposite sides of the creek throughout the afternoon, waiting expectantly for the action to resume. McClellan had found out what he came to learn: the

Confederates had little artillery capable of impeding his buildup but reacted quickly to any probes. John Magruder, who believed that the Federals had made "a serious effort to break through," turned in to Johnston the next day another pessimistic report on the strength of his lines.[15]

Johnston had earlier seen the rifle pits as the weakest links in Magruder's extended line. The unwelcome news that the enemy was also aware of this deficiency caused him to examine carefully his options for defending his positions. Counting detached forces at Gloucester Point, Williamsburg, and Jamestown Island, Johnston's army contained twenty-four brigades of infantry, one of cavalry, and two battalions of reserve artillery—at least 70,000 men "present for duty." The army roster contained four major generals: G. W. Smith, Longstreet, Magruder, and D. H. Hill, each of whom Johnston assigned to command a division of six brigades. That he thought such divisions overly large is evidenced by the fact that he allowed his four subordinates to subdivide their own commands and requested the promotion of W. H. C. Whiting. Johnston moved to improve the overall quality of his brigade commanders, recommending promotion for Col. Wade Hampton, permitting the elderly S. R. Anderson to resign, and campaigning to avoid the assignment of politican-general Henry A. Wise to the army.[16]

He decided to leave Hill in command of the Yorktown fortifications, because the North Carolinian was familiar with the strengths and weaknesses of the positions and because he had already begun to implement the orders to move a substantial number of heavy cannon from the river to the land side of the fort. Chief of Artillery William Pendleton was dispatched to assist him. Johnston limited Magruder's command to the far right side of the line—overlooking the Warwick River all the way to the James. He assigned Longstreet the center segment and G. W. Smith the reserve.

Moving Magruder, who had designed the entire defensive system, to the least critical point in the line appears to have been a tacit editorial comment by Johnston on "Prince John's" initial conduct of operations. Despite having commanded on the Peninsula for nearly a year and having held this line for several weeks, Magruder had allowed much necessary work to remain undone. He had retained too many guns facing the York River. The critical rifle pits in the center of the line had never been connected, improved, or drained. No telegraph lines had been run behind his front, and even locally no provisions seemed to have been made for commanders to react to a Federal attack. McClellan's probe of April 16, had it not been met by troops instinctively marching to the sound of the guns and the initiative of two colonels, might well have shattered the key point in the Yorktown line. "Labor enough has been expended here to make a very strong position," Johnston advised Lee on April 22, "but it has been wretchedly misapplied by the young engineer officers." He did not need to mention who had supervised the engineers.[17]

The methodical Longstreet received the assignment to shore up the middle of the line. Unlike Magruder, who had often halted labor on his fortifications when he could not find slaves to impress, the Georgian put his own troops to work. Shacks and other buildings behind the lines were dismantled, not to be fed into bonfires but to plank over the muddy bottoms of the trenches. His regiments worked in relays connecting and extending the rifle pits, erecting small redoubts every few hundred feet along the line. The rear walls of the two detached redoubts were filled in with a combination of earth, sandbags, and bales of cotton. Longstreet's men already knew how to walk—now he taught them to dig.[18]

The six brigades of G. W. Smith's division remained in reserve throughout the entire period of the army's stay in the trenches. The fact that his troops never had to rotate into the waterlogged front lines caused some resentment among the rest of the soldiers of Johnston's army, but the deployment represented sound military logic. Smith was Johnston's most trusted subordinate, the man he wanted instantly available to protect the army's flanks if McClellan's gunboats succeeded in opening either the James or York Rivers. Kept in their camps about a mile to the rear of the main line, Smith's brigades could be ready to march hours sooner than regiments that would have to be relieved in the trenches first. True, Johnston could have rotated the troops, brigade by brigade, to give the rest of his men more respite from disagreeable duty. Though such an action might have improved morale, it could also have left him with the fragments of two or more divisions as his reserve, not a single concentrated force of 10,000 to 15,000 men accustomed to working together. As usual, Johnston's dispositions were governed by military necessity; his primary failing was that he never saw the need to explain to anyone decisions he believed to be patently obvious.

Under ordinary circumstances, the perceived disparity in duties assigned might have passed with minor discontent. Between March and May 1862, however, the situation inside every Confederate army, including Johnston's, was hardly ordinary. In a desperate attempt to keep Southern brigades from melting away when the enlistments of the one-year regiments expired, the Confederate Congress had passed legislation requiring those units to reorganize for three years but had granted each company, battery, battalion, and regiment the right to reelect its officers.[19] It was a most peculiar exercise in democracy: men who could not vote for their own senators or even in some cases for president had demanded and won the right to select by popular vote the officers who would lead them into battle. For years after the war, veterans recalled the elections with reactions that ranged from wry humor to thinly veiled disgust. In the Eighteenth Mississippi, Captains S. G. Brown (ex-governor and senator) and O. R. Singleton (ex-congressman), both standing for higher office, "told us that if we should reorganize immediately they would 'wager their heads to brass pins the war would end in sixty days.'" An orderly sergeant campaigning for election to lieutenant in the First Virginia Cavalry performed the morning roll call while the men of his company lay in their bedrolls. He promised them that if they elected him he could get the company reorganized as artillery and sent on detached service to more favorable climes. "It was a comical sight," wrote a member of the Richmond Howitzers, "to see the officers of an army 'elected' by the people in ranks," but Col. John Brockenbrough of the Fortieth Virginia found nothing humorous in the situation: "We find worthless, intriguing, politicians, and those who have been defeated in company elections, taking advantage of all these conflicting bills and unsatisfactory constructions . . . using bribery, a great deal of flash plausibility, and arguments which any worthless demagogue is capable of making."[20]

The situation was hardly amusing to Joseph Johnston or his generals. The elections seriously disrupted discipline and consumed his senior officers' time supervising contests or puzzling out the finer points of byzantine Confederate election laws. More detrimental yet, the upheaval cost the army the service of hundreds of experienced officers in the midst of an active campaign, men often replaced by ciphers, demagogues, and aspirants with true potential but no training. No statistical study has ever quantified the precise effect of the elections on either the Department of Northern Virginia or the Southern forces as a whole, but rough approximations can be made. Over half the army on the Peninsula was affected by the reorganization: fifty of eighty-eight and one-half infantry regiments, three of four cavalry regiments, and probably twenty of thirty-eight field batteries. This represented roughly 35,600 officers and men, with about 2,175 officers forced to fight for reelection.[21] Spot samples, and research by Robert K. Krick, suggest that about 37 percent of the company officers and nearly 53 percent of the field officers were defeated, sending home more than 800 experienced officers during March, April, and May.[22] Certainly some of the defeated candidates had been overage, political appointees or deadwood better pruned from the army rosters, but dozens, if not hundreds, of competent men lost their positions. Among the able officers who left the army as a result of the elections were West Pointers Benjamin Stoddert Ewell, Robert Johnson, William E. "Grumble" Jones, Edward Murray, Stephen Dodson Ramseur, Beverly Robertson, and Armistead Rust, along with Virginia Military Institute graduates Charles Crump and Charles Lightfoot. Most of these men eventually returned to the army in other capacities, but for the moment they were as lost to Johnston as if Federal bullets had struck them in combat.[23]

It would be difficult to overstate the confusion caused by the elections. Several units, like Dreux's Louisiana Battalion and the Ninth South Carolina, simply ceased to exist when their companies attached to other regiments. The Fourth South Carolina lost so many men that it was barely saved by the expedient of reorganizing it as a battalion rather than as a regiment. Enough regiments to fill two brigades petitioned Johnston directly for discharge; he dutifully transmitted their request to the secretary of war.[24]

Meanwhile, aspiring officers probed for every favorable technicality in the poorly written rules and drove their brigadiers to distraction trying to adjudicate their claims. Captain David G. Houston of Company D, Eleventh Virginia, asserted that because his company had reorganized several days earlier than the remainder of the regiment, he was now, by law, the senior captain of the regiment and due for an automatic promotion to a vacant majority. When Brig. Gen. A. P. Hill forwarded this contention to Richmond, Cooper ruled that Houston was correct: "Officers take rank from the date of their election. It was the intention of the law to give this advantage to companies first organized." Later, this precedent was seized by Capt. Reuben Cleary of the Seventh Virginia—another of Hill's regiments—to claim likewise an open majority. The War Department upheld his right to the post, even though the company that elected him had disbanded.[25]

Hill's were among the more simple problems facing Confederate officers during the reorganization. In the Ninth Virginia, stationed at Norfolk, Company C held a disputed election for the captaincy. Ten of the seventy-seven men abstained, leaving one candidate with thirty-five votes, the other with thirty-two. But thirty-five votes, Maj. Mark Hardin pointed out, were only a majority of the sixty-seven men who actually voted, not of the entire company. Should the election stand? An anonymous endorsement from Cooper's office ratified the election.[26] Colonel Wade Hampton faced an even knottier problem in his brigade with the Sixteenth North Carolina, whose Company D entered the election season with 141 men. On April 22, Hampton presented Secretary of War George Randolph with the following conundrum: "Seventy four men of Company D 16 NC regt. re-enlisted & chose their officers under the bounty act leaving sixty-seven men in old company which is now Company D. What disposition shall be made of the residue?" He needed a quick answer, because the election—in whichever company the War Department decided really was Company D—was scheduled for the following day. Almost plaintively, he closed the telegram: "Do answer." There is no indication in the files that anyone ever did.[27]

The situation was even more muddled in regiments such as the First Texas and the Fifth Alabama, both of which had been so hastily assembled in fall 1861 that each contained five companies enlisted for one year and five that had signed on for three. "Does the 11th section of the Act of Congress require a new election of officers of the war companies and field officers," queried Brig. Gen. Jubal Early, whose brigade included the Alabamians, "or merely an election of officers of the 12 months companies?" Again, there is no reply extant; by mid-April 1862, it seemed as if the secretary of war and adjutant general had quietly given up and decided to ratify whatever the senior officer in the field decided fit the rules.[28]

The confusion was not confined to the infantry. Colonel Pendleton's effort to achieve consistent calibers in each company resulted not only in the constant transfer of guns between different batteries but also left the gunners with perplexing electoral questions as well. The Jeff Davis (Alabama) Artillery had originally boasted eight cannon but had been reduced by transfer to six. The problem was that the War Department had authorized the overstrength battery several additional lieutenants. Did their commissions expire with the loss of their guns? Nobody, including the secretary of war, seemed to be certain.[29]

Competition in the cavalry was even more keen than in the infantry or artillery. Of the seven Virginia regiments required to undergo reorganization, five voted out their colonels, all of whom had been professional soldiers before the war. This ousting included the colonels of Stuart's three regiments on the Peninsula. Jubal Early protested that "the bad effects of the election system has . . . been shown in the case of a Virginia Cavalry Regiment [the Third], in which, in my opinion by a mistaken [application] of the law, the election of field officers was held by the men, and the Colonel, an efficient officer from the old army, was beaten." Following its system of ratifying almost any outcome that did not result in the dissolution of the regiment in question, the War Department declined to overturn the election.[30]

Johnston, like Lee and almost every other professional officer in the army, viewed the elections with quiet apprehension. Even in his memoirs, Johnston remained mostly silent on the subject, noting only that the law "had the effect of weakening the army."[31] Despite their other differences, it is nearly certain that Johnston wholeheartedly agreed with the position stated by Lee, several months earlier:

> The best troops are ineffectual without good officers. Our volunteers, more than any other, require officers whom they can respect and trust. The best men for that position should be selected, and it is important to consider how it can be effected. It would be safe to trust men of the

intelligence and character of our volunteers to elect their officers, could they at the time of the election realize their dependent condition in the day of battle. But this they cannot do, and I have known them in the hour of danger to repudiate and disown officers of their choice and beg for others. Is it right then, for a State to throw upon its citizens a responsibility which they do not feel and cannot properly exercise?[32]

Regardless of his personal feelings, Johnston could do little to ameliorate the ill effects of the elections. He prevented disgruntled soldiers from simply leaving the army when they thought their enlistments had expired, employing Stuart's cavalry to round them up and return them to the ranks. He punctually forwarded the questions of his commanders to the appropriate departments in Richmond and enforced the ensuing decisions. He sanctioned the creation of boards of examination, in the hope that they would remove the most blatant incompetents before they could do severe harm to their own men.[33] Beyond these measures, there was little for the army commander to do but keep himself firmly focused on the military problem at hand: resisting McClellan.

There were certainly enough other issues facing Johnston, at least for one of which nothing in his entire military career had prepared him. In assuming command of the Peninsula and Norfolk, he had also acquired a navy. The *Virginia* and the other vessels under construction at Gosport were not really his concern. The talented if temperamental Flag Officer Josiah Tattnall had assumed command of the ironclad, whose mission was fairly simple: to cruise in the vicinity of Hampton Roads as often and as ostentatiously as possible. The *Richmond* and the other incomplete craft remained under the control of Capt. Sidney Smith Lee, the commandant of the navy yard. The remainder of the James River Squadron had been ordered out of Hampton Roads and up the James to support the far right of the Yorktown line.[34]

Compared to the massive flotilla with which Adm. Louis Goldsborough supported the Army of the Potomac, Comdr. John R. Tucker's five vessels seemed almost inconsequential. Only the partially armored *Patrick Henry,* mounting ten guns, could be considered a threat to any ship other than an undefended transport. Her sister ship, the *Jamestown,* sported no armor at all and carried but two cannon, which left her no more powerful than the smaller *Teazer,* which also carried two guns. The *Raleigh* and the *Beaufort* belonged to Navy Secretary Stephen Mallory's envisioned fleet of pesky little gunboats— converted tugs that, although light of draft and manueverable, were essentially impotent, having only a single rifled piece placed in each bow. As Tattnall informed the secretary of the navy on April 21: "I can not [*sic*] prevent the enemy's gunboats or light draft transports from entering and ascending the James River, or their army crossing it, except so far as the force of steamers I have placed in the river may prevent it." "On this, however," he remarked gloomily, "I have little reliance, as the enemy at any time can send a force so superior as to compel them to retire upon the river behind our forts."[35]

Johnston did realize that, helpless or not against the Federal navy, Tucker's squadron, until it was overwhelmed, could provide him with intelligence concerning operations on McClellan's left flank. The five vessels could also inhibit, if not prevent, any crossing of the lower Warwick River by unsupported Yankee infantry. Aside from that, Johnston instructed Tucker that "it would be well for your boats to do the enemy harm whenever they can." He also included the caution that "it is hardly worth while to fire, however, merely to annoy them." As with his most trusted subordinates, Johnston left the final decision up to the man in the field—or in this case, in the water—"You in the neighborhood can always judge when it is worth while to open fire." His trust proved to be well placed. A fifty-year-old Virginian, with thirty-five years experience afloat, including duty in the Mexican War, Tucker was cool under fire, meticulous about details, and a talented tactical improviser. Within a week of his first assignment to Johnston's command, the general praised Tucker's abilities to Tattnall: "I am much pleased with his intelligence and zeal." Both Johnston and the Confederate authorities in Richmond soon found even more reasons to appreciate his imagination and nerve.[36]

The normal details of army administration consumed much of the rest of Johnston's time. He ordered the few decent roads through Williamsburg kept clear of miscellaneous wagon traffic in order to ensure that they would be open if Smith's division had to move out quickly. Likewise, he insisted that the Engineer Bureau inspect and, if necessary, repair the major bridges over the Chickahominy. Johnston also had telegraph lines strung along the length of the army's rear. He badgered the secretary of war, requesting better cannon, and General Lee, asking him to inspect hospital accommodations for his sick men in Richmond and to push General Winder to sweep the city for soldiers absent without leave.[37]

For a man normally economical with words, the army commander virtually barraged his superiors with updates and requests: during his sixteen-day tenure at Yorktown, Johnston wrote Lee or Randolph at least fourteen times, and quite possibly more. He also attempted to maintain contact with his other subordinates. Several telegraphic messages and letters, some delivered by staff officers authorized to expand on their content, arrived at Norfolk for General Huger, Flag Officer Tattnall, and Captain Lee. Messages requiring Generals Jackson and Ewell to communicate through Cooper's office in Richmond had been dispatched before Johnston left the capital; Field received similar instructions during the following week. Despite his best efforts, Johnston soon found himself receiving less and less information from the rest of Virginia. By April 26 he would certainly have agreed with Col. Dorsey Pender of the Sixth North Carolina, who wrote to his wife: "We are about as near cut off from all communication with the world as we could well be. Our mail all seems to come by chance and I have not yet been able to find out from what post office it came."[38]

In Johnston's case, the culprit was not the Confederate Post Office—it was his superiors in Richmond, specifically Generals Cooper (though probably unintentionally) and Lee. Though Johnston had left instructions for his mail from Jackson, Ewell, and Field to be forwarded to him through the Adjutant General's Office, Cooper sent it to Lee. Neither the originals nor copies were posted to Johnston, who, unknowingly, found himself forced to rely upon letters from Lee, letters that subtly distorted not only the situation among Johnston's subordinates but also his own role in directing them. That Lee had the authority to intercept Johnston's correspondence and issue orders directly to his subordinates was indisputable; it was, however, his methods that were questionable.[39]

Many historians have assumed that Johnston simply neglected his detached subordinates, leaving a command vacuum into which Lee, Jefferson Davis's "military adviser," quietly inserted himself, guiding by suggestion in order to avoid rumpling Johnston's sensibilities. Clifford Dowdey entitled his chapter on the subject, "Lee Plays at Machiavelli," and Douglas Southall Freeman has asserted, without sources, that President Davis had instructed a reluctant Lee to intercept Johnston's correspondence and "supervise the movements of these two officers for as long as Johnston was at a distance from Richmond." Robert G. Tanner, in *Stonewall in the Valley,* has characterized Lee's intervention as being conducted "with great skill and little authority." More recently, Emory Thomas has portrayed Lee as working through "suggestions and ample encouragement" rather than by command prerogative.[40]

Clearly, Lee's position as commanding general was far less than nominal, and he hardly seems to have blinked at asserting his authority. Two letters from Ewell to Cooper, dated April 20 and intended for Johnston, announced that Jackson had called him from his post on the Rapidan toward the Shenandoah because the Federals were advancing. Johnston never saw the letters, which were diverted to Lee, who answered them most authoritatively: "If it is practicable to strike a speedy blow at General Banks and drive him back it will tend to relieve the pressure on Fredericksburg." The same day, Lee mailed a letter to Jackson, advising him that "if you can use General Ewell's division in an attack on General Banks, and to drive him back, it will prove a great relief to the pressure on Fredericksburg." If this was impracticable, Lee strongly suggested that Jackson return Ewell to supporting distance of Field's brigade south of the Rappahannock. Most important, Lee essentially cut Johnston out of the line of communication by telling Jackson to "please communicate with *me* on this subject."[41]

Nor did Lee inform Johnston, in a letter to the department commander on the same day, that he had written to both of Johnston's subordinates. Besides ignoring his own correspondence with Jackson, Lee neglected to announce that Field had abandoned Fredericksburg, and that he, standing on his authority as commanding general, had sent the young brigadier general explicit orders that were a far cry from the deferential suggestions of a military adviser. "I desire that you shall do everything in your power to prevent the enemy from advancing from Fredericksburg," Lee instructed Field on April 19, continuing: "You will use every exertion to ascertain the strength and movements of the enemy and keep me informed of the same. You will also communicate with General Ewell." These were positive directives, directives of which Lee did not advise Johnston.[42]

Lee did not even inform Johnston until April 23—six days after the fact—that the Confederates no longer held Fredericksburg. He vaguely detailed the reinforcements being dispatched to Field's position but in such a way that Johnston could not have estimated their numbers, even though Lee had an accurate count of the soldiers being sent north. Nor did he advise Johnston whether either of the brigade commanders, Maxcey Gregg or Joseph R. Anderson, ranked Field and would therefore take over his command. In the same pair of letters, Lee finally informed Johnston that Jackson had called Ewell into the Valley but omitted the date on which Jackson had done so and continued to ignore his own correspondence with the two generals.[43]

Lee's actions in regard to the Fredericksburg front became even more misleading on April 26. Brigadier General Joseph R. Anderson did indeed outrank Field and received his formal instructions from Lee when he passed through Richmond from North Carolina. "You will proceed with your brigade to the vicinity of Fredericksburg," Lee told Anderson, "where Brig. C. W. Field is now with the troops which have preceded you, and assume command of the operations of our army in that quarter, being the senior general officer." No mention was made by Lee that Field had been subordinate to Johnston, or that Anderson's command was a district in someone else's department. The appointment to command having been made, Lee continued with detailed strategic orders: "If it be impossible to drive the enemy from his present position, I desire you to lose no effort to keep him confined to the smallest possible margin."[44]

Anderson obviously considered himself the commander of one of the Confederacy's many small independent armies, answerable only to the commanding general. Lee neither corrected him when he styled his division the Army of the Rappahannock nor ever informed him that Johnston was his official superior. Johnston did not receive news of Anderson's assumption of command until May 8, when Lee responded to a direct question. On the other hand, Lee informed both Jackson and Ewell of Anderson's appointment in advance and ordered the three generals to communicate with each other.[45]

Lee's methods plainly discomfited both Jackson and Ewell. Jackson pointed out to him on April 23 that the options they had been discussing "would be departing from General Johnston's instructions." Three days later, Jackson, still uneasy about the lack of any word from his official superior, queried Ewell: "Do you make regular reports to General Johnston? The General directed me to send communications for him to you. Please acknowledge receipt of the accompanying one and let me know to what point you send it."[46]

Jackson's April 26 letter to Johnston did not survive to be included in either the *Official Records* or the files of the Adjutant and Inspector General's Office. Its timing suggests that Jackson, who had always kept Johnston carefully apprised of his movements, probably explained that he intended, on Lee's orders, to leave Ewell's division to observe Banks while he united with Brig. Gen. Edward Johnson west of Staunton to attack the Federals debouching from the mountains of western Virginia. As aggressive as he was, it would have been in character for Jackson to tell his superior that he intended to use the discretion granted him to pursue his plan unless he was overruled within a few days.[47] Four days later, having received no response, Jackson began the deceptive maneuvering that inaugurated the famous Valley campaign. It is impossible to determine whether Johnston would have sanctioned Jackson's offensive because he never received the letter.

Lee's disregard for the formal command structure also distressed Ewell. Dick Ewell's personality was such that his performance depended upon the receipt of explicit orders; ambiguity, or even an excess of personal discretion, unnerved him. Nobody, during April, May, and June 1862, ever seemed to want to explain to him where he was to march, why he was headed there, or who was in charge. He confided in one of his brigade commanders that "he never saw one of Jackson's couriers approach without expecting an order to assault the north pole." Lee's letters suited him little better; on April 26 he complained to the commanding general that "I have the honor to state that I don't clearly understand your letter of the 25th." This was followed by an extract and a series of detailed questions aimed at pinning down Lee's intent. Lee responded briefly on April 27 that the information had been more intended for Jackson than

Ewell and that Ewell had been informed almost as an afterthought.[48] Three days later, still disgruntled because he could not determine just who was in control of operations, Ewell shot back a rejoinder to Lee:

> I beg leave to say that it seems important to me that the whole line, including the forces south of Fredericksburg (Generals Field and Anderson), should be under one general, authorized to combine them against any point deemed advisable. This does not seem to be the case at present, and the enemy are exhausting the country at free cost.[49]

Johnston's continued ignorance of this situation raises two significant questions. First, why did Lee keep Johnston in the dark? Second, what efforts did Johnston make, or should he have made, to find out what was occurring in northern Virginia? There is no evidence extant to support Freeman's contention that Davis ordered Lee to take over coordination of the movements of Johnston's detached subordinates. Nor did there need to be such a directive—the correspondence of Jackson, Ewell, Anderson, and Field reveals the fact that each officer took Lee's title of commanding general quite seriously and assumed that he could legally issue their orders. If he had legal authority to command Johnston's subordinates, why did Lee not openly advise Johnston that he was doing so?

The correspondence between Johnston and Lee suggests a possible answer. Johnston had always been reluctant to commit his army to the Peninsula, and when Lee had written on April 21 that it might be necessary to detach units from Johnston's army to reinforce Field in order to protect the Fredericksburg line, Johnston had reacted negatively: "I think it anything but expedient to divide these forces." Further, Johnston responded on April 22:

> Should McDowell advance upon the capital, which is certainly probable, the only course for us, in my opinion, is . . . to assemble near Richmond as many troops as possible, those from Norfolk, North Carolina, and South Carolina to be joined by this army, then to endeavor to fight the enemy before all his forces are united. To detach troops from this position would be ruin to those left.[50]

His reaction caused Lee to tread lightly around the subject of a threat from Fredericksburg, primarily because his own preferred strategy involved holding the Peninsula as long as possible. Johnston's response would also have given Lee cause to believe that the general would respond negatively to any suggestion that Jackson and Ewell might actually march their divisions farther from

Richmond for any reason. Even allowing for the fact that Lee controlled much of Johnston's access to information about other fronts, why was there not a greater effort by Johnston to communicate directly with his own subordinates? Did his preoccupation with McClellan's army and growing siege train make him "lose touch" with the rest of his department, as Freeman believed?

The question of timing is critically important to resolving this issue. Johnston had last written to Jackson and Ewell on April 17, before leaving Richmond. Letters traveling from Richmond to the Rappahannock, Johnston knew from his own experience, usually required two or three days for delivery. A letter forwarded through Ewell to Jackson would take at least another day to reach the commander in the Shenandoah. Assuming that Jackson responded on the same day he received the letter, a minimum of three days could be expected in its return trip to the capital. Soon after arriving at Yorktown, Johnston discovered that the mail between Richmond and the Peninsula normally spent the better part of two additional days in transit. Therefore, even under the best of circumstances, Johnston would not have expected any reply from Jackson until April 24 or 25. A single missed connection or significant delay somewhere in the postal chain could have reasonably extended this period by two days; Johnston should not have had any cause to be anxious until after April 27.[51]

By that time, Johnston had already received Lee's letter of April 23, which seemed to update him on the positions of his subordinates. Jackson, he inferred incorrectly, had ordered Ewell toward the Valley on April 21, pursuant to Johnston's original orders to try to engage Banks near Swift Run Gap. Since it should take Ewell at least two days to join Jackson and Lee had "heard nothing . . . of the junction of Jackson and Ewell," Johnston had no real reason to expect either of his commanders to write unless some sort of action commenced.[52] Even if a battle took place immediately upon Ewell's reinforcement of Jackson—which Johnston believed would happen about April 24 or April 25—then a letter from Jackson could not reasonably be expected until April 29 or 30. The only problem with this series of assumptions was that it rested upon the mistaken belief that Jackson had ordered Ewell to march on April 21, when he had done so on April 17. Had Johnston known that events were progressing so rapidly in the Valley, it is unlikely that he would have remained so sanguine about the lack of correspondence.

Only by the last few days of April did Johnston begin to realize that something was dreadfully amiss with his lines of communication to his subordinates. Unfortunately, it was just then that another event occurred that rightfully riveted the army commander's eyes on the Yankee army directly in front of him: McClellan's siege artillery opened fire.

9
THE RETREAT
FROM YORKTOWN

The Farinholt House stood on a bluff overlooking Wormley's Creek, roughly 4,200 yards south of Yorktown. It was a large, colonial-style frame house with four white pillars on the front porch, chimneys at either end, and third-floor dormer windows. From the roof, an observer with a telescope could see over the ramparts protecting Yorktown, discern details of the water battery, and even watch the unloading of the schooners that glided down the upper York River to provide Joseph Johnston's army with provisions and ammunition. It had been a key observation point for George McClellan's engineers and artillery officers throughout the siege.[1]

Shortly after noon, on Wednesday, April 30, 1862, the roof was packed with far more men than usual. Battery no. 1—often informally known as the Farinholt Battery—was scheduled to open fire on the Confederates at 2:00 P.M. Brigadier General William F. Barry, chief of artillery of the Army of the Potomac, was there as was Col. Robert O. Tyler, organizer of the First Connecticut Heavy Artillery and commander of McClellan's siege train. Other officers from the First Connecticut, serving at batteries still incomplete, might have slipped away to watch the effect of the first heavy shells to drop into Yorktown, and beside them might well have been officers from the Fifth New York. The New Yorkers had a special interest in the guns in Battery no. 1: they had hauled them off the ships across paths so muddy that the monstrous cannon sunk in to their axles. Then they had dug them out and manhandled them, under the direction of the artillerymen, into the battery they had helped to excavate. Possibly McClellan himself, attended by his retinue of staff officers and foreign military observers, climbed onto the roof to watch what he hoped was the systematic destruction of Johnston's fortifications.[2]

Major Elisha F. Kellogg, also from the First Connecticut Artillery, did not have such a good view of Yorktown, even though what he saw was most important. Kellogg commanded Battery no. 1, and thus he was down inside the carefully dug traverses, calculating trajectories for his guns. His battery boasted five 100-pounder Parrotts and one monster 200-pounder. The smaller guns weighed 9,700 pounds and required 10 pounds of powder to throw a shell as far as 6,800 yards; the larger one weighed 16,500 pounds and lobbed its projectiles 8,000 yards on a charge of 16 pounds. The shells themselves weighed between 70 and 175 pounds. To hit the wharves or the batteries at Yorktown was well within their capability but called for careful ranging; missed shots were significant because the big guns took nearly an hour to reload.[3]

Kellogg's targets that Wednesday afternoon were the Yorktown wharves, where detailed soldiers struggled to unload half-a-dozen supply vessels. As the first shells plunged in, D. H. Hill's soldiers fled the docks in confusion, and the skippers of the schooners cast off and sailed behind Gloucester Point, a position that had previously represented safe haven from Yankee shells. But not that day. Kellogg's 200-pound Parrott slowly pivoted, and the gunners cranked it almost up to its thirty-five-degree maximum elevation. They loaded a shell and sent it crashing down among the anchored vessels some 6,200 yards up the river.[4]

Hill fired back. His men could sight Battery no. 1 quite easily, but McClellan's engineers had measured very carefully. An 8-inch Columbiad smoothbore was the largest piece that the Confederates could bring to bear, and the Yankee guns had been dug in just on the fringes of its most extreme range. Hill's gunners got close enough to rattle the teeth of the New Englanders inside the battery, but not close enough to hurt them. General Barry reported several days later: "The enemy's fire was well directed, but the protection afforded by the battery effective, and their fire caused us no casualties." Lowering the barrels of two of the 100-pounders slightly, Kellogg's men returned the favor. They could fire only once for every three times the Confederates did, but the greater range and shell weight of the Parrott rifles soon told; Hill's gun was quickly silenced. The firing continued throughout the afternoon and evening, thirty-nine heavy shells landing inside Hill's perimeter. The cannonade ceased with darkness. Gunnery with such heavy weapons in the mid-nineteenth century still required much direct sighting for accuracy, and McClellan hated to waste shells. Dense fog the next morning provided the Confederates a bit of a reprieve. Since no one could see where the shells were landing, Kellogg was ordered to limit himself to one shot an hour in the direction of the wharves, simply to discourage the unloading of supplies.[5]

Johnston knew the fog would not last, and his own observers confirmed that other heavy batteries across the Warwick were only days away from opening fire. Nothing in his own artillery park could seriously harm McClellan's batteries as they demolished his own positions piece by piece. In a classic siege, this would have been the moment for a sally against the enemy guns, but the inundations of the river to his front made an attack impossible.

Johnston had dreaded this moment. The day before Battery no. 1 opened fire, he had written to Robert E. Lee that "should the attack upon Yorktown be made earnestly, we cannot prevent its fall; nor can it hold out more than a few hours." He believed that McClellan would combine his bombardment with a rush up the James River by Federal ironclads, which, unlike the *Virginia,* had shallow enough drafts to follow the main channels. This "would enable him to reach Richmond three days before these troops, setting out at the same time. Should such a move be made, the fall of Richmond would be inevitable, unless we anticipate it." Anticipation meant withdrawal: "As two or three days, more or less, can signify little, I think it best for the safety of the capital to do it now, to put the army in position to defend Richmond." Yet he intended to move deliberately, "as soon as can be done conveniently, looking to the condition of the roads and the time necessary for the corresponding movement from Norfolk." Perhaps remembering Jefferson Davis's earlier disavowal of approving his withdrawal from Manassas, Johnston made sure that Lee understood the intent of his communication: "As this is an important movement, I think it necessary that the intention to make it be reported to the Government."[6]

The opening of Battery no. 1 forced Johnston's hand much more quickly than even he had expected. If the Federals could deny him the Yorktown docks, then the army became almost completely dependent on the trickle of supplies that could be landed at Jamestown Island. Further, he was faced with the prospect that this one battery could within days dismount all the Confederate cannon in the Yorktown water battery and those across the river at Gloucester Point. He called his senior officers to James Longstreet's headquarters on May 1: G. W. Smith, Longstreet, John Magruder, D. H. Hill, J. E. B. Stuart, William Pendleton, and Porter Alexander. Not one of them believed that the Yorktown line could or should be held longer than another forty-eight hours. Johnston had already ordered Benjamin Huger to prepare Norfolk for evacuation; he told his subordinates that the withdrawal would occur on the evening of May 2 and telegraphed Jefferson Davis to the same effect.[7]

Though aware that "the wretched condition of the roads may cause us heavy losses of materials on the march," Johnston determined to avoid leaving anything behind for McClellan that could be hauled away. As in northern Virginia, this did not include his heavy artillery, which, besides being nearly immobile, would have to cover the retirement of his divisions. He ordered Alexander to ship to Richmond all the extra ammunition and ordnance stores in depot beginning April 30. Pendleton's artillery was assigned the best of several poor roads and scheduled to march a few hours ahead of the main body. He ordered Col. Fitzhugh Lee's First Virginia Cavalry to precede the army to the vicinity of Eltham's Landing and West Point so that the army would be immediately alerted to the expected Federal amphibious landing, once Yorktown and Gloucester were evacuated.[8]

A Federal landing on the banks of the York River to his rear was Johnston's greatest concern. He believed that the *Virginia* could hold Adm. Louis Goldsborough's flotilla at bay on the James, at least for a few days. Even though he had ordered the batteries at Gloucester Point to be manned for several hours after the retreat of the bulk of the army, he harbored few illusions that this move would keep the Federals from ascending the York River. Thus he took what few precautionary measures he could. He ordered the supply vessels on the York River sailed upstream to critical points and sunk in the river as obstructions; fifty-three schooners were thus scuttled as Yorktown fell. The railroad bridge over the York River near West Point was burned, as were the docks at key points along the river. Johnston knew that such measures could at best delay, not prevent, an amphibious descent on his rear; he could count on having to fight McClellan's troops with part of his army before the rest had even cleared the vicinity of Williamsburg.[9]

Johnston wanted G. W. Smith's division available to oppose any Federal landing on the York River. The troops were the freshest in the army, and among Smith's brigade commanders were W. H. C. Whiting and Wade Hampton, two men whom he trusted implicitly. Thus he arranged that once the army passed through Williamsburg, Smith's division would be in the lead. Whiting's three brigades were scheduled to be among the first troops to march away from Yorktown on May 2. He also gave Smith control of the First Virginia Cavalry, as well as Magruder's division and part of the reserve artillery as soon as those units cleared Williamsburg. With half the army available to him, Smith should be able, Johnston hoped, to contain if not repulse a Yankee landing while Johnston supervised the rear guard and the evacuation of the army's guns and supplies.[10]

The pounding of heavy shells from Battery no. 1 resumed in earnest on the morning of May 2: Kellogg's men dropped sixty rounds on the Yorktown docks and the water battery; Hill's 8-inch Columbiad burst returning the fire. How many more days could the Yorktown fortifications withstand the shells of the Parrott guns? How long before more of McClellan's heavy artillery commenced battering the other sections of his line? Once the other Union batteries opened, Confederate withdrawal could potentially become a bloody disaster. Johnston's timetable was tight—much tighter than the one attempted in northern Virginia—because no movements near the front could be attempted until nightfall, lest they be observed. The orders for the retreat were carefully drawn and circulated to the division commanders on the morning of May 2.[11]

Delays and confusion among the trains of Longstreet's and Magruder's divisions forced Johnston to postpone the movement for twenty-four hours. It was a tense day: the First Connecticut Artillery poured another thirty-four rounds into Hill's fortifications at Yorktown, which now had no guns capable of reaching Battery no. 1 with return fire. Meanwhile, General Barry reported to McClellan that the next morning the ten 13-inch seacoast mortars of Battery no. 4, four more in Battery no. 11, five 10-inch siege mortars in Battery no. 12, six 30-pounder Parrotts in Battery no. 13, and three 100-pounder Parrotts in Battery no. 14 would be ready to open fire at dawn. Major Charles S. Wainwright of the First New York Light Artillery, who had dropped by Barry's headquarters, confided to his diary that evening that "it will be a splendid sight when all our guns and mortars open, especially if the rebs reply lively; one worth half a lifetime to see." Johnston had only hours left before the conflagration began.[12]

A heavy rain started to fall in the evening of May 3, as the first brigades slipped quietly out of their rifle pits. It was a decidedly mixed blessing; although it would disguise the movement to some extent, the downpour ruined the roads over which the army had to travel. Alexander wrote: "I recall that night's march as particularly disagreeable. The whole soil of that section seemed to have no bottom and no supporting power." The soil had been so soaked with the rain of previous weeks that the water could not even sink in; a private in George Pickett's brigade remembered that "the clay and sand of the roads was now worked into a liquid mortar, which overspread their entire surface, hiding the deep holes cut by heavy gun wheels, until man or beast discovered them by stumbling therein." The columns waded and struggled along at a pace that never exceeded one mile an hour, and that with exhausting effort. "The roads," said Alexander, "were but long strings of guns, wagons, and ambulances, mixed in with infantry, artillery, and cavalry, splashing and bogging through the darkness in a river of mud."[13]

At best, Johnston knew that his men might make seven or eight miles by sunrise. It was barely enough to give him a head start on the Federals, and even that was threatened by the constant stalling of wagons, caissons, and guns in the mud. Horses sank up to their bellies and wagons to their axles. Each time this happened, ropes had to be tied to other teams and their wagons brought back to assist in the rescue. Often this was not enough, and the infantry and gunners swarmed into the mud to manhandle wheels loose from the mire. Johnston himself dived into the muck to help pry loose a twelve-pounder of Snowden's (Georgia) Battery. Some of the horses drowned; others' hearts simply gave out. Wagons were abandoned and guns spiked. One private wrote later: "Sometimes I caught myself stumbling over a dead horse and sometimes upon a half-living man." Yet, somehow, the army kept moving, if only at a snail's pace, even though everyone was as tired as Col. William Pender, who told his wife, "I have seldom been more sleepy, hungry or tired than I am just now."[14]

The army kept moving, but many individual soldiers did not. The back-breaking work, combined with lack of sleep and the absence of rations for two days, caused many of Johnston's troops to collapse in an apathetic stupor. D. H. Hill counted more than 1,500 stragglers along his route of march through Williamsburg and told his wife, "There are thousands also scattered over the country engaged in plundering." When Hill attempted to encourage or intimidate them into rejoining the ranks, "some answered my entreaties with curses, some with 'I don't care if the Yankees do take me. I am starving to death and freezing with cold.' "[15] Well aware of the condition of his troops, Johnston knew that he could only retreat so far before he paused to give the men a rest. If not molested by Federal pursuit, he intended to halt between the Pamunkey and Chickahominy Rivers, and there await McClellan.[16]

The luxury of stopping depended on just how long McClellan would remain in front of empty entrenchments and how determined his pursuit would be. As the infantry evacuated Yorktown, Hill's cannoneers inaugurated their heaviest bombardment of the Yankee lines during the entire siege, firing off their stocks of powder and shot as if there were no tomorrow, because there was not. By midnight or soon thereafter the fire began to slacken, as the gunners spiked their pieces one by one and laid powder trails into their magazines. Major Bryan Grimes of the Fourth North Carolina commanded the last few companies of the infantry rear guard, which picked its way back from the picket line around 4:00 A.M. Grimes had to balance the speed necessary to clear the town before the fuses burned down against the need to avoid "torpedoes [that] had been planted on all the roads and streets leading into Yorktown."[17] The torpedoes—mostly 10-pounder shells rigged with pressure fuses and buried as mines—were the work of Brig. Gen. Gabriel J. Rains. Enraged by Federal shelling of his hometown, New Berne, North Carolina, Rains considered land mines a fair response. Almost everyone else, from Johnston to McClellan, disagreed, but they did so after the fact, for Rains had never informed his superiors of his intentions. Despite the fact that Johnston later disowned the tactic, Rains's explosives killed and wounded enough unwary Union soldiers to slow down the Federal penetration of Yorktown.[18]

For several hours after sunrise on May 4, as Johnston's infantry and artillery struggled up muddy roads, Stuart's depleted cavalry brigade was the only force actually facing the Army of the Potomac. Having detached the First Virginia Cavalry to cover Eltham's Landing, Stuart was left with just 1,500 sabers to slow down the pursuit. He deployed Lt. Col. Williams Wickham and the Fourth Virginia Cavalry, as well as part of Col. Thomas F. Goode's Third Virginia, to cover the Williamsburg Road. A few miles south of Wickham and Goode, on the Telegraph Road, Stuart himself took charge of the Jeff Davis (Mississippi) Legion and several companies of the Henry Wise (Virginia) Legion. There was little or no communication between the two wings of Stuart's brigade because the heavily wooded country "was exceedingly unfavorable for cavalry operations."[19]

Stuart was careful throughout the morning to keep Johnston informed of the advance of Federal cavalry under Brigadier Generals George Stoneman and William H. Emory on the Telegraph Road. What he did not know was that, on his left flank, Wickham and Goode were being pushed back steadily, until the blue-clad horsemen there had actually moved between Stuart and Johnston. This he discovered only when a courier returned with the news that it had been impossible to thread his way through Union lines with a message for the army commander. Resourceful in every extremity, Stuart trotted his men further south, detouring around the enemy by way of the beaches near Jamestown.[20]

Johnston, however, did not know that Stuart was extricating himself. About noon he realized that the courier was overdue. This was at roughly the same time the First and Fourth Virginia Cavalry found themselves pushed back to the outskirts of Williamsburg. In the densely forested terrain, there was no way to be certain that there was not a division of infantry on the heels of the Federal cavalry. Assuming the worst, at 1:00 P.M. Johnston himself rode to the rearmost unit in the line of march, Brig. Gen. Paul J. Semmes's Georgia-Kentucky Brigade, and ordered it into the forts around Williamsburg. About an hour later Johnston located Brig. Gen. Lafayette McLaws, who commanded part of Magruder's division. Johnston instructed him to send another brigade back to support Semmes and to go himself to supervise the line.[21]

McLaws, a Georgian who had graduated from West Point in Longstreet's class, selected the South Carolina brigade of lawyer-turned-soldier Joseph B. Kershaw for the assignment. Both arrived at Semmes's position about 3:00 P.M. McLaws was vaguely aware that the fortifications in front of Williamsburg were centered on a large earthwork—Fort Magruder—with minor works extending toward the rivers north and south at intervals of several hundred yards. Semmes had already occupied some of the redoubts to the right of the road, but neither he nor McLaws knew the exact location of all the forts. Fortunately for them, Col. Benjamin S. Ewell of the Thirty-second Virginia was at hand. Ewell had commanded the post of Williamsburg for months and was thoroughly familiar with the terrain. He quickly guided Kershaw's brigade into the correct positions.[22]

Even before the Confederates had deployed their second brigade, Stoneman's advance guard arrived. Federal cavalry, apparently unaware that it was probing a line now held by infantry, rode forward so boldly, McLaws reported, that "at first they were supposed to be our own men, so close were they and so confident in their advance." He soon realized his error, as Union horse artillery opened up in support of the horsemen. About this time Col. J. Lucius Davis, commanding the Wise Legion cavalry, and the first of Stuart's detachment to rejoin the army, arrived on the scene. McLaws ordered counterbattery fire against the Union artillery and a charge by Davis's men on the suddenly confused Federal cavalry. The charge routed the bluecoats with little loss to either side, and Kershaw's men finished occupying the forts along the road. No more probes were made against McLaws's positions for the rest of the afternoon.[23]

Johnston, who had been looking over McLaws's shoulder during the skirmish, knew that the Federal infantry could be, at best, a few hours behind the cavalry. When he thought of the condition of the roads and the tortuous progress of his army, he realized that he probably could not escape without fighting to slow down the pursuit. Inadequate as Magruder's line of redoubts may have been, it represented the only prepared fortification between Yorktown and Richmond, and he knew that he should make use of it. At sunset therefore, Johnston ordered McLaws to pull out his brigades, to be replaced by two from Longstreet's division. If he could get the army marching at the crack of dawn, the Confederates might yet elude McClellan without combat; if not, the action would be supervised by one of Johnston's most trusted subordinates. This arrangement evidently calmed any fears Johnston had that night, for he treated two of his staff officers to an impromptu, bare-chested display of saber-handling before retiring for the evening.[24]

Longstreet sent back Brig. Gen. Richard H. Anderson's South Carolinians and Col. Roger Pryor's mixed brigade of Alabamians, Virginians, and Louisianians. Anderson, a South Carolinian himself and a classmate of McLaws and Longstreet at West Point, met McLaws just after dark. The Georgian had already withdrawn his men from the line of redoubts in preparation to resume his march. Heavy rain was falling again. In the cold, wet darkness, Anderson made an error of judgment that the next day threatened the safety of Johnston's retreat. Although followed by suspicions of alcoholism throughout his regular army career, Anderson was a talented tactician and a brave leader of troops in battle, but he was not a man who paid a great deal of attention to details. "He was indolent," admitted Moxley Sorrel. "His capacity and intelligence [were] excellent, but it was hard to get him to use them." That night, he took the easiest course. Expecting that his men would be relieved soon after sunrise, he occupied all the forts to the right of the road but only two of the redoubts on the left. He did not send out scouts to find out how far the line extended; if he had done so, he would have discovered that there were at least four more fortifications around the boggy ground bordering the road to Allen's Wharf. If seized by the Federals, possession of these works would allow them to enfilade Fort Magruder.[25]

Neither Longstreet nor Johnston knew of this oversight. The division commander, having delegated the rear guard to Anderson, spent the night preparing his trains and the rest of his troops to move. He did authorize Anderson to call in other brigades from the division for reinforcements, if pressed, but he did not check on his subordinate's deployment or personally examine the line of redoubts until several hours after dawn. In fact, Longstreet did not even arrive on the field until a few minutes after noon.[26]

Anderson, his two brigades now reinforced by the brigades of Raleigh Colston, A. P. Hill, George Pickett, and Cadmus Wilcox—the remainder of Longstreet's division—had been fighting Brig. Gen. Joseph Hooker's Second Division, Third Corps, of the Army of the Potomac, since sunrise. "Being in pursuit of a retreating army," Hooker wrote five days later, "I deemed it my duty to lose no time in making disposition of my forces to attack, regardless of their number and position. . . . By doing so my division, if it did not capture the army before me, would at least hold them, in order that others might." "Hooker," Bruce Catton has observed, "was an army politician and a devious man . . . but as a fighter he was direct and straightforward." Without waiting to reconnoiter the strength of the Confederate defenses or to acquire authorization from his corps commander, Hooker waded in, attacking the fortifications that Anderson had already garrisoned. He drove in the Confederate skirmishers but foundered against Fort Magruder and began probing farther down Anderson's right flank. This move only succeeded in attracting the attention of Rebel reinforcements. Discounting his own brigade, which held Fort Magruder and the two redoubts on the far left, and Colston's, which was still marching up, by 10:00 A.M. Anderson had four brigades, numbering about 8,000 men, available for a counterattack. He also had Longstreet's permission.[27]

Anderson left Fort Magruder to assume personal command of the attack, which was quite successful despite being launched piecemeal. Wilcox advanced first against Hooker's left and became involved in a confusing fight in dense woods. Soon realizing that he was engaging a brigade against a division, Wilcox sent for assistance. Since he did not know that Anderson was riding to that part of the field to take command, he dispatched couriers directly to Pryor and A. P. Hill for support. Pryor, in the absence of orders from Anderson and still under obligation to hold two of the redoubts, could reinforce Wilcox's attack with only two of his three regiments. Hill, who had never received adequate orders from anybody, did not know exactly who was in command or what he should do. Consequently, he sent a courier to find Longstreet and waited. About half an hour later, Anderson arrived at his headquarters and ordered Hill to support Wilcox. Pickett's men meanwhile waited behind Fort Magruder until Anderson remembered to call them forward still later in the morning. With Anderson busy bringing up reinforcements, no one effectively assumed command of any group larger than a brigade for several hours.[28]

The consequences of such disorganization should have been disastrous, for there were probably 40,000 Federal troops within an hour's march of Hooker's beleaguered division. That morning, however, there was no one in effective command of the Union army either. McClellan was back in Yorktown, loading Brig. Gen. William B. Franklin's division on transports for an amphibious landing farther up the York River. The senior Federal officer at Williamsburg was the commander of the Second Corps, Maj. Gen. Edwin Vose Sumner, who sat in his headquarters at the nearby Adams House, "slightly befuddled." Because Sumner outranked him, the Fourth Corps commander, Maj. Gen. Erasmus Keyes, found himself allowed to do nothing to support Hooker, even though he had two divisions—those of William F. Smith and Darius Couch— nearby. Hooker's own commander, Maj. Gen. Samuel P. Heintzelman of the Third Corps, had been delayed while bringing forward his other division. Neither army, it seemed, had yet learned how to coordinate a battle. It was a perfect example of what Prince Henrí de Joinville ruefully characterized as "the American system of 'every man for himself.' "[29]

Numbers and Rebel enthusiasm seemed to be prevailing in the chaotic melee. After several hours of confused battle, Hill's First Virginia finally supplied the weight that forced Hooker's line back several hundred yards, capturing a battery of eight guns that the Yankees had time neither to spike nor to withdraw. Yet though the decision to the right of Fort Magruder went to the Confederates, they were too disorganized to profit from it. The regiments involved in the fighting had become intermingled and were difficult to maneuver. Most of the soldiers were low on ammunition, and the brigade commanders soon discovered that the reserve ammunition trains were heading in the other direction as rapidly as possible. A. P. Hill could not round up either enough horses to haul off his captured guns or axes to destroy their carriages.[30]

Meanwhile the attention of the senior officers of both armies had turned to the opposite flank, toward the redoubts north of Fort Magruder that

Anderson had failed to occupy. Brigadier General William F. Smith had finally prevailed upon Sumner to let him attempt a flanking maneuver. Sumner agreed to allow Smith to send a single brigade to probe the Confederate left. Smith chose Brig. Gen. Winfield Scott Hancock for this enterprise and quietly expanded both Hancock's strength and mission when the two were out of Sumner's earshot. Smith gave Hancock two additional regiments from an adjoining brigade and a battery of artillery. He then, Hancock reported, "authorized me to advance farther if I thought advantage could be obtained, and if I required them to send to him for re-enforcements." Hancock started at 11:00 A.M.; by noon his force had already outflanked Fort Magruder, taken two of the ungarrisoned redoubts, and was advancing toward one held by Anderson's men. Smith, sensing a decisive breakthrough, promised to order forward another four regiments and an additional battery. From his position Hancock's artillery could actually bombard Fort Magruder from the rear. If decisively reinforced, this attack could possibly succeed in cutting off Longstreet's entire division.[31]

Shortly after 12:00 P.M., as Anderson's attention was completely absorbed in the battle with Hooker on the right while Hancock crept up on the left, Longstreet finally rode back to the field. In his official report the Georgian contended that he did so because "it became evident that the trains would not be out of my way before night, and that I could, therefore, make battle without delaying the movement of the army." He asserted that he arrived on the field in time to see "the successful issue of the first grand assault" by Anderson's four brigades, which he complimented as having been "well arranged." It was the victory over Hooker's division, Longstreet claimed, that caused him to seek reinforcements: "The advanced positions so extended my lines that I found it necessary to bring other forces upon the field." Neither Longstreet's own memoirs nor the reports of his subordinates bear out this account. Anderson's attack was hardly well organized, nor was there any indication in any of the brigadiers' reports that Longstreet made it to their part of the field that early. The division commander admitted in his memoirs that it was "the swelling noise of battle" from which he "concluded that it would be well to ride to the front." When Hancock's artillery opened fire from several hundred yards in his rear, Longstreet quickly saw that "viewing the ground on the left, I thought it not so well protected as Anderson conceived."[32]

Even this was quite an understatement. With more than two-thirds of his division engaged with Hooker and the rest tied down holding the remaining redoubts, Longstreet suddenly realized that he had no troops of his own available to deal with Hancock. He sent an aide galloping back up the Williamsburg Road with orders for D. H. Hill's division to march back to support him.

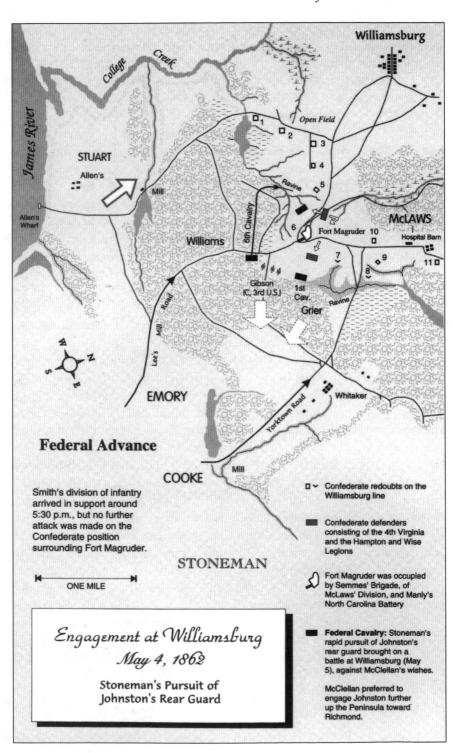

Federal Advance

Smith's division of infantry
arrived in support around
5:30 p.m., but no further
attack was made on the
Confederate position
surrounding Fort Magruder.

ONE MILE

Engagement at Williamsburg
May 4, 1862

Stoneman's Pursuit of
Johnston's Rear Guard

□ ⌄   Confederate redoubts on the
Williamsburg line

▬   Confederate defenders
consisting of the 4th Virginia
and the Hampton and Wise
Legions

𝄾   Fort Magruder was occupied
by Semmes' Brigade, of
McLaws' Division, and Manly's
North Carolina Battery

▬   **Federal Cavalry:** Stoneman's
rapid pursuit of Johnston's
rear guard brought on a
battle at Williamsburg (May
5), against McClellan's wishes.

McClellan preferred to
engage Johnston further
up the Peninsula toward
Richmond.

Longstreet sent this order directly to Hill because the North Carolinian had been subordinated to him during the retreat. For whatever reason, either haste or embarrassment at having been caught in the flank, Longstreet did not send any messages to Johnston.[33]

The first brigade of Hill's division to arrive was that of Jubal Early, at about 3:30 P.M. Along with his four regiments and a company of artillery, Early had in tow Col. George T. Ward's detachment, consisting of the Second Florida and the Second Mississippi Battalion. That Early's troops were the first to arrive added to Longstreet's unease, for he neither liked nor trusted the Virginia brigadier. When Early rode up, Longstreet was heading toward Anderson's disjointed battle, probably to find out if he could detach some of those regiments to safeguard the left flank. Quite to the contrary, the Georgian had discovered instead that most of Anderson's regiments were nearly out of ammunition, which forced him to commit his only divisional reserve, Colston's brigade, to hold the ground already won despite Hancock's threatening posture. Thus Longstreet reluctantly had to leave Early in charge of the left of his line, at least until Hill himself arrived.[34]

"I proceeded as near as practicable to the position designated by General Longstreet on the left and rear of Fort Magruder," Early reported, "and formed my regiments in line of battle on the crest of a ridge in a wheat field, and near a barn and some houses, with a woods some 200 or 300 yards in front." In that position "we were not in view of any body of the enemy, though we were soon informed by the firing from a battery in or beyond the woods toward Fort Magruder that a portion of the enemy were in our front." The battery firing at Early's men from beyond the woods was Company E, First New York Light Artillery, which had been attached to Hancock's force. Sumner had been unable to comprehend the opportunity that Hancock's advance against the unoccupied redoubts had given him, and believing that he was about to face another major Confederate counterattack the Second Corps commander had overruled Smith's wishes to reinforce Hancock. Even after Hancock sent one of his aides to explain the situation and to plead for more troops, Sumner remained adamant. Thus Hancock, since his augmented brigade was too small to risk a further advance on its own, could only open fire with his field artillery in hopes of diverting the attention of some of the Rebels from the other side of the line. The gambit was far more successful than he ever could have expected.[35]

Somehow, Jubal Early concluded that an unsupported Federal battery had located itself on the Confederate flank, and he decided that several Yankee cannon had situated themselves in just the right place for him to capture them. Hill had marched up with the remaining brigades of his division by this time, and Early brought the idea to his superior. What he did not tell him—and what Hill neglected to ask—was that he had done no reconnaissance to ascertain that the Federal battery was indeed unaccompanied. Indeed, Early still did not know the exact location of the guns he proposed to attack. After spending several weeks in Yorktown, impotently unable to strike back at enemy artillery, Hill was quickly caught up in Early's enthusiasm and set out to find Longstreet to get permission to launch the attack.[36]

It was at this point that Johnston finally arrived. He had been urging the rest of the army up the road all morning and afternoon, more concerned with a possible landing on the York River than with the Federals immediately to his rear. When he realized that a second division had become embroiled east of Williamsburg, the army commander spurred his horse in search of Longstreet and a report on the battle. Johnston, Longstreet, and Hill converged somewhere in the rear of Fort Magruder. Longstreet was feeling more confident by this time. With Colston's and Ward's regiments in line, supported by the reorganizing brigades that had made Anderson's attack, he felt that his right flank was secure, at least for the rest of the day. Hill reported that the brigades of Jubal Early, Winfield Scott Featherston, Gabriel Rains, and Robert Rodes were emplaced on the left. Thus, even if the redoubts on the far end of the line were in enemy hands, Longstreet's division no longer seemed to be in danger of being cut off. Unwilling to admit that events had slipped out of his control, Longstreet told Johnston that the battle had thus far proceeded exactly as he had planned it: a successful, limited rearguard action to discourage pursuit.[37]

Hill's proposal, then, came at what seemed an opportune moment. Success in the form of eight captured guns had already been achieved on the right. Why not attempt the same on the left, especially as the Yankees there appeared to have no idea what a potentially commanding position they held? Should not action be taken quickly, before the Federals realized their possible advantage and marched a division of infantry around the Rebel left? Johnston deferred to Longstreet's opinion, and the Georgian was willing to sanction the attack—with one condition. He did not have faith in Early to carry out the assault competently; later he claimed to have announced to the other generals that "the brigade you propose to use is not in safe hands."[38] He consented to the movement only if Hill directed it personally. Hill agreed, although with remarkable candor he admitted the next year that "neither Longstreet nor myself knew the precise location of the battery, and both were entirely ignorant of the ground." Despite this, the two "agreed in the general plan of getting in rear of the battery by passing through the woods to the left of its supposed position." Though he "could not distinctly locate the battery by the sound," Hill split Early's brigade into two detachments, and commanding one of them himself, marched the Fifth and Twenty-third North Carolina and the Twenty-fourth and Thirty-eighth Virginia into the woods in search of enemy guns.[39]

This ill-considered venture reaped exactly the kind of harvest that, in hindsight, might have been expected. Early's regiments came out of the woods one at a time, not facing, but flanked by, the New York guns, which were supported by five regiments of Federal infantry. Neither Hill nor Early could maintain any semblance of control over his regiments; Early's regiments actually attempted to charge a redoubt held by South Carolinians of Anderson's brigade before an officer from the Sixth South Carolina managed to get him turned in the right direction. Moments later, Early went down with a wound trying to lead the Twenty-fourth Virginia and the Fifth North Carolina in a desperate charge against Hancock's line. Hill remained in the woods attempting, without success, to organize the other two regiments to support him. The Twenty-fourth Virginia took 190 casualties, the Fifth North Carolina more than 300. Watching the Tarheels being mowed down, Hill always remembered that "the regiment was shot down like beeves, the Yankees cheering and laughing as they fired at the poor fellows."[40]

Ironically, the only circumstance that saved Early's men from even higher casualties was the fact that Hancock thought the Confederate regiments lost in the woods were about to envelop his own flank. He initially intended to charge out and capture the entire Fifth North Carolina:

The whole line advanced cheering, and on arriving . . . delivered two volleys, doing great execution. The order was then given to charge down the slope, and with reiterated cheers the whole command advanced in line of battle. A few of the leading spirits of the enemy were bayoneted; the remainder then broke and fled. The want of protection in my rear, and expecting an assault from that quarter every moment, I ordered a halt at the floor of the slope, and delivered a terrible fire along the whole line, expending 15 to 20 rounds. The plunging fire from the redoubt, the direct fire from the right, and the oblique fire from the left were so destructive that after it had been ordered to cease and the smoke arose it seemed that no man had left the ground unhurt who had advanced within 500 yards of our line.[41]

Satisfied that the battle was well in hand, Johnston had ridden off the field prior to Early's debacle, leaving Longstreet to close operations. Longstreet claimed that "this mishap could have been remedied by an extreme flank movement and complete victory won; but . . . we were not in a condition to increase our responsibilities, and a great delay might have endangered other operations of the army." D. H. Hill agreed, though for different reasons: "The turning of the Yankee position was still deemed practicable, but I soon found that the confusion was so great, arising mainly from the want of drill and discipline, that all idea of further advance was abandoned." Since Hill's division still had three fresh brigades, he was designated to take over rearguard responsibilities for the following day.[42]

The Battle of Williamsburg had cost the Army of the Potomac 2,233 casualties; Johnston's army lost 1,703. Johnston and his subordinates asserted that they had won a victory because they held the field at the end of the day, had captured eight guns and several hundred prisoners, and because the Federals did not contest the army's withdrawal the next morning. Both Johnston and Longstreet were in high spirits that evening. They spent the night together at the Bowden House, several miles west of Williamsburg. Johnston described the battle as merely a "pretty severe skirmish" and laughed off the lady of the house, who "said she had no room for retreating Generals."[43] Had Johnston taken the time to evaluate the engagement critically, he would have learned some disquieting facts. Longstreet, in whom he reposed great confidence, had allowed five of his six brigades to become committed to combat before he had even reached the field, leaving himself with few reserves and a left flank hanging in the air. Hill had shown himself to be aggressive to the point of rashness. Elections and service in the Yorktown trenches had taken their toll on drill and discipline; regiments from both divisions became entangled with each other and the woods around them. In fact, Confederate success at Williamsburg was more a matter of Union miscues than any brilliant moves by Johnston, Longstreet, or Hill.

Johnston had four reasons for not evaluating the performance of his army at Williamsburg. The first reason was victory—claiming to have won the battle, he hardly had much to stimulate him to seek out shortcomings. Longstreet was quick to reinforce this idea, effusively praising his subordinates and recommending promotions for Anderson, A. P. Hill, and Pryor.[44] Second, Johnston's supervision of the battlefield, it turned out, was not nearly as close as his supervision of administrative matters. Both on May 4 and 5, the army commander had felt comfortable delegating the entire responsibility for tactics on the field to a subordinate—first McLaws, then Longstreet. On May 5 in particular, Johnston had not bothered to be present until many hours after the battle had begun, and he accepted the judgments of Longstreet and Hill uncritically. Thus he did not know the details of the blunders that had marked the conduct of the battle. Was his behavior anomalous, caused by excessive concern about amphibious landings and the slow progress of the trains, or was it to be a consistent characteristic of Joseph Johnston as an army commander? There was no one nearby to ask the question.

A third reason why Johnston did not examine the army's performance more closely was that he would have had difficulty in doing so, at least for several days. Most of the brigadiers were tied up immediately in moving their exhausted commands through the torrential rain; few reports of the battle were written before May 10. Early did not complete his until June, and D. H. Hill's was not submitted until January of the following year. When Johnston wrote his official account of the battle, he had primarily Longstreet's recounting, which Douglas Southall Freeman has correctly labeled "casual, almost complacent," upon which to base his own narrative.[45] The final reason that Johnston turned his attention away from Williamsburg was probably the most influential. While he and Longstreet celebrated that night, an aide arrived at the Bowden House with unwelcome news. Johnston's worst fear had been realized: Federal transports had reached the mouth of the Pamunkey River, between his army and Richmond.

Union gunboats, as Johnston had predicted, wasted no time ascending the York River after the Confederates evacuated Yorktown. Lee wrote Johnston on May 5, even as Longstreet and Hill struggled with Yankees outside Williamsburg, that gunboats had been spotted at the mouth of the Pamunkey River. When that letter reached Johnston, probably on May 6, it confirmed what his cavalry pickets had already discovered: his line of communication was no longer clear. McClellan's intentions remained uncertain. Was the main weight of his pursuit following overland, as the battle at Williamsburg seemed to indicate, or had those Federal attacks been designed purely to delay Johnston long enough to envelop and isolate his army?[46]

Driven by the instinct to head for the battlefield, Johnston spurred his horse east toward New Kent Courthouse at a furious pace. Starting out with a full retinue of staff officers, he soon left everyone but Porter Alexander far behind. "I will remember that ride as long as I live," Alexander wrote. "The general seemed for some cause to be in a terrible temper—the only occasion I ever saw him exhibit it." The two men careened up the road, navigating "through the mud & around all the wagons, guns, ambulances" that constituted the baggage trains of the retreating army. After several hours of riding, Johnston found himself suddenly boxed in behind an ambulance that had inexplicably cut across his path and then stopped dead in the road. "I don't think I ever saw any one fly into such a fury in my life," recalled Alexander. "I had never heard the general use an oath, but now with his face as red as blood, 'God damn you!' he shouted, 'what do you mean? Give me a pistol & let me kill this infernal blanketty blank.'" The ordnance officer, thankfully, had the good sense to pretend he was not carrying a weapon.[47]

This was another battlefield that Johnston did not reach in time to influence the fighting. The commander on the spot was G. W. Smith, whose division had reached Barhamsville early on May 6. With the bulk of the army strung out all the way back to Williamsburg, it was Smith's responsibility to determine the Yankee intent. That evening, Smith and Whiting rode to Fitzhugh Lee's forward cavalry pickets in the woods above Eltham's Landing, where they had a clear view of the disembarking Federals. Blue-clad soldiers, in at least division strength, had already landed. The troops were the regiments of William Franklin's division, the first of four divisions that McClellan planned to advance by water to cut off Johnston's retreat. The Federal commander intended to follow up Franklin with Fitz-John Porter, Israel B. Richardson, and John Sedgwick. Fortunately for the Confederates, a shortage of transports forced McClellan to ship these divisions up the York River sequentially rather than simultaneously. Even more fortuitously, the lead division was commanded by the least aggressive of the four Union generals.[48] Though he began landing troops at 3:00 P.M. on May 6, Franklin was oppressed by "my ignorance of the topography of the place of landing, and the fact that the enemy's cavalry and infantry were seen in the woods surrounding the plain upon which we landed as soon as the landing began." As a result of his apprehension, the division commander sent out no scouts of his own and concentrated instead on "extraordinary precautions . . . to prevent the success of an attack." Thus he had no idea that the Confederate pickets he saw from the plain were virtually the only force available to oppose him during the first few hours after his landing.[49]

That did not long remain the case. Smith had immediately ordered up Whiting's three brigades from Barhamsville, though his object was not initially the attack that Franklin supposed. Smith hoped that the absence of any appreciable force to his front would lure Franklin into striking inland, away from the artillery support provided by his gunboats and allowing Whiting to engage him at a distance. When it became obvious on the morning of May 7 that the Yankees were entrenching and not moving forward, Smith had to change his plans; he ordered Whiting to attack Franklin's right flank and drive it back close enough to the river for his own artillery to fire on the gunboats. Whiting selected Brig. Gen. John Bell Hood's brigade to lead the attack. Though it also contained the Eighteenth Georgia during the Peninsula campaign, Hood's command earned its fame as "the Texas Brigade." Eltham's

Landing was the baptism of fire for the First, Fourth, and Fifth Texas and Hood's first battle.[50]

It was not much of a battle. Indeed, the action was little more than a skirmish between Hood's brigade, supported by a single battery, and Brig. Gen. John Newton's four regiments, attended by one company of artillery. Between 9:00 and 11:00 A.M., Hood drove in Newton's skirmishers, and the two lines traded volleys in the woods for another three or four hours. Meanwhile Hood's artillerymen determined that they could not hit the gunboats from an extended range, and Hood was ordered to withdraw. He had taken 37 casualties and inflicted 186, a tactical victory to be sure but hardly a devastating defeat for Franklin, who was reinforced by the lead brigade of Sedgwick's division that afternoon.[51]

Victory or defeat is often as much the commander's perception as it is reality. Within another twelve to twenty-four hours, approximately 25,000 Union soldiers had been concentrated near Eltham's, more than enough to engage Johnston and attempt to delay his retreat. Franklin, however, credited reports from Newton that he had been attacked by a full division supported by 20,000 additional troops and wrote McClellan's chief of staff, "I congratulate myself that we have maintained our position." He soon convinced McClellan that Johnston already had 80,000 to 120,000 in the area and cautiously awaited the arrival of the main body of the Army of the Potomac while the weary Rebel legions plodded unmolested past his position.[52]

Johnston himself breathed a sigh of relief when he halted his divisions near Baltimore Crossroads on May 10. He had originally desired to halt at New Kent Courthouse, six miles farther east, but the distance from the Richmond and York River Railroad—at this point his only line of supply—had forced the army to keep moving. To Johnston's jaded soldiers the halt represented the first chance for a hot meal and sleep in several days. Many of them, like D. H. Hill, were too exhausted to do more than collapse: "I slept nearly all day yesterday," Hill wrote to his wife on May 11, "just lying on the ground." Johnston could finally afford to rest his army because he had reached the position where he intended to await McClellan and offer battle. The area had many advantages for a smaller army fighting on the defensive. Johnston's left flank rested on the Pamunkey River, which, though navigable, was narrow enough to be blockaded by field artillery. His right was anchored by the Chickahominy, above the head of navigation but below the bridges that McClellan could have used for a rapid crossing. The Richmond and York River Railroad ran directly behind the Confederate lines, providing for relative ease of supply. Moreover, the terrain between the two rivers was heavily wooded; limited visibility would help to offset the Federal superiority in artillery. The only apparent weakness of the position was that it could be flanked by a waterborne advance up the James River, though this could not seriously endanger Johnston's army as long as the fortifications at Drewry's Bluff held out.[53]

As he waited for the Army of the Potomac to arrive, Johnston found the time to resume normal communications with the authorities in Richmond. He had not ceased to keep his superiors informed of his movements between the withdrawal from Yorktown and the skirmish at Eltham's Landing, as Freeman and other critics have asserted. The published correspondence in the *Official Records* does portray Johnston as silent between May 1 and May 7, but this is misleading. Numerous notes and endorsements signed by Johnston concerning routine administrative matters appear in the records of the adjutant and inspector general. Especially significant are the endorsements by Johnston on two letters by Longstreet to Samuel Cooper, dated May 7 and May 9, which indicate that he filed a preliminary report on the battles at Williamsburg. Though this document has not been found, its existence is further suggested by Johnston's immediate reports of the much smaller engagement at Eltham's Landing. Contextual evidence in Lee's letterbook also indicates that Johnston wrote him on May 6, referring to provisions for the army. The longest period during which Johnston remained incommunicado definitely did not exceed four days (May 2–5) and may well have been shorter.[54]

Johnston had notified Lee on May 7 that he could not provision the army near West Point but indicated that Federal naval power concerned him more. "The sight of the iron-clad boats make me apprehensive for Richmond, too, so I move on in two columns, one by the New Kent Road under Major-General Smith, the other by that of the Chickahominy under Major-General Longstreet." By the next day, when a brief halt at New Kent Courthouse had left him time for reflection, Johnston realized that events in his front had distracted his attention from the remainder of his command. He had received three letters from Lee that unfortunately had been signed for the general by Walter Taylor. This particularly upset Johnston because one of the letters gave him specific orders concerning his wagon trains, and another countermanded a portion of his own orders to Benjamin Huger for the transfer of certain troops from the south side of the James. None of the letters provided him with any intelligence concerning affairs in the Valley, central Virginia, or around Fredericksburg.[55]

"My authority does not extend beyond the troops immediately around me," Johnston complained. "I request therefore to be relieved of a merely nominal geographical command. The service will gain thereby unity of command, which is essential in war." Clifford Dowdey has misconstrued this paragraph as a "threatening gesture of 'resignation' " that "revealed an infantilism in Johnston's relations with the war office." The remainder of Johnston's letter and Lee's response, however, make it clear that he was only asking—albeit quite brusquely—either to have his orders to Huger obeyed or the Department of Norfolk removed from his command. Intemperate language aside, Johnston had a reasonable case against the Richmond authorities. Without ever informing him, they had delayed Huger's withdrawal from Norfolk, ordered a brigade from that command to central Virginia, and changed the objective of his eventual retreat from Richmond to Petersburg. Although each of these actions may have been defensible in terms of the overall strategic situation, ignoring Johnston's authority over Huger was a serious infraction of proper military procedure. That Johnston never intended to relinquish command of the Department of Northern Virginia was made clear in the next paragraph: "I have had in the Peninsula no means of obtaining direct information from the other departments of my command nor has the Government furnished it." He was especially worried about the forces south of Fredericksburg: "I wish to place them so that they may not be cut off by an army landing at West Point."[56]

This letter sparked a confusing exchange of correspondence between Johnston and Lee that lasted for nearly a week and that can only be satisfactorily explained if one assumes, as Lee finally did, that some of the letters miscarried and arrived out of order. The exchange centered on the question that had been deferred but not settled weeks earlier in Richmond: By what strategy should the Federal offensive be countered? Subsidiary issues included the control and positioning of Anderson's division near Fredericksburg and the proper thrust of operations in the Valley. The tone of the letters became steadily more antagonistic—particularly on Johnston's part—which ironically disguised the fact that by mid-May both Johnston and Lee had drawn a good deal closer in terms of their views on the proper conduct of operations.

Lee attempted to mollify Johnston on May 8 by assuring him, "I consider your authority to extend over the troops on both sides of the James River." At the same time, he also coolly denied having become Johnston's only conduit of information from the outlying districts. "I do not recollect your having requested information relating to the other departments of your command to be forwarded by any other means than the usual course of the mails, and supposed the commanders were in direct correspondence with you." This sentence ignored exactly such a request, made on April 22, which had alerted Lee to the fact that Johnston had no direct communication with either Stonewall Jackson or Richard Ewell and expected to depend on Lee to forward information. Lee also quietly overlooked that only in this letter did he finally tell Johnston that Joseph R. Anderson was in command below the Rappahannock, that Jackson had marched to attack the Federals west of Staunton, or that a brigade from Huger's department had been ordered to central Virginia. Nor did Lee explain that he himself had been the authority ordering these movements.[57]

Based on the intelligence provided by Lee, Johnston by May 10 had this picture of events in Virginia: McClellan was advancing cautiously up the Peninsula with over 100,000 men; from Fredericksburg, Maj. Gen. Irwin McDowell's corps, estimated accurately as containing nearly 40,000 soldiers, was threatening to march south; Nathaniel Banks, who had last been reported to Johnston as having 34,000 troops, was apparently leaving the Valley to unite with McDowell. Thus, the strategic scene Johnston viewed was one of at least 175,000 Yankees converging on Richmond from the north and east. In terms of what he knew of Confederate dispositions to receive them, Jackson had led a division of 8,000 into the mountains away from the main theater of war. Ewell's division, numbering 8,500 men, was positioned in Swift Run Gap, ostensibly outnumbered by four to one. At least one brigade was located at Gordonsville, observing nothing. Anderson's 12,000 soldiers south of Fredericksburg faced more than three times their own numbers. Huger's division had concentrated at Petersburg, where no enemy forces seemed to be. In front of McClellan, Johnston mustered only about 50,000 men in an army reduced by battle casualties and straggling. Thus, even though the Confederates deployed over 90,000 troops across the Old Dominion and still held a central position with interior lines, they had spread their forces too thin to hope for a victory without concentrating somewhere.[58]

Not knowing that Lee and Jackson had been considering the question since late April, Johnston saw three possible strategies for foiling the Federal offensive. United, the forces of Jackson, Ewell, L. O'Bryan Branch, and Edward Johnson (stationed at Monterey) might be able to attack Banks in the Valley, prevent him from reinforcing McDowell, and allow Jackson to march about 20,000 men to reinforce Anderson. This move would allow the force below Fredericksburg to meet McDowell's corps on essentially equal terms, removing the specter of a combination of the two Federal columns in eastern Virginia. Johnston dispatched orders to Jackson and Ewell on May 13 to pursue this course. If Jackson's force could not detain Banks in the Valley, then Johnston believed the proper course was for him to march directly "to join either the army near Fredericksburg, commanded by Brig. Gen. J. R. Anderson, or this one." If Huger were brought to Richmond at the same time, then Johnston would be able to deploy his 90,000 men in one army between enemy wings of roughly 75,000 and 100,000, separated by forty miles. He could then maneuver to engage either McDowell or McClellan in succession, with relative parity of numbers. The third option available to the Confederates was a simple concentration of all available troops to defend Richmond, including brigades from North Carolina and points farther south. "If the President will direct the concentration of all the troops of North Carolina and Eastern Virginia," Johnston told Lee on May 10, "we may be able to hold Middle Virginia at least. If we permit ourselves to be driven beyond Richmond we lose the means of maintaining this army." He concluded with a contention that only "a concentration of all our available forces may enable us to fight successfully." This focus has been traditionally cited as Johnston's preferred strategy, but a close reading of his correspondence from May 8 to May 13 suggests that he advocated it as much from frustration as from preference.[59]

Either of Johnston's other strategic choices depended on a single variable that he had not yet been able to master: the control of the detachments of his army at long distances. How could he expect to coordinate the operations of as many as six separate columns when he could not even reliably communicate with five of them? "I must be informed of your movements and progress, that your instructions may be modified as circumstances change," Johnston admonished Ewell on May 13. By this time that sentence had almost a plaintive ring to it, for since May 8 Johnston had been unable to reach Huger or Anderson. It must have seemed to Johnston that the only way he would ever be able to exert his authority over his widely spread divisions would be to gather them all in one place, where he could depend for success on the fighting qualities of his soldiers and not have to rely on a nonfunctional command system to orchestrate intricate maneuvers.[60]

Though Lee, like Johnston, never outlined his strategy for the defense of Richmond in a single sentence or paragraph, a sampling of his letters indicates that his intentions were now far less at odds with those of Johnston than they had been a month earlier. He suggested to Jackson on May 8 that at least Ewell's division should pursue Banks out of the Valley, attacking him en route if possible and eventually joining Anderson's force. On May 14 Lee was contemplating almost exactly the same strategy that Johnston had ordered the day before, authorizing Walter Taylor to write to Jackson that "if you can form a junction with General Ewell with your combined forces you should be able to drive Banks from the Valley."[61]

Lee also agreed with Johnston that the 12,000 Confederates near Fredericksburg should be united with Johnston's main army for the purpose of striking either McDowell or McClellan. He advised Johnston on May 10 that even President Davis held the "view that operations of its [Johnston's army] several divisions might be combined to attack the enemy, who seemed to have exposed himself and his line of communication, and to prevent any movement that might threaten your rear." On May 11, for the first time, Lee directed J. R. Anderson to "conform all your movements to the direction of General Johnston." The next day Lee asked Johnston, "Toward what point in the vicinity of Richmond do you desire [outlying troops] to concentrate?" The letter specified only Anderson's force but also implied that Lee understood that Johnston might need to draw in the divisions of Jackson and Ewell. Lee had apparently accepted Johnston's premise that more troops must be drawn from the coast to reinforce his army. In the last month, Lee had transferred Maxcey Gregg's brigade from South Carolina and those of Anderson and L. O'Bryan Branch from North Carolina. He then wrote the North Carolina governor, Henry Clark, and Maj. Gen. John C. Pemberton, commanding the Department of South Carolina and Georgia, that more brigades would have to be released to Virginia.[62]

Thus, when Davis and Lee rode out unannounced to Johnston's headquarters on May 12, there was more concord among the senior members of the Confederate command structure than had existed for months.[63] Davis contended in his memoirs that the conversation was "so inconclusive" that he and Lee were "unable to draw from it any more definite purpose than the policy was to improve his position as far as practicable, and wait for the enemy to leave his gunboats, so that the opportunity might be offered to meet him on land." The contemporary record reveals that the president's memory had become colored with the passage of two decades. Davis confided to his wife the following day misgivings about the speed of the withdrawals from Norfolk and Yorktown, but not about Johnston's operational strategy. The major fear he entertained then was that the slow pace of construction of the Drewry's Bluff fortifications might allow Federal ironclads to approach Richmond behind the army. Moreover, it is extremely doubtful that any discussion of operations would have excluded Johnston's instructions to Jackson and Ewell, posted the same morning the president rode back to Richmond. Respecting Johnston's assumption that McClellan would eventually have to leave his naval support to advance either north or south of the Chickahominy, Lee acknowledged on May 17, "I think there can be little doubt of the correctness of your views." Davis himself informed Johnston the same day that "if the enemy proceed as heretofore indicated, your position and policy, as you stated in our last interview, seems to me to require no modification." The president, Johnston later correctly asserted, left his army with "no cause to complain" about the conference, "especially as he suggested nothing better."[64] Whatever fragile harmony had been established among the three men soon disappeared, however, for on May 15 everyone's calculations were upset again. The much dreaded Federal ironclads had finally arrived at Drewry's Bluff.

10

DEFENDING RICHMOND

While Joseph Johnston's army retreated toward the Chickahominy, critical events transpired on the James River. When he determined to evacuate York-town, Johnston also dispatched orders to Comdr. John Tucker's James River squadron. Although the *Virginia* still closed the mouth of the James to the Union navy, Tucker was instructed to transport what he could save of the heavy guns at Jamestown Island back to Richmond. Eventually, Johnston knew, the *Virginia* would either have to be scuttled, lightened to run upriver, or under-take a final, suicidal dash into Hampton Roads to try to sell herself as dearly as possible among the Federal transports at anchor there. When that happened, Tucker and his command were to "continue to observe and control the upper James River as long as practicable, in order to prevent the enemy from cross-ing and attempting to cut off our forces retiring from Norfolk." It was an incredibly tall order: against Tucker's five vessels—only one of which was par-tially armored—mounting just sixteen guns among them, Adm. Louis Golds-borough would send Comdr. John Rodgers with nine vessels—including the ironclads *Monitor* and *Galena*—boasting forty-five cannon, five of which were the monstrous 100-pounder siege rifles. "When hard pressed," Johnston advised Tucker on May 2, "you will retire upon Richmond."[1]

After completing one trip hauling the artillery and ordnance stores from Jamestown Island to Richmond, Tucker received new orders, this time from Secretary of the Navy Stephen Mallory. James Longstreet was fighting his rear-guard action in front of Williamsburg; the Confederates on the Peninsula were in full retreat, yet Mallory's orders read: "Proceed to navy yard, Norfolk, with *Patrick Henry* and *Jamestown* and await orders."[2] The operation could be attempted only at night because it involved running past the heavy batteries at Newport News and avoiding detection by the Federal ships prowling Hampton Roads. As silently as possible, drifting more than steaming, Tucker steered the two vessels under the Yankee guns and picked his way around the obstructions in the Elizabeth River on the night of May 5.[3]

What Tucker found in Norfolk was chaos. The Department of Norfolk had always been a source of problems for the War Department: the army and navy constantly quarreled over spheres of authority, a disagreement still unsettled after the subordination of the naval forces in the department to Johnston in mid-April. The original commandant of Gosport Navy Yard had been replaced in March, primarily because of a perceived lack of energy in meeting construction deadlines. Benjamin Huger himself had survived calls for his resignation by his own officers, members of Congress, and even the vice-president, who labeled him "inefficient—indeed [an] imbecile." Jefferson Davis had sustained him, not from any great confidence but for lack of any better candidates to replace him. When the subject came up in a March cabinet meeting, with members calling for Huger to be superseded, Davis responded that "it was easy to say so, but the question was where to get one to take his place." Judah Benjamin, George Randolph, and Robert E. Lee found it constantly necessary to send Huger detailed orders to accomplish even the simplest of tasks.[4]

When Johnston directed Huger on April 28 to "be prepared for a prompt movement, and if compelled to move, as little public property as possible should be left for the enemy," the fifty-seven-year-old South Carolinian panicked. He wrote back to Lee, not to Johnston, that he could not remove or damage his guns, destroy his ammunition, relinquish any outlying parts of his garrison, or assist in the destruction of property in the navy yard. "It seems to me the best I can do is be prepared to repel promptly any attack and defend the position as long as I can." As the time for the withdrawal from Yorktown grew closer, Johnston sent more detailed orders to Huger, Josiah Tatnall, and Sidney Smith Lee; the orders were hand-carried by Col. George Lay, who was empowered to explain more fully his commander's intentions. When word of Johnston's instructions reached Richmond, Davis ordered Secretaries Mallory and Randolph to Norfolk to delay the evacuation long enough to ship out such supplies as could be saved and destroy those that could not.[5]

Thus occurred the confused situation in Norfolk on the night of May 5, when Commander Tucker quietly passed the obstructions near Craney Island. Two cabinet secretaries were personally supervising the shipment of supplies. Flag Officer Tatnall was trying to convince them that the *Virginia* could not possibly execute his orders to "protect Norfolk as well as James River, and if possible prevent the enemy from ascending it." At the same time, he was desperately attempting to find a pilot who could navigate the ironclad upriver if her draft was lightened. Captain Lee was dismantling the navy yard, and General Huger, by all accounts, was hardly capable of doing anything.[6]

Tucker discovered that his two steamers had been ordered to Norfolk to attempt to haul off the *Richmond,* ordnance supplies, and as many gunboats as possible before Gosport fell into Yankee hands. If sneaking into Norfolk had been difficult, steaming back upriver with several other vessels in tow was even more dangerous. Yet Tucker did not hesitate; the next night he re-entered Hampton Roads. The *Patrick Henry* towed the unfinished ironclad and a partially completed gunboat. The *Jamestown* had in tow another gunboat and the brig loaded down with the cannon and ammunition for the *Richmond*. The two gunboats, recalled Lt. Comdr. William H. Parker of the *Beaufort*, "had sawmill engines, and when they got underweigh [*sic*] there was such a wheezing and blowing that one would have supposed all hands had suddenly been attacked with the asthma or heaves." Miraculously, "they ran by the batteries at Newport News however without waking the sentinels up." The following morning, May 7, while John Bell Hood and John Newton traded volleys at Eltham's Landing, Tucker handed those vessels over to his smaller ships to be conveyed to Richmond and stationed himself to run the gauntlet again that night. By the evening of May 7, however, the Federals had more securely closed Hampton Roads; Tucker's vessels were spotted and forced to retreat soon after midnight.[7]

The next morning Tucker watched impotently as the *Galena*, the *Port Royal*, and the *Aroostook*, having themselves bypassed the *Virginia*, pounded the Confederate battery at Day's Bluff into submission. The Federal gunboats, Tucker wrote from his vantage point upriver, "silenced it in one hour." As he retreated slowly ahead of the Yankee vessels, Tucker warned Commander Ebenezer Farrand, commanding naval forces at Drewry's Bluff, that "the iron vessel the 'Galena' is one of them and can ascend the river to Richmond if she desires. I feel anxious for the fate of Richmond."[8]

Fort Huger, sitting atop Harden's Bluff with thirteen guns, several of which were rifled, proved too well entrenched to be silenced. Under orders from Admiral Goldsborough to ascend the James as rapidly as possible "to harass the retreat of the rebels wherever they can be reached," Commander Rodgers decided to bypass the second fort. The *Galena* capitalized on her relative invulnerability to the battery's ordnance, passing and repassing the Confederate position seven times to draw fire and distract attention from the two wooden vessels. Rodgers hoped that he could then quickly engage Tucker's squadron, guaranteeing Federal control of the lower James. However, the Confederates had moved the channel markers and managed to decoy the *Galena* into a sandbar near Hog Island. Her pipes filled with sand and water, choking the engines so effectively that she remained aground for thirty-six hours. Rodgers realized that without the ironclad the *Port Royal* and the *Aroostook* alone could not force the river against Tucker's five vessels, so he settled in to await repairs and reinforcements. While his engineers pumped out the *Galena*'s fouled plumbing, the Confederates finished the evacuation of Norfolk, and on May 10, a disconsolate Flag Officer Tatnall ordered the destruction of the *Virginia.*[9]

So far, Confederate operations on the James River had bought precious time to improve the fortifications at Drewry's Bluff. Rodgers did not move up the river from Hog Island until the evening of May 12, more than a week after Johnston's army had left the trenches at Yorktown.[10] The time would not have been half so critical had Johnston's suspicions not been well founded: despite having had nearly eight weeks available to perfect the fortifications at Drewry's Bluff, the Richmond authorities had allowed the work to proceed in a desultory and haphazard manner. Even as Commander Rodgers weighed anchor, it was questionable whether or not enough guns had been planted there to resist his passage.

Captain Augustus R. Drewry's Southside Heavy Artillery (Company C, Second Virginia Artillery) had been organized from overage volunteers in January 1862. Drewry believed that his company's first position, in Battery no. 19 on the turnpike between Richmond and Drewry's Bluff, "was unimportant, and that we would likely be called to field duty, for which I did not think my men were well suited." He requested an interview with General Lee in early March and convinced him to erect a battery on the James River below Richmond. Already conscious of the long-term weakness of Norfolk, Lee quickly agreed, sending Maj. Alfred Rives and Lt. Charles T. Mason of the Engineer Bureau downriver with Drewry to select a suitable location. The three men settled on the bluffs on Drewry's own farm, which bore his family name. The James River narrowed enough there to be obstructed, and the cliffs were high enough to allow for plunging fire into enemy vessels below. The Southside Artillery marched to its new post on March 17.[11]

Improving Drewry's Bluff, as with the rest of the defenses of Richmond, turned out to be a low priority for the Confederate authorities. Tredegar Iron Works provided the iron bolts and shoes for the pilings to reduce the channel in the river but only as a secondary effort. Lee did not request cannon for the battery until early April. Drewry could requisition neither wagons and teams nor supplementary labor; he quickly concluded that the government had no real interest in his project and set his men to building cabins for themselves instead of digging firing positions. There was a brief flicker of activity in mid-April when three guns, an additional company of artillery, and the commander of the Second Virginia Artillery, Col. Robert Tansill, showed up about the same time. But Tansill and the extra company were soon ordered to Fredericksburg, and Drewry recalled that after that "the work went on pretty much after the order of a private enterprise until a short while before Norfolk was evacuated."[12]

By the time Johnston began to speak of withdrawing from Yorktown, Lee and Naval Secretary Mallory took renewed interest in the project. Starting in late April, one or both would usually ride out daily to the bluffs to check on the work. Still, it was not until early May and the urgency caused by Johnston's retreat that Drewry's Bluff was granted any sort of priority, and by then it was almost too late. On May 2 Lee ordered a company of "sappers and miners" to augment Drewry's company. The day that Federal gunboats reduced Fort Huger, May 8, Mallory ordered Commander Farrand to take a detail of beached men to the position and take command of the works. The next day he ordered the crews of the James River squadron to the bluff to emplace cannon from the *Jamestown* and the *Patrick Henry*. On May 11, as Commander Rodgers's crews struggled to complete the repairs on the *Galena* and free her from the Hog Island sandbar, Lee ordered six more companies of heavy artillery to Chaffin's Bluff, just across the river from the original position, to begin digging in a new battery. The following morning, Mallory dispatched Lt. Catesby ap. R. Jones and the crew of the scuttled *Virginia* (minus only engineering officers) to the same location, followed a day or two later by Capt. John D. Sims and two companies of Confederate marines. A company of the Washington (Louisiana) Artillery was also transferred to Chaffin's Bluff on May 13. While Lee and Davis conferred with Johnston on May 14, Secretary Randolph ordered Huger—now in Petersburg—to send Brig. Gen. William A. Mahone's Virginia Brigade to the bluffs to support the artillery, in case transports carrying infantry followed the Yankee gunboats.[13]

By May 15 nearly 1,800 sailors and soldiers had gathered at Drewry's and Chaffin's Bluffs, and Mahone was marching up with nearly 4,000 more. Twelve guns had been placed in hastily dug embrasures; the heaviest were a 10-inch Columbiad and a 9-inch Dahlgren. After the *Patrick Henry* and the smaller gunboats had passed upriver, the *Jamestown* was sunk in the channel to close it completely to any but boats with the lightest of drafts. In material terms there were enough men and guns and obstructions to keep Rodgers's squadron from threatening Richmond, but there was no one in overall command. Farrand had been superseded by Sidney Smith Lee, who only arrived on the morning of May 15. Mahone was also coming to take command as Captain Drewry and the other army officers studiously ignored Commander Tucker, who had taken effective control of the navy work parties. It was almost as if the army and navy were preparing to fight two separate battles.[14]

Johnston discovered the true nature of the confusion at Drewry's Bluff only on May 15, when Federal ironclads had already tested the strength of the position. On May 13, from his headquarters near Baltimore Crossroads, he sent three staff officers to the Richmond area. Major A. H. Cole was to evaluate the logistical situation near the capital; Maj. Walter H. Stevens, an engineering officer, and Maj. Jasper Whiting, Smith's assistant adjutant general, were to examine the terrain of the upper Chickahominy and the preparations made to defend Drewry's Bluff. The responses from Stevens and Whiting were immediate and depressing: "There is nothing," reported Stevens on May 14, "to prevent [the Federals'] landing at City Point or above, up to Drewry's Bluff, in force." From Drewry's Bluff itself, Major Whiting wrote on the same day: "Stevens and I have done all we could to stir up the imbeciles. It is perfectly discouraging to see how absolutely nothing has been done." The next morning he sent an even gloomier assessment:

> It won't do to trust these people in any way. We can't get anything done. . . . If not too late, a good brigade under an energetic officer might perhaps save the city. A few more vessels sunk; a gun or two well placed, with bomb-proofs; some sharpshooters intelligently located—all with strong field artillery and infantry supports, and some *one* in charge— might give us, or somebody else, time to do something above. Everything now is at odds and ends; everybody frightened; and everybody looking out for his own affairs. I have never been so much ashamed of our people before.[15]

By the time Johnston read this report, the artillerymen at Drewry's Bluff had fought their first disjointed action. While President Davis, General Lee, and the general's brother, Captain Lee, watched, the *Galena,* reinforced by both the *Monitor* and the *Naugatuck,* steamed toward the obstructions in the river. Commander Rodgers, believing from past experience that his ironclads were invulnerable to Confederate fire, planned to remove the pilings in the river and then bypass the batteries.[16]

No one on the Confederate side coordinated the defense. Two separate parties of sharpshooters, one under Marine Captain Sims, the other led by Lt. John Taylor Wood of the *Virginia,* harassed Rodgers's working parties from the banks of the James, apparently without reference to each other. The army batteries fought under Captain Drewry's command; the navy guns were directed by Commander Farrand, Commander Tucker, and Lieutenant ap R. Jones. Nobody ordered any particular concentration of fire. Instead, the cannoneers simply blazed away at any targets they could hit.

The battle opened at 7:45 A.M. on May 15 and lasted just over three hours. The *Monitor* approached within 400 yards of the obstructions in the river, where it sat despite the fire of the batteries on the bluffs, prevented by the sharpshooters from sending out working parties. The *Naugatuck,* shrugging off the Rebel shells, retired only after the 100-pounder in its bow burst. Standing 600 yards out from the bluffs, however, the *Galena* finally showed that, under the right conditions, land batteries could stand against ironclads. Plunging fire from the Columbiad and the Dahlgren struck her forty-three times. Contrary to earlier opinion, Rodgers admitted the next day that the vessel "is not shot-proof; balls came through, and many men were killed with fragments of her own iron." At 11:05 A.M., Rodgers signaled his vessels to retreat. Yet he had not been convinced that the fortifications could not be taken; with infantry support to clear the banks of the river, he still thought that his ironclads could eventually steam past them to the Confederate capital. At any rate, he wrote to Admiral Goldsborough, "on James River an army can be landed within 10 miles of Richmond on either bank."[17]

This thought had haunted Johnston since late April and had kept reappearing in his correspondence over the past two weeks. It seemed that his worst fear was to be realized. Major Stevens reported on May 14 that "the danger is on the south side of James River." Unaware that Randolph had already done so, Johnston immediately "wrote to General Huger . . . desiring him to send a body of good riflemen . . . to shoot the crews of the enemy's gunboats near the 'obstruction' in James River." He also urged Lee to have any deployable forces in the Department of Henrico "placed near the battery." No sooner had he posted these letters than Johnston began receiving even more disturbing news from Drewry's Bluff. First came the warning from Major Whiting, and then, from Walter Taylor, the first notice of the battle. "The report given me by Captain Zimmer, who is connected with the Ordnance Department, and who was present," Taylor wrote, "is to the effect that the fire of the enemy was very bad." Lee sent a more restrained report later in the day, which emphasized that "only the two iron boats engaged. No one exposed and no chance for sharpshooters. No signs of landing." Lee admitted to Huger that he expected McClellan to "avail himself of the river as far up as possible. He may come beyond City Point."[18]

This information settled the matter for Johnston. He could not afford to wait north of the Chickahominy while the Federals possessed the ability to land in his rear and approach Richmond before he could react, especially when Lee informed him that "there is no force in this city" that could be rushed to oppose a landing. He called in G. W. Smith and Longstreet. The failure of the government to finish the fortifications at Drewry's Bluff, he told them, invalidated the premise under which they had been deployed to give battle between the Pamunkey and the Chickahominy. The army could not afford to engage with a superior force without secure flanks. Johnston ordered a withdrawal behind the river: Longstreet would move his own division to Drewry's Bluff and take over responsibility for the defense there while Smith assumed responsibility for defending the crossings of the upper Chickahominy.[19] Johnston promptly advised Lee of his apprehensions, his intention to move, and his general plan of action. He believed that McClellan would try to shift his base from the York to the James, which would require the Federal commander to order his troops across the Chickahominy. If so, there would come a moment of vulnerability for the larger Yankee army, when it would be split in two sections by the river, and the smaller Confederate army might engage one portion of it with parity or numerical superiority if it could maneuver swiftly enough.[20]

Both Lee and Davis accepted this strategy as valid, despite contentions to the contrary made by the president much later. Lee admitted that work at Drewry's Bluff was "progressing, but not satisfactorily." The heavy guns were "well posted, but not as perfectly protected as designed, for want of time." He hoped that Johnston, when he retired nearer Richmond, would rest the flank of his army there on the James to assist with the labor and protect the batteries. "It is fair for us to conclude," Lee continued in another letter, "that his operations in front of Yorktown will be re-enacted in front of the obstructions on James River, unless you can prevent it." As for Johnston's plan to strike McClellan when the Army of the Potomac moved toward the James, Lee wrote: "Should his course to James River be below the mouth of the Chickahominy this will be difficult, but should his march be across the Chickahominy his passage between that river and the James may furnish you the opportunity."[21]

Davis agreed with his generals. On May 17 he sent an aide, Col. G. W. C. Lee, to report to Johnston on the state of the defenses at Drewry's Bluff. In the letter that Colonel Lee hand-carried, the president told the general that if McClellan continued to advance with the York River as his base, then meeting the Federals between the Pamunkey and the Chickahominy was still a good plan. "But if, as reported here, he should change direction, and, leaving his boats on the Pamunkey, would cross the Peninsula to join those [boats] on the James River, the opportunity desired by you to meet him on the land will then be afforded." Like Lee, Davis suspected that the cautious "Little Napoleon" would sidestep down the east bank of the river until he came into contact with the Federal fleet on the James: "This diminishes the space within which his march will be exposed to your attack, unless he should cross the Chickahominy, which we can hardly hope." As late as May 17, the views of Johnston, Lee, and Davis were still in harmony.[22]

Events in the Shenandoah Valley had not ceased while Yankee ironclads pounded the Rebel batteries at Drewry's Bluff. Following his victory at the battle of McDowell, Stonewall Jackson headed back for the Valley to unite with Richard Ewell and attack Nathaniel Banks—a project endorsed both by Johnston and Lee. Banks, however, had split his forces is such a way as to confound the orders sent by the two Confederate generals. One division of 7,000 men, under Brig. Gen. James Shields, was marching out of the Valley to reinforce McDowell at Fredericksburg. The remainder of Banks's army had retreated to Strasburg—whether to fortify a position or to transfer troops by the Manassas Gap Railroad was not certain. Lee, who believed that Banks's ultimate objective was indeed to leave the Valley, still favored an attack on him by Jackson and Ewell. "Whatever movement you make against Banks do it speedily, and if successful drive him back toward the Potomac, and create the impression, as far as practicable, that you design threatening that line," Lee instructed Jackson. He also reminded Stonewall "not, in any demonstration you may make in that direction, [to] lose sight of the fact that it may become necessary for you to come to the support of General Johnston, and hold yourself in readiness to do so if required."[23]

Johnston was far less certain that the bulk of Banks's forces were intended to quit the Valley. To retreat to Strasburg, entrench, and essentially take himself out of the war would not be out of character for the political general from Massachusetts, based on his previous performance. "If Banks is fortifying near Strasburg the attack would be too hazardous," Johnston advised Ewell on May 17. "In such an event we must leave him in his works." Instead, Johnston proposed that Jackson and Ewell unite and strike Shields's detached division as it marched toward Fredericksburg, then for Ewell "to move on, while General Jackson should keep Banks away from McDowell." The letter concluded with several sentences that have remained the source of controversy for well over a century:

> We want troops here; none, therefore, must keep away, unless employing a greatly superior force of the enemy. In your march communicate with Brigadier-General Anderson, near Fredericksburg; he may require your assistance. My general idea is to gather here all the troops who do not keep away from McClellan's greatly superior forces. General Branch is ordered to Hanover Court-House. . . . After reading this send it to General Jackson, for whom it is intended as well as for yourself.[24]

Douglas Southall Freeman has contended that "Johnston could hardly have given more dangerous orders," which sprang from his "conservatism and his concern for his own army in front of Richmond." He has portrayed Lee, on the other hand, as following a natural "inclination . . . to take the lesser risks for the sake of the greater gain that would follow a defeat of Banks." Clifford

Dowdey quoted only one portion of Johnston's letter: "We want troops here; none, therefore, must be kept away unless employing a greatly superior force of the enemy," and has asserted that Johnston had posted the order, "knowing nothing of the conditions in the Valley." Dowdey has condemned Johnston for issuing "sporadic orders" that "had been contradictory, sometimes discretionary and sometimes arbitrary, with a day-to-day type of thinking that could not direct subordinates with a singleness of purpose." Also citing a portion of Johnston's orders, Robert G. Tanner has accused Johnston of trying to enforce on Jackson "his fundamental strategic preference for massing strength by giving up territory and fighting only when there was nowhere else to retreat and no other friendly force to muster." His letter, contends Tanner, "abandoned everything the Valley Army had striven for since the evacuation of Winchester."[25]

These criticisms share the central assumption that Johnston preferred a simplistic strategy of concentration of forces at Richmond and that he was unable to relate operations elsewhere to those of his own army. Such a case could be made if Johnston were shown to have advocated a purely passive course in the Valley and central Virginia and to have subordinated all other designs to the strengthening of his own army. This was far from true. Johnston's suggestion of a combined attack by Jackson and Ewell on Shields's division has been overlooked as a viable strategic option by his contemporaries and historians as well, because the attack on Banks and Jackson's raid down the Valley turned out to be such signal successes. Yet an attack on the lone Federal division had much to recommend it. Jackson and Ewell would have fought at favorable odds against an enemy caught on the march. Success would not only have prevented either Shields or Banks from reinforcing McDowell but also would have placed the Army of the Valley roughly at Thoroughfare Gap, threatening at once Banks's rear, McDowell's rear, and Washington. It was a position that would have allowed as aggressive a commander as Jackson to create fully as much panic north of the Potomac as his actual dash toward Harpers Ferry. Even had Johnston chosen, upon a defeat of Shields, to pursue the most conservative of choices—to return Jackson to the Valley, where he would meet Banks with relatively even numbers while Ewell cooperated with Joseph Anderson against McDowell—the victory would have borne substantial strategic fruit. McDowell, with 30,000 men and orders that included the protection of the capital, would have faced an uncomfortable situation at best. To his front would have been Anderson's 12,000 men, with 4,000 more under L. O'Bryan Branch in easy supporting distance at Hanover Courthouse. In his rear, between his main body and the capital, would have been Ewell with 6,000 to 8,000 troops. At the very least, Johnston's proposed maneuver would have prevented him from marching south and blithely brushing past Anderson with better than two-to-one odds.[26]

Johnston, as well as Lee and Jackson, could read a map, but he also had plenty of reasons to realize that communication lags could turn an apparently good plan in Richmond into one that was seriously out of date in Staunton. He had after all been the one who originally ordered Jackson and Ewell to work together and decide tactical questions on their own. So the very next day, May 18, before he could possibly have received the famous protest from Jackson that begged to be allowed to attack Banks, Johnston dispatched two more letters to the Valley District. In the first, Johnston reiterated that the mission of Jackson's army was to keep Banks's force from uniting with McDowell. If Jackson were too late to attack Banks successfully, then he must pursue the course that led east of the Valley. Johnston emphasized that he had full confidence in Jackson and Ewell themselves to choose whichever option held greater promise; he would not attempt to dictate a rigid course of action from the suburbs of Richmond. In the second letter, the army commander was even more explicit: "The whole question is, whether or not General Jackson and yourself are too late to attack Banks. If so the march eastward should be made. If not (supposing your strength sufficient) then attack."

Did Johnston, like Lee, anticipate Jackson following up the attack with an exploitation toward the Potomac? On May 18 it is difficult to say, for though he had already advocated threatening that line in April (albeit in quite different terms), Johnston did not actually authorize Jackson to strike north instead of east. At least by May 27 there was no question in Johnston's mind that Jackson should continue to pursue the most aggressive course possible: "If you can threaten Baltimore and Washington, do so. It may produce an important diversion. . . . Your movements depend, of course, upon the strength remaining in your neighborhood. Upon that depends the practicability of your advancing to the Potomac and crossing it. I know of no hostile force to prevent either." If Johnston and Lee sometimes differed on the exact operations to be pursued in the Valley and central Virginia, they never disagreed on the methods—striking exposed Federal forces as opportunity allowed—or the objective. In point of fact, when Johnston wrote, "We want troops here; none, therefore, must keep away, unless employing a greatly superior force of the enemy," he captured in a single sentence the essence of both men's strategy in May 1862.[27]

Federal operations over the next several days sustained the strategic insights of Johnston and Lee. McClellan said later that after Drewry's Bluff "the question now arose as to the line of operations to be followed: that of the James on one hand, and, on the other, the line from White House as a base, crossing the upper Chickahominy." He personally preferred the James because he thought it would give him an invulnerable supply line and because advancing on Richmond would be easier from the south. Yet the condition under which the Federal government was willing to reinforce him with McDowell's corps was that McDowell would join the Army of the Potomac by marching rather than by boat. Thus, reasoned Pres. Abraham Lincoln and Secretary of War Edwin Stanton, McDowell could still continue to safeguard Washington by pushing Anderson before him. McClellan was ordered to supply McDowell's corps from White House and to keep one wing extended north of the Chickahominy to meet him. Unwisely, the Federal commander attempted simultaneously to prepare to change his base to the James and to spread his right flank north to receive McDowell. He ordered the first troops across Bottom's Bridge on May 20 and within five days had divided his army into two unequal parts, precisely as the Confederates had wished but hardly dared to hope. The Third and Fourth Corps were south of the Chickahominy, and the Second, Fifth, and Sixth Corps remained on the north bank.[28]

McClellan still had not crossed the Chickahominy on May 18 or 19 when Davis rode again to Johnston's headquarters, this time without General Lee. He was, as usual, interested in knowing exactly what course Johnston intended to pursue and just how close he intended to bring his troops to Richmond. Johnston explained that he had pulled his lines in very close to the city in order to ensure a good water supply, ease of provision, and to put his troops into place to work on improving the battery at Drewry's Bluff and the Richmond defenses. He could not, however, have satisfied the president's curiosity about forthcoming operations, since McClellan had not yet revealed whether he would cross the Chickahominy.[29]

By May 21 there was no question that the Federal commander intended to accept the bait. Word of the Yankees south of the river reached Richmond, and almost immediately Davis had Lee write Johnston for details: "The President desires to know the number of troops around Richmond, how they are posted, and the organization of the divisions and brigades; also the programme of operation which you propose." Acknowledging that "your plan of operations, dependent upon circumstances perhaps yet to be developed, may not be so easily explained, nor may it be prudent to commit it to paper," Lee suggested that Johnston visit Richmond and communicate it in person. Johnston immediately replied with a memorandum showing the approximate strength of each of his brigades and the next day posted one letter and had another hand-carried to Lee by Maj. Jasper Whiting. Unfortunately, neither of these communications seems to have survived. It is impossible to tell by Lee's responses whether Johnston addressed any questions of strategy.[30]

His concern for the safety of the capital, however, did not allow Davis time to sit and wait for a reply. On the morning of May 22, before Johnston's answers—if indeed his letters answered Lee's inquiries—could have reached him, Davis again rode out to the army at Mechanicsville, this time with Lee. He found neither Johnston nor a situation calculated to instill in him confidence in his army commander: "I saw General Stuart and General Cobb," he wrote Johnston on his return,

> but as neither of them communicated to me any plan of operations, or appeared to know what troops were in front as we approached, I suppose neither of them could have been commanding in chief at that locality. My conclusion was, that if, as reported to be probable, General Franklin, with a division, was in that vicinity, he might easily have advanced over the turnpike toward if not to Richmond.[31]

He was upset enough with this appearance to order Lee back to the army on May 23 for a more thorough discussion of Johnston's plans.

By chance, Davis had ridden into the consequences of a dispute between G. W. Smith and John Magruder. Magruder, who had rejoined the army after a brief illness, was still irritated by the arrangement that subordinated his troops—temporarily, he contended—to Smith. As a result, every time Smith ordered regiments here or there, Magruder cooperated grudgingly, if at all. On May 22 and 23, their relationship had deteriorated to the point that, when Smith ordered two regiments from Lafayette McLaws's brigade to hold Mechanicsville, Magruder refused and insisted on using two regiments from Brig. Gen. D. R. Jones's brigade. Magruder's motivation seems to have come from a desire to be contentious rather than from any sound military reason. The two generals also issued a series of conflicting orders to the cavalry commanders in the area—not just J. E. B. Stuart, but also Fitzhugh Lee and Beverly H. Robertson. The result was confusion around Mechanicsville at the most inopportune of moments. Not only were the Yankees threatening to advance with at least a division, but Davis was present to witness a part of the army at loose ends. Johnston settled the internal dispute within a few days, but Davis's visit had definitely hurt his credibility with the chief executive.[32]

Possibly sensitive to the president's criticism, Johnston was more communicative than usual when Lee arrived at his headquarters on May 23. He definitely intended to strike one of the wings of the Army of the Potomac but had not yet decided which. Johnston himself seems to have consistently favored attacking south of the river, in the vicinity of Seven Pines. Three considerations made him lean on May 23, however, toward hitting the Federals on the north bank, in the vicinity of Beaver Dam Creek and Mechanicsville. First was the necessity of keeping McClellan and McDowell separated; an attack at Seven Pines might only have the effect of driving them together. Also in favor of a northern attack was the fact that the ground had already been thoroughly reconnoitered by Walter Stevens and Jasper Whiting a week earlier. Finally, Longstreet, in whose tactical judgment Johnston was inclined to have increasing confidence, had conducted a "careful study of the works and armaments at Drury's [*sic*] Bluff" and "ventured the suggestion that we recross the Chickahominy at Mechanicsville and stand behind Beaver Dam Creek." Johnston planned to wait a few days to find out just how much distance McClellan would voluntarily put between the sundered halves of his army, but he knew that he could not afford to delay too long. He told Lee that he intended to strike somewhere—probably but not definitely north of the river—by May 29.[33]

Lee evidently made two responses to Johnston's plan. First, he reiterated his suggestion that Johnston visit Richmond and communicate his strategy to the president directly. This Johnston did on May 24. In addition, Lee gave Johnston the welcome news that he would try, between then and the time of Johnston's attack, to reinforce the army with whatever troops could be scraped up in the Richmond area. Specifically, there were at least seven batteries of field artillery around the capital, which could be used to augment William Pendleton's artillery reserve. The Fourth Virginia Heavy Artillery Regiment and Lt. Col. Nicholas C. Harris's heavy artillery battalion were both assigned as infantry to Johnston's army. Likewise, Johnston was to receive Brig. Gen. Henry A. Wise's brigade, still in the process of rebuilding from its defeat at Roanoke Island. Aside from a complete regiment of cavalry, Wise's brigade had roughly the strength of two infantry regiments. But most significantly, Lee promised Johnston that he would try to stretch troops from Theophilus Holmes's Department of North Carolina to cover Petersburg, releasing the bulk of Huger's division for the offensive.[34]

The strategic situation began to change more and more rapidly after McClellan crossed the Chickahominy. On May 23 Jackson had initiated his attack on Banks by gobbling up a detached regiment at Front Royal and had swung around the Federal commander's left flank. By May 25 Banks was in full flight, and Jackson's brigades entered Winchester; within four days they had reached Harpers Ferry and the banks of the Potomac. It was not, however, the defeat of Banks that most affected events around Richmond. Jackson's raid had a much more profound consequence: at 5:00 P.M. on May 24, in a vain attempt to cut off the Confederate divisions in the lower Valley, President Lincoln ordered McDowell's corps to change front. Instead of marching south to link up with the Army of the Potomac, Lincoln instructed McDowell to head west in pursuit of Jackson. "At that moment," observes Robert G. Tanner, "the Valley Army won its Valley Campaign."[35]

This shift was not immediately evident in Richmond because all eyes were focused on McClellan. The same day that Lincoln authorized the diversion of McDowell, Brig. Gen. Erasmus Keyes advanced units of his Fourth Corps into the village of Seven Pines, and McClellan's cavalry finally pushed into Mechanicsville. Other Federal horsemen probed the swampland between Bottom's Bridge and the James on May 25 and 26 and Branch's position at Hanover Courthouse on May 26.[36] Johnston had begun pulling Anderson and Branch closer to the Chickahominy as early as May 23. Anderson sent the Forty-fifth Georgia to Ashland Station on May 23 and issued four days' rations to the rest of his troops. Johnston instructed Branch the same day to reconnoiter positions nearer to the Chickahominy (and the main body of the army) and advised him that "in a few days General J. R. Anderson will probably be near you." The following morning, Anderson issued marching orders to his regiments, culminating in the exhortation, "This Army after having waited long for an opportunity to meet the enemy who has sheltered himself behind the town of Fredericksburg and the river, now moves in pursuance of orders from higher authority to unite in the great battle of the issue of which depends the fate of the capital of our Country." Johnston told Branch to expect Anderson by May 27.[37]

Anderson was late, almost disastrously so for Branch. Fitz-John Porter's Fifth Corps, supported by William Emory's cavalry reserve—better than 16,000 troops—hit Branch's six regiments at noon on May 27. Branch held his position near Slash Church for several hours, until he determined that he was heavily outnumbered and that he had recovered all his detached units. Then, after suffering several hundred casualties, he withdrew in good order toward Johnston's lines. That same day his bloodied brigade, along with Anderson's command, was consolidated into a new division under just-promoted Maj. Gen. A. P. Hill.[38]

Still without reliable intelligence concerning McDowell's movements, Johnston reached an erroneous but understandable conclusion when Porter brushed Branch out of Hanover Courthouse. McClellan was extending his flank because he expected McDowell to march south within hours. This assumption was buttressed in Johnston's mind by an equally incorrect report on May 27 from Anderson that represented the Federals in Fredericksburg as having commenced their march to Richmond. "We must get ready to fight," Johnston told G. W. Smith and summoned his senior generals to conference.[39]

The moment of combat seemed to have been forced upon the Confederate army, and McClellan's dispositions invited attack. Three of his corps had been arrayed in a ten-mile line running southeast along the northern bank of the Chickahominy from Beaver Dam Creek to the Lower Bridge. Though Beaver Dam Creek was a formidable obstacle, if it could be breached quickly the opportunity existed to roll up the Federal corps in succession. The two corps south of the river were separated from each other by nearly five miles and would have to march several miles to reinforce the troops to the north. Johnston proposed that his army would slide suddenly to the left and that G. W. Smith would lead eleven brigades—his own division under Whiting, D. R. Jones's division, and A. P. Hill's division—across the Chickahominy above Mechanicsville, assault Beaver Dam Creek, and drive down the river. The remainder of Magruder's wing would hold the Chickahominy. D. H. Hill would be posted in front of Keyes's Fourth Corps on the Williamsburg Road, to pin him in position, and Longstreet would move northeast of Richmond to Nine Mile Road, available as a reserve on either flank.[40]

Despite being forced into an offensive, Johnston's spirits were high. D. H. Hill told one of his brigadiers that "I saw Genls. Johnston & Smith this afternoon. They think that tomorrow will be a great day in our history." It was the same day that Johnston learned that Jackson had routed Banks at Winchester and optimistically suggested that the Army of the Valley might attempt to cross the Potomac. He advised Lee that a battle probably would be fought on May 29, that he had ordered Huger to Drewry's Bluff to replace Longstreet, and requested that Holmes's division be brought to Richmond.[41]

The same day, Davis and one of his aides, Col. William Browne (formerly the acting secretary of state), visited Johnston at his headquarters. Johnston was out riding his lines when the president called, and a courier was dispatched to find him. The general sent back a polite note requesting that Davis return later in the afternoon, when he would have the time to acquaint the chief executive with his plans. Davis was then informed that an attack would take place on May 29.[42]

Yet once again, when the president rode out of the capital on May 29 expecting to witness a battle, he found consternation and confusion that recalled his May 22 visit to the front. As had been the case a week earlier, Howell Cobb had little idea what were the army commander's plans—nor did John Bell Hood. Davis could find neither Johnston nor G. W. Smith, who was supposed to be conducting the attack. Only Longstreet was where Davis thought he would be, and the massive Georgian was "walking to and fro in an impatient, it might be said fretful, manner." Longstreet was incensed because, when it came to the point of contact, Smith had balked at attacking.

Smith claimed that "I reported to General Johnston that I was satisfied the three divisions could carry the works at Beaver Dam Creek by open assault in front; but that it would be a bloody business." He did not think that ordering a wide flanking march by A. P. Hill's division was practical, suggesting as an alternative the rather fantastic idea that Jackson's divisions—then somewhere north of Winchester—be marched back to eastern Virginia for such a purpose. Rumors circulated that Smith had once again fallen ill with his mysterious neurological malady. The president returned to Richmond, his confidence in Johnston eroded once again.[43]

That evening the general called together his subordinates once more: Smith, Longstreet, Magruder, and Stuart. He announced that Stuart's outposts to the north reported that McDowell had turned back, which meant that there was no longer a pressing necessity for the attack. This satisfied Smith, who continued to express a negative opinion about the original plan. Longstreet, supported by Magruder and Stuart, demurred, believing that the concept of rolling up McClellan's right wing "was made stronger by the change of direction of McDowell's column, and should," in Longstreet's words, "suggest more prompt and vigorous action."[44]

According to Longstreet's recollection, the council of war continued for several hours, until, at last, Johnston grew disgusted and walked away. His fighting blood aroused by the prospect of action, Longstreet followed and suggested again the turning movement that Smith thought so impractical. With McClellan's inherent caution, there was little chance that the Federal commander would strike any detached Confederate divisions before they landed on his own flank. "General Johnston replied that he was aware of all that, but found that he had selected the wrong officer for the work," Longstreet asserted in his memoirs, adding that "this ended the talk."[45] Longstreet's account is somewhat suspect, as his memoirs were originally started as a refutation to charges made by Smith after the war. On the other hand, Johnston's opinion of Smith might well have already begun to decline by the evening of May 29, 1862. Several times Smith's health had forced him to alter plans. The Kentuckian quarreled with other generals, and twice within the past week Smith had caused Johnston to look less than capable in the president's eyes. The only action to his credit was the skirmish at Eltham's Landing, an engagement that, Johnston might have recalled, was directed entirely by Smith's subordinates.[46]

Longstreet, by contrast, had a fighting record that began at Manassas and had been extended by victory—at least in his own and Johnston's eyes—at Williamsburg. Now it was Longstreet who argued for the aggressive course.

Increasingly during May 1862, Johnston came to depend on Longstreet more than on Smith. He had always preferred striking McClellan's two isolated corps south of the river; suddenly in Johnston's mind, such an operation would have an extra benefit. Longstreet, not Smith, would be conducting the attack.

11
SEVEN PINES

Rain threatened Richmond again on May 30, 1862, but the ominous gray thunderheads seemed only slightly closer than the Yankee army. After the repulse of the ironclads at Drewry's Bluff, there had been a momentary rise in the city's morale. The *Richmond Examiner* asserted that "when the history of this war is reviewed, it will be found that the chief service the enemy has gotten from his gunboats has been to frighten bad officers and worse troops into surrendering positions which they might have continued to hold."[1] Then came news of Stonewall Jackson's success at Winchester and the hope that his dash toward the Potomac might force the recall of the Army of the Potomac to defend Washington. By that overcast Friday, however, the citizens of Richmond knew that no such reprieve lay in their future. George McClellan inched ever closer; if he were to be driven away, it would be by Joseph Johnston's outnumbered army, fighting from the outskirts of Richmond.

Hundreds, if not thousands, fled the capital. The cabinet debated where to locate the next line of defense if Johnston had to relinquish the city. Secretary of War George Randolph ordered the city council to conduct experiments to find the quickest and safest method of destroying tons of tobacco stored in Richmond warehouses, in order to prevent their falling into enemy hands. The specters of Nashville, New Orleans, Memphis, and Norfolk hung over the city.[2]

Yet there was a distinct difference between the feeling that gripped Richmond and the terror that had clutched at the hearts of the inhabitants of other Southern cities. "After the Confederate command's decision to evacuate their city without a fight, the people of Nashville had been panic-stricken," Walter T. Durham has written. "Citizens shared mixed emotions about the defense of the city. Certainly most wanted to be shielded from the Union Army; however, few wanted to be protected at the expense of the destruction of Nashville. The prevailing desire was to stop the Yankees—but not in the streets of the city." In New Orleans, when Flag Officer David G. Farragut's fleet had run the batteries and Maj. Gen. Mansfield Lovell's troops had withdrawn from the city, the mayor announced that "it would be proper to say that the withdrawal of troops rendering resistance impossible, no obstruction could be offered to the occupation of the place by the enemy." The citizens of Memphis watched from the banks of the Mississippi as their River Defense Fleet was destroyed and then surrendered without further resistance. Norfolk had also surrendered without a fight, once the army and navy left town.[3]

In Richmond the prevailing attitude was equally pessimistic, but underlying the gloom was a grim determination, in Jefferson Davis's words, "that the ancient and honored capital of Virginia, now the seat of the Confederate Government, shall not fall into the hands of the enemy. Many say rather let it be a heap of rubbish." Already Gov. John Letcher and Mayor Joseph Mayo had declared their determination to defend the city regardless of what the Confederacy did. Letcher visited Johnston's army on May 30 to spread his resolve to the Virginia regiments within its divisions. Mayo repeatedly stirred crowds by declaring that "rather than . . . surrender the city founded by his own ancestors, he would resign the office of the mayoralty, and though bending under the approach of three score years and ten, he would shoulder the musket himself in defense of the capital." "Some of the most wealthy of our population," recalled Sally Putnam, "declared they would fire their own beautiful residences, in preference to delivering up the city to our foes."[4]

The ultimate fate of Richmond, however, still lay with Johnston's army. When the army had halted between the Pamunkey and Chickahominy Rivers, it was plain that the retreat had taken its toll. "The army is very much demoralized," D. H. Hill told his wife. "Some five thousand threw away their guns and fled to Richmond to avoid a battle." There were other reasons besides cowardice for leaving the ranks. No rations had been issued since Williamsburg, reducing members of the Richmond Howitzers to stealing feed corn from their own starving horses. Even generals roamed the countryside foraging: Brig. Gen. Richard Griffith rode into the artillerymen's camp one night to beg an ear of corn for himself and several for his horse. Well-drilled soldiers might have been held in the ranks by veteran officers, but Hill pointed out that "the reorganization of the army at Yorktown, under the elective system, had thrown out of service many of our best officers." Johnston found himself faced with an army on the verge of melting away.[5]

Once again Johnston took immediate steps to improve the morale and efficiency of his army. With Robert E. Lee, he coordinated the delivery of rations and the return of the army's wagon trains. Armed with reports from his regimental and brigade commanders, Johnston finally managed to convince the

Richmond authorities to allow his own provost marshals into the city to recover his absentees. The army commander also began a thorough reorganization of both the artillery and cavalry serving under him, a reorganization that was greatly to strengthen those branches throughout the summer and fall.[6] Between May 13 and 30, Johnston's efforts, combined with those of Lee to reinforce him, caused the army to bounce back in terms of fighting spirit, organization, and numbers. James Longstreet, who had never ceased his own efforts to buttress morale, wrote that when his men "have their bellies full, also their cartridge boxes," then "I don't fear McClellan or anyone in Yankeedom." By the end of May he believed that his troops "were never so resolved" to fight as they were then; they "even asserted that they would dig bayous, to reach the enemy's trenches, if not allowed some other means of getting to him." The artillery reserve had been increased from fifty-six to nearly ninety guns, the cavalry brigade enlarged by the addition of several regiments. By May 31, with the addition of Benjamin Huger's and A. P. Hill's divisions, Johnston's army attained the greatest strength it had yet known: nearly 88,000 officers and men present for duty. Counting the brigades of Roswell S. Ripley and John G. Walker, both approaching Richmond on May 31, and adding in the garrison troops in the city itself, the Confederacy had managed, both through Johnston's administrative efficiency and Lee's herculean effort to secure reinforcements, to gather more than 97,000 men for the defense of the capital. On the same day, McClellan reported the Army of the Potomac as 103,382 strong. The overwhelming numerical advantage enjoyed by the Yankees in February had been almost completely neutralized.[7]

Given McClellan's normal caution, Johnston could have safely awaited Ripley's and Walker's brigades before attacking. He could have dropped upon Lee the responsibility for supporting Drewry's Bluff instead of leaving four of Huger's regiments there. To have done either would have been consistent with the stereotypical image of Johnston as always postponing battle to gather more strength. By May 30, however, he had finally been presented with the opportunity he had been seeking—Erasmus Keyes's Fourth Corps at Seven Pines was separated from the rest of the Federal army by several miles—and Johnston was not about to delay in striking a moment longer. "If nothing prevents we will fall upon the enemy in front of Major-General [D. H.] Hill," Johnston told G. W. Smith on May 30, "early in the morning—as early as practicable."[8]

Johnston's plan was simple. Three roads extended east from Richmond toward Keyes's position. Most of D. H. Hill's division was on the center route, the Williamsburg Road, which led directly to Seven Pines. He was to bring his flanking brigade up from Charles City Road to the south and attack toward

Seven Pines. The brigade on Charles City Road would be replaced by Huger's division, marching up from Drewry's Bluff. Huger's first task was to secure Hill's right flank, but if he found no opposition he was authorized to attack northeast to support Hill. Longstreet would march his own division down Nine Mile Road, which first paralleled and then intersected the Williamsburg Road, running through Fair Oaks Station to Seven Pines, and attack on Hill's left. Longstreet was to supervise the combined movements of these three divisions. Meanwhile, part of John Magruder's command and A. P. Hill's division would defend the upper bridges of the Chickahominy; W. H. C. Whiting's and Lafayette McLaws's divisions would be held in reserve either to support Longstreet or to engage any reinforcements McClellan attempted to send across the river.[9]

The sequence of events that led to the development of this plan and the methods by which the orders were distributed are critical to any understanding of what happened on May 31. About noon on May 30, D. H. Hill advised Johnston that Keyes's entire Fourth Corps was concentrated near Seven Pines and that there were apparently no Federal troops on the Charles City Road. "I received a prompt answer from him," Hill stated, "saying that, being satisfied by my report of the presence of the enemy in force in my immediate front, he had resolved to attack him, and directed me to serve with Major-General Longstreet and under his orders." Longstreet arrived at Johnston's headquarters soon after his commander had received Hill's intelligence, and the two generals began to discuss details of the upcoming attack.[10]

Not only by choosing Longstreet to command the attack, but also by failing to call Smith into the conference about its direction and coordination, Johnston sent a clear signal of just how far the Kentuckian had fallen in his estimation. There were other signs of Longstreet's rise and Smith's demise in the eyes of the army commander. Johnston's plan broke up Smith's "wing," leaving A. P. Hill on the upper Chickahominy and bringing Whiting up the Nine Mile Road as a reserve, with McLaws actually scheduled to be committed to battle first. The plan effectively reduced Smith to a division commander or a spectator, depending on whether or not he chose to supersede Whiting. Johnston obviously did not intend him to do so, sending Smith a not-so-subtle message by transmitting movement orders directly to Whiting.[11] Whether Johnston suspected that his nominal second-in-command lacked nerve—as Longstreet would later imply—or whether he simply feared a physical breakdown at a critical moment is impossible to determine. In either case, the effect was the same: Johnston deliberately cut Smith out of the attack.

Johnston and Longstreet no doubt discussed a variety of options for executing the attack. Any map of the Richmond area suggested the possibility of

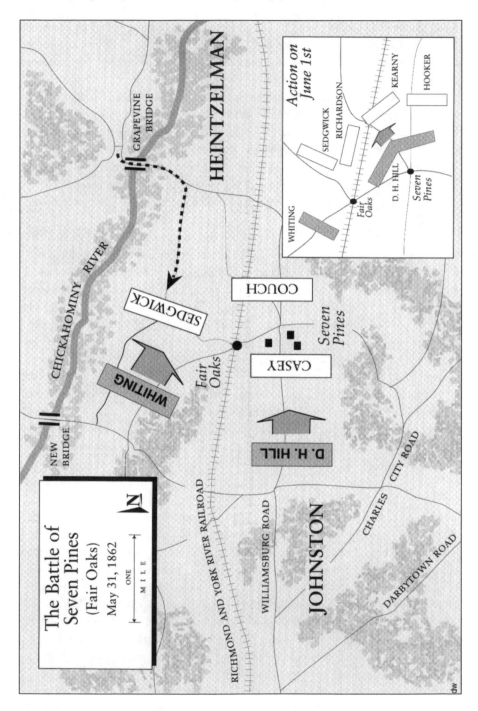

The Battle of
Seven Pines
(Fair Oaks)
May 31, 1862

ONE MILE

attacking Keyes simultaneously in front and flank by sending one division down the Williamsburg Road and another down the Nine Mile Road. This plan raised a serious question about the weight of D. H. Hill's frontal assault. At the moment, Hill had only three brigades on the Williamsburg Road; Robert Rodes's Mississippi-Alabama Brigade was stationed on the Charles City Road to protect his right flank.[12] Three brigades without reinforcements—fewer than 10,000 men—alone could hardly be expected to spearhead the crushing attack Johnston envisioned. How could the frontal attack be strengthened?

Three possible answers suggested themselves. First, Huger's division could be brought up from Drewry's Bluff along Charles City Road to relieve Rodes to participate in the attack. This would give Hill his full division for the attack, secure his right flank, and even hold out the possibility that Huger's three brigades might assist in enveloping the Federal left. The advantages of this approach were so clear that Johnston dispatched orders to Huger that evening.[13] This solution still left Hill attacking Keyes's front with only a single division. A second option for reinforcing his attack would be to bring some of Longstreet's brigades over to the Williamsburg Road to support the attack. If three of his six brigades marched across to support Hill, then the balance of forces in the attack would be seven brigades on the Williamsburg Road (Hill's division and half of Longstreet's) and seven on the Nine Mile Road (McLaws's division and the other half of Longstreet's). Against this plan there were two objections, one of command coordination and the other of Longstreet's ambition. With which column would Longstreet ride, and how would he coordinate the attack on the other road? If he chose the Williamsburg Road, the entire left prong of the attack would be left in the hands of McLaws, one of the most junior division commanders in the army. McLaws had just received his commission a week earlier and had not, with the exception of the skirmish at Williamsburg on May 4, maneuvered even a single brigade in combat. On the other hand, if Longstreet personally commanded operations on the Nine Mile Road, there remained a question of delegating the responsibility for opening the action entirely to Hill. Given Hill's performance at Williamsburg, which his critics could well have characterized as rash, how safe would it be to leave to him the command of half the forces involved in the attack?

There was, however, a third possibility. Hill could be reinforced on the Williamsburg Road with Longstreet's entire division. This would put ten brigades in the main attack under Longstreet's direct supervision. The assault of McLaws's four brigades on the Nine Mile Road would then be relegated to the status of a supporting attack. Should greater weight be needed there,

Johnston could always draw on Whiting's five brigades. The advantages of this plan, from an operational perspective, were the added weight to the attack on the center of the Fourth Corps and Longstreet's personal supervision of the attack. As a disadvantage, such a maneuver required six of Longstreet's and three of Huger's brigades to share one constricted stretch of the Williamsburg Road, upon which both divisions would have to travel until Huger's men turned off on the Charles City Road. Without careful coordination, confusion could delay the opening of the attack.

When Longstreet left Johnston's headquarters, the army commander had decided to follow the simplest of the plans discussed: Longstreet would follow the Nine Mile Road, Hill the Williamsburg Road. Huger would relieve Rodes's brigade, and when Rodes reported to Hill, the North Carolinian would fire a signal gun to start the attack. The noise was to alert Longstreet's division on the Nine Mile Road to begin its advance. The sequence of events was to begin as early as possible after dawn.[14] With the advantage of hindsight, it is easy to fault Johnston's faith in the ability of his army to perform such a complex maneuver with clockwork efficiency, since his divisions were separated by several miles of dense woodland and murky swamps. Yet such convoluted arrangements for opening battles by an intricate succession of attacks were a regular feature of Civil War combat. Lee attempted to start the battles of Cheat Mountain and Mechanicsville with just such maneuvers. Braxton Bragg routinely employed complicated echelon movements to begin battles: he did so at Perryville, Stone's River, and on the second day at Chickamauga. Upon his promotion to command of the Army of Tennessee, John Bell Hood did the same at Peachtree Creek and the Battle of Atlanta. Nor was faith in the abilities of their divisions to conduct themselves flawlessly in battle maneuvers that would have taxed their skills on the parade ground strictly a Confederate delusion. McClellan at Antietam, Joseph Hooker at Chancellorsville, and George G. Meade at Mine Run provide only three of a great number of examples of an equal Yankee fascination with overly complex opening gambits.

Johnston committed two far greater mistakes in planning his battle. Though he wrote Huger two letters—one on the evening of May 30 and one very early in the morning of May 31—he neglected to make clear either the scope of the battle or the fact that Huger would be responsible for starting it. Instead of telling Huger on May 30 that an attack was planned, Johnston merely informed him that "the reports of Maj. Gen. D. H. Hill give me the impression that the enemy is in considerable strength in his front. It seems to me necessary that we should increase our force also." Even when he assigned Huger his post, Johnston did not specify that an attack by Hill's division was contemplated: "For that object I wish to concentrate the troops of your division on the Charles City Road and concentrate the troops of Major-General Hill on that to Williamsburg." After providing Huger with directions, Johnston ended the letter with the only sentence, ambiguous as it was, that even hinted at his plans for attack: "Be ready, if an action should be begun on your left, to fall upon the enemy's left flank." There was no doubt in Johnston's mind that he intended to attack the next morning; thirty-five minutes after he wrote Huger, he sent much more explicit orders to Smith and Whiting. "If nothing prevents we will fall upon the enemy in front of Major-General Hill," he told them.[15] Why did he fail to reveal his intentions to Huger?

Why also, in the predawn hours of May 31, did Johnston suddenly decide to limit Huger's actions even more strictly? The following confused note would have found Huger as he put his brigades into motion:

GENERAL: I fear that in my note of last evening, of which there is no copy, I was too positive on the subject of your attacking the enemy's left flank. It will, of course, be necessary for you to know what force is before you first. I hope to be able to have that ascertained for you by cavalry. As our main force will be on your left, it will be necessary for your progress to conform at first to that of General Hill; but then a strong reserve should be retained to cover our right.[16]

This letter more clearly implied an attack but disregarded several points. Huger was not informed that his relief of Rodes would signal the beginning of the battle; he was not even told which brigade he would replace in Hill's division. Cavalry was to scout the area in front of him, but what cavalry, and when would it report to him? Most critically, the message did not alert Huger that a major attack by fourteen brigades had been ordered or that Longstreet was in overall command. Johnston, it almost seemed, expected Huger to divine his intentions by telepathy. The army commander, anxious over the impending battle, may well have dashed off the first note without thinking it through. By the time he dispatched the second letter, he admitted that he could no longer quite remember what he had written and revealed that he had not had a copy entered in his letterbooks. It was a failure of both the individual and of his mediocre staff; everyone simply assumed that the correct information had been disseminated, and no one bothered to check. Yet, as Douglas Southall Freeman has pointed out, Huger's orders, "while not models of their kind," could reasonably be expected to put him in approximately the right place at roughly the correct hour. If he commenced his march early enough, if the roads were clear and the bridges intact, and if D. H. Hill had guides awaiting him as instructed, then Johnston's plan might not be irrevocably injured.[17]

Johnston's second significant miscue on the day before the battle had the potential for far worse consequences. He had discussed with Longstreet several variations of his original plan, and though he had finally decided on his original concept, he failed to make sure that his division commander left the meeting with the same understanding. Longstreet returned to his own camps and ordered his brigadiers to issue ammunition, have rations cooked, and prepare for an early march. Yet along what route? As Longstreet pondered the attack, more and more he thought of the personal and strategic advantages that would accrue from sending his division down the Williamsburg Road and supervising the combined attack of his and Hill's brigades. There could be no question of credit for a victory if Longstreet commanded both divisions. Combined with his defensive success at Williamsburg, an offensive triumph at Seven Pines would secure his own reputation as the army's chief fighting general and cement his place as Johnston's most trusted subordinate. Rationalizations come easily to an ambitious man: unity of command, weight of attack, and the possible need to restrain the sometimes overly aggressive Hill would have offered themselves to the Georgian that night.[18]

By what authority could he modify the plan upon which Johnston had settled? At some point in the night, Longstreet convinced himself that as commander of the "right wing" he had been given the assignment to attack the enemy in front of Hill and that he and the army commander had discussed alternatives for that attack without ever firmly deciding on one. It would have been in character for Johnston to have told Longstreet at some point in the discussion that he depended on him to use his own best judgment in controlling the attack. From such an expression of confidence, Longstreet could easily have derived the idea that Johnston had entrusted to him the authority to change plans as circumstances might dictate. Without notifying Johnston, Longstreet sent a message to Hill informing the other division commander that his six brigades would march to the Williamsburg Road in the morning to support the attack.[19]

The only other possible explanations of Longstreet's conduct are that either he completely misunderstood Johnston's instructions or that he coolly and consciously disobeyed orders. Neither seems satisfactory. As poorly conceived as was his correspondence with Huger, the idea that, in a conversation that must have consumed hours, Johnston could not make clear to Longstreet on which of two roads he wished his division to march stretches plausibility beyond the breaking point. Nor did Longstreet ever admit that he altered Johnston's original design. In both his official report of the battle and his memoirs, he steadfastly maintained that his dispositions were precisely those directed by the army commander. The account of the conference with Johnston and the outline of the plan of attack that Longstreet published in his memoirs demonstrate, however, a striking similarity to those passages in which he depicted Lee as firmly agreeing to fight only defensive battles during the Gettysburg campaign. Throughout his career, the Georgian repeatedly proved that he was quite capable, upon reflection, of hearing what he wished to have heard. Unfortunately, the army commander had no inkling that such was the case. To paraphrase Freeman on Lee and Longstreet in Pennsylvania, Johnston never had intended to commit himself to any changes that Longstreet might introduce to his plan of battle, and he did not know that Longstreet considered him so pledged.[20]

In his ignorance that the general to whom he had assigned responsibility for the next day's attack had decided to change the plan, Johnston found several omens that apparently augured for resounding success. The primary one was rain—a hard, driving, drenching rain accompanied by pounding thunder. The downpour began within hours of the time Johnston decided to take the offensive and raised the prospect that the Chickahominy would overflow its banks, rendering communication between the two parts of McClellan's army not difficult but impossible. It did not seem to occur to him that the same deluge might also swell the streams to his rear and slow the approach of Huger's division or flood the low-lying countryside to such an extent that troop movements would be hindered.[21]

More news that Johnston considered good came to headquarters in the person of Col. Armistead L. Long, Lee's military secretary, who rode from Richmond with two messages from the commanding general. First, Long informed the army commander that Ripley's South Carolina Brigade had been ordered to report to him when it arrived in Richmond, probably the next day.[22] The other communication that Long brought was a personal message from Lee, "to tell him that he would be glad to participate in the battle. He had no desire to interfere with [Johnston's] command, but simply wished to aid him on the field to the best of his ability and in any manner in which his services would be of most value."[23] The offer both pleased and embarrassed Johnston. For two weeks, the generals had been growing closer together in their strategic appreciation of the military situation. Lee's request to serve under Johnston was a heartening vote of confidence, but at the same time it was an awkward proposition. Lee could be relied upon to keep his word not to interfere, but his presence would raise a thorny issue of credit if a victory were gained. Johnston could scarcely have forgotten that the public awarded P. G. T. Beauregard the lion's share of the praise for Manassas; would it be said that Lee had been forced to ride out to Johnston's army to save Richmond? To Long, none of this internal struggle was apparent. He recorded that "General Johnston expressed gratification at this message, and the hope that General Lee would ride out to the field, with the desire that he would send him all the reinforcements he could." Johnston then informed Long that the battle would open the following day, though he did not elaborate on his plans.[24]

Few soldiers and even fewer officers in the divisions of Longstreet, D. H. Hill, Huger, or Whiting got much sleep that night; a morning attack required preparations that consumed the hours of darkness. Huger, whose men had the longest distance to travel, was on the march soon after 3:00 A.M. Longstreet's men started toward the Williamsburg Road before 6:30 A.M. On the Williamsburg and Charles City Roads, D. H. Hill had already roused his own troops and awaited the arrival of Huger's lead brigade to relieve Rodes and allow him to open the attack. Whiting, who had been cast in the role of reserve on the Nine Mile Road, began his own march at first light.[25]

Nor had the sun risen when G. W. Smith met Johnston just outside the city limits at his headquarters on the Nine Mile Road. Smith's arrival was an event that Johnston knew must eventually occur but that he had not anticipated with pleasure. The previous day he had essentially removed the Kentuckian—the man he once described as fit to command in chief—from the command structure of the army. Yet since Smith remained legally his second-in-command, Johnston felt constrained to explain to him the details of the attack.[26] Johnston's evident expectation was that Smith would take the hint of his de facto demotion and avail himself of one of two face-saving alternatives. Either he would personally resume command of Whiting's division, or he would return to the upper Chickahominy and supervise the four brigades of A. P. Hill's division guarding the bridges. If he chose to supersede Whiting, Johnston was willing to allow him a part, albeit a very small one, in the battle. The army commander could do so without fear, for if Smith lost his taste for attacking or suffered an attack of his illness, there was always Whiting to replace him. Should Smith decide to retire to the far left of the army, he would be out of the way entirely.

Smith confounded Johnston before the first light had streaked across the Virginia sky. Calmly ignoring the choices that his superior had tacitly laid before him, Smith told Johnston that he had left A. P. Hill in charge of observing bridges and that he "did not propose relieving General Whiting of the command of the division." Instead, he "would accompany it to the designated point, and take whatever part circumstances might require of him in the coming contest."[27] Whiting was scheduled to march down the Nine Mile Road to the point where it split, the left fork heading toward New Bridge, the right to Fair Oaks Station. Since it was from this location Johnston intended to oversee the battle, Smith's announcement meant that he planned to remain at Johnston's shoulder all day. This was not a prospect that pleased Johnston, and he cast about quickly for an assignment for the Kentuckian. Smith recalled that Johnston decided that if the Federals "attempted to cross anywhere above New Bridge, he would place me in command of all our troops on that side, and that I must repel any attack they might make on Richmond, whilst the mass of our army was engaged with McClellan's left wing."[28]

The next news that Johnston received was far more welcome. Theophilus Holmes, whom Johnston had not seen since he departed to command in North Carolina, rode up to headquarters, accompanied by Lt. Col. Archer Anderson, his chief of staff. Holmes advised Johnston that he had received definitive orders from the secretary of war to reinforce the army in front of Richmond with three of his brigades—more than 8,000 men. The leading troops, 3,000 soldiers of Walker's brigade, would reach Drewry's Bluff sometime that day, which would allow Johnston to call up immediately the four regiments that he had been forced to leave there.[29] Not only would there be reinforcements available the next day to follow up a successful battle, but it also must have seemed to Johnston that the administration had finally decided to strip its coastal garrisons in order to defeat McClellan.

His satisfaction, however, was short-lived. Only minutes after Holmes and Anderson had departed, a frustrated inquiry from Whiting arrived by courier. Whiting had attempted to start his division down the Nine Mile Road at daybreak but found Longstreet's brigades blocking his march. Quickly becoming impatient, he directed his complaint to Smith. Unfortunately, not knowing the entire battle plan, Whiting omitted one key detail from his message: he did not tell Smith that Longstreet was marching *south* across his lines, instead of *east* down the Nine Mile Road.[30] Johnston was standing beside Smith when the latter received the message. For Johnston, it was the first notice that something had gone awry with his plan. Whiting had sent his letter after 6:00 A.M. and his courier had consumed the better part of an hour in finding Johnston and Smith. The chances for a near-dawn attack were diminishing rapidly. Johnston directed Smith to send an aide to Longstreet to find out what had caused the delay. Lieutenant Robert F. Beckham was chosen for the mission. When Beckham asked Smith where Longstreet's headquarters could be found, Smith referred him back to the army commander. Johnston's answer was abrupt: Longstreet's division was assigned to the Nine Mile Road, and Longstreet, "in all probability," was at its head. Beckham was to hurry Longstreet along and reassure Whiting that Longstreet was to precede him.[31]

A tense hour passed before word came back from Beckham. It was not good news. He had ridden as far up the Nine Mile Road as Whiting's division and could find no sign of the Georgian or his six brigades. Either from an interview with Whiting, or from his own observations, Beckham realized what had happened: Longstreet was marching toward the Williamsburg Road. On his own initiative, he set off cross-country in search of the missing division.[32]

Even after the receipt of Beckham's intelligence, Johnston resisted the idea that Longstreet had ignored the plan of attack. Perhaps the troops that had delayed Whiting were other brigades—in all events, Longstreet *should* have marched hours earlier—and the Georgian's division had passed down the Nine Mile Road in the dark and was already *east* of the position where Johnston and Smith were standing. The lack of any noise from in front was inconclusive because Longstreet would have kept troops in position as quiet as possible until Hill's attack began. Having convinced himself that Beckham could well be mistaken, Johnston dispatched one of his own aides east down the Nine Mile Road, *toward* the Federal position at Seven Pines. If Lt. J. B. Washington could not find Longstreet on that part of the road either, the army commander instructed him to cut across to the Williamsburg Road. There he was to order Longstreet, if he found him, to send at least three brigades back to the Nine Mile Road if the attack had not yet opened.[33]

That he would order three of Longstreet's brigades to countermarch back to the Nine Mile Road when the attack was already several hours late in opening revealed much about Johnston's state of mind on May 31. Either he forgot that he still had four brigades under McLaws and five under Whiting available for the left wing of his attack, or he had become fixed upon the idea of keeping Smith from having an active role in the battle. It is also possible that, in the moment of his first offensive battle, Johnston proved unable to impose his will upon events. He had proven his ability to direct strategy, administer a department, maneuver his troops, and supervise (if loosely) a defensive battle. Attacking—turning a plan into reality, despite the fact that troops took the wrong roads and generals misunderstood their orders—was a much more strenuous exercise. So far his reactions could be excused as those of a novice commanding his first attack; but with his orders to Lieutenant Washington, legitimate suspicions about Johnston's capacity to command an attack begin to surface.

Three hours had already passed since Whiting's initial complaint when Washington spurred his horse toward Seven Pines, just after 9:00 A.M. No one at headquarters saw him again that day. Washington became so absorbed in looking for Longstreet's brigades that he completely overshot Confederate lines and delivered himself as a prisoner into the hands of the 100th New York, the regiment picketing the far right of Brig. Gen. Silas Casey's Second Division of the Fourth Corps. Although Washington said nothing of his mission or the impending attack to his captors, the capture of an army commander's aide could not help but make the Yankees suspicious. "This circumstance," reported Casey, "in connection with the fact that Colonel Hunt, my general officer of the day, had reported to me that his outer pickets had heard cars running nearly all night on the Richmond end of the railroad, led me to exercise increased vigilance."[34]

All Johnston knew was that Washington had simply disappeared. In the meantime, Lieutenant Beckham rode back to the army commander's field headquarters with the news that he had found not only General Longstreet but his entire division and all its trains on the Williamsburg Road. Since Beckham had pursued Longstreet on his own initiative, however, he had no orders to pass on to the commander of the right wing. It was now nearly 10:00 A.M. To send a courier back to Longstreet with orders to transfer three brigades to the Nine Mile Road would consume at least another hour (by which time the frontal attack by Hill's and Huger's divisions should have commenced) and would risk even more confusion. In Johnston's mind there would have been only two viable options at this point: call off the attack entirely and regroup or follow Longstreet's lead.

Johnston vacillated. As he told Maj. S. B. French, Smith's chief commissary, to post himself outside his advanced headquarters and listen for the sound of musketry from the south, he made a remark that revealed an inclination to cancel the attack. "He said that he wished the troops were back in their camps," recalled French.[35] Left to himself, Johnston might well have called off the offensive, but within a few minutes another incident occurred, an event that rendered such a course impossible in Johnston's mind: Robert E. Lee appeared on the field.

Lee could not bring himself to remain in Richmond, doing nothing but shifting papers while the army battled for the city. He made sure that the orders forwarding Walker's and Ripley's troops had gone out and ordered John Pemberton to send an additional pair of regiments from South Carolina. Sometime during the morning, his patience exhausted, the commanding general mounted Traveler and rode out toward Johnston's headquarters. Eventually, probably about 11:00 A.M., Lee arrived at Johnston's forward command post in a house just off to the right of the Nine Mile Road, where the road to New Bridge turned off.[36]

There is little doubt that Lee approached Johnston on May 31 with exactly the same intentions in mind that he had sent Colonel Long to communicate the previous day. He wanted to help. He needed, for his own peace of mind, to be involved in the defense of Richmond. He had told Johnston he would be happy to serve in any capacity, and he did not seek to usurp the command. The remainder of Lee's military career provides mute testimony to his sincerity: he rarely interfered directly in the tactical conduct of his corps, division, or brigade commanders. He would have been far less likely to do so in the case of a general—a peer and a friend—commanding an army. Johnston, growing more anxious each moment for the success of his plan, was hardly in a state to appreciate this fact. His design had already begun to go awry with Gustavus Smith as an unwelcome witness. As he waited for the guns that would herald the belated attack on the Williamsburg Road, his confidence further unraveled. Johnston perceived Lee only as a threat to his reputation and his command. Would Lee take some sort of action if he found out about the morning's miscues? If the attack commenced after Lee's arrival, would he somehow be accorded the credit?

"There was a tenseness in the air" between the two men at that moment, writes Douglas Southall Freeman. It was obvious that an attack was brewing, although not yet under way, but Johnston was hardly in a mood to confide his plans or his problems to Lee. Lee was caught in the prison of his own hands-off attitude; he would not ask until Johnston seemed willing to answer. The net result was that Johnston found himself with two pairs of eyes gazing directly over his shoulders.[37]

He waited. Longstreet had nearly 30,000 soldiers, counting his own and the divisions of Hill and Huger. There was no reason that even an attack delayed into midday might not crush Keyes. He "still had full faith," he told Smith, possibly with more bravura than he actually felt as noon approached, that Longstreet's attack would destroy the Fourth Corps. Smith, who had the luxury of being very nearly an uninvolved bystander, was not so sure.[38] The minutes dragged silently past until sometime in the early afternoon Johnston finally decided that he needed another update on Longstreet's position and progress. He directed Smith to send Maj. Jasper Whiting cross-country to check on the Georgian. About 2:00 P.M., the staff officer spurred his mount south through the woods toward the Williamsburg Road.[39] Everyone else— Johnston and his staff, Smith and his, and Lee—waited nervously as their apprehension grew. Something must have gone horribly wrong.

A dull roar sounded in the woods to the south shortly before 4:00 P.M. Johnston listened but heard only cannon. An artillery duel, he concluded. To Lee's ear the noise contained the faint echo of musketry, and he said as much. Johnston could not discern it.[40] More than two-thirds of the day had elapsed without combat. With only a few hours of daylight left, it seemed almost as if the army commander was hoping that Longstreet had the sense to postpone an assault that would be made too late to be decisive.

Lee was correct: a bloody battle was rolling down the Williamsburg Road. Major Whiting confirmed this at 4:00 P.M. when he galloped back to headquarters with an urgent message from Longstreet. The full text has been lost, but Smith's report summarized its substance:

He had attacked and beaten the enemy after several hours, severe fighting; that he had been disappointed in not receiving assistance upon his
left; and, although it was now nearly too late, that an attack, by the Nine
Mile Road, upon the right flank and rear of the enemy would probably
enable him to drive them into the Chickahominy before dark.[41]

Johnston was taken aback. Longstreet's attack had been launched several
hours earlier. How was it possible that neither the report of a signal gun nor
sounds beyond the barely audible noise heard half an hour ago had penetrated
to the Nine Mile Road? After reading the Georgian's note, Johnston concluded
that perhaps, with swift action, he might yet achieve his goal that afternoon.
Three of Whiting's brigades, those of Hood, J. J. Pettigrew, and Whiting's own
under its senior colonel, had halted in the vicinity of headquarters. The need
for haste drove all thoughts of proper chain of command from Johnston's
mind. Without pausing to locate Whiting, he began to order those units into
line. He dispatched Smith back up the road to bring forward the remainder of
the division: the brigades of Wade Hampton and Robert Hatton.[42]

What had happened on the Williamsburg Road?
Longstreet's impromptu change of the attack plan had required three divisions to share at least a part of that road as they deployed for battle. When
Huger's lead brigade arrived at rain-swollen Gillies Creek, the soldiers discovered Longstreet's troops had beaten them to the ford, which they were
crossing single file on a plank laid across a wagon bed. There was ample reason for Huger to be surprised. He had never even been informed that
Longstreet's division was involved in the attack and could claim precedence
at the crossing—his troops had the assignment of relieving Rodes on the
Charles City Road so that the battle could commence. Longstreet's men
refused: they had built the bridge and intended to cross it first.[43]
Impatient at this delay, Huger asked for the location of Longstreet's command post and urged his horse across the creek to the Poe House, farther down
the Williamsburg Road. There he found Longstreet and D. H. Hill. Huger
voiced his complaint and probably demanded to know what other parts of the
plan had been kept from him. Hill, by far the most junior of the three generals,
would have had little to say. Longstreet, as he often did when challenged, fell
back on his authority as commander of the right wing to justify his division
passing the creek first. Huger then played what he considered to be his trump
card. He asked Longstreet his date of commission which, if junior to his own,
would give Huger the overall command despite Johnston's intentions. Both
men had the same date of rank as major and brigadier generals, which put the
issue back either to their standings in the skeletal Confederate regular army or

the prewar U.S. Army. Longstreet was suspiciously vague on the dates of his own commissions. Huger, with old-army rank-consciousness, had no trouble providing his first, at which point—without citing specifics—Longstreet flatly asserted his own seniority. Huger was personally unconvinced but found himself maneuvered into a position where it seemed necessary to drop the issue. Longstreet retained command, and Huger's troops continued to cool their heels as his men inched across the precarious bridge.[44]

Longstreet then decided to modify further Johnston's simple plan of attack. As wing commander, controlling three divisions, he evidently did not feel that his proper place was the direct tactical supervision of a single division. So he divided his six brigades into two demidivisions, under Richard Anderson and Cadmus Wilcox. Wilcox would take his own troops, plus those of Raleigh Colston and Roger Pryor, down the Charles City Road and support Huger on the extreme right of the attack, operating under the now-disgruntled major general's orders. Anderson, with his own brigade and James Kemper's (A. P. Hill's old brigade), would support D. H. Hill's attack. George Pickett was deployed independently along the line of the York River Railroad in a half-hearted attempt to connect Hill's left with the right flank of the troops on the Nine Mile Road.

Longstreet's revised dispositions eradicated any possible advantage of increased weight of numbers gained by sending his division down the Williamsburg Road. Pickett's brigade was wasted. Rodes had not yet rejoined Hill, leaving his main attack with only five brigades—three of his own and two of Longstreet's. The possibility of the six brigades under Huger achieving any decisive action on the Charles City Road was questionable: the ground there was exceedingly swampy, and Hill had reported on May 30 that he did not believe there was any significant body of Federal troops within reach. Worse, the new attack plan entailed even more delays. Longstreet, Huger, and Hill met around 10:00 A.M. When the meeting adjourned, Longstreet's division—including Wilcox's detachment—pulled off to the side of the road and watched Huger's division march past.[45] This pointless leapfrog arrangement consumed still more precious time.

The continuing delays weighed more heavily in the mind of D. H. Hill than they apparently did in those of Longstreet or Huger. The aggressive North Carolinian had been waiting all morning to strike his blow, and following the meeting of the three generals he decided to take some actions of his own. He correctly reasoned that his right flank would be secured by Huger's six brigades quickly enough to risk recalling his own detached brigade to strengthen his attack. Either he asked Longstreet for permission, or on his own authority as division commander, Hill sent orders to Rodes not to wait for Huger's division to relieve him before rejoining the main body of the division. Even so, Rodes's Alabama and Mississippi regiments took a great deal of time struggling north through White Oak Swamp. "The men had to wade in water waist-deep and a large number were entirely submerged," Hill reported. "It was absolutely necessary to proceed with great caution to prevent the loss of both ammunition and life."[46]

Longstreet had not relieved Hill of the necessity of awaiting Huger's deployment on the right to initiate the attack, but by 1:00 P.M. Hill could not wait any longer. He lined his division up in a two-brigade front: Rodes's brigade south of the Williamsburg Road and Samuel Garland's to the north, supported by the brigades of Gabriel Rains and George B. Anderson. There was still no word from Huger, and only Rodes's skirmishers had arrived. Nonetheless, apparently on his own initiative, D. H. Hill fired his signal guns and sent his division forward.[47]

Advancing at the sound of the signal guns, Samuel Garland was unaware that, across the road, only Rodes's skirmishers were present and that for the first fifteen minutes his brigades would be attacking the Federal Fourth Corps by itself. The woods were too dense for Garland's regiments to keep their alignment, much less to discover that the brigade on their right had not moved. "The difficulties of the ground were almost insurmountable," Garland stated four days later:

The recent rains had formed ponds of water throughout the woods with mud at the bottom, through which the men waded forward knee-deep, and occasionally sinking to the hips in boggy places, almost beyond the point of extrication. The forest was so thick and the undergrowth so tangled that it was impracticable to see the heads of several regiments as they moved forward, and the deploying intervals were consequently very imperfectly preserved.[48]

Nonetheless, Garland's 2,200 men, unaware that they currently constituted the entire attacking force of Johnston's army, moved out aggressively. The Second Mississippi Battalion had been ordered out as skirmishers, with directions to remain at least 150 yards ahead of the main body of the brigade. In the confusion caused by the limited visibility, as the Mississippians became engaged with the first line of Yankee pickets, the remaining five regiments closed the distance and moved up through them. The Second Mississippi Battalion ceased to exist as a separate fighting force, even though it had taken as yet few casualties; individual companies and squads attached themselves to the nearest regiment and fought on their own for the remainder of the afternoon.[49]

This was only the beginning of the disintegration of the formal command structure of Garland's brigade and Hill's division. Within minutes, as his brigade hit the first line of Federal abatis, Garland began to lose control of events. His senior colonel, Duncan McRae of the Fifth North Carolina, who had been entrusted with the supervision of the brigade's right flank, had not completely recovered from his wound at Williamsburg. Physical exhaustion caused him to leave the field and forced Garland to move personally to the far right of his lines. It only required a few minutes for the brigade commander to restore order to the Tarheels, but while he did so Col. Daniel H. Christie's Twenty-third North Carolina had halted, believing it heard an order to retreat. Simultaneously, the only field officer in the Twenty-fourth Virginia, Maj. Richard L. Maury, was hit by Federal fire, leaving the brigade's largest regiment in confusion. His troops by then heavily engaged with the enemy and somewhat out of control, Garland began to wonder where his supporting brigade was. He wanted to send a courier back to speed Anderson's march to the battle but discovered that his entire staff was busy just trying to straighten out his own line of battle. "I trusted to Colonel Anderson's intuition as an accomplished soldier to perceive that we were hotly engaged," wrote Garland—trusting Anderson's instincts more likely from necessity than from choice. He was not disappointed: "As I anticipated, he arrived upon the scene just at the proper time."[50]

Colonel Anderson brought up his own 1,835 men, reinforced by two regiments from Richard Anderson's brigade of Longstreet's division, adding weight to Garland's attack just as it stalled. Yet the addition of six more regiments to the fight was only a mixed blessing. The impenetrability of the woods caused Anderson's regiments, like Garland's before them, to march forward in a somewhat haphazard fashion. The Twenty-eighth Georgia, for example, ended up on the right of the Forty-ninth Virginia when it entered the battle, after beginning the approach march on the Virginians' left. When Anderson's augmented brigade arrived at the forward line of the battle, the ability of Confederate commanders to control the attack diminished even further. Garland explained in his official report that "the passage of lines being a feat in tactics which had never been practiced by any of us, large fragments of those regiments who were left without field or company officers were joined in and continued forward with that brigade."[51]

Much the same thing occurred on the north side of the Williamsburg Road as had happened with Longstreet's division at Williamsburg several weeks earlier. Inadequate reconnaissance left regimental commanders blind. The attacking brigades became so intermingled that no one retained effective control. Brigade commanders scurried about the field rallying and reorganizing individual companies and regiments. The senior generals, in this case D. H. Hill and Richard Anderson, found themselves able to do little more than continue to pour reinforcements into the battle.

The brigades on the left of Hill's division, however, continued to make headway throughout the afternoon because Federal reactions were equally disjointed. Though he claimed that the capture of Lieutenant Washington alerted him to the possibility of an attack, the only action that Brig. Gen. Silas Casey took to prepare the troops in front of Garland was to support his picket line with a single regiment, the 430-man-strong 103d Pennsylvania. Casey did not order his division under arms until two Confederate artillery shells "were thrown over my camp," by which time the 103d Pennsylvania was trying to resist five times its own numbers. It held for about fifteen minutes. As Casey began to order his division into line—still in piecemeal fashion—the Pennsylvanians "came down the road in some confusion, having suffered considerable loss."[52] Nonetheless, with more than 4,200 men in his own three brigades, reinforced by as many men as Fourth Corps commander Erasmus Keyes could spare while organizing a second line of defense, Casey might have succeeded in holding his own against the Confederates attacking north of the Williamsburg Road. But fifteen minutes after Samuel Garland's men assaulted the 103d Pennsylvania, Robert Rodes finally brought his own brigade into the battle.

In his haste to open the battle, D. H. Hill committed an error very similar to that of Richard Anderson at Williamsburg: he did not pay enough attention to one of his flanks. By the time Garland's brigade had deployed in the line of battle, Hill could see elements of two regiments from Rodes's brigade on the south side of the Williamsburg Road. Colonel John B. Gordon's Sixth Alabama had spread out in front as skirmishers, and Col. William H. Taylor's Twelfth Mississippi had fallen in about 150 yards behind them. Rodes warned Hill that he could not possibly have the remainder of the brigade in place for at least another fifteen minutes and possibly as much as half an hour. Nonetheless, Hill had resolved to order the attack.

This decision presented Rodes with the difficult tactical problem of just how to get his brigade, arriving unit by unit and already exhausted by its passage through the swamps, into the battle as quickly as possible. He could already hear the sound of musketry on his left to indicate that Garland was engaged. In an instant, Rodes reacted with the type of decisiveness that began that day to mark him as one of the premier, small-unit tacticians of the army: he determined to attack immediately en echelon, bringing each regiment through the dense woods into the battle in successive lines. As he closed with the Yankees—literally under their guns—Rodes intended to redeploy his units from parallel lines into a brigade front with all five regiments abreast.[53] The maneuver was more than audacious; it was downright dangerous. Garland's brigade to his left had already proven unable to perform a passage of the lines of its own skirmishers and had been thrown into total disorder by its reinforcements. What Rodes prepared to do was more complicated by several orders of magnitude.

Yet despite appalling casualties, Rodes's brigade managed to implement its commander's plan. Gordon's Sixth Alabama capitalized on the fact that the Federal pickets to the north of the road were distracted by the firing there, advanced without pause over the first line of abatis, and threatened Casey's main line of rifle pits almost before anyone knew they had attacked. Gordon himself was the first man through Casey's line of outposts, leaping his horse over the abatis and shouting for his men to follow him through. Though the cry "Shoot that man on horseback!" echoed through the Federal line, the colonel miraculously continued to press home his attack unscathed.[54]

Union resistance stiffened beyond the first pickets, however, and the Sixth Alabama and Twelfth Mississippi stalled in front of Casey's main line of defense. Rodes placed himself at the head of the Fifth Alabama as it struggled up from its trek from the Charles City Road and led it to support the Mississippians. His remaining two infantry units—a heavy artillery battalion under Capt. C. C. Otey and the Twelfth Alabama—had been instructed to enter the line of battle at predesignated points as they marched up. If everything proceeded as planned, the 2,200 men of the brigade would be in action within half an hour.

Of course the conditions under which Rodes operated were no better than those that bedeviled Garland on the far side of the road. The woods were so thick that Rodes himself lost track of half the Fifth Alabama, ending up on the flank of the Twelfth Mississippi with only five companies. The heavy artillery battalion, new to the army and composed primarily of older men who had never intended to be infantry in the first place, decided that it had been given orders to halt short of the battle. The Twelfth Alabama, ordered to the far right flank, had discovered easier ground and advanced out of step with the rest of the brigade, to the point of crowding Gordon's skirmishers.[55]

Rodes's brigade was poised, at that moment, on the point of the same degenerating confusion that had already made a shambles of the command structure on the left of the division. That did not happen here, however, due to Rodes's skill, the high standard of training in his brigade, the movements of his supporting brigade, and a healthy dose of luck. The lost companies of the Fifth Alabama, under their field officers, reoriented themselves and arrived as a unit on the opposite side of the Twelfth Mississippi, allowing Rodes to reunite the entire regiment during a momentary break in the firing. He personally bullied the heavy artillery battalion into the fight. Colonel Robert T. Jones of the Twelfth Alabama joined Gordon's Sixth Alabama on the far right of the brigade, and without orders, provided enfilading fire against the Federal line.

At this juncture, Rodes's original orders called for him to sidestep his entire brigade to the right, allowing Rains's brigade to attack through his lines. Rains had perceptively noticed that Rodes had his hands full just forming his brigade under fire and was certainly not preparing to perform a right oblique march. So the commander of the supporting brigade swung his own regiments around the right of Rodes's units. The maneuver proved decisive, despite the considerable amount of time it took Rains's men to pick their way through the swamps and Rodes's later complaints that Rains had left his men without support for too long a period. Rains's attack, when it came, rolled up Casey's left flank and levered his entire division from its line.[56]

It had taken about two hours to drive the Federals from their defensive line, and the Confederate attack continued to roll forward far more because of momentum than from planning or organization. Hill's main role after 3:00 P.M. was to try to keep his brigades separate and moving forward at roughly the same pace. He fed reinforcements into the battle more cautiously now, paying close attention to avoiding the kind of snafu that had threatened to paralyze his left in the early going.

Longstreet's role in the battle after it opened was far less significant than Hill's. He had released Anderson and Kemper to the division commander before the opening of the attack, so when Hill committed their troops it was on his own initiative. Longstreet never appeared anywhere near the front line of the battle. His sole contribution to Hill's attack seems to have been to order Wilcox's brigade to countermarch yet again, back from Charles City Road to the Williamsburg Road, where it arrived too late to make any real contribution to the battle. By the time Longstreet wrote his 4:00 P.M. note to Johnston that his men were driving the enemy, Hill had supervised—if loosely—all the fighting. That fighting had been done, thanks to Longstreet's orders, by just six of thirteen available brigades.[57]

Yet there was more than a kernel of truth in Longstreet's contention that he had defeated the Yankees and that they needed only one more sharp push to disintegrate the Fourth Corps, if not also the Third. Despite substantial reinforcements from Samuel Heintzelman's Third Corps, which had arrived to bolster his position, and the fact that he had enjoyed several hours to deploy Darius Couch's division as Casey's men slowly crumbled, Keyes could not hold his second line. Hill's men, admittedly at the cost of murderous casualties, sent the Yankees reeling back again. By this point Hill's reinforced division had captured ten cannon and held a field scattered with "6,700 muskets and rifles in fine con-dition, ordnance, commissary, and medical stores."[58] A flank attack down the Nine Mile Road might well have delivered the coup de grâce, at least to the extent of routing two Federal corps back to the Chickahominy.

By the time that Johnston received Longstreet's message, the conditions under which such an attack would have been possible had changed. Even as Johnston frantically prepared to attack with Whiting's division, another Fed-eral corps commander took decisive action to save the day for the Army of the Potomac. Edward Sumner's Second Corps, deployed along the north bank of the Chickahominy between the Upper and Lower Bridges, was the portion of McClellan's army closest to the fighting. The bridges were underwater, and Sumner was the commander who had vacillated so long at Williamsburg that he allowed Winfield Scott Hancock's flanking action to accomplish nothing. It should have been a recipe for disaster, yet when the moment came on May 31, Sumner did not hesitate. At 1:00 P.M., McClellan advised him that an attack had commenced south of the river and ordered Sumner "to be in readi-ness to move at a moment's warning." At 2:30 P.M. the call came to cross the bridges and march to support Keyes and Heintzelman. Perhaps here the dif-ference from Williamsburg was that Sumner was not in overall command; he merely had to react to orders. His division commanders, Israel B. Richardson and John Sedgwick, were instructed to cross the Chickahominy, regardless of the condition of the bridges. "Our men," reported Richardson, "were obliged to wade (part of the bridge having been swept away) nearly up to their mid-dles in water, and of course could follow but slowly."[59] By 4:00 P.M. Sedg-wick's division was marching into position on the Federal right at Seven Pines, and the advance by Whiting's division did not hit the flank of a defeated enemy but encountered three fresh brigades of unbloodied Yankees.

Johnston ordered Hood's brigade into the woods and swamps between the Nine Mile and Williamsburg Roads in an attempt to link Whiting's right flank with Hill's left. The Texans obligingly angled off into the forest and promptly got lost, removing themselves from the remainder of the battle. The army commander planned to send J. J. Pettigrew's and Whiting's brigades abreast in line of battle down the Nine Mile Road. When Smith brought up Wade Hampton and Robert Hatton, the former would extend the line and the lat-ter would become the division reserve.[60] It was a relatively orthodox deploy-ment for those four brigades, marred only by two facts: there were three different generals supervising the move, and nobody knew that Sedgwick's division was in the woods.

By taking personal command of the division, Johnston, in his anxiety, had both abdicated his role as army commander and also reduced Smith and Whiting to high-ranking supernumeraries. He sent Smith dashing back and forth—first to bring up Hampton and Hatton; again to modify their marching orders; and finally, when contact was made at Fair Oaks Station, to detach brigades from John Magruder farther down the river. These were errands that any competent lieutenant serving as an aide de camp should have been able to handle. Johnston kept Whiting at his side; although he issued his own orders through the division commander, Johnston did not allow him to function as a commanding general. In the case of Smith, Johnston's actions were understandable, if not laudable. In the case of Whiting, who was one of Johnston's most trusted subordinates, his usurpation of the brigadier general's command revealed just how severely he was feeling the strain of battle. As a result of these unwieldy command arrangements, Whiting's division took far longer than it should have to deploy for battle. Hood had simply disappeared. Hampton's brigade, blundering around in the woods, almost engaged in a fire fight with Pettigrew's men.[61] As the sun began to sink, the division finally moved forward, only to run into the unexpected fire of Sedgwick's division.

Two batteries of Federal artillery, supported by two of Sedgwick's brigades, the First under Brig. Gen. Willis A. Gorman and the Third under Brig. Gen. Napoleon J. T. Dana, had arrived in the vicinity of Fair Oaks Station. Sedgwick himself was farther down the line, supervising the movement of his other brigade as it connected with the right flank of the hard-pressed Third and Fourth Corps at Seven Pines. This left the immediate direction of the bulk of his division in Sumner's hands.[62]

Whiting, ever pessimistic, had warned Johnston that the Federals might have crossed the river. Sensing a chance to win a victory regardless of the day's miscues, Johnston ignored him. "Oh!" one of Whiting's staff officers recalled the army commander exclaiming, "General Whiting, you are too cautious." When the Union artillery opened on the unsuspecting Confederates, the response of the leading brigades was an immediate, uncoordinated attack. This assault failed in short order. Since it had occurred more or less spontaneously and had not involved all the personnel of the three brigades, the troops rallied quickly. They were ordered in again.[63]

This attack involved the four available brigades and was pressed with a great deal more vigor. Gorman, whose troops supported one of the batteries, reported "as severe a fire of musketry as ever was witnessed or heard, perhaps, by the oldest officers of the army." Virtually invisible in the woods and supported by twelve cannon, the Federal troops at Fair Oaks made up for the ignominious retreat of their comrades at Seven Pines. Neither Gorman's nor Dana's brigades suffered more than 200 casualties; the four brigades of Whiting's division took nearly 1,300. Three of his four engaged brigadiers went down: Hatton killed, Pettigrew seriously wounded and captured, Hampton shot in the foot. As dusk began to fall, it was no longer a question of whether Whiting's men could break through the enemy but whether they could hold their ground.[64]

The abortive attack of Whiting's division highlighted the tactical mismanagement of the Battle of Seven Pines. Johnston started his brigades forward without any attempt to reconnoiter for Yankees along their route of march. By accompanying the division personally, the army commander not only confused its chain of command but also removed himself from the best location on the field from which to coordinate reinforcements. There was no one left at his former headquarters with either complete knowledge of the battle plan or authority to shift troops in Johnston's absence. If McClellan had been industrious enough to counterattack Johnston's far left flank, there would have been no way for A. P. Hill to request reinforcements quickly. Given these circumstances, why did Johnston decide to supervise Whiting's attack in person?

Three answers suggest themselves, all of which may have affected the army commander's choice, and they rest upon a clear understanding of the mental strain Johnston felt in the late afternoon hours of May 31. Johnston had been conscious of his growing cadre of observers since before dawn. Smith, who had every reason to be a critical witness, had been with him since first light, accompanied by his entire staff. Whiting, who had ridden up as his division approached at midmorning, also hovered around headquarters all day. Though Johnston counted him as a friend, Whiting represented another officer whose opinion of the army commander's capabilities might suffer as the result of a botched battle. Then Lee arrived sometime around noon—his rank and his position both made his presence disconcerting to Johnston as he waited for the battle to open. Finally, about 4:00 P.M., as Johnston received Longstreet's note, Davis himself cantered down the Nine Mile Road to join the impromptu entourage that had gathered.[65]

The president's arrival may have been the last straw for Johnston. He knew that Davis's opinion of his administrative ability had been marred by the recent excursions to the front when the chief executive had been greeted by disorganization and nonexistent attacks. He could also be sure that Davis, unlike Lee, would immediately open any conversation with direct inquiries into the progress of the battle. With Smith around and fully aware of the original design, Johnston would be forced to admit that nothing had thus far transpired in accordance with his wishes. He would have to tell Davis that Longstreet had taken the wrong road, that the attack had opened six to eight hours late, and that no one on the Nine Mile Road had been sure enough that the fight had begun to launch the left wing into action promptly. On the other hand, if Johnston rode off with Whiting's division he would escape such a painful situation, at least for the moment. If Whiting's attack succeeded, and he could bring back tidings that included the destruction of at least one Federal corps, then he could reasonably expect that the embarrassing post mortems would be delayed for a much longer time and might be avoided forever in the flush of a desperately needed victory.

It is also possible that Johnston, whose ambitious strain always made him consider the question of personal reputation and ultimate credit for battles won, rode with Whiting's division not because he feared the president's inquisition, but because he scented victory. Johnston never forgot that at Manassas he had dispatched Beauregard to the threatened flank instead of going there himself. In his *Narrative* he wrote, "After assigning Beauregard to the command of the troops immediately engaged, which he properly suggested belonged to the second in rank, not to the commander of the army, I returned to the supervision of the whole field." After that battle, notes Freeman, "there was praise for Johnston, to be sure," yet "the concentration of the two armies, not less than the victory itself, was assumed to be the work of Beauregard." Nothing that Johnston said or wrote, then or later, ever managed to dispel this impression. If Whiting or Longstreet delivered the knockout blow at Seven Pines while Johnston remained again at headquarters, it must have occurred to him that history might well repeat itself.[66]

Both explanations reflect less than favorably on Johnston's personal integrity. They imply that the army commander might base his actions on personal motives—and not on purely military considerations—even under the strain of a battle that had spiraled out of his control. There is also the possibility that the overriding concern in Johnston's mind was one of command. His two most trusted lieutenants had each botched a major operation: Smith by declining to attack on May 28, and Longstreet that morning by following the wrong road. The Kentuckian and the Georgian were the two generals whom Johnston had always considered not only competent but absolutely indispensable. If he could not safely assign missions to them, how could he rely on their juniors? When the instant came in which Johnston expected to strike the decisive blow, he may well have acted on a belief that the only way to ensure himself an immediate and aggressive movement was to lead it himself.

It should be emphasized, however, that Johnston's choice to accompany Whiting's division was made in minutes if not seconds. The preceding considerations may have influenced him to a greater or lesser degree, but in the necessity for haste that he felt on the receipt of Longstreet's note Johnston had precious little time to think the options through. He did not have the luxury of hours to brood and rationalize, as Longstreet had had the previous night—he had to determine his course as immediately as did Rodes when he brought his brigade into the fighting south of the Williamsburg Road. It is quite possible that these considerations passed so rapidly through the army commander's mind that later, upon reflection, he could not reconstruct his reasons even to himself.[67]

Certainly there was no occasion for such reflection that evening. As it became obvious that Whiting's division had been stalemated and as the evening shadows grew longer and longer, Johnston realized that his army could not follow up the blow that had sent two Federal corps reeling, at least not that day, though despite the result at Fair Oaks Station, Longstreet's partial victory might be completed with another attack the following morning. "So I announced to my staff officers," Johnston recalled, "that each regiment must sleep where it might be standing when the contest ceased for the night, to be ready to renew it at dawn next morning."[68]

The battle, if it was to continue on June 1, would have to do so in his absence. Johnston had hardly given those orders when a stray musket ball hit him in the right shoulder. Though it inflicted little more than a superficial wound, the effects of the random fragment of a Federal artillery shell that then slammed into his chest were far more serious. The impact unseated him from his saddle, and though he never lost consciousness it was a dazed and severely wounded Johnston that his aides carried off the field.

He did not yet realize it, but Joseph E. Johnston's campaign in the defense of Richmond had abruptly ended.

12

JOHNSTON'S CAMPAIGN: AN ASSESSMENT

As cynical as the proposition appears, dying in battle at the proper moment can do great things for a general's reputation, but surviving even a great victory can be a dreadful mistake. The American Civil War was full of examples that prove both assertions. The death of Albert Sidney Johnston from the fatal wound he received on the first day of the Battle of Shiloh deflected the criticism of his conduct of operations during the months preceding the battle. From the standpoint of his entrance into the pantheon of Confederate legends, no novelist or scriptwriter could have imagined a more dramatic end for Stonewall Jackson than to be shot down by his own men at Chancellorsville, in the hour of one of his most audacious and successful maneuvers.

On the opposite side of the coin, by surviving Gettysburg both George Meade and George Pickett found themselves forced to endure the decline of their reputations from glory into mediocrity. Meade lived to be castigated for failing to pursue Robert E. Lee's beaten army, raked over the coals by an unsympathetic congressional committee, superseded by Ulysses S. Grant, and eventually denied the post of commanding general of the postwar U.S. Army in favor of a man who had been his junior throughout the war. Pickett faced humiliation and defeat at Five Forks and questions after the war about how he, among all the generals and all but one of the field officers in his three brigades, had avoided Yankee fire in the charge that destroyed his division. Ironically, the verdict of peers and historians on both men would probably have been much more favorable if Meade had fallen defending Cemetery Ridge and Pickett had died assaulting it.

Joseph E. Johnston's recuperation from the wounds he received at Seven Pines landed him in the company of Meade and Pickett rather than with Jackson or the other Johnston. By the time Johnston had recovered sufficiently to return to active duty, Lee had an undisputable claim to command of the Army of Northern Virginia. He had driven George McClellan away from

Richmond in the Seven Days Battles, routed John Pope at Second Manassas, invaded Maryland, and fought the Army of the Potomac to a bloody stand-still at Antietam Creek. When Lee's accomplishments were compared to Johnston's record—partial credit for victory at First Manassas, a minor defensive success at Williamsburg, and the disjointed stalemate at Seven Pines—it was obvious that no one could expect Jefferson Davis to remove Lee from command in order to reinstate Johnston. Yet the president could hardly be accused of injustice to the man who had become the Confederacy's second ranking field general. Johnston was assigned in November 1862 to command Department no. 2, a vast theater that included both Braxton Bragg's Army of Tennessee and John Pemberton's army defending Vicksburg. It was not a fortunate assignment. Johnston, who would have preferred to lead any single field army, saw his authority as "little more than nominal."[1] He quarreled with the president over strategy, complained that he could never get Pemberton to follow his orders, and presided over the Confederate debacle at Vicksburg. With defeat came frenzied rounds of mutual recriminations that extended to generals and politicians alike; Johnston did not escape unscathed.

Yet Vicksburg did not end Johnston's career as it did Pemberton's. After the disastrous defeat at Missionary Ridge in November 1863, the president set personal rancor aside and appointed Johnston to succeed Bragg in command of the Army of Tennessee. Johnston's administrative abilities paid immediate dividends in the restoration of morale and efficiency to his dispirited divisions, and when the campaign of 1864 opened he was back in the spotlight again, defending Atlanta against William Tecumseh Sherman while Lee resisted Grant before Richmond. Old disagreements and mutual distrust quickly resurfaced between the president and the general. Johnston's Fabian policy of retreating, with the avowed intent of drawing Sherman deeply enough into Confederate territory to ensure his army's destruction, did not suit Davis at all. By mid-July, Johnston had backed up to the suburbs of Atlanta, and when Jefferson could not get from the army commander what he considered to be sufficient guarantees of offensive action, the president sacked Johnston in favor of John Bell Hood. Hood attacked, losing thousands of men and the city. Johnston claimed that he had been on the verge of launching a successful offensive when relieved; Davis countered that the general in fact had been on the verge of abandoning Atlanta without a fight.

The final postscript to Johnston's career was his recall in February 1865, this time at the insistence of Lee, to undertake the hopeless task of trying to halt Sherman's rampage through the Carolinas. His reputation and his administrative capabilities allowed Johnston to cobble together the last army the Confederacy ever fielded. With it, Johnston scored a small tactical victory at the Battle of Bentonville on March 19, attacking an isolated wing of Sherman's army, but it was far too late to have any effect on the course of the war.

When the war ended it was followed in remarkably short order by a war of words among former Confederate politicians and military officers, scrambling to avoid being assessed the responsibility for the South's defeat. Men who once had fought and bled together divided into new camps and attacked each other with a petty vindictiveness that often served more to diminish their reputations than to protect them. Carefully worded statements of fact—as misleading as they were true—along with innuendo, edited documents, artfully doctored reminiscences, and outright lies were the weapons in this second, far less honorable conflict.

None of the principals in Johnston's defense of Richmond managed to remain above the mudslinging. The memoirs and articles of Joseph Johnston, Jefferson Davis, Gustavus Smith, and James Longstreet were colored by self-justification and marred by inaccuracies, as were those of lower ranking officers from Jubal Early to John Gordon, Armistead Long to John Bell Hood. For anyone determined to pick his way through the literary charges and counter-charges in order to reconcile all the discrepancies, the task represents an assignment as hazardous as that handed to the Yankee pickets who had to enter Yorktown after Gabriel Rains had booby-trapped the town with explosives.

The campaign to defend Richmond represents a particular problem for the historian intent on assessing Johnston's performance as a general, for the course of events leading up to Seven Pines has received relatively little attention, even among the writers of memoirs. This neglect stems in part from the fact that the defense of Richmond in 1862 ended successfully, but those of Vicksburg and Atlanta did not. Generals rarely feel the need to defend victorious campaigns. When the question of Johnston's Peninsula campaign did arise in memoirs, it was often merely as a blind for some argument about Vicksburg or Atlanta. Hood, for example, voiced the contention that Johnston had supposedly contemplated the evacuation in 1862 as a rationale for believing that he would have deserted Atlanta in 1864.[2] To evaluate Johnston's performance in 1862 fairly then, it is necessary to approach that campaign as much as possible without reference to later battles or subsequent controversies. In one sense, it is almost necessary to pretend that Johnston's wound at Seven Pines indeed proved fatal in order to reach a judgment on his capacity as a general at that time.

Johnston quickly convinced himself that his injuries had snatched victory from his grasp. In his initial report, filed June 24, 1862, Johnston ignored James Longstreet's mistake in following the Williamsburg Road (he also asked Gustavus Smith to purge a reference to it from his own report) and relied heavily on the Georgian's recounting of the fighting in front of Seven Pines. Longstreet, anxious to find a scapegoat for his delay in opening the attack, blamed Benjamin Huger for not marching into position on time. Johnston picked this up and asserted that had "Major-General Huger's Division been in position and ready for action when those of Smith, Longstreet, and Hill moved, I am satisfied that Keyes's corps would have been destroyed instead of being merely defeated."[3]

Eventually, due primarily to the efforts of Gustavus Smith, Huger was exonerated of the charge that he did not arrive at his designated objective on time. Johnston, still convinced that a decisive success had only narrowly eluded him, shifted the ground of his argument and laid the blame on Smith. "*Darkness only*" halted the battle on May 31, Johnston contended, but after the army was turned over to Smith there was "no serious fighting" on June 1, even though "advantage of position and superiority of numbers would have enabled them to defeat [Keyes's] corps had the engagement been renewed on Sunday morning." Smith spent thirty years presenting evidence to disprove this assertion, arguing that he had attempted to attack on the second day, only to be frustrated by Longstreet's inaction; but he never managed to escape the image of a general who folded under the strain of combat. Douglas Southall Freeman, the first historian to examine the evidence closely, has condemned Smith for "vacillation, overcaution and conflicting orders" on June 1. Though Johnston's rationalizations changed, he enjoyed great success for many years in advancing the idea that, like P. G. T. Beauregard, who was almost universally blamed for not pressing home the attack on Grant after Sidney Johnston fell at Shiloh, Smith was the culprit for not delivering the coup de grâce at Seven Pines.[4]

Though there was in truth very little to praise in Smith's conduct of the battle on June 1, Johnston's accusation that he forfeited the fruits of a hard-won victory was without any factual basis. By Sunday morning there were equal numbers of Federal and Confederate soldiers on the field south of the Chickahominy, including fresh troops on both sides who had not participated in the previous day's fighting. Of the Union units that had been bloodied in D. H. Hill's attack, only a portion of Silas Casey's division had not been sufficiently reorganized to go into combat again. The Confederate advantage of surprise had certainly been lost. Casualties among general officers had been severe for a battle of no more than five hours and included the army commander and four of the ten brigade commanders actually engaged. Yankee confidence, far from being shattered, remained solid enough that almost all the actions of June 1 were Federal attacks.

The opportunity to smash at least Erasmus Keyes's Fourth Corps on May 31, on the other hand, had been very real. Had Johnston's original plan been executed, Keyes's six brigades would have been assaulted by thirteen Confederate brigades: three under Huger, four under Hill, and six under Longstreet. Union reinforcements available in the first two hours would only have been Samuel Heintzelman's six brigades; Johnston had four under Lafayette McLaws and five under W. H. C. Whiting in reserve. However, Johnston's relatively simple plan went hopelessly awry from the very beginning.

It is questionable to what extent Johnston may be faulted for Longstreet's carefully rationalized disobedience. Both Lee and Bragg discovered in turn that Longstreet, though undeniably talented, was incredibly willful, and his cooperation in operations of which he did not approve was notoriously poor. Nonetheless, given the vague nature of the orders Johnston dispatched to Huger, it is possible to suspect that Johnston may well have employed ambiguous language in his final oral orders to his wing commander. Although it is a military truism that no plan survives contact with the enemy, the army commander bears the responsibility to adapt to unexpected events. The delegation of an important mission such as Longstreet's supervisory authority over the attack of the right wing does not relieve the commanding general from the responsibility to maintain control of the various detachments of his army. In these terms, at the Battle of Seven Pines, Johnston failed miserably.

Johnston made no provisions for couriers or staff officers to move on a regular basis between the separated wings of his army so that he could be kept updated on the progress of each division. When the first reports arrived that Longstreet had taken the wrong road, Johnston wasted precious hours without deciding on a modified plan or a cancellation of the attack. In the event the sound of the signal guns did not carry, there was no backup plan for alerting units on the Nine Mile Road that the attack to the south had begun. Finally, Johnston totally abdicated his responsibility for the overall conduct of the battle when he led Whiting's division down the Nine Mile Road toward Fair Oaks Station.

It must be noted that similar failings bedeviled almost every commanding general, Confederate or Union, in his first offensive battle. Civil War battles were almost all planned and fought by generals who had never commanded more than a single regiment under fire before 1861. Lee at Mechanicsville, Bragg at Stone's River, Hood at Peachtree Creek, and Beauregard at Drewry's Bluff committed the same or comparable mistakes, as did George McClellan at Antietam, Joseph Hooker at Chancellorsville, Meade at Mine Run, Sherman at Chickasaw Bluffs, and Grant at Belmont. The good generals learned from their mistakes and slowly, painfully, improved their performances in subsequent battles. This process was, however, as Bruce Catton has pointed out with regard to Ulysses Grant, "at a prodigious cost to himself and to some thousands of young men who, without quite realizing it, had joined the Union Army in order to pay for his education."[5] In almost every case, it was difficult to render a valid judgment on the basis of the first offensive battle, because almost no one ever performed well. The value of a general could best be determined by observing whether he was able to improve upon this performance.

If Johnston had botched Seven Pines, he had not done so in a disastrous manner: he had not won, but he had not been defeated either, and his army survived to fight again. A man as realistic as Davis would have known that the proof would come the next time, and that, of course, was eventually the rub. Lee handled the Battle of Mechanicsville on June 26, 1862, little if any better than Johnston managed the Battle of Seven Pines. Lee's second attack, the Battle of Gaines's Mill, came the following day and proved that if he had not grown perfect overnight he was clearly capable of learning from his own mistakes. Johnston might well have been as able to learn from his own mistakes as Lee and might have proved it on June 1 had he not been wounded. Through choice or circumstance, however, Johnston did not fight another offensive battle until nearly three years later, at Bentonville.

That three-year gap between Seven Pines and Bentonville is the crux of the case for or against Johnston as a successful field general. Johnston's critics, who are currently in the ascendant and include historians of the quality of Albert Castel, William C. Davis, Joseph Glathaar, Richard McMurry, and Steven Woodworth, argue that the record reveals the general's fatal flaw: his personal inability to risk defeat on the battlefield. They argue that it requires not only rationalization but special pleading to discount every single opportunity to attack that existed in Mississippi in 1863 and Georgia in 1864. On the other hand, Johnston's partisans (a small group these days, restricted in great measure to Craig Symonds and myself, although the case can be made for Stephen Sears in this narrow regard) contend that Johnston did order several attacks, notably in 1864 at Resaca, Cassville, and Pickett's Mill. At Resaca half of Johnston's army *did* take the offensive, and a larger assault was planned for the second day, only to be canceled when Sherman flanked his communications. The abortive attacks at Cassville and Pickett's Mill foundered within the peculiar relationship between Johnston and Hood, which has depths that still remain unexplored.

The problem with Johnston's critics is not that they do not have a case, especially in 1863 and 1864, but that they insist on interpreting every single incident in the general's career from a particular perspective: that he was a man temperamentally incapable of committing himself to offensive battle. Having created this caricature, they maintain there is nothing that cannot be explained by it—even at the expense of chronology. For example, consider

Steven Woodworth's assessment of Johnston in an article on the Battle of Williamsburg: "He was the sort of general who could fearlessly expose his person to enemy fire but was paralyzed by fear at the thought of exposing his reputation to mishap in the ultimate test of an army commander's skill— pitched battle. For him, tomorrow was always a better day for fighting than today, and the day after was better still." It is possible to reach this conclusion only by arguing backward in time, explaining the general's actions in early May 1862 by his conduct two years later and by considering Johnston's personality, character, and capabilities as immutable constants that never changed throughout four years of war. For Woodworth, the entirety of Johnston's strategy on the Peninsula (or anywhere else) can be reduced to the following formulation: "Since defending the Peninsula meant immediate confrontation with the hostile army, Johnston preferred retreat, staying well clear of the enemy as long as possible and hoping in the shadow of Richmond to find more troops—or at least more nerve." In a similar vein, Richard McMurry asserts that "all of the great disasters that came during Johnston's 1862–1864 command in the West were adumbrated in the time that he directed operations in the Old Dominion."[6]

The chief problem with this interpretation of Joseph Johnston is that it does not explain anything about the man himself. If Johnston did possess an aversion to attacking, how did it develop? His record before the war suggests an ambitious man, perhaps obsessively so, but nothing that even hinted at a phobia about professional failure in battle. Indeed, Johnston, like most of his peers, seems to have entered the war with the naive belief that he was completely prepared and wholly competent to direct a great army in combat. Nothing prior to Seven Pines occurred that would have shaken this conviction, not Manassas, Yorktown, or Williamsburg. Johnston may be accused of flaws in his generalship but not of lacking confidence in his own abilities. By May 30, as he planned the next day's attack, Johnston thought he would solidify his reputation, not risk it.

A study of Johnston's defense of Richmond suggests that the first day of offensive battle at Seven Pines, interrupted by his wounding, may have had a more profound effect on the general than has heretofore been acknowledged. Had he been forced, like Lee, to absorb the lessons of May 31 and go back into battle the next day, much might have been different about the later career of Joseph Johnston. His wounds, however, stopped this process and almost froze his development as a field general forever. As he lay in his bed recovering from his wounds, Johnston began to rationalize his conduct of the attack into a position he could publicly defend, a stance from which he did not retreat for the remainder of his life. Yet he could not have escaped the personal knowledge that he had utterly failed to impose his will on events. How this conflict between Johnston's public image as the master general and the interior doubts left from Seven Pines affected his conduct of later campaigns has never been satisfactorily examined. Until it is, historians will lack a complete appreciation of one of the most important figures in Confederate history and his contribution to his nation's defeat.[7]

On the evening of May 31, 1862, however, these questions lay far in the future, and my purpose here is to evaluate the general's conduct within the confines of the Peninsula campaign. Based solely on his performance at Seven Pines (which was, after all, what Davis had to work with), a verdict on Johnston as battlefield commander would have been provisional: if he had not proved to be an immediate savant, he had not been an unmitigated disaster. His conduct rated another opportunity, and throughout the war Davis made good-faith efforts to give him that chance.

Johnston also claimed that, even allowing for his failure to crush Keyes's corps, the Battle of Seven Pines resulted in two favorable advantages for his successor. The attack had rocked McClellan enough to freeze him in his tracks for about three weeks, and this period of inaction provided enough time for Lee to receive substantial reinforcements: "General Lee did not attack the enemy until June 26th, because he was engaged from June 1st until then in forming a great army."[8] The first of these contentions was valid: McClellan's first reaction in the battle's aftermath was to demand that more troops be sent to him before he could advance.[9] Johnston's insistence that Lee benefited from this time to build a great army, which he had been denied, was inaccurate. Johnston cited the Army of Northern Virginia as having been augmented between June 1 and 26 by the divisions of Theophilus Holmes, Jackson, and Richard Ewell as well as by the brigades of Roswell Ripley and Alexander Lawton and miscellaneous troops. Johnston's argument here was spurious. Holmes and Ripley were in the Richmond area on May 31 and already subject to his orders. If he considered their participation critical to success, it required but a single day's delay in his battle plan. Jackson and Ewell were also under Johnston's command; they were unavailable at the end of May because Johnston himself had approved the operations in the Shenandoah Valley that detained them. In May 1862 Johnston clearly considered the absence of those two divisions to be compensated for by the corresponding absence of the armies of Nathaniel Banks and Irwin McDowell on his flanks. Thus, in Johnston's catalog of units sent to Lee during June, only Lawton's Georgia Brigade had not actually been near his army or under his control on May 31, and Lawton's regiments did not quite muster enough men—even by Johnston's own optimistic estimate—to do more than replace the battle losses of Seven Pines. The time won at Seven Pines benefited Lee by allowing Jackson to finish the Valley campaign, the troops already in transit to arrive, and to dig substantial entrenchments in front of Richmond.

The successes and failures of Seven Pines, however, were hardly the whole measure of Johnston's defense of Richmond up to May 31, 1862. Between the February conference in Richmond and Johnston's fall from his horse beside the Nine Mile Road, the Confederates had gained several important strategic advantages. Primarily, the campaign had bought three months of valuable time—time to produce or import weapons, time to muster and train new troops, and time to reorganize the army onto a wartime footing. The second material result of Johnston's campaign was that by the end of May the overwhelming numerical advantage of Union numbers—nearly a four-to-one superiority in February—had been reduced so far at the point of contact that Johnston's inferiority to the Army of the Potomac was roughly 10,000 men. In armies of 80,000 to 100,000 troops, this difference hardly represented a decisive disadvantage. Lee fared even better the next month, entering the Seven Days Battles with a slight numerical superiority and fielding the largest army the Confederacy ever sent into battle. This feat had been achieved by a combination of strategic juggling in Virginia and along the Atlantic Coast, where garrisons were stripped to bare essentials, and by the operational maneuvers of Confederate forces in Virginia, which led to the immobilization of Banks and McDowell. Finally, from the nucleus of detached garrisons, strung out across the Potomac frontier throughout winter 1861–1862, a solid, well-organized, maneuverable army had been formed: the Army of Northern Virginia. It was not, and it never became, a perfect organization, but the army that Johnston unknowingly and unwillingly bequeathed to Lee stood upon a firm foundation. These accomplishments cannot be ascribed to Joseph Johnston simply because he commanded the Department of Northern Virginia. Other key leaders, from Davis to Lee, Jackson to John Magruder, played essential roles in the defense of Virginia. To what extent therefore did Joseph Johnston contribute to the successes of early 1862?

The breathing spell won for the Confederacy in the Peninsula campaign was chiefly the result of three events: the Valley campaign, the siege of Yorktown, and the retreat up the Peninsula. Johnston's role in the Valley campaign was supportive but not seminal. He clearly envisioned the potential for combined operations between Jackson and Ewell when the rest of the army left northern Virginia for the Yorktown line, though he did not map out a specific strategy. He expected Jackson and Ewell to react opportunistically to Federal miscues. It was the correspondence of Lee and Jackson in late April that developed the original premises of the campaign that paralyzed several Federal armies and terrorized Washington. Nonetheless, Johnston supported the general thrust of the operation when he found out about it, and though his mid-May strategic concepts were slightly at variance with those of Lee and Jackson, they were equally workable. Johnston certainly never lost sight of the important contribution that active forces in the Valley and central Virginia could make to the defense of Richmond, and he never pursued a myopic strategy of concentration of all the troops in Virginia under his immediate control as a panacea to overcome his own manpower deficiencies.

Initial credit for the delay of McClellan at Yorktown has to be accorded without question to John B. Magruder. In the critical two weeks between March 17 and 31, he held his line with bravado and a paltry number of troops while Lee wrestled with the problems of determining McClellan's intentions and reinforced Magruder with agonizing slowness. From April 1 through Johnston's evacuation on May 3, 35,000 soldiers on the Peninsula would probably have bought the Confederacy as much time as the 70,000 eventually committed there. The only requirement of a commanding general throughout most of the month was a stolid resolution to defend the trenches and redoubts. Magruder himself, Longstreet, Smith, or even D. H. Hill had the skill and tenacity to maintain that line during April 1862. Johnston's contribution was twofold: he provided the only realistic evaluation of just how long Yorktown could be held and the insight to know exactly when it must be abandoned. The first, even though Johnston's views did not prevail during the April conference in Richmond, alerted both Lee and Davis to the amount of time that they could continue to defer making some tough choices. The second, if McClellan's own engineers are to be believed, at least saved the army thousands of casualties and possibly avoided its capture. Had Johnston's army remained in the Yorktown entrenchments when the Confederate batteries at Gloucester Point were dismounted, there would have been no troops far enough up the Peninsula to resist William Franklin's landing at West Point: the army would have been cut off from Richmond and assailed from both front and rear. Johnston's was the key decision that kept the siege of Yorktown from turning into an irredeemable disaster.

The month that the Army of the Potomac required to creep from Yorktown to Seven Pines must be attributed equally to Joseph Johnston and George McClellan. It is arguable that had Johnston merely decamped from Yorktown and never looked back, the Federal commander could have taken, in his own timidity, almost as long to approach Richmond as he did with Johnston retreating slowly and stopping periodically to offer battle. That possibility does not diminish Johnston's efficiency—only extremely incompetent generals depend on their enemies to do the wrong thing. Despite his failure to supervise the Battle of Williamsburg closely, Johnston's retreat was marked by skillful maneuver and strategic insight under difficult conditions. Clear thinking and careful supervision of the army's movements were needed to overcome the muddy roads and general scarcity of transportation. Johnston was able to overcome these hindrances and to balance the deployment of his four divisions so that two were present to handle the rearguard contest at Williamsburg and two were close enough to oppose an amphibious landing near West Point. The point between the Pamunkey and Chickahominy Rivers at which Johnston chose to end his retreat and await McClellan was selected based on a sound appreciation of his strategic position. His lines were clear of navigable water, logistically convenient to Richmond, and heavily enough wooded to negate partially McClellan's numerical advantage. It was also a line that, for as long as he held it, kept Johnston's army solidly between McClellan and McDowell. If the failure of the Richmond authorities to press the completion of the fortifications at Drewry's Bluff had not compelled Johnston to retreat across the Chickahominy, McClellan would have been faced with a serious operational dilemma. He would either have had to attack on ground of Johnston's own choosing, where his soldiers had been digging entrenchments and laying out abatis for three to five days, forfeiting the advantages of naval and heavy artillery, or he would have had to risk crossing the Chickahominy with the Confederates on his flank. Ultimately, fear of Federal ironclads and not McClellan forced Johnston from this position.

Thus, from an operational standpoint, Johnston performed quite well. He contributed to the Valley campaign, made the key decision at Yorktown, and handled the retreat up the Peninsula with efficiency and aplomb. If his initial conception of strategy in the Valley was somewhat hazy, he knew how to exploit the opportunities presented him. Confronted with multiple threats, his instincts were consistently sound, and, as in the case of his timing of the Yorktown evacuation, sometimes inspired.

As the commanding general of the Confederate army, it was Lee and not Johnston who found the steady stream of troops to reinforce the army between March and June. Lee made the best possible use of the time won by Johnston, Jackson, and Magruder to muster new troops and cajole governors and generals alike into accepting smaller forces in Georgia and the Carolinas. Lee took pains to see that when new regiments were organized they went to the static garrisons to replace more seasoned troops to reinforce the army in Virginia. Thus Johnston consistently received the best-trained brigades available in the eastern Confederacy. Yet Johnston had been the one participant in the April conference who insisted that it was feasible to reduce the coastal garrisons. He had argued his point adamantly; as an army commander there was really nothing else he could do.

Johnston consistently used his administrative skills to maintain the army assembled under him at the highest possible strength. From the winter through the spring, Joseph Johnston proved himself an exceptionally capable administrator, managing his limited supplies as efficiently as possible and combating desertion, malingering, sickness, malnutrition, and disaffection every day. Johnston conducted both the retreat from the Potomac and the retreat from Yorktown with minimal losses of critical supplies and supervised the transitional elections required by the Conscription Act in a manner that minimized their damage to the army's efficiency.

His instincts for command organization were sound but continually thwarted by Confederate law. He did not favor operating his army as separate divisions, realizing that such an arrangement was terminally unwieldy for an army in battle or on the march. His original organization of the army in northern Virginia had been in two corps of two divisions each, with a strong reserve division, which he maintained until the president ruled that the law did not recognize the position of corps commander. This glaring defect in Confederate military organization was not remedied until October 1862, with the creation of the rank of lieutenant general, but Johnston—like Lee after him—circumvented the statutes by creating unofficial wing commands under his senior division commanders. Gustavus Smith and James Longstreet commanded wings of two divisions each in the Manassas and Yorktown withdrawals. As his army grew when stationed on the Chickahominy by the subdivision of Magruder's command into two divisions and the addition of A. P. Hill and Huger, Johnston reorganized his army into three unofficial corps with an army artillery reserve and an independent cavalry force—an organization strikingly similar to the one employed by Lee after Chancellorsville.

Johnston's choices for command of wings and divisions proved that he had a keen if occasionally myopic eye for picking talented commanders. Discounting Magruder, who was incorporated into his army by virtue of his former departmental command, of Johnston's choices for senior positions, only Gustavus Smith failed in the rest of the war to justify his confidence. Longstreet, Jackson, Stuart, Ewell, A. P. Hill, Richard Anderson, Early, and Wade Hampton rose to corps command under Lee; D. H. Hill achieved the same position in the Army of Tennessee. Though he never advanced beyond division command, Whiting competently carried out the thankless task of defending the critical port city of Wilmington until the last months of the war. These men owed their initial recommendations for promotion to Johnston.

The allegation that Johnston turned over a demoralized and disorganized body of troops to Lee, who had to whip it quickly into shape, has persisted to the present day. Colonel Robert H. Chilton, who served faithfully on Lee's staff, contended after the war that the condition of the Army of Northern Virginia on June 1, 1862,

> appeared to me to be in a very disorganized condition. Large unauthorized absences of officers and men greatly weakened its force, exhausting wastefulness pervaded all departments, especially apparent with each change of camp, in the abandonment of supplies of different kinds, and a laxity of discipline prevailed, which greatly impaired the efficiency of this Army.[10]

Two facts should be noted about Chilton's statement, which is typical of the assertions made about the army's state in early June. First, Chilton himself later attributed these conditions not to any deficiencies in Johnston but to the deleterious effects of the recent elections and the necessity for fighting two battles in the same month. Second, Chilton's accusation conveniently ignored the fact that several of the staff officers whose departments he castigated, notably William Pendleton and Porter Alexander, were the same men who rapidly gained reputations for administrative excellence under Lee.

Douglas Southall Freeman has made a point of emphasizing Lee's administrative ability by exaggerating the condition of Johnston's army at the end of May:

> In some of its aspects discipline had been lax under Johnston; drunkenness had been frequent; many things were at loose ends. Some of the regiments reported a third of the troops sick. Lee worked as fast as he could to improve the condition of the men. The commissary and the quartermaster's service were improved. Favoritism in granting details for service in the rear was ended.[11]

Freeman's own footnotes reveal just how misleading this paragraph is. The allegation concerning drunkenness was supported only by a passage from gossipy War Office clerk J. B. Jones and a Confederate army regulation on stern penalties for drunkenness that was only issued on May 22, 1862. It neither referred specifically to the Army of Northern Virginia, nor was it available to support Johnston's own efforts to combat intoxication throughout his tenure in command. The statement regarding excessive sickness is buttressed not by army returns but by a single regimental history. Nothing is cited to support Freeman's contention that Lee made immediate improvement in the army's logistical services. The praise given Lee for ending "favoritism" in details comes from several documents that Lee submitted to the War Office complaining that the Richmond authorities had been the offenders, not Johnston and his officers, as Freeman's passage subtly implies. Indeed, Lee's missives to George Randolph and Samuel Cooper echoed complaints that Johnston had been making since fall 1861.

In one aspect and one aspect only did the status of the army immediately improve under Lee: relations with his civil superiors. Johnston and Davis both suffered from the same kind of stiff neck; neither could admit a fault gracefully. Nor could either man readily forgive transgressions. As the friction slowly built between the army commander and the chief executive over spring 1862, the necessary trust for a desperate campaign quietly eroded. Although Davis did not lose his respect for Johnston as a general, and Johnston never ceased to be formally respectful in his dealings with the president, from March through May Lee constantly had to intervene between them. Johnston was a prickly subordinate, and Davis was not an easy master to serve. In the necessary aspects of civil diplomacy required of a senior military officer in a republic, Johnston was plainly deficient and Lee was patently gifted. It was a failing that haunted Johnston for the rest of his career.

On balance, Johnston's performance as an army commander in Virginia should be rated as a success. He was far from perfect, and his two greatest deficiencies—the ability to control a battlefield closely and a knack for getting along with his superiors—would eventually develop into fatal flaws, but they were not such during the Peninsula campaign. Three years later, in a report drafted with the intention of humiliating Johnston, an embittered John Bell Hood said that "the results of a campaign do not always show how the General in command has discharged his duty. Their enquiry [*sic*] should be not what he has done, but what he should have accomplished with the means under his control."[12] Hood's standard was one that governments cannot always afford but that historians usually employ. By either standard, concrete results or credible performance, Joseph Johnston's defense of Richmond fares quite well.

Appendix A
The Deleted Paragraph from Joseph E. Johnston to Jefferson Davis, September 12, 1862
(Original in the Robert Morton Hughes Papers, Old Dominion University, Norfolk, Virginia)

"The spectacle which is presented in the conduct of the Governments on the two sides of the Potomac towards their Commanding Generals cannot fail to arrest our attention. The Commanding General of the Northern army, a veteran of more than fifty years is superseded by his junior of half his years, of scarcely one-fourth of his period of service, because defeated. He is merely removed, however, from the direct command. His superior rank is left him. When we look to the South of the same line, what do we see? The greatest and most important battle ever fought in America has been won. It has been won by a general [holding] the highest rank in his republic. It has been won by his leaving the District in which he commanded, making a forced march (of —— miles), forming a junction with an army too weak to maintain its ground, and by their united force, against immense odds, winning a victory, which in the minds of all men and nations establishes the glory and independence of the Confederate States, and crowns the army and its generals with the highest honor to which they could aspire: The applauding acclamation of the country, the Thanks of Congress, voted unanimously. Such is the first result presented to our view. What is the next reaped by the victorious General? What next? The General was already first in the highest grade known to the service—He could not be advanced. Something should be done—so he was degraded. Three officers, his inferiors in grade, and in service, for neither of them had fought or won a battle for the Republic, were placed above him. Besides all this, a study in dignity is offered him. His noble Compeer in the battle has his preferment connected with the victory won by their common toils and dangers. His commission bears the date of the 21st of July. But care is taken to exclude the idea that the general commanding had any part in winning our triumph. His commission is made to bear such a date that his once inferiors in the service of the United States, and of the Confederate States, shall be above him. But it must not be dated as of the 21st July. It shall (must) not suggest the victory of Manassas."

Appendix B
The Strength of Johnston's Army at Yorktown and Seven Pines

The only relatively complete return for Joseph Johnston's army on the Peninsula is dated April 30, 1862, lists the army as having 55,633 "effectives," and is the figure usually accepted for the army at Yorktown. It is defective, however, in several respects that render it far too low. First, it does not include any numbers for the Third Virginia Cavalry or the reserve artillery. Second, being effective returns, as the Confederates figured them, this return excluded officers and detailed men normally carried under the heading "present for duty" (PFD). Finally, these figures do not allow for the fact that the memorandum was compiled about two weeks after the balance of the army arrived at Yorktown. Hundreds, if not thousands, of men had been returned to Richmond hospitals or had wandered off in the interim.

In order to reconstruct Johnston's actual strength on the Peninsula it is necessary to account in some way for each of these factors. The strength of the Third Virginia Cavalry can be determined from John Magruder's April 23, 1862, return, which gives it, and two other independent companies of cavalry 923 enlisted men. Jennings Wise used the average strength of Johnston's other field batteries to calculate that there were 1,050 enlisted men in the reserve artillery. Thomas Livermore argued quite convincingly that the effective force of Confederate units represented between 85 percent (cavalry) and 93 percent (infantry and artillery) of the enlisted PFD. Thus 54,344 effective infantry and artillery equate with 58,434 enlisted PFD. Likewise, 2,221 effective cavalry equate with 2,613 enlisted PFD, giving a total enlisted PFD strength of 61,047 men. If one allows the lowest percentage that Livermore cites for officers in the Confederate army (6.5 percent), these men were probably accompanied by 3,968 officers, for a total PFD strength on April 30 of 65,015.

This figure still does not account for two weeks of debilitating sickness and desertions. From Magruder's report of April 23, only two units—the heavy artillery battalion and the artillery from Lafayette McLaws's division—can be determined with relative certainty to have had the same composition as they had a week later. The heavy artillerymen suffered a 10 percent decline in strength, and the field gunners, who presumably saw more service in the trenches, lost 20 percent. The lower of the two would correlate closely with the rate of illness and absence in the Department of Northern Virginia during the winter and seems therefore an acceptable percentage. If one takes the lower figure of 10 percent as a working number, then Johnston originally had 72,739 officers and men PFD when he assumed command.

Calculations of Johnston's strength around Richmond in late May 1862 begin with his May 21 memorandum of army composition and strength. Many of the figures had been drawn directly from the April 30 return at Yorktown just before the retreat, so it is certain that the army had lost several thousand men from those figures between April 30 and May 21. It is equally certain that many of the stragglers returned to the ranks, and many more were dragooned in Richmond by Johnston's or John Winder's provosts, so the figures for the four divisions, William Pendleton's artillery reserve, and the cavalry brigade still offer good approximation for the effective strength of the army on May 21. This figure is 53,688.

Significant reinforcements joined the army during the last ten days. Nine artillery batteries left Richmond for that purpose, which, calculated at the average effective strength of artillery companies at that time, would have fielded 560 men. The Fourth Virginia Heavy Artillery and four more companies of heavy artillery were also assigned to the army as infantry. The Fourth, with ten companies, had a strength of 466 men in late June, after Seven Pines. It is not disproportionate therefore to credit the other four companies with at least 200 men. Seventeen infantry companies of the Henry Wise Legion also joined the army. Fifteen of them reported their strength in late June, and adding in the other two at the average company strength yields 942 effectives. The Third Virginia Cavalry, which numbered at least 300 men, the Wise Legion Cavalry (later the Tenth Virginia), mustering at least 400, and several other miscellaneous companies of cavalry around Richmond—probably at least 240 men—are not accounted for in Johnston's memorandum, which would increase the size of the cavalry force by another 940 effectives.

Benjamin Huger's division at Seven Pines has been estimated anywhere from 5,008 effectives by G. W. Smith and Jefferson Davis to 7,000 by Johnston himself. A more likely strength seems to be 6,257, calculated by Livermore. This excludes the Sixth, Sixteenth, Fifty-sixth, and Fifty-seventh Virginia, left at Drewry's and Chaffin's Bluffs. Assuming these regiments to have averaged the same as Huger's other regiments, this number would add another 1,200 troops to his roster.

A. P. Hill's division has been underestimated by almost all authorities since G. W. Smith placed its numbers at a ludicrously low 4,000 men. This figure is hardly possible, considering the four brigades and other miscellaneous troops that composed the division. Charles Field's brigade (augmented by the Ninth Virginia Cavalry) reported 2,200 men. Joseph Anderson's brigade came to Virginia with 2,873 effectives and had seen no combat to reduce its numbers. Robert E. Lee had sent more than 3,000 men from Richmond to the Rappahannock in mid-April, and Maxcey Gregg's brigade, by subtraction in one of Lee's letters, should be credited with 2,127 men. From these figures should be subtracted about 900 casualties—the highest estimate—incurred at Hanover Courthouse.

All these figures, however, are for effectives. Converting them to PFD strength yields a total number of troops in Johnston's army on May 31 of 87,890. This total is still short of Confederate manpower resources available near the capital. In Richmond there were between 2,600 and 4,800 officers and men. The lower figure allows 700 for the heavy artillery, 500 for the militia, 400 for the Tredegar battalion, and 1,000 for the miscellaneous troops. The higher number counts the heavy artillery at 1,400, the militia at 1,000, the Tredegar battalion still at 400, and the other troops at 2,000. From contemporary evidence it is difficult to hone these estimates any closer. Roswell Ripley's brigade, estimated by Livermore at 2,356 effectives, and John Walker's, reported in mid-April as having 3,693 effectives, were both approaching Richmond that afternoon. Following the same conversion process for these brigades, and adding in the troops at Richmond, would result in an additional 6,923 PFD—even excluding the heavy artillerymen, marines, and naval troops still at Drewry's Bluff. The total number then would be at least 94,813 PFD in the vicinity of Richmond.

These figures are an approximation, and each of the precise calculations could be challenged, but the methodology is that which is most widely accepted and indicates that Johnston's army on the Peninsula was indeed much stronger than has heretofore been suggested.

See *OR*, 9: 459; 11 (Part 3): 204, 458, 460, 523, 525, 530–33, 539, 540, 542, 558, 563, 615; 12 (Part 1): 434; Livermore, *Numbers and Losses,* pp. 67–70, 81–86; Smith, *Seven Pines,* pp. 172–73; Davis, *Rise and Fall,* 2: 153; Johnston, "Manassas to Seven Pines," *B&L,* 2: 208–9; Archer Anderson to

Joseph E. Johnston, September 14, 1887, in RMH; Robert E. Lee to Abraham C. Myers, April 29, 1862, Robert E. Lee to Samuel P. Moore, April 29, 1862, Robert E. Lee to John H. Winder, May 3, 1862, in *Lee Letterbook;* Returns of the Department of Northern Virginia, October–December 1861, in JJWM.

NOTES

1. THE GENERAL

1. Joseph E. Johnston, *Narrative of Military Operations Directed During the Late War Between the States* (Bloomington: Indiana University Press, 1959), 139–43; Joseph E. Johnston, "Manassas to Seven Pines," in *Battles and Leaders of the Civil War,* ed. Robert U. Johnson and Clarence C. Buel, 4 vols. (New York: Century, 1887), 2: 215 (hereafter cited as *B&L*).

2. Benjamin S. Ewell to Joseph E. Johnston, May 4, 1885, in Robert Morton Hughes Collection, Old Dominion University, Norfolk, Virginia (hereafter cited as RMH); Gustavus W. Smith, "Two Days of Battle at Seven Pines," *B&L*, 2: 227; Gustavus W. Smith, *The Battle of Seven Pines* (New York: C. C. Crawford, 1985), 66; see also U.S. War Department, *The War of the Rebellion: A Compilation of the Official Records of the Union and Confederate Armies,* 128 vols. (Washington, DC: Government Printing Office, 1880–1891), Series 1, 11 (Part 1): 943–46 (hereafter cited as *OR;* all references are to Series 1 unless otherwise indicated).

3. Jefferson Davis, *The Rise and Fall of the Confederate Government,* 2 vols. (New York: D. Appleton, 1881), 2: 120; John B. Hood, *Advance and Retreat* (1880; rpt., Secaucus, NJ: Blue and Grey, 1985), 153–55; Stephen W. Sears, *To the Gates of Richmond* (New York: Ticknor and Fields, 1992), 120; Steven E. Woodworth, *Davis and Lee at War* (Lawrence: University Press of Kansas, 1995), 103–8, 132–35; Richard M. McMurry, "Ole Joe in Virginia: Gen. Joseph E. Johnston's 1861–1862 Period of Command in the East," in *Leadership and Command in the American Civil War,* ed. Steven E. Woodworth (Campbell, CA: Savas Woodbury, 1995), 14–21; Joseph T. Glathaar, *Partners in Command, The Relationships Between Leaders in the Civil War* (New York: Free Press, 1994), 112–17. One of the relatively scarce pro-Johnston viewpoints is presented in Craig L. Symonds, *Joseph E. Johnston, A Civil War Biography* (New York: W. W. Norton, 1992), 140–75.

4. Tredegar Iron Works cast 164 pieces of field artillery and 39 heavy guns between January and June 1862; the Richmond arsenal produced at least 6,000 muskets. Between April 27 and August 16, 1862, more than 48,000 small arms slipped through the blockade into Wilmington, Charleston, or Savannah, more than three times the number of weapons imported between September 1861 and February 1862. See Charles B. Dew, *Ironmaker to the Confederacy: Joseph R. Anderson and the Tredegar Iron Works* (1966; rpt., Wilmington, NC: Broadfoot, 1987), 111; Richard D. Goff,

Confederate Supply (Durham, NC: Duke University Press, 1969), 31; Larry J. Daniel, "Manufacturing Cannon in the Confederacy," *Civil War Times Illustrated* 12, no. 7 (November 1973): 10; Frank Vandiver, ed., *Confederate Blockade Running Through Bermuda, 1861–1865, Letters and Cargo Manifests* (Austin: University of Texas Press, 1947), xviii, xxiv; Stephen R. Wise, *Lifeline of the Confederacy: Blockade Running During the Civil War* (Columbia: University of South Carolina Press, 1988), 55–73; Thomas L. Livermore, *Numbers and Losses in the Civil War in America, 1861–1865* (1900; rpt., Dayton OH: Morningside, 1986), 86.

5. Gilbert Govan and James W. Livingood, *A Different Valor: The Story of General Joseph E. Johnston, C.S.A.* (New York: Bobbs-Merrill, 1956), 11–28; Edward Johnston to John W. Johnston, January 2, 1848, in RMH; Winfield Scott, *Memoirs of Lieut.-General Scott, LL. D., Written by Himself,* 2 vols. (New York: Sheldon, 1864), 2: 517; Govan and Livingood, *Different Valor,* 20; Dabney H. Maury, "Interesting Reminiscences of General Johnston," *Southern Historical Society Papers* 28 (1890): 178–79 (hereafter cited as *SHSP*); Jay Luvaas, "An Appraisal of Joseph E. Johnston," *Civil War Times Illustrated* 4, no. 9 (January 1966): 7.

6. Walter Lord, ed., *The Fremantle Diary* (Boston: Little, Brown, 1954), 93; P. W. Alexander, "Confederate Chieftains," *Southern Literary Messenger* 35, no. 1 (January 1863): 35.

7. Lord, ed., *Fremantle,* 93; Henry Kyd Douglas, *I Rode with Stonewall* (Chapel Hill: University of North Carolina Press, 1940), 234; Richard Taylor, *Destruction and Reconstruction* (New York: Longman's, Green, 1955), 42; undated notes for a talk by Benjamin S. Ewell before the Magruder-Ewell Camp, United Confederate Veterans, Benjamin Stoddert Ewell Papers, Swem Library, College of William and Mary, Williamsburg, Virginia.

8. Robert Stiles, *Four Years Under Marse Robert* (Washington, DC: n.p., 1903), 90; Bradley T. Johnson, *A Memoir of the Life and Public Service of General Johnston* (Baltimore: R. H. Woodward, 1891), 268, 301–2, 313; Lord, ed., *Fremantle,* 93.

9. Lord, ed., *Fremantle,* 93; James Longstreet, *From Manassas to Appomattox* (1896; rpt., Secaucus, NJ: Blue and Grey, 1984), 100; Donald B. Sanger and Thomas Robson Hay, *James Longstreet* (Baton Rouge: Louisiana State University Press, 1952), 426; H. J. Eckenrode and Bryan Conrad, *James Longstreet, Lee's War Horse* (Chapel Hill: University of North Carolina Press, 1936), 326–27; Taylor, *Destruction,* 28; Wade Hampton, "The Battle of Bentonville," *B&L,* 4: 703; Manly Wade Wellman, *Giant in Gray: A Biography of Wade Hampton of South Carolina* (New York: Charles Scribner's, 1949), 165; Stiles, *Four Years,* 90; Douglas, *Stonewall,* 66.

10. Stephen Vincent Benet, *John Brown's Body* (New York: Book of the Month Club, 1980), 93.

11. Johnston's department contained 62,112 "effectives" on the last day of 1861, compared to 54,004 "present for duty" in Albert Sidney Johnston's Western Department on about the same date. The difference between the equipment and organization of the two armies was also considerable, with the balance in favor of Joseph Johnston's army by a large margin. See *OR,* 5: 913–14; and 7: 813; Richard M. McMurry, *Two Great Rebel Armies: An Essay in Confederate Military History* (Chapel Hill: University of North Carolina Press, 1989), 74–86.

12. Douglas Southall Freeman, *Lee's Lieutenants: A Study in Command,* 3 vols. (New York: Charles Scribner's, 1942–1944), 1: 117–18; Johnston, *Narrative,* 59–63.

13. Douglas Southall Freeman, *R. E. Lee: A Biography*, 4 vols. (New York: Charles Scribner's, 1935), 1: 559; Johnson, *Johnston*, 251; McMurry, "Johnston in Virginia," 11–13.

14. James D. Richardson, ed., *The Messages and Papers of Jefferson Davis and the Confederacy, Including Diplomatic Correspondence, 1861–1865*, 2 vols. (New York: R. R. Bowker, 1966), 1: 129; *OR*, Series 4, 1: 605, 607–8.

15. An incomplete draft of the letter, in the handwriting of Beverly Johnston, is in RMH. Aside from the deleted paragraph, marked out with a large X (see Appendix A), the differences between the draft and the published copy are mostly details of syntax. Johnston, *Narrative*, 72–73; *OR*, Series 4, 1: 607–9.

16. *OR*, Series 4, 1: 164.

17. Johnston, *Narrative*, 72.

18. Davis, a longtime opponent of brevet rank, had never believed that staff officers should be entitled to exercise command. In contrast to U.S. Army regulations, therefore, Confederate law specifically prohibited staff officers from asserting the seniority of their rank to assume command. See Robert M. Utley, *Frontiersmen in Blue: The United States Army and the Indian, 1848–1865* (Lincoln: University of Nebraska Press, 1967), 33; Dunbar Rowland, ed., *Jefferson Davis, Constitutionalist: His Letters, Papers, and Speeches*, 10 vols. (Jackson, MS: n.p., 1923), 8: 257; "Report of Board of Officers, November, 1850," and "Opinion of Secretary of War Charles M. Conrad, 1851," both in *Letters and Telegrams Received, Secretary of War, Main Series, 1801–1870*, National Archives, M-567, Reel 192; *OR*, Series 4, 1: 115; *Official Army Register for August 1, 1855* (Washington, DC: Adjutant General's Office, 1855), 9.

19. One element of the controversy over rank that has received scant attention is the fact that Johnston's instincts in claiming that he had been intentionally slighted in favor of Cooper, Sidney Johnston, and Lee, however intemperately stated, were more accurate than many historians have been willing to admit. There is significant evidence, as suggested by William C. Davis and Steven Woodworth among others, that the president did manipulate his interpretation of the statutes in order to favor Sidney Johnston in particular and to a lesser extent Cooper and Lee. Although Johnston's "momentary laspe of self-control" is emphasized, very little analysis is given to the possibility that Davis first responded so sharply and then tacitly agreed to avoid the issue because he *had* been caught in an act of favoritism. Davis could rarely suffer himself to be corrected, even tactfully, and the absence of a detailed self-justification, which the president willingly employed on many similar occasions, could with some justice be construed almost as an admission of at least guilty feelings, if not guilt. See William C. Davis, *Jefferson Davis, the Man and His Hour: A Biography* (New York: HarperCollins, 1991), 356–61; Woodworth, *Davis and Lee at War*, 53–58; Symonds, *Johnston*, 128–29; Rembert W. Patrick, *Jefferson Davis and His Cabinet* (Baton Rouge: Louisiana State University Press, 1944), 36; *OR*, 5: 829–30, 833–34, and Series 4, 1: 611.

20. Glathaar, *Partners in Command*, 105; McMurry, "Ole Joe in Virginia," 13; Symonds, *Johnston*, 129.

21. Davis gave the letter to Assistant Secretary of War Albert Bledsoe with instructions not to file it. Stephen Mallory was the only cabinet member who mentioned the incident at the time, though Judah Benjamin must have been aware of it. In Johnston's entourage only A. H. Cole seems to have commented on the issue at the time, in an

October 1861 letter to Brig. Gen. Roswell S. Ripley in Charleston. Mary Chesnut, as close as she and her husband were both to the Davis and the Johnston families, caught no hint of the feud; C. Vann Woodward dismisses the entry in the first publication of her diary as an afterthought, probably inserted in the 1880s. Joseph E. Johnston, "Responsibilities of the First Bull Run," *B&L*, 2: 240n; entry for September 18, 1861, Stephen Mallory Diary, Southern Historical Collection, University of North Carolina, Chapel Hill: C. Vann Woodward, ed., *Mary Chesnut's Civil War* (New Haven: Yale University Press, 1981), 136n; Ellsworth Elliot, *West Point in the Confederacy* (New York: G. A. Baker, 1914), 84–86.

22. The correspondence between Davis and his two other senior generals, Lee and A. S. Johnston, can be cited as examples of the lessening of direct presidential communication. Between November 8, 1861, and March 3, 1862, the *OR* shows only a single letter between Lee and Davis, against fifteen between Lee and the War Department; see *OR*, 6: 928–29. Between November 20, 1861, and March 4, 1862, the number of entries for correspondence between the other Johnston and Davis is three, versus thirty-one between the general and the War Department. See *OR*, 7: 980; see also Patrick, *Jefferson Davis and His Cabinet*, 164–65.

23. *OR*, 2: 511–51; 5: 1062, 1072; 51 (Part 2): 374; Series 4, 1: 999.

24. *Richmond Enquirer*, January 10, 1862, 3, and May 30, 1862, 2.

2. THE DEPARTMENT OF NORTHERN VIRGINIA

1. See the train schedules published daily in the Richmond newspapers, for example, *Richmond Examiner*, February 13, 1862, 1.

2. Robert C. Black III, *The Railroads of the Confederacy* (Chapel Hill: University of North Carolina Press, 1952), 12–14, 31–32; John F. Stover, *Iron Road to the West: American Railroads in the 1850s* (New York: Columbia University Press, 1987), 65, 203; Angus J. Johnston II, *Virginia Railroads in the Civil War* (Chapel Hill: University of North Carolina Press, 1961), 9–17; Charles W. Turner, "The Virginia Central Railroad at War, 1861–1865," *Journal of Southern History* 12, no. 4 (November 1946): 510–33.

3. George B. Davis, Leslie J. Perry, Joseph W. Kirkley, and Calvin D. Cowles, *The Official Military Atlas of the Civil War* (1891–1895; rept., New York: Arno, 1978), Plate 137 (hereafter cited as *OR Atlas*).

4. *Richmond Examiner*, February 10, 13, and 19, 1862, 1.

5. *OR*, 5: 1028, 1079; Joseph Johnston to Abraham Myers, January 14, 1862, in *Letters and Telegrams Received, Adjutant and Inspector-General's Office, Confederate States of America*, National Archives, M-474, Reel 27 (hereafter cited as *LR–AIGO*); Mary Conner Moffett, ed., *Letters of General James Conner, C.S.A.* (Columbia, SC: R. L. Bryan, 1950), 60; 37th Congress, 3d sess., *Report of the Joint Committee on the Conduct of the War* (Washington, DC: Government Printing Office, 1863), 1: 244 (hereafter cited as *JCCW*; all references are to vol. 1 unless otherwise indicated); Augustus P. Dickert, *History of Kershaw's Brigade* (Newberry, SC: Elber H. Aull, 1899), 89.

6. Jeffrey N. Lash, *Destroyer of the Iron Horse: General Joseph E. Johnston and Confederate Rail Transport, 1861–1865* (Kent, OH: Kent State University Press,

1991), 21–23; Joseph M. Hanson, *Bull Run Remembers: The History, Traditions, and Landmarks of the Manassas (Bull Run) Campaigns Before Washington, 1861–1862* (Manassas, VA: National Capitol Publishers, 1953), 40–41; Dew, *Ironmaker,* 128; Joseph E. Johnston to A. W. Barbour, February 12, 1862, in Joseph E. Johnston Papers, Swem Library, College of William and Mary, Williamsburg, Virginia (hereafter cited as JJWM); Assistant Adjutant General to Stephen W. Presstman, January 9, 1862, in *Letters and Telegrams Sent, Army of Northern Virginia, January 1862–March 1863,* National Archives (hereafter cited as *LTS-ANVA*); Secretary of the Congress to Jefferson Davis, February 17, 1862, in *LR–AIGO,* M-474, Reel 11; James L. Nichols, *Confederate Engineers* (Tuscaloosa, AL: Confederate Publishing, 1957), 97; George Wise, *History of the Seventeenth Virginia Infantry, C.S.A.* (Baltimore: Kelly, Piet, 1870), 18.

7. Though there are few written sources on the railroad, it shows up in maps made by Federal engineers after Second Manassas and in photographs taken either upon McClellan's occupation of the Centreville position in March 1862 or during Maj. Gen. Irwin McDowell's operations during the summer. See Hanson, *Bull Run,* 40–41; Lash, *Destroyer,* 21–24; *OR Atlas,* Plates 22 (3), (4), (6), (7), 23 (1); William C. Davis, ed., *The Image of War, 1861–1865,* 6 vols. (Garden City, NY: Doubleday, 1982), 2: 406, 407; Abraham Myers to Joseph Johnston, January 20, 1862, in *Letters and Telegrams Sent, Quartermaster-General, Confederate States of America,* National Archives, T-131, Reel 8 (hereafter cited as *LS-QMG*).

8. Johnston, *Narrative,* 96.

9. Joseph Johnston to Jefferson Davis, February 16, 1862, in JJWM; *OR,* 5: 1074.

10. *OR,* 5: 985–87, 1086; 51 (Part 2): 465; D. H. Hill to Samuel Cooper, February 7, 1862, D. H. Hill to Judah P. Benjamin, February 22, 1862, in *LR–AIGO,* M-474, Reel 23; D. H. Hill, "The Haversack," in *Land We Love,* 1, no. 2 (June 1866): 116; Joseph Johnston to Judah Benjamin, January 3, 1862, in *Letters and Telegrams Received, Secretary of War, Confederate States of America,* National Archives, M-618, Reel 8 (hereafter cited as *LR–SW*).

11. *OR,* 5: 12; Prince Henrí de Joinville, *The Army of the Potomac: Its Organization, Its Commander, and Its Campaign* (New York: Anson D. F. Randolph, 1862), 13; William Swinton, *Campaigns of the Army of the Potomac: A Critical History of Operations in Virginia, Maryland, and Pennsylvania from the Commencement to the Close of the War, 1861–1865,* rev. ed. (New York: University Publishing, 1881), 67.

12. U. B. Phillips, ed., *The Correspondence of Robert Toombs, Alexander H. Stephens, and Howell Cobb* (Washington DC: n.p., 1913), 57; *OR,* 5: 883, 1045–6, 1089; Freeman, *R. E. Lee,* 2: 87; Clifford Dowdey, *The Seven Days, The Emergence of Robert E. Lee* (Boston: Little Brown, 1964), 36; Glathaar, *Partners in Command,* 105.

13. This estimate of Johnston's cannon may be on the high side, for there is reason to believe it includes thirty-five to forty heavy guns along the lower Potomac. See Stephen Z. Starr, *The Union Cavalry in the Civil War,* 3 vols. (Baton Rouge: Louisiana State University Press, 1979), 1: 218–21; Jennings C. Wise, *The Long Arm of Lee, or the History of the Artillery of the Army of Northern Virginia,* 1 vol. ed. (1915; rpt., New York: Oxford University Press, 1959), 67, 71–72, 79, 110, 136, 143, 145; J. Thomas Scharf, *History of the Confederate States Navy from Its Organization to the Surrender of Its Last Vessel* (New York: Rogers and Sherwood, 1887), 95–99; *OR,* 5: 777, 784, 886, 921, 958, 1051–2; Series 4, 1: 971; Daniel, "Manufacturing Cannon," 40; Jack Cog-

gins, *Arms and Equipment of the Civil War* (Garden City, NY: Doubleday, 1962), 63–64, 66.

14. Samuel G. French, *Two Wars: An Autobiography of Gen. Samuel G. French* (Nashville, TN: Confederate Veteran, 1901), 143; Samuel French to Samuel Cooper, February 12 and February 14, 1862, in *LR–AIGO,* M-474, Reel 18; J. B. Walton to Samuel Cooper, January 17, 1862, in *LR–AIGO,* M-474, Reel 52; Wise, *Long Arm,* 144.

15. This information cannot be derived from the "extracts" of monthly departmental returns in *OR* but shows up in the originals. The originals of the monthly returns for the Department of Northern Virginia for October, November, and December 1861 are in JJWM.

16. Two examples of regiments that suffered so heavily were the Thirty-fifth Georgia and the Fourteenth Alabama. Disease in the latter was so prevalent that Benjamin ordered it to Richmond in December 1861 in order for it to recover. Bell I. Wiley, *The Life of Johnny Reb, the Common Soldier of the Confederacy* (1943; rpt. Baton Rouge: Louisiana State University Press, 1978), 251–54; Phillips, ed., *Correspondence,* 575, 578; Jeffrey Wert, "I Am So Unlike Other Folks," *Civil War Times Illustrated* 28, no. 2 (April 1989): 16; *OR,* 5: 891, 893, 896–97, 934, 941–42, 948–49, 951, 962, 998–99, 1020, and Series 4, 1: 887–90.

17. *OR,* 5: 529, 857, 867, 871–73, 1028.

18. The First (Provisional), Seventh, and Fourteenth Tennessee, as well as the Fourth Alabama, petitioned the government that winter for reassignment. Judah Benjamin to Joseph Johnston, February 12, 1862, in *Letters and Telegrams Sent, Secretary of War, Confederate States of America,* National Archives, M-522, Reel 3 (hereafter cited as *LS–WD*); Thomas Bragg Diary, typescript, Southern Historical Collection, University of North Carolina, Chapel Hill, 104, 123, 127, 141–44; Phillips, ed., *Correspondence,* 592; W. D. Camp to Samuel Cooper, February 13, 1862, in *LR–AIGO,* M-474, Reel 11; Joseph Johnston to Samuel Cooper, January 10, 1862, in *LR–AIGO,* M-474, Reel 27; Johnston, *Narrative,* 90–91, 99–101; *OR,* 5: 1028–32, 1036–37, 1045–46, 1057–58; 7: 901–3; 10 (Part 2): 397; Series 4, 1: 788–90, 859–61, 962–64.

19. Johnson, *Johnston,* 78.

20. This final order, regarding preliminary entrenchments along the Rappahannock, is one of the best early indicators that Johnston was not half so ill-informed about the country in his rear as his critics have maintained. Joseph Johnston to Thomas Jackson, January 24, 1862, Joseph Johnston to Samuel Cooper, February 9, 1862, in *LR–AIGO,* M-474, Reel 27; A. P. Mason to W. H. C. Whiting, February 4, 1862, in *LS–ANVA; OR,* 5: 982, 986–87; Hanson, *Bull Run,* 37; Joseph Johnston to R. W. Hughes, April 9, 1867, in RMH; Johnston, *Narrative,* 445.

21. *JCCW,* 243, 247, 248; Robert T. Bell, *Eleventh Virginia Infantry,* 1st ed., (Lynchburg, VA: H. E. Howard, 1985), 18; Davis, *Image of War,* 2: 398; A. M. Barbour to Abraham Myers, January 23, 1862, in *Letters and Telegrams Received, Quartermaster-General, Confederate States of America,* National Archives, M-469, Reel 1 (hereafter cited as *LR–QMG*); Robert Rodes to Lieutenant Ingraham, December 25, 1861, in Jubal A. Early Papers, Virginia Historical Society, Richmond; U.S. Navy Department, *Official Records of the Union and Confederate Navies in the War of the Rebellion,* 30 vols. (Washington, DC: Government Printing Office, 1921), Series 1, 5: 4–5, 7–8 (hereafter cited as *NOR;* all citations are from Series 1 unless otherwise

indicated); Naval History Division, Navy Department, compilers, *Civil War Naval Chronology, 1861–1865,* 1 vol. (Washington, DC: Government Printing Office, 1971), 6: 237; Samuel French to Samuel Cooper, February 7, 1862, in *LR–AIGO,* M-474, Reel 18; *OR,* 5: 53.

22. A. P. Mason to H. Cole, January 25, 1862, in *LS–ANVA;* Susan P. Lee, ed., *Memoirs of William Nelson Pendleton* (Philadelphia: n.p., 1893), 155–56; Edward Porter Alexander, *Military Memoirs of a Confederate* (New York: n.p., 1907), 52–53.

23. For a typical example of Johnston's staff remonstrating with subordinates over their paperwork, see A. P. Mason to E. K. Smith, January 6, 1862, in *LS–ANVA;* there are letters extant in this book to every senior commander in January and February. See also Joseph Johnston to Theophilus Holmes on January 31 and February 13, 1862, as well as Joseph Johnston to Thomas J. Jackson, February 13, 1862, Joseph Johnston to A. W. Barbour, February 1 and February 1, 1862, Joseph Johnston to Abraham Myers, February 1 and February 3, 1862, in JJWM; Joseph E. Johnston to Samuel Cooper, January 14, 1862, in *LR–AIGO,* Reel 10; *OR,* 51: 48; Joseph Johnston to P. G. T. Beauregard, December 9, 1861, in E. Murray Smith Collection, U.S. Military History Institute, Carlisle Barracks, Pennsylvania.

24. William W. Hassler, ed., *The General to His Lady: The Civil War Letters of William Dorsey Pender to Fanny Pender* (Chapel Hill: University of North Carolina Press, 1962), 59, 96–97; Wise, *Seventeenth Virginia,* 43–44, 49; Samuel French to Theophilus Holmes, February 13, 1862, in *LR–AIGO,* M-474, Reel 17; Richard M. McMurry, *John Bell Hood and the War for Southern Independence* (Lexington: University Press of Kentucky, 1982), 30–31; Donald B. Sanger and Thomas R. Hay, *James Longstreet* (Baton Rouge: Louisiana State University Press, 1952), 33.

25. F. N. Boney, *John Letcher of Virginia* (University: University of Alabama Press, 1966), 149; *OR,* 5: 1057–59, 1062; A. P. Mason to Thomas J. Jackson, January 4, 1862, A. P. Mason to E. K. Smith, January 6, 1862, A. P. Mason to P. G. T. Beauregard, January 7, 1862, in *LS–ANVA.*

26. Joseph Johnston to Samuel Cooper, January 10, 1862, in *LR–AIGO,* M-474, Reel 27; W. D. Camp to Samuel Cooper, February 13, 1862, in *LR–AIGO,* M-474, Reel 11; Phillips, ed., *Correspondence,* 592; Terry L. Jones, *Lee's Tigers: The Louisiana Infantry in the Army of Northern Virginia* (Baton Rouge: Louisiana State University Press, 1987), 35–39, 40–42; Taylor, *Destruction,* 25.

27. There remains among modern historians critical of Johnston a remarkable double standard in dealing with the issue of his administrative competence. With the exception of Jeffrey Lash, who makes a detailed although not a conclusive case for the general's mismanagement of his railroads (Lash, *Destroyer,* 38–39), the course chosen by most historians is to condemn Johnston by implication rather than to examine his specific accomplishments, or simply to ignore the question of his technical competence as an administrator while highlighting his conflicts with the Richmond authorities (see Woodworth, *Davis and Lee at War,* 82–84; Glathaar, *Partners in Command,* 108–11). Possibly this tack has been taken because very little of the tedious correspondence with regard to the details of his activities has been published. The most significant letters remain in poorly indexed collections of personal papers, and without this evidence it is easy to portray Johnston as ineffective or even disinterested by relying on the testimony of his enemies. Ironically, however, the one point that even Johnston's staunchest critics seem to agree on is that in early 1864 he

proved exceptionally capable in administering the Army of Tennessee under similar conditions (compare McMurry, "Ole Joe in Virginia," 15, with McMurry, "A Policy So Disastrous," 226). How the man who is castigated for such a poor showing in 1862 suddenly developed his abilities in 1864 is a question that is never satisfactorily answered. For the generally accepted view of Johnston's handling of administration in northern Georgia, see Albert Castel, *Decision in the West: The Atlanta Campaign of 1864* (Lawrence, University Press of Kansas, 1992), 37–38.

28. *OR*, 5: 897, 905, 921, 1043, 1049, 1050, 1059, 1069; Bragg Diary, 116; Thomas J. Jackson to A. R. Boteler, January 24, 1862, in Thomas J. Jackson Papers, Virginia Historical Society, Richmond.

29. Dew, *Ironmaker*, 111, 114.

30. A. P. Mason to R. H. Cole, January 25, 1862, A. P. Mason to A. P. Hill, February 10, 1862, in *LS–ANVA;* Judah Benjamin to P. G. T. Beauregard, January 12, 1862, in *LS–SW;* Samuel Cooper to P. G. T. Beauregard, January ?, 1862, Braxton Bragg to Samuel Cooper, January 8, 1862, in *LR–AIGO,* M-474, Reel 5; John B. Magruder to Samuel Cooper, January 10 and January 16, 1862, in *LR–AIGO,* M-474, Reel 32; Abraham Myers to William Cabell, December 21, 1861, in *LS–QMG,* T-131, Reel 8; Phillips, ed., *Correspondence,* 586.

31. D. H. Hill to Judah Benjamin, February 12, 1862, in *LR–AIGO,* M-474, Reel 23; Nathan Evans to R. H. Chilton, January 3, 1862, A. W. Barbour to Abraham Myers, February 8, 1862, in *LR–AIGO,* M-474, Reel 22; Thomas T. Fisher to Samuel Cooper, January 27, 1862, in *LR–AIGO,* M-474, Reel 17; Abraham Myers to Joseph Johnston, December 11, 1862, Abraham Myers to William Cabell, December 21, 1861, Abraham Myers to Joseph Johnston, January 2, 1862, in *LS–QMG,* T-131, Reel 8; Joseph Johnston to P. G. T. Beauregard, December 9, 1861, in Smith Collection.

32. Richard D. Goff, *Confederate Supply* (Durham, NC: Duke University Press, 1969), 18–19; Joseph Johnston to Samuel Cooper, January 14, 1862, in *LR–AIGO,* M-474, Reel 10; Joseph Johnston to Abraham Myers, January 14, 1862, in *LR–AIGO,* M-474, Reel 27; James Longstreet to Samuel Cooper, April 9, 1862, in *LR–AIGO,* M-474, Reel 30; *OR,* 5: 883, 835–36, and 51 (Part 2): 468.

33. *OR*, 5: 877, 894, 904–6, 930, 1036, 1053, 1075; Series 4, 1: 626–33, 902, 946–47; A. T. Rainey to Judah Benjamin, February 8, 1862, in *LR–SW,* M-618, Reel 8; D. H. Hill to Judah Benjamin, January 22, 1862, in *LR–AIGO,* M-474, Reel 23; Joseph Johnston to Samuel Cooper, January 10, 1862, in *LR–AIGO,* M-474, Reel 27; Judah Benjamin to Joseph Johnston, February 12, 1862, in *LS–SW,* M-522, Reel 3; "Copy of endorsement on letter of Col. Radford of Feb. 5, 1862, to the Adjt. & Inptr. Genl.," in JJWM.

34. Glathaar criticizes Johnston for his stance on furloughs, arguing that he was short-sighted in attempting "to maintain a maximum level of preparedness" and that "like many Confederate generals, he opted for temporary readiness over the long-range benefits of an expansive leave policy." This analysis subtly misconstrues the logic of Johnston's resistance. Johnston believed—as did most commanders—that he was in the best position to decide which units could afford to grant furloughs at any given time. He did not refuse, on any wholesale basis, to honor the furloughs approved by Benjamin but declined to grant any additional leaves while the secretary was issuing the orders without reference to his tactical or operational requirements. Glathaar also

appears to ignore the fact that, under Benjamin's system, many of the men availing themselves of these furloughs did so as a preliminary to joining new organizations stationed elsewhere: they had no intention of coming back and therefore represented a permanent loss to Johnston's army. That Johnston did not in principle oppose the idea of liberal furloughs during the winter months can be supported by reference to his policies at Dalton in 1864. See *OR*, 5: 1057; Glathaar, *Partners in Command*, 108, 111.

35. *OR*, V: 1089, but see literally dozens of Benjamin-approved furloughs in *LS–SW*, M-522, Reel 3.

36. D. H. Hill to Samuel Cooper, March 5, 1862, in *LR–AIGO*, M-474, Reel 23.

37. Rowland, ed., *Jefferson Davis*, 8: 139–40; James Longstreet to Samuel Cooper, February ?, 1862, in *LR–AIGO*, M-474, Reel 30; Percy G. Hamlin, *"Old Bald Head" (General R. S. Ewell): The Portrait of a Soldier* (Strasburg, VA: Shenandoah Publishing House, 1940), 78.

38. Benjamin told Davis in early March that "he has not granted leaves of absence or furloughs to soldiers for a month past." This was technically true; Benjamin himself had stopped granting furloughs, but he had continued to allow recruiters to enter Johnston's department with documents that empowered them to grant furloughs and leaves of absence in his name. Davis told Johnston, "The authority to re-enlist and change from infantry to artillery, the Secretary informs me, has been given but in four cases." This was simply not true. Not only had Benjamin permitted twelve rather than four infantry companies to convert into artillery, but he also continued well into February to authorize ambitious officers to recruit throughout Johnston's command for new companies of heavy artillery and cavalry—at least ten in the six weeks prior to Johnston's protest to Davis (see authorizations in *LS–SW*, M-522, Reel 3 and *OR*, 5: 1089.

39. *OR*, 5: 892.

40. Ibid., 893, 907, 913, 960–61.

41. Ibid., 894, 907, 985; Freeman, *Lee's Lieutenants*, 1: 119.

42. *OR*, 5: 894, 897–98.

43. Ibid., 1011–12, 1015–16, 1020, 1028, 1035, 1091–92; Joseph E. Johnston to Samuel Cooper, January 12 and January 13, 1862, Joseph E. Johnston to Judah P. Benjamin, January 13, 1862, in *LR–SW*, M-437, Reel 21; Joseph E. Johnston to Samuel Cooper, January 7, 1862, in *LR–AIGO*, M-474, Reel 27, W. H. C. Whiting to Samuel Cooper, January 5, 1862, in *LR–AIGO*, M-474, Reel 52.

44. Here again it is important to note that Johnston in his correspondence reserved his primary ire for Benjamin, Cooper et al. and only secondarily for Jefferson Davis after the president refused to intervene in his behalf. To an army commander with an outnumbered force on an exposed frontier, the failure of his commander in chief to rein in his subordinates represented a substantially more significant cause of division than concerns about his date of rank. To argue otherwise is to assert, on extremely flimsy evidence, that Johnston from October 1861 to March 1862 was consistently more concerned with his own career than with his professional responsibilities. Although there is a case to be made that this indeed occurred in 1863 or 1864 (though the case is not as conclusive in that regard as many scholars have asserted), it requires a significant chronological inversion of the evidence to make the argument in the first year of the war (see *OR*, 5: 884–87, 944, 949–50, 990).

3. DECISION IN RICHMOND

1. Charles W. Turner, ed., *Captain Greenlee Davidson, CSA, Diary and Letters, 1851–1863* (Verona, VA: McClure, 1975), 34–35; Bragg Diary, 156.

2. Emory M. Thomas, *The Confederate State of Richmond* (Austin: University of Texas Press, 1971), 24, 59–62, 78; Virginius Dabney, *Richmond: The Story of a City* (Garden City, NY: Doubleday, 1976), 166–68; Rudolph von Abele, *Alexander H. Stephens: A Biography* (New York: Alfred A. Knopf, 1946), 206; *Richmond Examiner*, February 21, 1862, 3.

3. *Richmond Religious Herald*, February 20, 1862, 2; *Richmond Whig*, January 1, 1862, 1; Ernest B. Ferguson, *Ashes of Glory: Richmond at War* (New York: Vintage, 1996), 100–101.

4. Wilfred Buck Yearns, *The Confederate Congress* (Athens: University of Georgia Press, 1960), 14; Thomas, *Richmond*, 73–74.

5. *Richmond Examiner*, February 21 and 22, 1862, 3; *Richmond Dispatch*, February 21, 1862.

6. *Richmond Dispatch*, February 20, 1862, 3; *Richmond Whig*, February 20, 1862, 2; *Richmond Examiner*, February 20, 1862, 2–3.

7. Johnston, *Narrative*, 96; Thomas, *Richmond*, 44.

8. In his memoirs Johnston erroneously stated that his visit to Richmond consumed only a single day: February 20. Bragg's diary, however, makes it clear that the general arrived on February 19 and was present at cabinet sessions on both February 19 and 20 (Johnston, *Narrative*, 96; Bragg Diary, 154–57; Turner, "Virginia Central," 510–33).

9. Johnson, *Johnston*, 78; Johnston, *Narrative*, 96; Govan and Livingood, *Different Valor*, 93; Bragg Diary, 154.

10. *Richmond Whig*, February 22, 1862, 2.

11. Davis's policy in 1861 has often been discounted derisively as a cordon defense, adopted as the result of the combination of the president's mediocre strategic insight, demands for local defense by Confederate governors, and an unwillingness by the administration to recognize a substantial Federal threat in the west. The most vigorous recent proponent of the viewpoint that Davis had no coordinated grand strategy during the first year of the war is Steven Woodworth, who maintains that "although this stratagem was undoubtedly used by Albert Sidney Johnston in Kentucky, it is difficult if not impossible to make any connection between it and a deliberate policy of the president." This argument ignores material written by the president, either during or after the war, in which he explained his concept. See *OR*, 5: 884–87; Series 4, 1: 998–99; and Davis, *Rise and Fall*, 1: 406, 449–52, and 2: 43.

12. *OR*, 4: 531; Charles Roland, *Albert Sidney Johnston: Soldier of Three Republics* (Austin: University of Texas Press, 1964), 261–77; Thomas L. Connelly, *Army of the Heartland: The Army of Tennessee, 1861–1862* (Baton Rouge: Louisiana State University Press, 1967), 63.

13. War Department returns for December 31, 1961, indicated that 59.3 percent of the Confederate army was under the command of either Joseph Johnston or Albert Sidney Johnston. Roughly 36.2 percent defended the coasts, and 4.5 percent were deployed in western Virginia. These percentages were only approximate, as the returns upon which they were based were somewhat fragmentary, omitting both H. H. Sib-

ley's brigade in New Mexico and Sterling Price's division in Missouri; adding those forces to the rest would only emphasize more clearly that Davis had pushed the bulk of his armies to the periphery of the Confederacy. See *OR*, Series 4, 1: 822.

14. *OR*, 4: 332; 5: 53, 1086; 7: 450–52, 511, 520–21, 528–29, 813.

15. Vandiver, *Confederate Blockade Running Through Bermuda*, xiv; Wise, *Lifeline*, 52–55; Goff, *Confederate Supply*, 31; Bragg Diary, 99, 110, 112.

16. *OR*, 5: 1074.

17. Ibid., Series 4, 1: 998–99.

18. *OR*, 6: 367, 380.

19. Ibid., 826.

20. Roland, *Albert Sidney Johnston*, 227; see also *OR*, 7: 890.

21. *OR*, 6: 828, 829, and 9: 436.

22. Ibid., 7: 894.

23. Ibid., 4: 188.

24. Bragg Diary, 115; see also Boney, *Letcher*, 132–34; Frank L. Owsley, "Local Defense and the Overthrow of the Confederacy," *Mississippi Valley Historical Review* 11, no. 4 (March 1925): 493–94, 498.

25. *Richmond Examiner*, February 20, 1862, 2.

26. Bragg Diary, 153.

27. *NOR*, 6: 776–77, 780–81.

28. Bragg Diary, 152–54.

29. Johnston had lost three Tennessee regiments in early February from the Army of the Northwest, which was then attached to Jackson in the Valley District. Though this transfer was partly motivated by Grant's expedition against Fort Henry, disaffection among those regiments over their winter quarters and the belief that they would not reenlist if stationed in Virginia were the primary motivations for the War Department's orders. See *OR*, 5: 1066–67.

30. Bragg Diary, 154.

31. Peter J. Parish, *The American Civil War* (New York: Holmes and Meier, 1975), 307; Thomas, *Richmond*, 21, 23; Thomas S. Berry, "The Rise of Flour Milling in Richmond," *Virginia Magazine of History and Biography* 77, no. 4 (October 1970): 387–408; Goff, *Confederate Supply*, 15, 31.

32. Thomas, *Richmond*, 23.

33. Dew, *Ironmaker*, 86, 88, 111, 119.

34. Ibid., 86, 124–35; Kathleen Bruce, *Virginia Iron Manufacture in the Slave Era* (New York: Century, 1931), 331, 39.

35. Compare Johnston *Narrative*, 96, with the draft of *Narrative*, Box 28, Folder 4, in RMH; Joseph E. Johnston to Jefferson Davis, February 16, 1862, in Joseph E. Johnston Letterbook, JJWM; *OR*, 5: 1073–74, 1077–78, and 6: 879; Bragg Diary, 154.

36. Bragg Diary, 154; compare with Johnston, *Narrative*, 96.

37. Bragg Diary, 154.

38. Ibid., 154–55.

39. Johnston, *Narrative*, 97; Hassler, ed., *General to His Lady*, 113–14.

40. Bragg Diary, 157.

41. Johnston, *Narrative*, 96; Johnston's memory of the events changed by the time he prepared an article for the *Century*. In it he contended that "the President directed me to prepare to fall back from Manassas, and to do so as soon as the condition of the

country should make the marching of troops practicable." His first recollection more nearly matches the contemporary evidence. See Johnston, "Responsibilities," *B&L*, 1: 256; Bragg Diary, 157.

42. As with many of Davis's best misstatements, this account undoubtedly rests on a flawed reconstruction of an actual conversation. Johnston's correspondence with Lee over the next two months makes it clear that he was dealing with the question in strategic terms, and in that context it made sense to ask Davis to specify just how far he should withdraw. The president, however, chose to interpret Johnston's comments in a tactical/operational sense and to read into them confessions of incompetence that were not there. See Rowland, ed., *Jefferson Davis, Constitutionalist*, 6: 493–94.

43. Joseph E. Johnston to Samuel Cooper, February 9, 1862, in *LR–AIGO*, M-474, Reel 27; Joseph E. Johnston to R. W. Hughes, April 9, 1867, in RMH; Johnston, *Narrative*, 445.

44. Samuel Cooper to Theophilus Holmes, February 20, 1862, in *LS–AIGO*, vol. 36, Reel 2.

45. Patricia J. Faust, "Henry Stuart Foote," in *Historical Times Illustrated Encyclopedia of the Civil War*, ed. Patricia J. Faust (New York: Harper and Row, 1986), 266; Eli N. Evans, *Judah P. Benjamin, the Jewish Confederate* (New York: Macmillan, 1988), 148; *Richmond Examiner*, February 21, 1862, 3.

46. Henry S. Foote, *War of the Rebellion: or Scylla and Charybdis* (New York: Harper and Brothers, 1866), 356.

47. Rober Douthat Meade, *Judah P. Benjamin, Confederate Statesman* (New York: Oxford University Press, 1943), 235; Foote, *Scylla and Charybdis*, 479–80; "Proceedings of the First Confederate Congress–First Session," in *SHSP* 44 (June 1923): 50.

48. Rowland, *Jefferson Davis, Constitutionalist*, 9: 326; Johnston, *Narrative*, 97; Johnston, draft of *Narrative*, 18, Box 28, Folder 1, RMH.

4. WITHDRAWAL FROM THE FRONTIER

1. Sally Putnam, *Richmond During the War: Four Years of Personal Observation by a Richmond Lady* (New York: G. W. Carleton, 1867), 106–7; James M. McPherson, *Battle Cry of Freedom: The Civil War Era* (New York: Oxford University, 1988), 403; Bragg Diary, 156, 160-A.

2. *OR*, 5: 1081.

3. Ibid., 797; Longstreet, *Manassas to Appomattox*, 103; Phillips, ed., *Correspondence*, 579; Joseph E. Johnston to Jefferson Davis, February 16, 1862, in JJWM.

4. W. W. Blackford, *War Years with Jeb Stuart* (New York: Charles Scribner's, 1945), 47; Wise, *Seventeenth Virginia*, 49.

5. G. Moxley Sorrel, *Recollections of a Confederate Staff Officer* (New York: Neale, 1905), 37–38; Sanger and Hay, *James Longstreet*, 36–37; William Garrett Piston, *Lee's Tarnished Lieutenant: James Longstreet and His Place in Southern History* (Athens: University of Georgia Press, 1987), 18, 193; *OR*, 5: 1074; Longstreet, *Manassas to Appomattox*, 60.

6. Samuel J. Martin, "The Complex Confederate," *Civil War Times Illustrated* 25, no. 2 (April 1986): 26–33; Sorrel, *Recollections*, 53; Douglas, *Stonewall*, 53; Taylor, *Destruction*, 37; *OR*, 5: 892, 893–94, 960–61, 1008, 1023.

7. Walter F. Fleming, "Jefferson Davis at West Point," *Publications of the Mississippi Historical Society* 10 (1909): 267; *Official Army Register for 1861* (Washington, DC: Adjutant General's Office, 1861); *OR,* 5: 797.

8. Bragg Diary, 130; *OR,* 5: 1046–47, 1050, 1054–56, 1065–66; Douglas, *Stonewall,* 226; A. P. Hill to J. E. B. Stuart, November 14, 1862, in James Ewell Brown Stuart Papers, Virginia Historical Society, Richmond; see also Mark Grimsley, "Jackson: The Wrath of God," *Civil War Times Illustrated* 23, no. 1 (March 1984): 10–17.

9. *OR,* 5: 966, 1053, 1059–60.

10. It has often been assumed that Longstreet's assertions in his memoirs and other postwar writings about his distrust of and dislike for Early were primarily reflections of postwar feuds and not of wartime realities. An examination of Longstreet's (not Early's!) service record in the National Archives makes it clear that Longstreet did express himself negatively about the Virginian as early as fall 1861. Longstreet's poor opinion of Early seems to have stemmed from an inability to make him follow orders on outpost at Fairfax Courthouse in late summer 1861. See James Longstreet to Thomas Jordan, undated but by context from August or September 1861, in James Longstreet, Compiled Service Record, Record Group 94, National Archives; see also Longstreet, *Manassas to Appomattox,* 78; Sorrel, *Recollections,* 56; Ezra J. Warner, *Generals in Gray: Lives of the Confederate Commanders* (Baton Rouge: Lousiana State University Press, 1959), 79; *OR,* 5: 1061–62.

11. Stiles, *Four Years,* 67; *OR,* 51 (Part 2): 513; D. H. Hill to Joseph E. Johnston, May 25, 1862, in RMH.

12. Emory Thomas, *Bold Dragoon: The Life of J. E. B. Stuart* (New York: Harper and Row, 1961), 40, 47, 60, 69–73, 90–93; Rowland, ed., *Jefferson Davis, Constitutionalist,* 8: 370–71; Govan and Livingood, *Different Valor,* 21–23; Stephen W. Sears, *George B. McClellan: The Young Napoleon* (New York: Ticknor and Fields, 1988), 50; Albert Gallatin Brackett, *History of the United States Cavalry* (New York: Harper and Brothers, 1865), 141–45, 177; Joseph E. Johnston to Flora Cook Stuart, September 28, 1861, in James Ewell Brown Stuart Papers; *OR,* 5: 777.

13. *NOR,* 5: 4–5, 7–8, 25.

14. C. B. Denson, "William Henry Chase Whiting," *SHSP,* 26 (1898): 140; Longstreet, *Manassas to Appomattox,* 113; *OR,* 5: 1011–12, 1015–16, 1020, 1028, 1035, 1091–92; Joseph E. Johnston to Samuel Cooper, January 12 and January 13, 1862, Joseph E. Johnston to Judah P. Benjamin, January 13, 1862, in *LR–SW,* M-437, Reel 21; Joseph E. Johnston to Samuel Cooper, January 7, 1862, in *LR–AIGO,* M-474, Reel 27, W. H. C. Whiting to Samuel Cooper, January 5, 1862, in *LR–AIGO,* M-474, Reel 52.

15. *OR,* 5: 1074; Return of the Department of Northern Virginia, December 31, 1861, in JJWM; Russell F. Weigley, *History of the United States Army,* enlarged ed. (Bloomington: Indiana University Press, 1984), 240–41; 36th Cong., 2d sess., *Report of the Commission Appointed under the eighth section of the Act of Congress of June 21, 1860, to examine into the organization, system of discipline, and course of instruction of the United States Military Academy at West Point* (Washington DC: Government Printing Office, 1860), 85, 86, 236–37, 330–31, 334, 345; J. D. Hittle, *The Military Staff, Its History and Development* (Harrisburg, PA: Stackpole, 1961), 67.

16. J. B. Jones, *A Rebel War Clerk's Diary at the Confederate State Capital,* ed., Howard Swiggett, 2 vols. (New York: Old Hickory Bookshop, 1935), 2: 249, 278;

Mrs. Burton Harrison, *Recollections Grave and Grey* (New York: Charles Scribner's, 1911), 79; Edward Younger, ed., *Inside the Confederate Government: The Diary of Robert Garlick Hill Kean* (New York: Oxford University Press, 1957), 84–85; *OR*, Series 4, 2: 609–10; Elliot, *West Point*, 370–71; Joseph H. Crute Jr., *Confederate Staff Officers, 1861–1865* (Powhatan, VA: Derwent Books, 1982), 19, 104; Francis Heitman, *Historical Register and Dictionary of the United States Army, from Its Organization . . . to 1903* (Washington, DC: Government Printing Office, 1903), 1: 620; Jon Wakelyn, *Biographical Dictionary of the Confederacy* (Westport, CT: Greenwood, 1977), 122–23; C. Vann Woodward and Elisabeth Muhlenfeld, eds., *The Private Mary Chestnut: The Unpublished Civil War Diaries* (New York: Oxford University Press, 1984), 28n; Woodward, ed., *Mary Chesnut's Civil War*, 28n, 121, 125.

17. Charles E. Cauthen, *South Carolina Goes to War, 1860–1865* (Chapel Hill: University of North Carolina Press, 1950), 115; Laura A. White, *Robert Barnwell Rhett: Father of Secession* (New York: Century, 1931), 220n; Elliot, *West Point*, 417; Heitman, *Historical Register*, 1: 641, 826; Crute, *Staff Officers*, 104, 178; Woodward and Muhlenfeld, eds., *Private Mary Chesnut*, 65n, 150n; Wakelyn, *Biographical Dictionary*, 314, 367–68; Burton J. Kendrick, *Statesmen of the Lost Cause, Jefferson Davis and His Cabinet* (Boston: Little, Brown, 1939), 237–40; Robert E. Lee to Samuel Cooper, June 3, 1862, in *LR–AIGO*, M-474, Reel 3.

18. H. H. Cunningham, *Doctors in Gray: The Confederate Medical Service* (Gloucester, MA: Peter Smith, 1970), 34, 161, 249; Richard B. Stark, "Surgeons and Surgical Care of the Confederate States Army," *Virginia Medical Monthly* 88, no. 10: (1973) 607; Warner, *Generals in Gray*, 3–4, 234–35; Elliot, *West Point*, 271–72, 287, 316–17, 408; Sorrel, *Recollections*, 114; Larry J. Daniel, *Cannoneers in Gray: The Field Artillery of the Army of Tennessee, 1861–1865* (University: University of Alabama Press, 1984), 135; Wise, *Long Arm*, 76–78, 193–95; Crute, *Staff Officers*, 14, 21, 103, 115, 189; Heitman, *Historical Register*, 1: 426, 503.

19. Woodward and Muhlenfeld, eds., *Private Mary Chesnut*, 65n; Stewart Sifakis, *Who Was Who in the Civil War* (New York: Facts on File, 1988), 436; Crute, *Staff Officers*, 103, 104, 116; Wakelyn, *Biographical Dictionary*, 314; Kendrick, *Statesmen*, 237–40; *OR*, 5: 789–90; Johnston, *Narrative*, 67–68.

20. Johnston, *Narrative*, 98; Carlton McCarthy, *Detailed Minutiae of Soldier Life in the Army of Northern Virginia, 1861–1865* (Richmond: Carlton McCarthy, 1882), 16–20; see also Jubal A. Early, *War Memoirs: Autobiographical Sketch and Narrative of the War Between the States* (Bloomington: Indiana University Press, 1960), 53–54.

21. Moffet, ed., *Conner*, 62; Taylor, *Destruction*, 40; Phillips, ed., *Correspondence*, 582–83.

22. Bragg Diary, 156; Scharf, *Confederate States Navy*, 95–99; *OR*, 5: 529.

23. Johnston, *Narrative*, 98–99; *OR*, Series 4, 1: 1038–39, and 2: 522.

24. Bragg Diary, 154; *OR*, 5: 732, 1086; Joseph E. Johnston to Samuel Cooper, February 27 and March 3, 1862, in JJWM.

25. *OR*, Series 4, 1: 1039.

26. A. P. Mason to Richard S. Ewell, March 2, 1862, in *LS–ANVA;* Abraham C. Myers to Joseph E. Johnston, March 7, 1862, in *LS–QMG*, T-131, Reel 8; Rowland, ed., *Jefferson Davis, Constitutionalist*, 8: 3; Warner, *Generals in Gray*, 310; *OR*, 5: 1091.

27. *OR*, 5: 1087–88, 1092–93; Joseph E. Johnston to T. H. Williams, February 27, 1862, in JJWM; Robert G. Tanner, *Stonewall in the Valley: Thomas J. "Stone-*

wall" Jackson's Shenandoah Valley Campaign of 1862 (Garden City, NY: Doubleday, 1976), 106.

28. *OR*, 5: 830, 1099, and 51 (Part 2): 497; Archer Anderson to W. H. F. Lee, March 11, 1862, in George Bolling Lee Papers, Virginia Historical Society.

29. *OR*, 5: 1095.

30. Ibid., 1091; Stiles, *Four Years*, 71–72.

31. Coggins, *Arms and Equipment*, 88; *OR*, 5: 1081, and 51 (Part 2): 477–78.

32. Johnston, *Virginia Railroads*, 11; Black, *Railroads*, 18, 76; Turner, "Virginia Central Railroad at War," 521–22.

33. Lash, *Destroyer*, 28.

34. *OR*, Series 4, 1: 1039–40.

35. Early, *War Memoirs*, 54–55; *OR*, 50 (Part 2): 1073–74; Freeman, *Lee's Lieutenants*, 1: 140; Tanner, *Stonewall in the Valley*, 98; Lash, *Destroyer*, viii, 33; Glathaar, *Partners in Command*, 112; Woodworth, *Davis and Lee at War*, 105.

36. *OR*, 5: 1086, and Series 4, 1: 1038–39; Goff, *Confederate Supply*, 17–18n.

37. Joseph E. Johnston to Abraham C. Myers, March 2, 1862, in JJWM; Abraham C. Myers to Joseph E. Johnston, March 7, 1862, in *LS–QMG*, T-131, Reel 8; *OR*, 5: 1093.

38. Johnston, *Narrative*, 98–99n; see also Davis, *Image of War*, 2: 370–73.

39. *JCCCW*, 244.

40. *OR*, V: 742 (emphasis added).

41. Freeman, *Lee's Lieutenants*, 1: 140.

42. Moffet, ed., *Conner*, 84–85; *OR*, 5: 1091; Taylor, *Destruction*, 38.

43. Joseph E. Johnston to Abraham C. Myers, February 26, 1862, in JJWM; Abraham C. Myers to Joseph E. Johnston, March 2, 1862, Abraham C. Myers to Thomas R. Sharpe, March 8, 1862, in *LS–QMG*, T-131, Reel 8; Taylor, *Destruction*, 36, 38; Dickert, *Kershaw's Brigade*, 93; *OR*, 5: 1082–83, 1085, 1090–93, and 51 (Part 2): 481, 487, 488; McHenry Howard, *Recollections of a Maryland Confederate Soldier and Staff Officer Under Johnston, Jackson, and Lee* (Baltimore: Williams and Wilkins, 1914), 68; Gary W. Gallagher, ed., *Fighting for the Confederacy: The Personal Recollections of General Edward Porter Alexander* (Chapel Hill: University of North Carolina Press, 1989), 72.

44. French, *Two Wars*, 143; *OR*, 5: 1082–83, 1085, 1090–93, and 51 (Part 2): 481, 487, 488.

45. *OR*, 51 (Part 2): 497.

46. Johnston, draft of *Narrative*, Box 28, Folder 3, in RMH; *OR*, 5: 524, 526–27, 537, 549; *Richmond Examiner*, March 11, 1862, 2; Bragg Diary, 178.

5. ENTER LEE

1. Freeman, *R. E. Lee*, 1: 628; Clifford Dowdey and Louis H. Manarin, eds., *The Wartime Papers of Robert E. Lee* (New York: Bramhall House, 1961), 124.

2. George H. Reese, ed., *Proceedings of the Virginia State Convention of 1861; February 13–May*, 18 vols. (Richmond: n.p., n.d.), 4: 363.

3. Dowdey and Manarin, eds., *Wartime Papers*, 18.

4. Ibid., 63, 70.

5. Freeman, *R. E. Lee*, 1: 602–3; Dowdey and Manarin, eds., *Wartime Papers*, 71, 80.

6. *OR*, 6: 106, 394, 397–400; Emory M. Thomas, *Robert E. Lee, A Biography* (New York: W. W. Norton, 1995), 213.

7. Dowdey and Manarin, eds., *Wartime Papers*, 121–22.

8. *OR*, 6: 397–400.

9. Freeman, *R. E. Lee*, 1: 628; *OR*, 6: 400–401.

10. John Taylor Wood, "The First Fight of Ironclads," *B&L*, 1: 696.

11. R. E. Colston, "Watching the 'Merrimac,'" *B&L*, 1: 713.

12. Shelby Foote, *The Civil War: A Narrative*, 3 vols. (New York: Random House, 1958), 1: 255; *Richmond Examiner*, March 11, 1862, 2; Putnam, *Richmond*, 111–12.

13. *NOR*, 7: 793; *OR*, 9: 57, 65, and 11 (Part 3): 386–88.

14. *OR*, 5: 1096, and 9: 68; *NOR*, 6: 776–77, 780–81, and 7: 224, 761.

15. *OR*, 5: 527, 1096; Woodworth, *Davis and Lee at War*, 103; Bragg Diary, 178.

16. Former editor R. W. Hughes had married Johnston's niece Eliza, the adopted daughter of John Floyd. The current editor, John Daniel, had served the first few months of the war on Floyd's staff. See Robert M. Hughes, ed., "Some Letters from the Papers of General Joseph E. Johnston," *William and Mary Quarterly* 2d Series, 11, no. 4 (October 1931): 320; Jedediah Hotchkiss, *Virginia*, vol. 3, *Confederate Military History*, expanded edition (Dayton, OH: Morningside, 1975), 949.

17. *Richmond Examiner*, March 11, 1862, 2.

18. Ibid.; Robert G. Cleland, "Jefferson Davis and the Confederate Cabinet," *Southwestern Historical Quarterly* 19, no. 3 (January 1916): 216; Bragg Diary, 94, 104–5, 135; *OR*, 5: 526–27, 1099–1100.

19. Rowland, ed., *Jefferson Davis, Constitutionalist*, 6: 502–4; Johnston, *Narrative*, 100–101, 482–83.

20. *OR*, 5: 1083–85.

21. This letter was erroneously dated February 6, 1862, when printed in *OR*; a careful reading of Joseph E. Johnston to Jefferson Davis, March 3, 1862, with particular reference to comments about Stuart, reveals that the letter should carry the date March 6, 1862; *OR*, 5: 1063–64, 1088.

22. Davis, *Rise and Fall*, 2: 88.

23. Freeman, *R. E. Lee*, 1: 479–86, 497–500; Davis made his opinion of Lee freely known throughout *Rise and Fall*; see also Arthur Martin Shaw, ed., "Some Post-War Letters from Jefferson Davis to His Former Aide-de-Camp, William Preston Johnston," *Virginia Magazine of History and Biography* 51, no. 2 (April 1943): 152.

24. *Richmond Examiner*, March 6, 1862, 2; Yearns, *Confederate Congress*, 108; *OR*, Series 4, 1: 997–98; Freeman, *R. E. Lee*, 2: 5.

25. *OR*, 5: 1099, and Series 4, 1: 997; Bragg Diary, 183–84.

26. Dowdey and Manarin, eds., *Wartime Papers*, 124, 127–28; Freeman, *R. E. Lee*, 2: 6–7; Hermann Hattaway and Archer Jones, *How the North Won: A Military History of the Civil War* (Urbana: University of Illinois Press, 1983), 124.

27. The correspondence preserved in *OR* is not necessarily representative of Lee's habits in signing his letters or with respect to his personal command authority. Many of the direct orders that he issued during the period under consideration were of a technical nature and not chosen for inclusion. See Robert E. Lee to Benjamin Huger, March 18, 1862, Robert E. Lee to Joseph E. Johnston, March 18, 1862, Robert E.

Lee to Theophilus Holmes, March 19, 1862, Walter Taylor to Benjamin Huger, March 25, 1862, Robert E. Lee to Gustavus Smith, April 1, 1862, in *Robert E. Lee Letterbook,* National Archives, Washington, DC (hereafter cited as *Lee Letterbook*); T. A. Washington to Samuel Cooper, April 4, 1862, Robert E. Lee to Samuel Cooper, April 17, 1862, Robert E. Lee to George W. Randolph, April 20, 1862, in *LR–AIGO,* M-474, Reel 30.

28. For the best explanation of the U.S. Army's precedent for the conduct of the commanding general, see Robert F. Stohlman Jr., *The Powerless Position: The Commanding General of the Army of the United States, 1864–1903* (Manhattan: Kansas State University Press, 1975), 2–12, in which he discusses the position in the prewar army. For an early situation in which rank distinctions played a part in limiting the commanding general's authority, see Weigley, *History of the United States Army,* 170–72.

29. *OR,* 33: 1239.

30. Freeman, *R. E. Lee,* 1: 434; Connelly and Jones, *Politics of Command,* 46.

31. Dowdey and Manarin, eds., *Wartime Papers,* 105, 142.

32. Charles Wells Russell, ed., *The Memoirs of Colonel John. S. Mosby* (Boston: Little, Brown, 1947), 375; Bragg Diary, 178.

33. *OR,* 5: 1103 (emphasis added).

34. Bragg Diary, 156; Johnston, *Narrative,* 445.

35. *OR,* 51 (Part 2): 1073–74; Rowland, ed., *Jefferson Davis, Constitutionalist,* 6: 493–94.

36. *OR,* 5: 527–28.

37. Steven Woodworth represents the views of most modern historians when he writes that "Davis's behavior patterns throughout his presidency give ample reason to believe that the original purpose of the trip was as he stated [to review the topography and assist in selecting a defensive line]. Johnston was apparently embarrassed enough about the purpose of Davis's visit to deny after the war that it had ever taken place" (*Davis and Lee at War,* 353n). This interpretation ignores the distinction that Johnston and his aides made between the president's visiting the main army and in visiting an outpost near Fredericksburg, which was never specifically denied. The testimony of Johnston's aides was omitted in the abridgement of his article from *Century Magazine* when published in *B&L;* see Johnston, "Responsibilities," *B&L,* 1: 257; Joseph E. Johnston, "Manassas to Seven Pines," *Century Magazine,* 30, no. 1 (May 1885): 109–10; Davis, *Rise and Fall,* 1: 465; Dowdey and Manarin, eds., *Wartime Papers,* 133–34; Bragg Diary, 190–91; Rowland, ed., *Jefferson Davis, Constitutionalist,* 9: 377–78, 381–83; Woodworth, *Davis and Lee at War,* 353n; Ann Eliza Gordon to Doubleday A. Gordon, March 22, 1862, provided by Robert K. Krick, to whom I am indebted for the information.

38. *OR,* 9 (Part 3): 385–86, and 51 (Part 2): 512.

39. *OR,* 5: 392; Joseph E. Johnston to Samuel Cooper, March 24, 1862, in *LR–AIGO,* M-474, Reel 27.

40. Two letters from Holmes to Lee for March 14 and 15, 1862, are preserved in *OR;* Lee's correspondence in reply indicates that Holmes also wrote on March 16 and 17; see *OR,* 5: 1100, 1103, 1104–5; Warner, *Generals in Gray,* 84, 141, 151, 192, 281; Johnston, *Narrative,* 109.

41. Rowland, ed., *Jefferson Davis, Constitutionalist,* 9: 377–78; *OR,* 5: 392.

42. Johnston, *Narrative,* 109.

6. SHOULD YORKTOWN BE DEFENDED?

1. *OR*, 9: 269–70; Sifakis, *Who Was Who*, 624.
2. Swinton, *Campaigns*, 100.
3. *OR*, 11 (Part 3): 388, 392–93, 394; de Joinville, *Army of the Potomac*, 14.
4. *OR*, 9: 450–51; and 11 (Part 3): 393–94, 396–97.
5. John Morgan Dederer, "The Origins of Robert E. Lee's Bold Generalship: A Reinterpretation," *Military Affairs* 46 (1985): 117–23; Connelly and Jones, *Politics of Command*, 31–33; see also Louis H. Manarin, "Lee in Command: Strategical and Tactical Policies" (Ph.D. diss., Duke University, 1965).
6. Interestingly enough, some of the consensus has begun to shift from Freeman's interpretation of Lee's actions during the period. Stephen Sears and Emory Thomas both glide by the period of concentration on the Peninsula with little comment, and Steven Woodworth advances the idea that everything Lee sent to Johnston during the period was a product of the strategic waffling of Davis. Woodworth ignores the dynamic tension between the Lee and Davis concepts of strategy here, which is highly unusual, since that dynamic is the theme of his book. See Freeman, *R. E. Lee*, 2: 14, 17, 19; Sears, *To the Gates of Richmond*, 20–39; Thomas, *Robert E. Lee*, 219; Woodworth, *Davis and Lee at War*, 108–9, 354n.
7. *OR*, 11 (part 3): 389–90, 397 (emphases added).
8. Ibid., 398 (emphasis added).
9. Ibid., 400–401.
10. Ibid., 401.
11. Lee's telegram to Johnston has not been preserved, but Johnston's response is in ibid., 405.
12. Ibid., 406–7, and 12 (Part 3): 840.
13. *OR*, 11 (Part 3): 408.
14. Ibid., 409.
15. Phillips, ed., *Correspondence*, 593.
16. The letters from Johnston to Jackson are not reprinted in *OR*, but he briefed Davis on his instructions in *OR*, 12 (Part 3): 838.
17. *OR*, 11 (Part 3): 419–20.
18. The last indication of Johnston's presence at Rapidan is in A. P. Mason to Jubal Early, March 30, 1862. After that, the orders and correspondence indicate that Johnston had left Longstreet in command there. See *OR*, 11 (Part 3): 412, 415–16; 12 (Part 3): 842–44; 51 (Part 2): 527–28; Hassler, ed., *General to His Lady*, 131; Longstreet, *Manassas to Appomattox*, 65.
19. The existence of this telegram is to be inferred from Johnston's response to Lee on April 4; see *OR*, 11 (Part 3): 419.
20. *OR*, 9: 455; 11 (Part 3): 418–19, 420; 51 (Part 2): 528.
21. Swinton, *Campaigns*, 100–102; *OR*, 11 (Part 1): 403–4.
22. *OR*, 11 (Part 1): 403–4; (Part 3): 422; see also *OR Atlas*, Plates 14–19.
23. *OR*, 11 (Part 3): 419–20, 424–25, 426–27.
24. Ibid., 11: 419–20, and 51 (Part 2): 527–28.
25. Ibid., 11 (Part 3): 419–20.
26. Even Johnston's more ardent advocates such as Craig Symonds have oversimplified the nature of the general's strategic thought: "The essence of Johnston's strate-

gic vision can be stated in a single phrase: concentration of force" (Symonds, Johnston, p.3) What is important about these interchanges with Lee and the later exchanges regarding proper strategy in the Shenandoah is the insight provided into Johnston's thinking, which turns out to be considerably more flexible and realistic than is usually credited. The quoted remark was made in reference to the Vicksburg campaign; see Johnston, *Narrative*, 221; *OR*, 11 (Part 3): 420, 423.

27. *OR*, 11 (Part 3): 423.

28. McClellan erroneously believed that Johnston and his army had already arrived in Yorktown by April 7; see *OR*, 11 (Part 1): 11–12.

29. Ibid., (Part 3): 422, 425, 426–27, 422–33, 435–36.

30. Johnston, *Narrative*, 110; *OR*, 11 (Part 3): 435–36.

31. Johnston, *Narrative*, 110; Longstreet, *Manassas to Appomattox*, 66.

32. Tanner, *Stonewall in the Valley*, 152; Jubal Early, "Strength of Ewell's Division in the Campaign of 1862—Field Return," *SHSP* 8 (1880): 302–3; *OR*, 12 (Part 3): 434.

33. Such had been the case when Johnston suggested that while he was in Fredericksburg Longstreet might detach two or more brigades to reinforce Jackson quickly for a surprise attack. See *OR*, 12 (Part 3): 838; Johnston, *Narrative*, 110.

34. Modern writers have a tendency to ignore Johnston's arrangements for the defense of northern Virginia as he left for the Peninsula, which is unfortunate because his instructions reveal much about his strengths and weaknesses as a general. Symonds ignores the issue, and Woodworth inverts chronology to the extent that he considers Jackson's March 23 attack at Kernstown to be in response to Johnston's strategic directives upon leaving for Richmond—even though the general did not leave his headquarters for Fredericksburg until March 29 or depart for Richmond until April 11. Stuart took the First and Fourth Virginia and the Jefferson Davis (Mississippi) Legion from his own brigade; the Hampton (South Carolina) Legion cavalry accompanied Smith's division. Remaining in northern Virginia were the Seventh Virginia in the Valley (about 1,000 strong); the Second and Sixth Virginia with Ewell's division (totaling about 900); and the Ninth Virginia with Field's brigade (probably about 400 to 500). Thus Johnston left approximately 2,300 cavalrymen along the frontier—roughly 1,000 more than he took with him to Yorktown. See Tanner, *Stonewall in the Valley*, 152; Early, "Ewell's Division," 302–3; *OR*, 11 (Part 3): 484, and 12 (Part 1): 434, and (Part 3): 848, 852; Symonds, *Johnston*, 150; Woodworth, *Davis and Lee at War*, 120–21.

35. That the strength of Magruder's line and the capabilities of the *Virginia* were stressed is inferred from previous statements by the principals on the ironclad's potential (see chapter 5) and from their subsequent position at the meeting on April 14 (see chapter 7). Johnston, *Narrative*, 110; Davis, *Rise and Fall*, 2: 86.

36. Johnston, *Narrative*, 110, and Davis, *Rise and Fall*, 2: 86.

37. For indications of just how close the Federal gunboats were willing to approach the Yorktown fortifications during early April, see *NOR*, 7: 208, 209–10, 212–13; Johnston, *Narrative*, 111.

38. *OR Atlas*, Plates 14, 15, 19; *OR*, 11 (Part 1): 316, 317, 337, and (Part 3): 439, 441–42.

39. On the other hand, as Ludwell H. Johnson has pointed out to me, Magruder could well have had the offending trees girdled and burned. *OR*, 11 (Part 3): 438, 439, 441–42; Dew, *Ironmaker*, 179–80.

40. D. H. Hill to Joseph E. Johnston, May 25, 1862, in RMH.

41. Ibid.; *OR,* 11 (Part 3): 441–42.

42. *OR,* 11 (Part 1): 316, 317, and (Part 3): 441–42; *OR Atlas,* Plates 14, 15, 19; Edward P. Alexander, "Sketch of Longstreet's Division, Yorktown and Williamsburg," *SHSP* 10 (1882): 36.

43. *OR,* 11 (Part 1): 316, 317, and (Part 3): 432.

44. Ibid. (Part 3): 432; *OR Atlas,* Plates 14, 15, 19.

45. Among the more glaring inconsistencies of the case that Early attempted in postwar years to build against Johnston is his widely accepted criticism of the general for retreating so precipitously from Yorktown that he wasted supplies and lost heavy ordnance. This censure blithely ignores the fact that, if Early had had his way in April 1862, Magruder's army would have pulled back before Johnston ever arrived. Under those circumstances the material losses could only have been worse. See Rowland, ed., *Jefferson Davis, Constitutionalist,* 8: 3.

46. *OR,* 11 (Part 1): 275.

47. Ibid., (Part 3): 422, 436.

48. Johnston, *Narrative,* 110; Davis, *Rise and Fall,* 2: 86; *OR,* 11 (Part 3): 455.

7. DECISION IN RICHMOND II

1. Stanley F. Horn, *The Army of Tennessee* (1952; rpt., Wilmington, NC: Broadfoot, 1987), 99–121; Connelly, *Army of the Heartland,* 126–57; James L. McDonough, *Shiloh—In Hell Before Night* (Knoxville: University of Tennessee Press, 1977), 3–26, 84; *OR,* 10 (Part 1): 384, and (Part 2): 394, 403, 407.

2. *OR,* 10 (Part 1): 403

3. Johnston, *Narrative,* 112–13.

4. Ibid. (emphasis added).

5. Davis, *Rise and Fall,* 2: 86–87; Johnston, *Narrative,* 114.

6. This account is taken from a report of a conversation that Smith held with Johnston's older brother Beverly in 1863. See Beverly Johnston to Joseph E. Johnston, September 14, 1867, in RMH.

7. Smith later claimed that his memorandum had called for a counterinvasion across the Potomac and that this option received considerable attention. The bulk of the evidence points to this as being a postwar addition to the record. Neither Johnston, Davis, nor Longstreet recalled any such discussion, and in several discussions with Beverly Johnston during the war, Smith failed to mention any such plan. As Beverly wrote to Joseph in 1868, "Nothing was said by him expressing or hinting at any other idea as being proposed or suggested by him. I am perfectly confident that I could not have forgotten so daring and eccentric a scheme as he says (in the passage you quote) he presented to the council." Perhaps Smith conflated this meeting with the October 1861 conference held among himself, Johnston, Beauregard, and Davis when he had in fact put forth such a plan. See Gustavus W. Smith, *Confederate War Papers; Fairfax Court House, New Orleans, Seven Pines, Richmond and North Carolina,* 2d ed. (New York: Atlantic, 1884), 41–42; Johnston, *Narrative,* 113–14; Davis, *Rise and Fall,* 2: 87; Longstreet, *Manassas to Appomattox,* 65; Beverly Johnston to Joseph E. Johnston, September 14, 1867, and February 23, 1868 (two letters of same date), in RMH.

8. Even though he did not mention such an action, it is to be assumed as consistent with his general strategic outlook that he favored such; Smith, *Confederate War Papers,* 41–42; Longstreet, *Manassas to Appomattox,* 66; Davis, *Rise and Fall,* 2: 87.

9. Beverly Johnston to Joseph Johnston, September 14, 1867; February 23, 1868 (two letters of the same date); Joseph E. Johnston to [Gustavus W. Smith], January 6 and January 21, 1868, all in RMH.

10. Longstreet himself admitted that "it was the first time that I had been called to such august presence, to deliberate on momentous matters" (Longstreet, *Manassas to Appomattox,* 66).

11. Johnston denied the rumor after the war but in language that was singularly unconvincing, writing to Smith: "You say that I told Genl. Whiting that if you had not gone to sleep the army would not have been sent to that position (of Yorktown). I cannot pretend to remember what I may have said in casual conversation at that time. But such an opinion seems to me now so unreasonable that I cannot imagine that it was ever entertained by me. I hope, therefore—indeed think that Genl. Whiting must have misunderstood me" (Joseph E. Johnston to G. W. Smith, January 21, 1868, in JJWM).

12. Johnston, *Narrative,* 115.

13. Patrick, *Jefferson Davis and His Cabinet,* 122, 124; J. B. Jones, *Rebel War Clerk's Diary,* 1: 117; H. J. Eckenrode, *The Randolphs: The Story of a Virginia Family* (New York: Bobbs-Merrill, 1946), 257–58; Bragg Diary, 192; Freeman, *R. E. Lee,* 2: 28–29; Archer Jones, *Confederate Strategy from Shiloh to Vicksburg* (Baton Rouge: Louisiana State University Press, 1961), 42–49; Sifakis, *Who Was Who,* 530–31.

14. Smith, *Confederate War Papers,* 42.

15. Lewis P. Summers, *History of Southwest Virginia, 1746–1786, Washington County, 1777–1870* (Richmond: J. L. Hill, 1903), 768–69; Edgar E. Hume, *Peter Johnston, Junior: Virginia Soldier and Jurist* (Charlottesville, VA: Historical Publishing Company, 1935), 7–10; Armistead C. Gordon, "Peter Johnston," in *Dictionary of American Biography* (New York: Charles Scribner's Sons, 1955), 5: 147–48; Connelly and Jones, *Politics of Command,* 54–60.

16. Freeman, *R. E. Lee,* 1: 74; James A. Bethune to Robert M. Hughes, February 25, 1910; George B. Johnston to Robert M. Hughes, December 12, 1912, Robert M. Hughes to Gameliel Bradford, December 16, 1912, in RMH; Fleming, "Jefferson Davis at West Point," 266; Govan and Livingood, *Different Valor,* 14, 20.

17. Johnston's original regiment, the Fourth Artillery, was nicknamed the Immortal Fourth by junior officers waiting for their superannuated superiors to die. Johnston's obsession with promotion seems clearly to have exceeded that of many of his peers. His correspondence and discussions with his brothers, Edward and Beverly, make this abundantly clear. Govan and Livingood, *Different Valor,* 16; Joseph E. Johnston to Beverly Johnston, June 13, 1837, in JJWM; Edward Johnston to John Warfield Johnston, January 2, 1848, in RMH; Edward N. Coffman, *The Old Army, A Portrait of the American Army in Peacetime, 1784–1898* (New York: Oxford University Press, 1985), 49, 52, 56.

18. Joseph E. Johnston to J. Preston Johnston, August 31, 1839, and May 25, 1843; Joseph E. Johnston to Edward Johnston, January 6, 1851, all in JJWM. A slightly edited version of the August 1839 letter to Preston appears in Robert M. Hughes, ed., "Some Letters from the Papers of General Joseph E. Johnston," *William and Mary Quarterly* 2d Series, 11, no. 4 (October 1931): 320.

19. The first application Johnston made in January 1851 when there was a rumor that two new regiments would soon be formed. When that did not happen, he applied again in 1855 when four regiments were added to the existing structure. See Joseph E. Johnston to J. Preston Johnston, November 27, 1842, Joseph E. Johnston to Edward Johnston, January 6, 1851, undated opinions of Secretary of War John B. Floyd and Adjutant General Samuel Cooper, in JJWM; Joseph E. Johnston to Samuel Cooper, February 24, 1855, in the Joseph E. Johnston Papers, Duke University, Durham, NC; Samuel Cooper to Jefferson Davis, July 13, 1855, in *SW–MS*, M-567, Reel 581 (abstracted in Haskell Monroe Jr., James T. McIntosh, Linda Lasswell Crist et al., eds. *The Papers of Jefferson Davis*, vols. to date Baton Rouge: Louisiana State University Press, 1985), 5: 440–41; Govan and Livingood, *Different Valor*, 16–25; Jack Bauer, *The Mexican War, 1846–1848* (New York: Macmillan, 1974), 276.

20. Johnston, *Narrative*, 10; Alfred P. James, "General Joseph E. Johnston, Storm Center of the Confederacy," *Mississippi Valley Historical Review* 14, no. 3 (December 1927): 345.

21. Robert E. Lee to Joseph E. Johnston, July 30, 1860, in JJWM; Freeman, *R. E. Lee*, 1: 41; J. William Jones, *Life and Letters of Robert Edward Lee, Soldier and Man* (New York: Neale, 1906), 414.

22. A. L. Long, *Memoirs of Robert E. Lee* (New York: J. M. Stoddart, 1886), 151.

23. *NOR*, 6: 740–41, and Series 2 (Part 4): 77, 716–17; *OR*, 11 (Part 3): 429–30; Davis, *Rise and Fall*, 2: 87; William H. Parker, *Recollections of a Naval Officer, 1841–1865* (New York: Charles Scribner's, 1883), 247.

24. *NOR*, Series 2 (Part 2): 254, 255, 261–65.

25. Ibid., 6: 604–5; *OR Atlas*, Plates 137, 138; *OR*, 11 (Part 3): 474.

26. Johnston, "Manassas to Seven Pines," 209; *OR*, 11 (Part 3): 477.

27. *NOR*, Series 2 (Part 4): 716–17.

28. *OR*, 11 (Part 1): 275; (Part 3): 408–11.

29. Freeman, *R. E. Lee*, 2: 18; *OR*, 9: 61–62, 68; and 11 (Part 3): 398–99; Davis, *Rise and Fall*, 2: 87; *NOR*, 6: 699.

30. *OR*, 11 (Part 3): 398–99, 433–34.

31. Ibid., 9: 45–48, 61–62; John H. Winder to Samuel Cooper, February 28, 1862, in *LR–AIGO*, M-474, Reel 52; John H. Winder to Samuel Cooper, February 28, 1862 (second letter same date), in *LR–SW*, M-437, Reel 76.

32. *OR*, 9: 61–62, and 11 (Part 3): 485, 500–501; undated manuscript for speech by Benjamin Stoddert Ewell before the Magruder-Hill Camp, United Confederate Veterans, in Ewell Papers.

33. Nichols. *Confederate Engineers*, 84; *NOR*, 7: 435; *OR*, 9: 61–62; Davis, *Rise and Fall*, 2: 103.

34. For the argument that such numbers were habitually understated, see the section on Johnston's army in the appendixes; *OR*, 6: 422, and 9: 38, 419.

35. Davis, *Rise and Fall*, 2: 87; *OR*, Series 4, 1: 987–88.

36. Davis, *Rise and Fall*, 2: 87; Patrick, *Jefferson Davis and His Cabinet*, 124; Freeman, *R. E. Lee*, 2: 28–29; Archer Jones, *Confederate Strategy*, 42–49.

37. *OR*, 5: 1083; Black, *Railroads*, inset map.

38. Black, *Railroads*, 98.

39. This calculation assumes a reduction in North Carolina from 20,000 to 12,000 troops, and along the lower coast from 29,000 to 19,000 men. Neither decrease in

troop strength would have rendered the Confederates incapable of defending the major ports from the Union forces threatening them. See *OR*, 6: 263, and 9: 381.

40. Hattaway and Jones, *How the North Won*, 218; *OR*, II (Part 3): 477.

41. Davis, *Rise and Fall*, 2: 87.

42. Livermore, *Numbers and Losses*, 77.

43. Davis, *Rise and Fall*, 2: 88; Johnston, *Narrative,*, 116; Freeman, *Lee's Lieutenants*, 1: 151; Dowdey, *Seven Days*, 35.

44. Draft of *Narrative*, 18, Box 28, Folder 2, in RMH (emphasis added); see also Joseph E. Johnston to Gustavus W. Smith, January 21, 1868, in JJWM.

45. Beverly Johnston to Joseph E. Johnston, September 14, 1867, February 23, 1868, and a second letter February 23, 1868, in RMH.

8. ISOLATED ON THE PENINSULA

1. Putnam, *Richmond*, 29.

2. Bragg Diary, 201–2, 205.

3. John B. Gordon, *Reminiscences of the Civil War* (New York: Charles Scribner's, 1903), 52; Moffett, ed., *Conner*, 88.

4. Putnam, *Richmond*, 119–20; Foote, *Civil War*, 1: 403.

5. J. G. de Roulhac Hamilton, ed., *The Papers of Randolph Abbot Shotwell*, 3 vols. (Raleigh: North Carolina Historical Commission, 1929), 1: 175–76; Putnam, *Richmond*, 119–20.

6. Thomas, *Bold Dragoon*, 103; Putnam, *Richmond*, 120; Sorrel, *Recollections*, 59.

7. River transportation was so strained during the redeployment of Johnston's army that only 4,000 troops could be moved down the river during any twenty-four-hour period; see *OR*, 11 (Part 3): 400; Dickert, *Kershaw's Brigade*, 93; Hamilton, ed., *Shotwell*, 1: 177.

8. Joel Cook, *The Siege of Richmond: A Narrative of the Military Operations of Major-General George B. McClellan During May and June, 1862* (Philadelphia: G. W. Childs, 1862), 144–45; Hamilton, ed., *Shotwell*, 1: 180–81; Dickert, *Kershaw's Brigade*, 95; Edward P. Alexander, *Military Memoirs of a Confederate* (New York: n.p., 1907), 64.

9. *OR*, 12 (Part 3): 852.

10. Robert E. Lee to John H. Winder, April 27, 1862, in *Lee Letterbook*.

11. *NOR*, Series 2, 3: 122–23; Robert G. Cleland, "Jefferson Davis and the Confederate Cabinet," *Southwestern Historical Quarterly* 19, no. 3 (January 1916): 216; *OR*, 11 (Part 3): 403, 499; A. P. Hill to Samuel Cooper, April 27, 11862, *LR–AIGO*, M-474, Reel 24; Robert E. Lee to John H. Winder, May 3, 1862, in *Lee Letterbook*.

12. *OR*, 11 (Part 1): 364–65.

13. Ibid., 417, 421–22.

14. Ibid., 375, and (Part 3): 480.

15. Ibid., (Part 1): 375.

16. For a detailed analysis of Johnston's numbers on the Peninsula, see the appendixes; see also *OR*, 11 (Part 3): 460; Wise, *Long Arm*, 186; Livermore, *Numbers and Losses*, 67–70; Robert E. Lee to Abraham C. Myers, April 29, 1862; Robert E. Lee to Samuel P. Moore, April 29, 1862; Robert E. Lee to John H. Winder, May 3, 1862,

in *Lee Letterbook;* Louis T. Wigfall to Joseph E. Johnston, May [April] 21, 1862, Returns of the Department of Northern Virginia, October, November, and December 1861, in JJWM; Joseph E. Johnston to George W. Randolph, April 20, 1862, in W. H. C. Whiting, Compiled Service Record; S. R. Anderson to Samuel Cooper, March 5, 1862; S. R. Anderson to Jefferson Davis, March 8, 1862, in *LR–AIGO,* M-474, Reel 23.

17. *IR,* 11 (Part 3): 448, 455–56.

18. Ibid., 51 (Part 2): 543; David F. Riggs, *Seventh Virginia Infantry* (Lynchburg VA: H. E. Howard, 1982), 22; Robert T. Bell, *Eleventh Virginia Infantry* (Lynchburg VA: H. E. Howard, 1985), 19; Hamilton, ed., *Shotwell,* 1: 180–81; Alexander, "Sketch," 36; Alexander, *Military Memoirs,* 64.

19. Patrick, *Jefferson Davis and His Cabinet,* 124; Freeman, *R. E. Lee,* 2: 28–29; Jones, *Confederate Strategy,* 42–49.

20. W. Gart Johnson, "The Barksdale-Humphrey Brigade," *Confederate Veteran,* April 1894 supplemental issue, 25; Blackford, *War Years,* 62–63; *Richmond Howitzers in the War: Four Years Campaigning with the Army of Northern Virginia, by a Member of the Company* (Richmond: n.p., 1891), 55; *OR,* 12 (Part 3): 832–33.

21. These numbers result from a comparison of the Confederate regiments in Virginia during April 1862 and the December 13, 1861 list provided by the Secretary of War, which enumerated the enlistment status of all Confederate regiments. The following regiments on the Peninsula were therefore affected (with battalions and regiments split between war companies, and twelve-month companies counted as half a regiment): Gracie's Battalion, 4, 5 (1/2), 6, 26 Alabama; Arkansas Battalion; 2 Florida; 7 Georgia; 1 Kentucky; 2 Louisiana; 2, 11, 12, 13, 17, 18 Mississippi; 13, 14, 15, 16, 22, 23 North Carolina; 1, 7, 14 Tennessee; 1 (1/2) Texas; Noland's Battalion, 1, 1 Cavalry, 3, 3 Cavalry, 4 Cavalry, 7, 8, 11, 17, 18, 19, 24, 26, 28, 32, 46, 47, 49 Virginia. In the other components of the Department of Northern Virginia the percentage of units affected was even higher. In Jackson's and Ewell's divisions, twenty-three of thirty-two regiments had to reorganize; in Huger's division, eleven of twelve; and among the units gathered around Fredericksburg, eleven of twenty-one. In total, at least 98 of 152.5 infantry and cavalry regiments, or more than 62 percent, underwent the throes of reorganization.

22. The figure of 37 percent of company officers was originally derived from Robert K. Krick, *Thirtieth Virginia Infantry* (Lynchburg, VA: H. E. Howard, 1983), 13, and was confirmed by spot-checking other entries in the H. E. Howard regimental series as well as muster rolls in the National Archives. Krick's biographical dictionary—Robert K. Krick, *Lee's Colonels: A Biographical Register of the Field Officers of the Army of Northern Virginia,* 2d ed. (Dayton, OH: Morningside, 1984)—makes it possible to determine the number of field officers ousted with some precision. Eliminating Gracie's Alabama Battalion, Noland's Virginia Battalion, and the First Kentucky, which Krick does not cover, 8 field officers lost their positions of 152 required to stand the elections.

23. Ramseur did not leave the army because he had lost an election but because he had won one. He had been serving as captain of the Ellis (North Carolina) Light Artillery when he learned of his election to the colonelcy of the Forty-ninth North Carolina and left the army to return to his home state and finish the regiment's training. See Gary W. Gallagher, *Stephen Dodson Ramseur, Lee's Gallant General* (Chapel

Hill: University of North Carolina Press, 1985), 37. The other cases are drawn from Krick or Warner; see Krick, *Lee's Colonels,* 90–91, 114–15, 181, 205, 245–46, 283–84; Warner, *Generals in Gray,* 167, 260.

24. Krick, *Lee's Colonels,* 48, 452; R. G. Lowe, "The Dreux Battalion," *Confederate Veteran* 5, no. 2 (February 1897): 55; Thomas G. Rhett to James Longstreet, April 27 and April 28, 1862, in *LS–ANVA;* Joseph Johnston to George W. Randolph, April 28 and April 29, 1862, in *LR–SW,* M-618, Reel 9.

25. David G. Houston Jr. to Samuel Cooper, May 24, 1862, in *LR–AIGO,* M-474, Reel 25. Robert Cleary to W. T. Patton, June 10, 1862, in *LR–AIGO,* M-474, Reel 29.

26. Mark Hardin to Samuel Cooper, March 25, 1862, in *LR–AIGO,* M-474, Reel 24.

27. Wade Hampton to George W. Randolph, April 22, 1862, in *LR–SW,* M-618, Reel 9.

28. Jubal Early to George W. Randolph, April 21, 1862, in *LR–AIGO,* M-474, Reel 13.

29. Ibid., Reel 17.

30. Krick, *Lee's Colonels,* 181; Warner, *Generals in Gray,* 167, 260; Jubal Early to George W. Randolph, April 21, 1862, in *LR–AIGO,* M-474, Reel 13.

31. Johnston, *Narrative,* 90.

32. *OR,* 6: 350.

33. Thomas G. Rhett to J. E. B. Stuart, April 24, 1862, in *LS–ANVA;* Lewis Armistead to Samuel Cooper, May 24, 1862, in *LR–AIGO,* M-474, Reel 3.

34. Bragg Diary, 201; *NOR,* 7: 748, 749, 768.

35. *OR,* 9: 8; *NOR,* 7: 769–70, and Series 2, 2: 77.

36. *NOR,* 7: 769–70, 775–76; Series 2, 2: 633; Sifakis, *Who Was Who,* 662.

37. Thomas G. Rhett to Benjamin S. Ewell, April 21, 1862, in *LS–ANVA; OR,* 11 (Part 3): 456; *NOR,* 7: 775; Joseph Johnston to George W. Randolph, April 25, 1862, in *LR–AIGO,* M-474, Reel 27; Robert E. Lee to Samuel P Moore, April 29, 1862, Robert E. Lee to Abraham C, Myers, April 29, 1862, Robert E. Lee to John H. Winder, May 3, 1862, in *Lee Letterbook.*

38. Johnston's correspondence on the Peninsula has to be reconstructed with care, given the fact that many of his letters did not make it into *OR* and that others, to which Lee specifically refers, may not have survived at all. A close survey of the *OR, LR–AIGO, LR–ANVA,* and the *Lee Letterbook,* however, makes it possible to determine that Johnston wrote substantively either to Lee or Randolph on the following dates (asterisks mark letters not preserved but mentioned by Lee): April 20 (two letters/one preserved)*, April 22 (two letters), April 24 (two letters), April 25, April 27, April 28 (three letters), April 29, April 30, May 1.* This list omits at least thirty endorsements on letters by other officers, forwarded to Lee, Cooper, or Randolph, in which Johnston sometimes made important remarks. Johnston's correspondence with his subordinates is contained in *OR,* 11 (Part 3): 469–70, 474, 475; *NOR,* Series 2, 2: 633–34; Thomas G. Rhett to Charles W. Field, April 24, 1862, in *LS–ANVA.* Pender's comment on April 26, 1862, is from Hassler, ed., *General to His Lady,* 137.

39. Although a few of the letters as recorded in *OR* show endorsements of Lee forwarding them to Johnston, most of the letters were never forwarded to Johnston, and several, when they were copied for *OR,* either had their endorsements omitted or

were apparently copied from the sender's files, not the recipient's. See Richard S. Ewell to Samuel Cooper, May 9, 1862, in *LR–AIGO*, M-474, Reel 17, for an example of a letter forwarded by Cooper to Lee and not to Johnston. Compare the version of Richard S. Ewell to Robert E. Lee on May 14, 1862, in *OR*, 12 (Part 3): 890, with the version in *LR–AIGO*, M-474, Reel 17, which contains an endorsement by Lee forwarding it for the information of Cooper but not sending it to Johnston. That this process did not begin after Johnston's withdrawal from Yorktown is evident from an examination of A. Blanchard to Samuel Cooper, April 28, 1862, in *LR–AIGO*, M-474, Reel 6. Blanchard commanded a brigade in the Department of Norfolk and was therefore Johnston's subordinate, but the letter was sent to Lee instead. See also arguments on communications with Ewell and Jackson in the rest of this chapter.

40. Dowdey, *Seven Days*, 63; Freeman, *R. E. Lee*, 2: 131; Tanner, *Stonewall in the Valley*, 156; Thomas, *Lee*, 224.

41. *OR*, 12 (Part 3): 857–60 (emphasis added).

42. Ibid., 11 (Part 3): 452; and 12 (Part 1): 433.

43. Lee did not give Johnston the numbers of either Gregg's or Anderson's brigades, both of which he would have known from departmental returns in Cooper's office. The strength of the regiments sent from Richmond he knew exactly because he had the muster rolls. See *OR*, 11 (Part 3): 458–59; Robert E. Lee to Samuel Cooper, April 24, 1862, in *LR–AIGO*, M-474, Reel 30.

44. *OR*, 12 (Part 3): 867.

45. Ibid., 11 (Part 3): 500–501, and 12 (Part 3): 865–66, 873; see also J. R. Anderson Brigade Order Book, Virginia Historical Society, Richmond.

46. *OR*, 12 (Part 3): 863, 868.

47. Jackson, for instance, had always kept Johnston well informed during his Romney campaign the previous winter. Nor would the content have been much different from his April 29 letter to Lee in *OR*, 12 (Part 3): 872; Tanner, *Stonewall in the Valley*, 161–62.

48. Freeman, *Lee's Lieutenants*, 1: 350–52; Taylor, *Destruction*, 36; *OR*, 12 (Part 3): 867, 869.

49. *OR*, 12 (Part 3): 876.

50. Ibid., 11 (Part 3): 456.

51. These times have been derived from a study of the transmittal and reception dates of the correspondence cited earlier in the chapter.

52. *OR*, 11 (Part 3): 458–59.

9. THE RETREAT FROM YORKTOWN

1. William C. Davis, ed., *The Image of War, 1861–1865*, 6 vols. (Garden City: Doubleday, 1982), 2: 45.

2. *OR*, 11 (Part 1): 345, 348.

3. Ibid., 348; Coggins, *Arms and Equipment*, 86; David G. Martin, "Civil War Artillery," *Strategy and Tactics* no. 81 (July–August 1980): 18–19.

4. *OR*, 11 (Part 1): 345; Martin, "Artillery," 18.

5. *OR*, 11 (Part 1): 345.

6. Ibid., (Part 3): 473.

7. The telegram to Davis has not been preserved but may be inferred from Jefferson Davis to Joseph Johnston on May 1. See Early, *War Memoirs*, 15; *OR*, 11 (Part 3): 469–70, 473, 484–85.

8. *OR*, 11 (Part 3): 473; E. P. Alexander to Edwin Taliaferro, April 30, 1862, in Beverly Randolph Wellford Papers, Virginia Historical Society, Richmond; Lee, *Memoirs*, 183; H. B. McClellan, *The Life and Campaigns of Major-General J. E. B. Stuart* (Boston: Houghton Mifflin, 1885), 47–48.

9. *OR*, 11 (Part 3): 473; Naval History Division, *Civil War Naval Chronology*, VI: 33–333; *NOR*, 7: 310–11, 313.

10. *OR*, 11 (Part 3): 486; Smith, *Confederate War Papers*, 45–48.

11. The orders as given in *OR* omit the distribution notes in "General Orders no. ____, Department of Northern Virginia, May 2, 1862," in *LS–ANVA;* see *OR*, 11 (Part 1): 347, and (Part 3): 489–90.

12. *OR*, 11 (Part 1): 347–48; Allan Nevins, ed. *A Diary of Battle: The Personal Journals of Colonel Charles S. Wainwright, 1861–1865* (New York: Harcourt, Brace, and World, 1962), 42.

13. Smith, *Confederate War Papers*, 46; Alexander, *Military Memoirs*, 68; Hamilton, ed., *Shotwell*, 199–200.

14. Stiles, *Four Years*, 83; Edgar Warfield, *A Confederate Soldier's Memoirs* (Richmond: Masonic Home Press, 1936), 84; Hamilton, ed., *Shotwell*, 199–200; F. Y. Dabney, "General Johnston to the Rescue," *B&L*, 2: 25–276; Hassler, ed., *General to His Lady*, 140.

15. D. H. Hill to "My Dear Wife," May 11, 1862, in D. H. Hill Papers, College of William and Mary, Williamsburg, Virginia.

16. Smith, *Confederate War Papers*, 48.

17. *OR*, 11 (Part 1): 398; Pulaski Cowper, ed., *Extracts of Letters of Major-General Bryan Grimes to his Wife, written while in Active Service in the Army of Northern Virginia, together with some personal recollections of the war written by him after its close* (Raleigh, NC: Alfred Williams, 1884), 12.

18. *OR*, 11 (Part 1): 349–50, 399–400; and (Part 3): 509–10, 511, 516–17.

19. Ibid., 444.

20. Ibid., 444; Thomas, *Bold Dragoon*, 104–5.

21. *OR*, 11 (Part 1): 441–42, 445.

22. The information about Ewell conducting McLaws's troops into the line is from interlineal notes by Benjamin S. Ewell in the original of Johnston's report, which is in JJWM. Ewell habitually wrote notes inside Johnston's reports when he served on the general's staff later in the war; see Joseph Johnston to Benjamin S. Ewell, October 12, 1868, in Ewell Papers; *OR*, 11 (Part 1): 275, 441–42; Thomas, *Bold Dragoon*, 105.

23. *OR*, 11 (Part 1): 275, 441–42; Thomas, *Bold Dragoon*, 105.

24. Johnston had actually ordered Longstreet to send one brigade, but thinking his brigades too small the Georgian dispatched two. See Johnston, *Narrative*, 120; Longstreet, *Manassas to Appomattox*, 72; Gary W. Gallagher, ed., *Fighting for the Confederacy: The Personal Recollections of Gen. Edward Porter Alexander* (Chapel Hill: University of North Carolina Press, 1989), 49, 80–81.

25. Longstreet, *Manassas to Appomattox*, 72–73; Sorrel, *Recollections*, 128; Freeman, *Lee's Lieutenants*, 1: 177–78; *OR*, 11 (Part 1): 564–65.

26. Longstreet, *Manassas to Appomattox*, 72; *OR*, 11 (Part 1): 564–65.

27. *OR,* 11 (Part 1): 465, 564–65, 580; Bruce Catton, *Mr. Lincoln's Army* (Garden City NY: Doubleday, 1951), 266; Mark Grimsley, "Rear Guard at Williamsburg," *Civil War Times Illustrated,* 24, no. 3 (May 1985): 12–13.

28. *OR,* 11 (Part 1): 576, 580–81, 584–85, 587–88, 591.

29. Grimsley, "Rear Guard," 27; de Joinville, *Army of the Potomac,* 52.

30. *OR,* 11 (Part 1): 577–78; Longstreet, *Manassas to Appomattox,* 74–77.

31. *OR,* 11 (Part 1): 535.

32. The question of when Hancock's artillery opened fire is critical to understanding how concerned Longstreet would have been about his left flank. It has usually been assumed that the Federals did not begin firing until late in the afternoon, when Early's brigade had already been deployed on the left. Hancock says that he took the first unoccupied redoubt about noon, and fired his first shots with his guns while advancing on the second. This would place the action between noon and 1:00 P.M. Micah Jenkins, left in command at Fort Magruder, mentions Hancock opening on the rear of the fort between 3:00 and 4:00 P.M., but this does not rule out earlier fire from that direction. If, as Johnston later suggested, the Confederates did not even know that Hancock had moved into their left and rear, there is little to explain Longstreet's examination of the ground to his left on first arriving on the field (while an active battle was in progress on the right) or his deployment of the bulk of Hill's division on the left. See *OR,* 11 (Part 1): 536–37, 564–65, 580, 602–3, 606–7; Longstreet, *Manassas to Appomattox,* 74; Johnston, *Narrative,* 124–25.

33. Longstreet claimed in his memoirs that he first sent for a single brigade from Hill's division, but Hill's report makes it clear that his entire division was ordered back. That Johnston had not received any messages from Longstreet is inferred from Longstreet's memoirs and report and from Johnston's own report, none of which mentions sending any dispatches to the army commander. In his report, Johnston only said that he returned to the area of Fort Magruder after hearing Hill's division ordered back, and the timing of his arrival supports this. In his memoirs, Johnston claimed that "at noon the fighting was reported by Longstreet and Stuart to be so sharp, that D. H. Hill's division, which had marched several miles, was ordered back to Williamsburg, and I returned myself; for at ten o'clock, when the action had lasted more than four hours, there seemed to be so little vigor in the enemy's conduct, that I became convinced that it was a mere demonstration, intended to delay our march . . . and had ridden forward to join the leading troops." By 10:00 A.M. no one was making any reports from which Johnston could have concluded this; read literally, Johnston's paragraph only implies but does not emphatically state that he had received messages from Longstreet and Stuart. See *OR,* 11 (Part 1): 275, 564–65, 602; Longstreet, *Manassas to Appomattox,* 74; Johnston, *Narrative,* 120.

34. *OR,* 11 (Part 1): 602–3, 606–7.

35. Ibid., 535, 606–7; Grimsley, "Rear Guard," 28.

36. Early denied in his report that this was his idea, attributing it instead to D. H. Hill. But Hill, Longstreet, and Johnston agreed—though their accounts did differ on other particulars—that the original idea to capture the battery was Early's. See *OR,* 11 (Part 1): 275, 564–65, 602, 607; Longstreet, *Manassas to Appomattox,* 78; Johnston, *Narrative,* 121; Grimsley, "Rear Guard," 29.

37. The tenor of Longstreet's report may be inferred from Johnston's comments on the Georgian's conduct of the battle: "I rode upon the field, but found myself com-

pelled to be a mere spectator, for General Longstreet's clear head and brave heart left me no apology for interference." That was the official report, and though Johnston rewrote himself a much larger part in the *Narrative*, it was one that was not borne out by contemporary accounts. See *OR*, 11 (Part 1): 275, 602–3; Johnston, *Narrative*, 122–25; Longstreet, *Manassas to Appomattox*, 77.

38. Many historians assume that Longstreet's postwar statements concerning his mistrust of Early at Williamsburg are a case of projecting later feuds to the earliest part of the war. That this is not so can be seen from an examination of Jubal A. Early, Compiled Service Record, National Archives, that contain several pieces of correspondence dated in late 1861 in which Longstreet is critical of Early. See Longstreet, *Manassas to Appomattox*, 78.

39. *OR*, 11 (Part 1): 603; Janet B. Hewett, Noah Andre Trudeau, and Bryce A. Suderow, eds., *Supplement to the Official Records of the Union and Confederate Armies*, 54 vols. to date (Wilmington, NC: Broadfoot, 1994–1997), 2: 335 (hereafter cited as *SOR*).

40. *OR*, 11 (Part 1): 602–3, 606–7; Freeman, *Lee's Lieutenants*, 1: 182–89; Grimsley, "Rear Guard," 29–30; *SOR*, 2: 335–36.

41. *OR*, 11 (Part 1): 540.

42. Ibid., 564–65, 604.

43. Livermore, *Numbers and Losses*, 80–81; Johnston, *Narrative*, 124–25; Longstreet, *Manassas to Appomattox*, 79; *JCCW*, 1: 583; undated notes for a speech by Benjamin S. Ewell before the Magruder-Ewell Camp, United Confederate Veterans, Ewell Papers.

44. Longstreet's ulterior motive in recommending Hill and Anderson for promotion was that it would split his division into two commands of three brigades each, under a permanently established army corps that he would control. See James Longstreet to Samuel Cooper, May 9, 1862, in *LR–AIGO*, M-474, Reel 30; Robert E. Lee to James Longstreet, May 28, 1862, in *Lee Letterbook*.

45. Freeman, *Lee's Lieutenants*, 1: 189.

46. Robert E. Lee to Joseph Johnston, May 5, 1862, in *Lee Letterbook*. This letter does appear in *OR* but was incorrectly dated March 5, 1862, and therefore published in the wrong volume; *OR*, 5: 1090.

47. Gallagher, ed., *Fighting for the Confederacy*, 82.

48. The other Federal division commanders waiting to steam up the York River were Fitz-John Porter, Israel B. Richardson, and John Sedgwick, all of whom would later earn reputations for more combativeness than Franklin. See *OR*, 11 (Part 1): 23, 627, 629; Smith, *Confederate War Papers*, 47.

49. *OR*, 11 (Part 1): 615.

50. Smith, *Confederate War Papers*, 47; *OR*, 11 (Part 1): 627, 629.

51. A few supporting troops were engaged on both sides beyond the two brigades—the Fifth Maine and First New Jersey for the Federals and Hampton's (South Carolina) Legion and two regiments of Anderson's Tennessee Brigade for the Confederates—but these units had little to do with the actual contest. See *OR*, 11 (Part 1): 615–17, 623–25, 627, 631–32; McMurry, *Hood*, 38–39; Hood, *Advance and Retreat*, 21–22.

52. *OR*, 11 (Part 1): 151, 614, 625, and (Part 3): 184.

53. D. H. Hill to "My Dear Wife," May 11, 1862, in Hill Papers; Smith, *Confederate War Papers*, 48; *OR Atlas*, Plate 19 (1).

54. Johnston had announced his intention to evacuate Yorktown to Lee on May 1 (not preserved, but mentioned by Lee the following day). He evidently attempted to communicate his plan to delay the withdrawal by one day on May 2 or 3 but discovered that the Williamsburg telegraph office had been broken up. If Johnston then attempted to post a letter on the same subject to Richmond, it has been lost. During May 3 to 5, the retreat from Yorktown and the two engagements in front of Williamsburg, Johnston apparently found no time to write, but by May 7 his endorsement on Longstreet's letter indicates that he had already filed his Williamsburg report, as does the context of his May 7 letter to Lee. This was probably a different letter from his May 6 letter to Lee concerning provisions, which had been posted twelve miles west of Williamsburg and would have been written either on the evening of May 5 or the morning of May 6. Here then is a tentative reconstruction of Johnston's correspondence during the withdrawal period:

May 1: Johnston to Lee (mentioned by Lee);
May 3: Johnston to Lee (telegram that could not be sent; inferred from Johnston to D. H. Hill, May 3);
May 3: Johnston to Lee (conjectural; letter sent in place of telegram?);
May 5 or 6: Johnston to Lee or Cooper (inferred from endorsements on Longstreet's letters);
May 6: Johnston to Lee or Cooper (mentioned in *Lee Letterbook*).

See Freeman, *R. E. Lee*, 2: 43–44; James Longstreet to Samuel Cooper, May 7 and May 9, 1862, in *LR–AIGO*, M-474, Reel 30; *OR*, 11 (Part 3): 488, 491, 496, 499–500 and 51 (Part 2): 552–53; Robert E. Lee to Joseph Johnston, May 7, 1862, Robert E. Lee to Lucius B. Northrop, May 7, 1862, in *Lee Letterbook*.

55. Only one of these letters is printed in *OR*—Lee to Johnston, May 7. A second is in the *Lee Letterbook*. The third has not been found, but it may be inferred from Johnston's response that it did not provide information on the activities of Jackson, Ewell, or Anderson. See *OR*, 11 (Part 3): 497, and 51 (Part 2): 552–53.

56. Dowdey, *Seven Days*, 66; *OR*, 11 (Part 3): 490, 497, 499–501.

57. *OR*, 11 (Part 3): 455, 500–501.

58. The last intelligence Johnston had from Jackson on Banks's strength was dated March 27, and though Johnston had no way of knowing, it was quite out of date by May 10. See *OR*, 11 (Part 3): 503, 505, and 12 (Part 3): 840–41.

59. For the more traditional interpretation of Johnston's intention to concentrate, see Freeman, *Lee's Lieutenants*, 1: 202; *OR*, 11 (Part 3): 506, and 12 (Part 3): 888.

60. *OR*, 11 (Part 3): 506, and 12 (Part 3): 888.

61. Ibid., 12 (Part 3): 883–84, 889.

62. Ibid., 11 (Part 3): 505, 511, 512–13, and 12 (Part 3): 887.

63. The traditional dating of this meeting has always been May 14, which has been accepted by virtually every historian since Freeman. Recent publication of a May 13 letter from Davis to his wife, however, has pinned the date with certainty to May 12. See Freeman, *Lee's Lieutenants*, 1: 210; *OR*, 11 (Part 3): 512–13, 518; 12 (Part 3): 889; 51 (Part 2): 556; Linda Lasswell Crist, Mary Seaton Dix, and Kenneth H. Williams, eds., *The Papers of Jefferson Davis*, 9 vols. (Baton Rouge: Louisiana State University, 1995), 8: 174–75.

64. Davis, *Rise and Fall,* 2: 101–2; *OR,* 11 (Part 3): 523–24; Johnston, "Manassas to Seven Pines," *B&L,* 2: 206.

10. DEFENDING RICHMOND

1. The Federal vessels were the *Monitor* (two guns), *Galena* (six guns), *Wachusett* (10 guns), *E. A. Stevens* (one gun), *Aroostook* (three guns), *Port Royal* (eight guns), *Maratanza* (six guns), *Mahaska* (six guns), and *Dragon* (two guns). *OR,* 11 (Part 3): 488–89; NOR, Series 2, 2: 39, 62, 90, 132, 134, 148, 182, 215, 235.

2. *NOR,* 7: 784.

3. Ibid., 786.

4. *OR,* 9: 45, 55–56, 68, and 11 (Part 3): 384–85, 411, 412–13, 414, 425–26, 474; *NOR,* 7: 747–49, 776; George W. Randolph to T. M. R. Talcott, April 4, 1862, in Talcott Family Papers, Virginia Historical Society, Richmond.

5. *OR,* 11 (Part 3): 474, 488, 682; *NOR,* 7: 782; Series 2, 1: 716–17.

6. *NOR,* 7: 796–97; Series 2, 1: 716–17; Wood, "First Fight," *B&L,* 1: 709.

7. William H. Parker, *Recollections of a Naval Officer, 1841–1865* (New York: Charles Scribner's, 1883), 278; *NOR,* 7: 786.

8. John R. Tucker to Ebenezer Farrand, May 8, 1862, in Charles T. Mason Papers, Virginia Historical Society, Richmond; *SOR,* 2: 347–49.

9. *NOR,* 7: 327–29, 797; *SOR,* 2: 349–50.

10. *NOR,* 7: 345.

11. William Izard Clopton, "New Light on the Great Drewry's Bluff Fight," *SHSP* 24 (1901): 284–85.

12. Dew, *Ironmaker,* 182; *OR,* 11 (Part 3): 421; Clopton, "New Light," 83–84.

13. W. H. Fry to Samuel Cooper, May 14, 1862, in *LR–AIGO,* M-474, Reel 18; Robert E. Lee to Samuel Cooper, May 2, 1862, in *LR–AIGO,* M-474, Reel 30; *NOR,* Series 2, 1: 635–36; Scharf, *History of the Confederate Navy,* 711; *OR,* 51 (Part 2): 555.

14. Drewry's company, the company of sappers and miners, and the company from the Washington Artillery probably numbered less than 300 men. The six companies of heavy artillery added 668 more, and the muster rolls of the three vessels attest to over 700 sailors, to which should be added at least another 150 men for the two companies of marines and Farrand's original work party. See *NOR,* Series 2, 1: 289–90, 299–301, 308–11; *OR,* 9: 38; Scharf, *History of the Confederate Navy,* 711; Clopton, "New Light," 88; Drewry, "Drewry's Bluff Fight," *SHSP* 29 (1901): 285–86; Robert Wright, "Sinking of the Jamestown," *SHSP* 29 (1901): 372.

15. All quoted in Smith, *Confederate War Papers,* 48–49 (emphasis in original).

16. *NOR,* 7: 357–58.

17. Ibid., 357–58, 359–60, 369–70.

18. *OR,* 11 (Part 3): 473, 499–500, 503–4, 518, 519, 520; Joseph Johnston to Robert E. Lee, May 15, 1862, in Wellford Papers.

19. *OR,* 11 (Part 3): 520–22; Longstreet, *Manassas to Appomattox,* 81–82; Smith, *Confederate War Papers,* 49.

20. Johnston's second May 15 letter has not been found, but its substance can be easily inferred from Lee's two letters of May 16 and 17 and Davis's letter of May 17, all in *OR,* 11 (Part 3): 521, 523–24. Lee's remark that "I have supposed that if your

army took a position so near this city its right would rest in that vicinity [Drewry's Bluff]" implies that Johnston had advised him of the position he intended to take near Richmond. Lee's second letter agrees with Johnston that McClellan would probably try to cross the Chickahominy, and the Davis letter reiterates the same point.

21. *OR,* 11 (Part 3): 521, 523.

22. Davis implied in his memoirs that he had sent Custis Lee primarily to confer upon strategy rather than as a courier instructed to present and receive information. This interpretation strains the wording in Davis's letter to the breaking point. He also stated that Johnston did not ever inform either Colonel Lee or himself as to an intention to cross the Chickahominy. Yet not only had Johnston already informed General Lee of the impending move, he had already begun it when Custis arrived and in fact received Davis's aide on the near bank of the river. See Davis, *Rise and Fall,* 2: 103; Johnston, "Manassas to Seven Pines," 207; *OR,* 11 (Part 3): 523–24.

23. *OR,* 12 (Part 3): 892–93.

24. Ibid., 896–97.

25. Freeman, *R. E. Lee,* 2: 55–56; Dowdey, *Seven Days,* 74–75; Tanner, *Stonewall in the Valley,* 199.

26. For evidence that such a plan can reasonably be inferred from existing documents, see Joseph R. Anderson to Richard S. Ewell, May 17, 1862, in which Anderson, who was then in contact with Johnston, suggests procedures very similar; *OR,* 12 (Part 3): 896.

27. The suggestion for crossing the Potomac came in Johnston's April 10 letter to Lee, wherein Johnston argued that instead of defending Yorktown the Confederates should "take the offensive, collect all the troops we have in the East and cross the Potomac with them." Admittedly the letter was written in a much different context from that of the Valley campaign, but it does show that Johnston had begun almost as early as Lee to think about the advantage of distracting the enemy with a march north. See *OR,* 11 (Part 3): 477; Freeman, *Lee's Lieutenants,* 1: 371n; Douglas, *Stonewall,* 72.

28. George B. McClellan, "The Peninsular Campaign," *B&L,* 2: 173–74; *OR,* 11 (Part 1): 25–26; Swinton, *Campaigns,* 129.

29. Davis's postwar contention that he was surprised to find the army on the south bank of the Chickahominy and that the topic of why Johnston had crossed the river dominated the conversation was dismissed even by Freeman, who charitably credits the president with confusing his dates. The only support for that account came from the gossipy and undependable memoirs of Postmaster General John H. Reagan, who claimed to have accompanied the president and to have seen a "look of surprise" sweep over his face, revealing "a trace of pain." The actual topics of discussion can be inferred from Reagan, however, when read in conjunction with later accounts by Johnston and a letter to Lee on May 18. See *OR,* 11 (Part 3): 526; Davis, *Rise and Fall,* 2: 103–4; Freeman, *Lee's Lieutenants,* 1: 210n; John H. Reagan, *Memoirs, with Special Reference to Secession and the Civil War* (New York: n. p., 1906), 138–39; Johnston, "Manassas to Seven Pines," 208; Longstreet, *Manassas to Appomattox,* 82; Lee, ed., *Pendleton,* 184.

30. Johnston himself admitted that the return he provided Lee was approximate, and a superficial examination reveals that the numbers had been taken directly from his return of effectives on April 30, before the battle of Williamsburg. That Johnston

wrote twice to Lee on May 22 can be determined from Lee's two May 22 letters in response. See *OR*, 11 (Part 3): 530–34.

31. Ibid., 536.

32. Johnston resolved the situation by an almost cosmetic expedient, "elevating" Magruder on May 28 to command of the "Centre" of the army, which nominally made him the equal of Smith and Longstreet. Magruder still commanded only six brigades; Smith and Longstreet each supervised eleven and twelve. *OR*, 11 (Part 1): 663–68, and (Part 3): 537–39; Smith, *Battle of Seven Pines*, 8.

33. That Johnston planned to attack by May 29 and that he favored an assault north of the river can be determined from Davis's memoirs, although, as G. W. Smith later pointed out, Davis apparently confused the elements of several different plans. It is far more likely that Johnston was still waiting for the Federals to make themselves vulnerable in one locale or the other. See Smith, *Confederate War Papers*, 48–49; Longstreet, *Manassas to Appomattox*, 82; Davis, *Rise and Fall*, 2: 120–21; Smith, *Seven Pines*, 10–11; Freeman, *Lee's Lieutenants*, 1: 313; *OR*, 11 (Part 3): 541–42. Freeman, apparently misreading Davis's memoirs and letter to Johnston on May 23, incorrectly places this visit by Lee on May 24.

34. There may have been as many as nine batteries in the Richmond area—the statements of A. L. Long and Pendleton disagree. See *OR*, 11 (Part 3): 539–40, 542, 552; Lee, ed., *Pendleton*, 185.

35. Douglas, *Stonewall*, 58–74; Tanner, *Stonewall in the Valley*, 239.

36. *OR*, 11 (Part 1): 668–69, 675–77; Johnston, *Narrative*, 130.

37. Special Orders no. 26, Army of the Rappahannock, May 23, 1862, General Orders no. 13, Army of the Rappahannock, May 24, 1862, in Anderson Brigade Order Book; *OR*, 11 (Part 3): 537, 543.

38. Branch reported 243 casualties, excluding those in the Twenty-eighth North Carolina and the Fourth Virginia Cavalry. Porter claimed to have found 200 dead and taken more than 700 prisoners. For a discussion of this discrepancy, see Freeman, *Lee's Lieutenants*, 1: 270n; *OR*, 11 (Part 3): 184, 546–47, 554; Robert E. Lee to Samuel Cooper, May 25, 1862, in *LR–AIGO*, M-474, Reel 25; Robert E. Lee to James Longstreet, May 28, 1862, in *Lee Letterbook*.

39. Smith, *Seven Pines*, 12–13.

40. Johnston in his memoirs mistakenly recalled that Huger's division and not that of D. R. Jones would be brought to reinforce Smith's attack. Otherwise, the accounts of Johnston, Smith, and Longstreet are remarkably consistent to this point. See Johnston, *Narrative*, 131; Smith, *Seven Pines*, 15; Longstreet, *Manassas to Appomattox*, 85.

41. D. H. Hill to Winfield Scott Featherston, May 27, 1862, Hill Letters; Douglas, *Stonewall*, 72; *OR*, 11 (Part 3): 555.

42. No record of the conference has survived, though the fact that it happened is established by Joseph Johnston to William Browne, May 27, 1862, in Jefferson Davis Papers, Chicago Historical Society. It may be inferred that Davis was informed of the proposed date of the attack from the fact that he rode out again on May 29, for which his erroneous chronology of the last half of May in his memoirs fails to account satisfactorily. See Davis, *Rise and Fall*, 2: 121.

43. Davis, *Rise and Fall*, 2: 121; Smith, *Seven Pines*, 14.

44. Curiously, given the postwar antipathy between them, both Smith and

Longstreet agree fairly closely regarding the conference to this point. See Longstreet, *Manassas to Appomattox,* 85–86; Smith, *Seven Pines,* 15.

45. Longstreet, *Manassas to Appomattox,* 86.

46. James Longstreet to Osmun Latrobe, February 10, 1886, in Osmun Latrobe Diary Virginia Historical Society, Richmond.

11. SEVEN PINES

1. *Richmond Examiner,* May 19, 1862, 2.

2. The only extant record of the cabinet meeting in which the possible abandonment of Richmond was discussed is that of John H. Reagan, who painted the picture of an emotional Robert E. Lee declaring that "Richmond must not be given up." Even ignoring the fact that Lee knew Johnston had no intention of giving up the capital and that such an outburst would have been totally out of character for Lee, it should be sufficient to note that the anecdote is sandwiched between two others of doubtful credibility. Without any supporting evidence, Reagan's description of the scene is best relegated to the status of colorful apocrypha. See Reagan, *Memoirs,* 138; Manarin, ed., *Richmond at War,* 176–77.

3. Walter T. Durham, *Nashville, the Occupied City: The First Eighteen Months, February 16, 1862, to June 30, 1863* (Nashville: Tennessee Historical Society, 1985): 1, 14; Marion A. Baker, "Farragut's Demands for the Surrender of New Orleans," *B&L,* 2: 95; Samuel Carter III, *The Final Fortress: The Campaign for Vicksburg, 1862–1863* (New York: St. Martin's Press, 1980), 51–52.

4. *OR,* 11 (Part 3): 524; Boney, *John Letcher,* 163; Putnam, *Richmond,* 131.

5. D. H. Hill to "My Dear Wife," May 11, 1862, in Hill Papers, Stiles, *Four Years,* 85–86; *OR,* 11 (Part 1): 605.

6. Johnston inaugurated the practice of consolidating understrength batteries, and, from contextual evidence, seems to have envisioned separate artillery battalions supporting each division. His calls for the independent companies of cavalry around the state to be gathered together into regiments led Confederate authorities from May to July 1862 to issue orders creating the Fifth, Tenth, Twelfth, and Thirteenth Virginia Cavalry Regiments, and the Fourteenth, Fifteenth, and Seventeenth Virginia Cavalry Battalions. See Robert E. Lee to Joseph Johnston, May 7, 1862, Robert E. Lee to Abraham C. Myers, May 7, 1862, Robert E. Lee to Lucius Northrop, May 7, 1862, Robert E. Lee to Abraham C. Myers, May 8, 1862, Robert E. Lee to Lucius B. Northrop, May 8, 1862, Walter Taylor to John H. Winder, May 14, 1862, in *Lee Letterbook; OR,* 11 (Part 3): 512, 513; George T. Anderson to George W. Randolph, May 16, 1862, in *LR–AIGO,* M-474, Reel 3; John B. Gordon to George W. Randolph, May 13, 1862, in *LR–AIGO,* M-474, Reel 21; A. P. Hill to Samuel Cooper, May 13 and May 24, 1862, in *LR–AIGO,* M-474, Reel 24; D. H. Hill to John Trapier, May 28, 1862, in *LR–AIGO,* M-474, Reel 25; Lee, ed., *Pendleton,* 185; Wise, *Long Arm,* 186–87.

7. For the detailed calculation of Johnston's strength in late May, see the appendixes. McClellan reported only 98,008 "present for duty," but in a spurious bookkeeping maneuver omitted from this total 5,374 officers and men actually present and available to him. Smith, *Confederate War Papers,* 145; Rowland, ed., *Jefferson Davis,*

Constitutionalist, 9: 594–95; Lee, ed., *Pendleton,* 185; *OR,* 11 (Part 3): 204, 539, 558, and 51 (Part 2): 564.

8. *OR,* 11 (Part 3): 563.

9. This interpretation follows G. W. Smith rather than Johnston or Longstreet, both of whom maintained in official reports and postwar memoirs that Longstreet was supposed to support Hill on the Williamsburg Road instead of moving down Nine Mile Road. Smith's account is accepted for purposes of establishing Johnston's original intentions because of Johnston's June 28, 1862, letter to Smith in which Johnston referred to "the misunderstanding between Longstreet and myself in regard to the direction of his division" and asked that Smith remove several paragraphs from his official report. See Smith, *Seven Pines,* 19–22; *OR,* 11 (Part 1): 933–41; Johnston, *Narrative,* 132–33; Longstreet, *Manassas to Appomattox,* 87–88; Johnston, "Manassas to Seven Pines," 211–12; G. W. Smith, "Two Days of Battle at Seven Pines," *B&L,* 2: 225–26, 228.

10. *OR,* 11 (Part 1): 943; Longstreet, *Manassas to Appomattox,* 87.

11. *OR,* 11 (Part 3): 563.

12. Ibid., (Part 1): 943.

13. Ibid., 938.

14. Ibid., 942.

15. Ibid., 938, and (Part 3): 563.

16. Ibid., (Part 1): 538.

17. Freeman, *Lee's Lieutenants,* 1: 228; *OR,* 11 (Part 1): 938.

18. Longstreet's ambition for promotion and independent command later in the war has been argued by historians for years. It is evident upon reading the barrage of correspondence with General Cooper during the three weeks following May 5 that Longstreet's design for carving from Johnston's army a permanent command larger than a single division began with the battle of Williamsburg. See James Longstreet to Samuel Cooper, May 7, May 9, and May 27, 1862, in *LR–AIGO,* M-474, Reel 30; James Longstreet to Samuel Cooper, May 12, 1862, in Richard H. Anderson, Compiled Service Record, National Archives. It was no slip of the pen that Longstreet cited himself in these letters as commanding the "Second Corps" of the army.

19. Johnston's willingness to delegate, even to extremes, has already been demonstrated within the context of Williamsburg and northern Virginia. The message to Hill can be inferred from the fact that the North Carolinian stated in his report that "I was directed by General Longstreet to move with my whole division at dawn on the Williamsburg Road and to *lead* the attack on the Yankees" [emphasis added]. That Hill would "lead" the attack on the Williamsburg Road implies that he had been informed there would be other troops following his. See *OR,* 11 (Part 1): 943.

20. *OR,* 11 (Part 1): 939; Longstreet, *Manassas to Appomattox,* 87–88, 331; Freeman, *Lee's Lieutenants,* 3: 50.

21. *OR,* 11 (Part 3): 563; Smith, *Seven Pines,,* 146; Longstreet, *Manassas to Appomattox,* 87.

22. That Long brought this news may be inferred from three facts. First, Lee did not include it in the letter he sent later in the day. Second, the order had just been issued at headquarters that morning, and it would have been natural for Long to carry it out with him. Third, Long and Johnston eventually got around to discussing reinforcements, at which point if not before it would have occurred to Long to mention

Ripley's force even if he did not bring along a copy of the order. See *OR,* 11 (Part 3): 560, 563; Long, *Personal Memoirs,* 158–59.

23. Long, *Memoirs,* 158–59.

24. Both Freeman and Dowdey find much in Long's account for which to castigate Johnston. Freeman has described Long as returning to Richmond with "a polite but indefinite answer to his message: Johnston would be happy to have Lee ride out to the field, and, meantime, would Lee send him all the reinforcements he could collect?" Thus far, Freeman is well inside the bounds of legitimate if arguable interpretation of Long's statement, which he cited as his authority for the sentence. But in the next pair of sentences—unsupported by any references—Freeman asserts that "Johnston did not tell Long, nor did Long learn from any other source, when the battle for Richmond would open. Still uncertainty; still suspense!" Dowdey has gone further afield, distorting the entire exchange: "To Lee's offer of his services, Johnston answered civilly enough that Lee would be welcome at headquarters, *but that the only service he could perform would be to send reinforcements. For what purpose he did not tell Colonel Long* [emphasis added]."

Johnston could not have revealed the full details of his plans, even had he been willing to do so, because when Long approached him, the army commander had not yet held his conference with Longstreet to iron out the essentials of the attack. This may be inferred by the fact that Long did not mention Longstreet's presence and Longstreet did not mention Long. For Long to have arrived after Longstreet left Johnston's headquarters would have placed the visit into the early evening, far later than Long's memoirs suggest. Thus Johnston could not have confided the specifics of his operational planning to Long.

It again stretches credibility to suggest that Johnston told Long nothing about his intentions. Lee already knew that Johnston planned to attack McClellan and that he preferred to strike south of the river. That Lee knew some sort of attack was impending is implied by Long's statement that Lee "would be glad to participate in *the* battle" [emphasis added]. It also makes little sense to believe that Johnston, who wanted Ripley's brigade and any other reinforcements he could get, did not tell Lee when he expected to need them, particularly when the two men had been in daily contact since the first week of May, and Johnston had always advised Lee in advance of major movements, from the evacuation of Yorktown to the aborted attack on May 29. See Freeman, *R. E. Lee,* 2: 67; Dowdey, *Seven Days,* 86.

25. *OR,* 11 (Part 1): 943, 986, and (Part 3): 563; Smith, *Seven Pines,* 23.

26. Smith, *Confederate War Papers,* 162.

27. Ibid.

28. Smith, *Seven Pines,* 23.

29. *OR,* 11 (Part 3): 565.

30. Smith, *Confederate War Papers,* 164.

31. Smith, *Seven Pines,* 24; Smith, *Confederate War Papers,* 564.

32. Smith, *Seven Pines,* 24.

33. Smith, *Confederate War Papers,* 169; Smith, *Seven Pines,* 25.

34. *OR,* 11 (Part 1): 914.

35. Smith, *Seven Pines,* 26.

36. Freeman, *R. E. Lee,* 2: 68.

37. Freeman, *Lee's Lieutenants,* 1: 236; Freeman, *R. E. Lee,* 68.

38. Smith, *Confederate War Papers*, 171.

39. Smith did not specify a time for Whiting's departure in his memoirs. Freeman guessed at 2:00 P.M., which seems logical enough since the trip should have consumed about an hour each way, and the major returned at 4:00 P.M. See ibid., 167, and Freeman, *Lee's Lieutenants*, 1: 236.

40. Davis, *Rise and Fall*, 2: 122.

41. This sentence is from the version of Smith's report printed in his memoirs, not the one that he submitted to the adjutant general after Johnston later requested several omissions. See Smith, *Confederate War Papers*, 170.

42. Johnston never admitted later that he personally assumed command of Whiting's division, but on this point Smith and Davis agreed convincingly. See ibid., 174, and Davis, *Rise and Fall*, 2: 122–23.

43. Longstreet, *Manassas to Appomattox*, 91; Smith, "Two Days," 229; OR, 11 (Part 1): 942.

44. Most historians have correctly dismissed Longstreet's contention in his memoirs that he had admitted to Huger that he was the junior officer and that Huger had declined to command, citing Huger's endorsement on Longstreet's report. There is, however, even more compelling evidence to support Huger's position, a letter he addressed to Lee the next week concerning Longstreet's rank and the response from the adjutant general's office, which reveals that the discussion had extended to dates of rank in the Confederate regular army. It may also be inferred from this document that Longstreet did not give Huger specific dates for his own commissions, or else Huger would have phrased his letter to confirm them rather than to ascertain them. See Benjamin Huger to Robert E. Lee, June 7, 1862, Samuel Cooper to Benjamin Huger, June 8, 1862, in *LR–AIGO*, M-474, Reel 27.

45. The best reconstruction of these orders is in Freeman, *Lee's Lieutenants*, 1: 239; OR, 11 (Part 1): 939–43, 986; Longstreet, *Manassas to Appomattox*, 92; Smith, "Two Days," 229; Smith, *Seven Pines*, 77.

46. OR, 11 (Part 1): 971.

47. Ibid., 943, 971.

48. Ibid., 961.

49. This and the succeeding paragraphs are based on Garland's report in OR, 11 (Part 1): 961–63.

50. Ibid.

51. Ibid., 951, 953, 961.

52. Ibid., 914, 238.

53. Ibid., 971.

54. Ibid., 979; Gordon, *Reminiscences*, 56.

55. OR, 11 (Part 1): 971–72.

56. Ibid., 969–70.

57. Smith, *Seven Pines*, 66; OR, 11 (Part 1): 986–87.

58. OR, 11 (Part 1): 945.

59. Ibid., 763–64.

60. McMurry, *Hood*, 41; Smith, *Confederate War Papers*, 174–75.

61. OR, 11 (Part 1): 175.

62. Ibid., 792.

63. Smith, *Confederate War Papers*, 179.

64. *OR,* 11 (Part 1): 758, 800; Smith, *Confederate War Papers,* 176–77.

65. Davis, *Rise and Fall,* 2: 122.

66. Johnston, *Narrative,* 48–49; Freeman, *Lee's Lieutenants,* 1: 80.

67. The manner in which Johnston rewrote his role at the key moment in the battle during the postwar years gives a strong indication of just how uncomfortable the general was with his rather rash decision to lead Whiting's division himself. In both the *Narrative* and his article for *B&L,* Johnston related that he had directed that the division be sent forward, omitting the fact that he accompanied it and issued orders directly to its brigadiers. See Johnston, *Narrative,* 136–37; Johnston, "Manassas to Seven Pines," *B&L,* 2: 214.

68. Johnston, *Narrative,* 138.

12. JOHNSTON'S CAMPAIGN

1. Johnston, *Narrative,* 154.

2. Hood, *Advance and Retreat,* 21, 154–56.

3. *OR,* 11 (Part 1): 935, 939–41; Smith, *Confederate War Papers,* 165–71.

4. Smith dealt with Huger's "alleged 'slow movements'" in everything he wrote about the battle, more from an interest in smearing Longstreet's name than from any regard for or friendship with Huger. That Johnston did not initially blame Smith for the failure to gain a victory on June 1 is evident from the tone of his June 24, 1862, report. See Smith, *Seven Pines,* 64–82; *OR,* 11 (Part 1): 933–35; Johnston, *Narrative,* 139, 141; Freeman, *Lee's Lieutenants,* 1: 243.

5. Bruce Catton, *Grant Moves South* (Boston: Little, Brown, 1960), 216–17.

6. Steven E. Woodworth, "Dark Portents: Confederate Command at the Battle of Williamsburg," in *The Peninsula Campaign: Yorktown to Seven Days,* ed. William J. Miller, 3 vols. to date (Campbell, CA: Savas, 1997), 3: 3; McMurry, "Ole Joe in Virginia," 26.

7. It is an intriguing fact, never to my knowledge investigated or even remarked upon, that Johnston's wounding at Seven Pines was a unique occurrence in the war. No other commanding general of a major army suffered such a wound (and recovered) in his first battle. The effect of major wounds on the psyche of men such as Richard S. Ewell and John B. Hood has been considered at length by a number of historians, but between their cases and that of Johnston there are significant differences. Neither Ewell nor Hood held top command (and therefore final responsibility) when so wounded, and neither man was wounded in his first major attack. Yet both men suffered severe personality changes that affected their generalship throughout the remainder of the war. If this was the case, then it is hard to escape the conclusion that Johnston's wounds must have had an equal impact on him.

8. Johnston, "Manassas to Seven Pines," *B&L,* 2: 217.

9. Sears, *McClellan,* 196–97.

10. Rowland, ed., *Jefferson Davis, Constitutionalist,* 8: 60.

11. Freeman, *R. E. Lee,* 2: 87–88.

12. Hood, *Advance and Retreat,* 317.

BIBLIOGRAPHY

MANUSCRIPT SOURCES

Chicago Historical Society, Chicago, IL
    Jefferson Davis Papers
College of William and Mary, Civil War Collection, Williamsburg, VA
    Benjamin Stoddert Ewell Papers
    John Buchanan Floyd Papers
    Daniel Harvey Hill Papers
    Robert Morton Hughes Papers
    Joseph Eggleston Johnston Papers
    Stephen Russell Mallory Papers
Duke University, Durham, NC
    Joseph E. Johnston Papers
Library of Congress, Manuscript Division, Washington, DC
    Judah P. Benjamin Diary
    Alexander Hugh Holmes Stuart Papers
    Louis T. Wigfall Papers
National Archives, Washington, DC
    Richard H. Anderson, Compiled Service Record
    Jubal A. Early, Compiled Service Record
    Richard Stoddert Ewell, Compiled Service Record
    Daniel Harvey Hill, Compiled Service Record
    Thomas Jonathan Jackson, Compiled Service Record
    Joseph Eggleston Johnston, Compiled Service Record
    Robert Edward Lee, Compiled Service Record
    Robert Edward Lee, Letterbook, 1862–1864
    Letters and Telegrams Received, Confederate Quartermaster-General
    Letters and Telegrams Received, Office of the Adjutant and Inspector General, Con-
        federate States of America
    Letters and Telegrams Received, Secretary of War, Confederate States of America
    Letters and Telegrams Sent, Army of Northern Virginia, January 1862–March 1863
    Letters and Telegrams Sent, Confederate Quartermaster-General
    Letters and Telegrams Sent, Office of the Adjutant and Inspector General, Con-
        federate States of America

Letters and Telegrams Sent, Secretary of War, Confederate States of America
Letters and Telegrams Received, Secretary of War, Main Series, 1801–1870
Letters Sent, Secretary of War, Main Series, 1801–1870
Letters Sent, W. H. C. Whiting, March–July 1862
James Longstreet, Compiled Service Record
John Bankhead Magruder, Compiled Service Record
Gustavus Woodson Smith, Compiled Service Record
William Henry Chase Whiting, Compiled Service Record
Old Dominion University, Norfolk, VA
    Robert Morton Hughes Collection
University of Alabama, University, W. Stanley Hoole Special Collections
    Jefferson Davis Papers
University of Michigan, Ann Arbor, William L. Clements Library
    Joseph Eggleston Johnston Papers
University of North Carolina, Chapel Hill, Southern Historical Collection
    Thomas Bragg Diary
    Stephen R. Mallory Diary
University of Virginia, Charlottesville, Aldermann Library
    Robert Mercer Taliaferro Hunter Papers
U.S. Military History Institute, Carlisle Barracks, PA
    Murray J. Smith Collection
Virginia Historical Society, Richmond
    J. R. Anderson, Brigade Order Book, 1862
    Carter Family Papers
    Early Family Papers
    Harwood Family Papers
    Daniel Harvey Hill Letter
    Thomas Jonathan Jackson Papers
    Osmun Latrobe Diary, 1862–1865 (typescript)
    George Bolling Lee Papers
    Charles T. Mason Papers
    James Ewell Brown Stuart Papers
    Talcott Family Papers
    Beverly Randolph Wellford Papers

PRIMARY SOURCES (PRINTED)

Adjutant General. *Official Army Register for 1843–1862.* Washington, DC: Adjutant
    General's Office, January of appropriate year, except for additional August 1855
    edition.
Alexander, E. P. *Military Memoirs of a Confederate.* New York: n.p., 1907.
———. "Sketch of Longstreet's Division, Yorktown and Williamsburg." *Southern
    Historical Society Papers* 10 (1882): 35–39.
Armistead, Drury. "The Battle in Which General Johnston Was Wounded." *Southern
    Historical Society Papers* 18 (1890): 185–88.
Blackford, W. W. *War Years with Jeb Stuart.* New York: Charles Scribner's, 1945.

Clopton, William Izard. "New Light on the Great Drewry's Bluff Fight." *Southern Historical Society Papers* 24 (1901): 283–87.

Cook, Joel. *The Siege of Richmond: A Narrative of the military operations of Major-General George B. McClellan during May and June, 1862.* Philadelphia, 1862.

Cowper, Pulaski, ed. *Extracts of Letters of Major-General Bryan Grimes to his wife, written while in Active Service in the Army of Northern Virginia, together with some personal recollections of the war written by him after its close.* Raleigh, NC, 1884.

Crist, Linda Lasswell, Mary Seaton Dix, and Kenneth H. Williams, eds. *The Papers of Jefferson Davis.* 9 vols. to date. Baton Rouge: Louisiana State University Press, 1981–1996.

Davis, George B., Leslie J. Perry, Joseph W. Kirkly, and Calvin D. Cowles, compilers. *The Official Military Atlas of the Civil War.* 1891–1895. Reprint, New York: Arno Press, 1978.

Davis, Jefferson F. *The Rise and Fall of the Confederate Government.* 2 vols. New York: D. Appleton, 1881.

Douglas, Henry Kyd. *I Rode with Stonewall.* Chapel Hill: University of North Carolina Press, 1940.

Dowdy, Clifford, and Louis H. Manarin, eds. *The Wartime Papers of Robert E. Lee.* New York: Bramhall House, 1961.

Drewry, A. H. "Drewry's Bluff Fight." *Southern Historical Society Papers* 29 (1901): 285–87.

Early, Jubal A. "Strength of Ewell's Division in the Campaign of 1862—Field Return." *Southern Historical Society Papers* 8 (1880): 302–3.

———. *War Memoirs; Autobiographical Sketch and Narrative of the War Between the States.* Bloomington: Indiana University Press, 1960.

Foote, Henry S. *War of the Rebellion; or Scylla and Charybdis.* New York, 1866.

Freeman, Douglas Southall, ed. *Lee's Dispatches to Jefferson Davis, 1862–1865.* New edition, enlarged, with foreword by Grady McWhiney. New York: G. P. Putnam's, 1957.

French, Samuel G. *Two Wars: An Autobiography of Gen. Samuel G. French.* Nashville, TN: Confederate Veteran, 1901.

Gallagher, Gary W., ed. *Fighting for the Confederacy: The Personal Recollections of General Edward Porter Alexander.* Chapel Hill, University of North Carolina Press, 1989.

———. " 'We are our own Trumpeters': Robert E. Lee Describes Winfield Scott's Campaign to Mexico City." *Virginia Magazine of History and Biography* 95, no. 3 (July 1987): 123–27.

Gordon, John B. *Reminiscences of the Civil War.* 1903. Reprint, New York: Charles Scribner's, 1928.

Gorgas, Josiah. "Ordnance Department of the Confederate Government." *The Confederate Soldier in the Civil War.* New York, n.d.

Grimsley, Mark, ed. " 'We prepare to Receive the Enemy Where We Stand': The Journal of the Comte de Paris." Translated by Bernatello Glod. *Civil War Times Illustrated* 24, no. 3 (May 1985): 18–31.

Hamilton, J. G. de Roulhac, ed. *The Papers of Randolph Abbot Shotwell.* 3 vols. Raleigh: North Carolina Historical Commission, 1929.

Harrison, Mrs. Burton. *Recollections Grave and Grey.* New York: Charles Scribner's, 1911.

Hassler, William W., ed. *The General to His Lady: The Civil War Letters of William Dorsey Pender to Fanny Pender*. Chapel Hill: University of North Carolina Press, 1962.

Hewett, Janet B., Noah Andre Trudeau, and Bryce A. Suderow, eds. *Supplement to the Official Records of the Union and Confederate Armies*. 54 vols. to date. Wilmington, NC: 1994–1997.

Hill, Daniel Harvey. "The Haversack." *Land We Love* 1, no. 1 (May 1866): 15.

———. "The Haversack." *Land We Love* 1, no. 2 (June 1866).

Hood, John Bell. *Advance and Retreat*. 1880. Reprint, Secausus, NJ: Blue and Grey, 1985.

Howard, McHenry. *Recollections of a Maryland Confederate Soldier and Staff Officer Under Johnston, Jackson, and Lee*. Baltimore: Williams and Wilkins, 1914.

Hughes, Robert M., ed. "Some Letters from the Papers of General Joseph E. Johnston," *William and Mary Quarterly* 2d ser., 11, no. 4 (October 1931): 318–24.

Jennings, T. D. "Incidents in the Battle of Williamsburg." *Confederate Veteran* 5, no. 9 (September 1897): 477–78.

Johnson, Robert U., and Clarence C. Buell, eds. *Battles and Leaders of the Civil War*. 4 vols. New York: Century, 1887.

Johnson, W. Gart. "The Barksdale-Humphrey Brigade." *Confederate Veteran*. April 1894 Supplemental Issue.

Johnston, Joseph E. "Manassas to Seven Pines," *Century Magazine* 30, no. 1 (May 1885). (An abridged version of this article was published under the same title in Johnson and Buell, eds., *Battles and Leaders of the Civil War*, vol. 2: 93–114.)

———. *Narrative of Military Operations Directed During the Late War Between the States*. Bloomington: Indiana University Press, 1959.

———. "Responsibilities of the First Bull Run." In Johnson and Buell, eds., *Battles and Leaders of the Civil War*. Vol 2: 240–58.

de Joinville, Prince Henrí. *The Army of the Potomac: Its Organization, Its Commander, and Its Campaign*. New York: Anson D. F. Randolph, 1862.

Jones, John B. *A Rebel War Clerk's Diary at the Confederate States Capital*. Edited by Howard Swiggett. 2 vols. New York: Old Hickory Bookshop, 1935.

Laswell, Mary, ed. *Rags and Hope: The Recollections of Val C. Giles, Four Years with Hood's Brigade, Fourth Texas Infantry, 1861–1865*. New York: Coward-McCann, 1961.

Lee, Susan P., ed. *Memoirs of William Nelson Pendleton*. Philadelphia, 1893.

Longstreet, James. *From Manassas to Appomattox*. 1896. Reprint, Secaucus, NJ: Blue and Grey, 1984.

Lord, Walter, ed. *The Fremantle Diary*. Boston: Little, Brown, 1954.

Lowe, R. G. "The Dreux Battalion," *Confederate Veteran* 5, no. 2 (February 1897): 55.

———. "Magruder's Defense of the Peninsula." *Confederate Veteran* 8, no. 3 (March 1900): 72–73.

McCarthy, Carlton. *Detailed Minutiae of Soldier Life in the Army of Northern Virginia, 1861–1865*. Richmond: Carlton McCarthy, 1882.

McClellan, H. B. *The Life and Campaigns of Major-General J. E. B. Stuart*. Boston, 1885.

McKinney, J. W. "My First Experience at the Front." *Confederate Veteran* 3, no. 1 (January 1985): 13–14.

Manarin, Louis H., ed. *Richmond at War: The Minutes of the City Council, 1861–1865.* Chapel Hill: University of North Carolina Press, 1966.

Maury, Dabney H. "Interesting Reminiscences of General Johnston." *Southern Historical Society Papers* 18 (1890): 171–79.

———. *Recollections of a Virginian in the Mexican, Indian, and Civil Wars.* New York, 1894.

Moffett, Mary Conner, ed. *Letters of General James Conner, C.S.A.* Columbia, SC: R. L. Bryan, 1950.

Monroe, Haskell, Jr., James T. McIntosh, Linda Lasswell Crist et al., eds. *The Papers of Jefferson Davis.* 9 vols. to date. Baton Rouge: Louisiana State University Press, 1981–1997.

Northrop, Lucius B. "A Statement from the Confederate Commissary General." *Century Magazine* 31, no. 5 (March 1886): 114.

Oates, William C. *The War Between the Union and the Confederacy and Its Lost Opportunities.* n.p., n.d.

Parker, William H. *Recollections of a Naval Officer, 1841–1865.* New York, 1883.

Pendleton, S. H. "Seven Pines, or Fair Oaks." *Confederate Veteran.* April 1894 Supplemental Issue.

Phillips, U. B., ed. *The Correspondence of Robert Toombs, Alexander H. Stephens, and Howell Cobb.* Washington, DC: n.p., 1913.

"Proceedings of the First Confederate Congress—First Session." *Southern Historical Society Papers* 44 (June 1923): 1–246.

Putnam, Sally. *Richmond During the War: Four Years of Personal Observations by a Richmond Lady.* New York, 1867.

Reagan, John H. *Memoirs, with Special Reference to Secession and the Civil War.* New York: n.p., 1906.

Reese, George H., ed. *Proceedings of the Virginia State Convention of 1861.* 18 vols. Richmond: n.p., n.d.

Report of the Commission Appointed Under the eighth section of the Act of Congress of June 21, 1860, to examine into the organization, system of discipline, and course in instruction of the United States Military Academy at West Point. Washington, DC, 1860.

Report of the Joint Committee on the Conduct of the War. 37th Congress, 3d Session, House of Representatives. 3 vols. Washington, DC: GPO, 1863.

Richardson, James D., ed. *The Messages and Papers of Jefferson Davis and the Confederacy, Including Diplomatic Correspondence.* 2 vols. 1906. Reprint, New York: R. R. Bowker, 1966.

Richmond Howitzers in the War; Four Years Campaigning with the Army of Northern Virginia, by a Member of the Company. Richmond, 1891.

Rowland, Dunbar, ed. *Jefferson Davis, Constitutionalist: His Letters, Papers and Speeches.* 10 vols. Jackson, MS, 1923.

Scott, Winfield. *Memoirs of Lieut.-General Scott, LL.D., Written by Himself.* 2 vols. New York: Sheldon, 1864.

Shaw, Arthur Marvin, ed. "Some Post-War Letters from Jefferson Davis to His Former Aide-de-Camp William Preston Johnston." *Virginia Magazine of History and Biography.* 51, no. 2 (April 1943): 149–55.

Smith, Gustavus Woodson. *The Battle of Seven Pines.* 1891. Reprint, New York: C. C. Crawford, 1985.

————. *Confederate War Papers: Fairfax Court House, New Orleans, Seven Pines, Richmond, and North Carolina.* 2d ed. New York, 1884.

Sorrel, G. Moxley. *Recollections of a Confederate Staff Officer.* New York: Neale, 1905.

Stiles, Robert. *Four Years Under Marse Robert.* Washington, DC, 1903.

Tapscott, J. B. "Early War Incidents on the James." *Confederate Veteran* 7, no. 1 (January 1898): 27–28.

Taylor, Richard. *Destruction and Reconstruction.* 1889. Reprint, New York: Longman's, Green, 1955.

Taylor, Walter H. *Four Years with General Lee.* New York: D. Appleton, 1877.

————. *General Lee, His Campaigns in Virginia, 1861–1865, with Personal Reminiscences.* Norfolk, VA: Nusbaum, 1906.

Tower, R. Lockwood, ed. *Lee's Adjutant: The Wartime Letters of Colonel Walter Herron Taylor, 1862–1865.* Columbia: University of South Carolina Press, 1995.

Trout, Robert J., ed. *With Pen and Saber: The Letters and Diaries of J. E. B. Stuart's Staff Officers.* Mechanicsburg, PA: Stackpole, 1995.

Turner, Charles W., ed. *Captain Greenlee Davidson, CSA, Diary and Letters, 1851–1861.* Verona, VA: McClure, 1975.

Vandiver, Frank, ed. *Confederate Blockade Running Through Bermuda, 1861–1865, Letters and Cargo Manifests.* Austin: University of Texas Press, 1947.

Warfield, Edgar. *A Confederate Soldier's Memoirs.* Richmond: Masonic Home Press, 1936.

Woodward, C. Vann, ed. *Mary Chesnut's Civil War.* New Haven: Yale University Press, 1981.

Woodward, C. Vann, and Elisabeth Muhlenfeld, eds. *The Private Mary Chesnut: The Unpublished Civil War Diaries.* New York: Oxford University Press, 1984.

Wright, Robert. "Sinking of the Jamestown." *Southern Historical Society Papers* 29 (1901): 371–72.

Younger, Edward, ed. *Inside the Confederate Government: The Diary of Robert Garlick Hill Kean.* New York: Oxford University Press, 1957.

SECONDARY SOURCES

Abele, Rudolph von. *Alexander H. Stephens: A Biography.* New York: Alfred A. Knopf, 1946.

Alexander, P. W. "Confederate Chieftains." *Southern Literary Messenger* 35, no. 1 (January 1863): 11–12.

Allan, William. *History of the Campaign of Gen. T. J. (Stonewall) Jackson in the Shenandoah Valley of Virginia.* Dayton, OH: Morningside, 1974.

Bauer, Jack. *The Mexican War, 1846–1848.* New York: Macmillan, 1974.

Bell, Robert T. *Eleventh Virginia Infantry.* Lynchburg, VA: H. E. Howard, 1985.

Benet, Stephen Vincent. *John Brown's Body.* 1943. Reprint, New York: Book of the Month Club, 1980.

Berry, Thomas S. "The Rise of Flour Milling in Richmond." *Virginia Magazine of History and Biography* 77, no. 4 (October 1970): 387–408.

Black, Robert C., III. *The Railroads of the Confederacy.* Chapel Hill: University of North Carolina Press, 1952.

Boatner, Mark Mayo, III. *The Civil War Dictionary*. New York: David McKay, 1959.

Boney, F. N. *John Letcher of Virginia*. University: University of Alabama Press, 1966.

Brackett, Albert Gallatin. *History of the United States Cavalry*. New York: Harper and Brothers, 1865.

Bradford, Gameliel. *Confederate Portraits*. Boston, 1912.

Bruce, Kathleen. *Virginia Iron Manufacture in the Slave Era*. New York: Century, 1931.

Bryan, Charles F. Jr. "Stalemate at Seven Pines." *Civil War Times Illustrated* 12, no. 5 (August 1973): 4–11.

Carter, Samuel C., III. *The Final Fortress: The Campaign for Vicksburg. 1862–1863*. New York: St. Martin's Press, 1980.

Casdorph, Paul D. *Prince John Magruder, His Life and Campaigns*. New York: John Wiley and Sons, 1996.

Castel, Albert. *Decision in the West: The Atlanta Campaign of 1864*. Lawrence: University Press of Kansas, 1992.

Catton, Bruce. *Grant Moves South*. Boston: Little, Brown, 1960.

———. *Mr. Lincoln's Army*. Garden City: Doubleday, 1951.

Cauthen, Charles E. *South Carolina Goes to War, 1860–1865*. Chapel Hill: University of North Carolina Press, 1950.

Chapla, John D. *Forty-second Virginia Infantry*. Lynchburg, VA: H. E. Howard, 1983.

Cleland, Robert G. "Jefferson Davis and the Confederate Cabinet." *Southwestern Historical Quarterly* 19, no. 3 (January 1916): 189–235.

Coffman, Edward N. *The Old Army: A Portrait of the American Army in Peacetime, 1784–1898*. New York: Oxford University Press, 1985.

Coggins, Jack. *Arms and Equipment of the Civil War*. New York: Doubleday, 1962.

Connelly, Thomas Lawrence. *Army of the Heartland; The Army of Tennessee, 1861–1862*. Baton Rouge: Louisiana State University Press, 1967.

Crute, Joseph H. Jr. *Confederate Staff Officers, 1861–1865*. Powhatan, VA: Derwent Books, 1982.

Cunningham, H. H. *Doctors in Gray: The Confederate Medical Service*. Gloucester, MA: Peter Smith, 1970.

Dabney, Virginius. *Richmond: The Story of a City*. Garden City: Doubleday, 1976.

Daniel, Larry J. *Cannoneers in Grey: The Field Artillery of the Army of Tennessee, 1861–1865*. University: University of Alabama Press, 1984.

———. "Manufacturing Cannon in the Confederacy." *Civil War Times Illustrated* 12, no. 7 (November 1973): 4–11.

Davis, William C. *Duel Between the First Ironclads*. Baton Rouge: Louisiana State University Press, 1975.

———. *Jefferson Davis, the Man and His Hour: A Biography*. New York: Harper-Collins, 1991.

———. ed. *The Image of War, 1861–1865*. 6 vols. Garden City: Doubleday, 1982.

Dederer, John Morgan. "The Origins of Robert E. Lee's Bold Generalship: A Reinterpretation." *Military Affairs* 46 (1985): 117–23.

Denson, C. B. "William Henry Chase Whiting." *Southern Historical Society Papers* 26 (1898): 137–49.

Dew, Charles B. *Ironmaker to the Confederacy: Joseph R. Anderson and the Tredegar Iron Works*. Wilmington, NC: Broadfoot, 1987.

Dickert, Augustus P. *History of Kershaw's Brigade*. Newberry, SC: Elber H. Aull, 1899.

Dictionary of American Biography. 11 vols. Edited by Dumas Malone et al. New York: E. P. Dutton, 1955.

Divine, John E. *Eighth Virginia Infantry.* 1st ed. Lynchburg, VA: H. E. Howard, 1983.

Dowdey, Clifford. *The Seven Days: The Emergence of Robert E. Lee.* New York: Bonanza, 1978.

Driver, Robert J. Jr. *Fifty-second Virginia Infantry.* Lynchburg, VA: H. E. Howard, 1986.

Durham, Walter T. *Nashville, the Occupied City: The First Eighteen Months, February 16, 1862 to June 30, 1863.* Nashville: Tennessee Historical Society, 1985.

Durkin, Joseph T. *The Randolphs: The Story of a Virginia Family.* New York: Bobbs-Merrill, 1946.

————. *Stephen R. Mallory, Confederate Naval Chief.* Chapel Hill: University of North Carolina Press, 1936.

Eckenrode, *The Randolphs: The Story of a Virginia Family.* New York: Bobbs-Merrill, 1946.

Elliot, Ellsworth. *West Point in the Confederacy.* New York: G. A. Baker, 1914.

Evans, Eli N. *Judah P. Benjamin, the Jewish Confederate.* New York: Macmillan, 1988.

Faust, Patricia, ed. *Historical Times Illustrated Encyclopedia of the Civil War.* New York: Harper and Row, 1986.

Ferguson, Ernest. *Ashes of Glory: Richmond at War.* New York: Vintage, 1996.

Fields, Frank E. Jr. *Twenty-eighth Virginia Infantry.* 1st ed. Lynchburg, VA: H. E. Howard, 1985.

Fleming, Walter L. "Jefferson Davis at West Point." *Publications of the Mississippi Historical Society* 10 (1909): 261–89.

Foote, Shelby. *The Civil War: A Narrative.* 3 vols. New York: Random House, 1974.

Freeman, Douglas Southall. *Lee's Lieutenants: A Study in Command.* 3 vols. New York: Charles Scribner's, 1942–1944.

————. *R. E. Lee: A Biography.* 4 vols. New York: Charles Scribner's, 1935.

Frye, Dennis E. *Second Virginia Infantry.* Lynchburg, VA: H. E. Howard, 1984.

Gallagher, Gary W. *Stephen Dodson Ramseur, Lee's Gallant General.* Chapel Hill: University of North Carolina Press, 1985.

Glathaar, Joseph T. *Partners in Command: The Relationships Between Leaders in the Civil War.* New York: Free Press, 1994.

Goff, Richard D. *Confederate Supply.* Durham, NC: Duke University Press, 1969.

Govan, Gilbert, and James W. Livingood. *A Different Valor: The Story of General Joseph E. Johnston, C.S.A.* New York: Bobbs-Merrill, 1956.

Grimsley, Mark. "Jackson: The Wrath of God." *Civil War Times Illustrated* 23, no. 1 (March 1984): 1–19.

————. "Rear Guard at Williamsburg." *Civil War Times Illustrated* 24, no. 3 (May 1985): 10–13.

Hattaway, Hermann, and Archer Jones. *How the North Won: A Military History of the Civil War.* Urbana: University of Illinois Press, 1983.

Hamlin, Percy Gatling. *"Old Bald Head" (General R. S. Ewell): The Portrait of a Soldier.* Strasburg, VA: Shenandoah Publishing House, 1940.

Hanson, Joseph Mills. *Bull Run Remembers: The History, Traditions and Landmarks of the Manassas (Bull Run) Campaigns Before Washington, 1861–1862 .* Manassas, VA: National Capitol Publishers, 1953.

Hay, Thomas Robson. "The Davis-Hood-Johnston Controversy of 1864." *Mississippi Valley Historical Review* 11 (June 1924): 116–44.

Heitman, Francis B. *Historical Register and Dictionary of the United States Army.* 2 vols. Washington, DC: GPO, 1903.

Hittle, J. D. *The Military Staff, Its History and Development.* Harrisburg, PA: Stackpole, 1961.

Horn, Stanley F. *The Army of Tennessee.* 1952. Reprint, Wilmington, NC: Broadfoot, 1987.

Hotchkiss, Jedediah. *Virginia.* Vol. 3 of *Confederate Military History.* Edited by Clement Evans. Expanded edition. Dayton, OH: Morningside, 1975.

Hughes, Robert M. *General Johnston.* New York, 1893.

Hume, Edgar Erskine. *Peter Johnston, Junior: Virginia Soldier and Jurist.* Charlottesville, VA: Historical Publishing Company, 1935.

James, Alfred P. "General Joseph Eggleston Johnston, Storm Center of the Confederacy." *Mississippi Valley Historical Review* 14, no. 3 (December 1927): 223–49.

Johnson, Bradley T. *A Memoir of the Life and Public Service of Joseph E. Johnston.* Baltimore: R. H. Woodward, 1891.

Johnston, Angus James, II. *Virginia Railroads in the Civil War.* Chapel Hill: University of North Carolina Press, 1961.

Jones, Archer. *Confederate Strategy from Shiloh to Vicksburg.* Baton Rouge: Louisiana State University Press, 1961.

Jones, J. William. *Life and Letters of Robert Edward Lee, Soldier and Man.* New York: Neale, 1906.

Jones, Terry L. *Lee's Tigers: The Louisiana Infantry in the Army of Northern Virginia.* Baton Rouge: Louisiana State University Press, 1987.

Kendrick, Burton J. *Statesmen of the Lost Cause: Jefferson Davis and His Cabinet.* Boston: Little, Brown, 1939.

Klein, Maury. *Edward Porter Alexander.* Athens: University of Georgia Press, 1971.

Krick, Robert E. L. *Fortieth Virginia Infantry.* Lynchburg, VA: H. E. Howard, 1985.

Krick, Robert K. *Lee's Colonels: A Biographical Register of the Field Officers of the Army of Northern Virginia.* 2d ed., rev. Dayton, OH: Morningside, 1984.

———. *Ninth Virginia Cavalry.* Lynchburg, VA: H. E. Howard, 1982.

———. *Thirtieth Virginia Infantry.* Lynchburg, VA: H. E. Howard, 1983.

Lash, Jeffrey N. *Destroyer of the Iron Horse: General Joseph E. Johnston and Confederate Rail Transport, 1861–1865.* Kent, OH: Kent State University Press, 1991.

Livermore, Thomas L. *Numbers and Losses in the Civil War in America, 1861–1865.* 1900. Reprint, Dayton, OH: Morningside, 1986.

Long, Armistead L. *Memoirs of Robert E. Lee.* New York, 1886.

Luvaas, Jay. "An Appraisal of Joseph E. Johnston." *Civil War Times Illustrated* 4, no. 9 (January 1966): 4–11.

McDonough, James L. *Shiloh—In Hell Before Night.* Knoxville: University of Tennessee Press, 1977.

McMurry, Richard M. "'The *Enemy* at Richmond': Joseph E. Johnston and the Confederate Government." *Civil War History* 28 (March 1981): 5–31.

———. *John Bell Hood and the War for Southern Independence.* Lexington: University Press of Kentucky, 1982.

———. "Ole Joe in Virginia: Gen. Joseph E. Johnston's 1861–1862 Period of Command in the East." In *Leadership and Command in the American Civil War*. Edited by Steven E. Woodworth. Campbell, CA: Savas Woodbury, 1995.

————. "A Policy So Disastrous: Gen. Joseph E. Johnston's Atlanta Campaign." In *The Campaign for Atlanta and Sherman's March to the Sea*. Edited by Theodore Savas and David A. Woodbury. Vol. 2. Campbell, CA: Savas Woodbury, 1994.

————. *Two Great Rebel Armies: An Essay in Confederate Military History*. Chapel Hill: University of North Carolina Press, 1989.

McPherson, James M. *Battle Cry of Freedom: The Civil War Era*. New York: Oxford University Press, 1988.

Manarin, Louis H. "Lee in Command: Strategical and Tactical Policies." Ph.D. diss., Duke University, 1965.

Martin, David G. "Civil War Artillery." *Strategy and Tactics* 81 (July/August 1980): 18–19.

Martin, Samuel J. "The Complex Confederate." *Civil War Times Illustrated* 25, no. 2 (April 1986): 26–35.

Maurice, Frederick. *Robert E. Lee the Soldier*. Boston: Houghton Mifflin, 1925.

Meade, Robert Douthat. *Judah P. Benjamin, Confederate Statesman*. New York: Oxford University Press, 1943.

————. "The Relations Between Judah P. Benjamin and Jefferson Davis: Some New Light on the Working of the Confederate Machine." *Journal of Southern History* 5, no. 4 (November 1939): 367–79.

Melvin, Philip. "Stephen Russell Mallory, Southern Naval Statesman." *Journal of Southern History* 10, no. 2 (May 1944): 185–202.

Miller, William J., ed. *The Peninsula Campaign: Yorktown to Seven Days*. 3 vols. to date. Campbell, CA: Savas, 1997.

Naval History Division, Naval Department, compilers. *Civil War Naval Chronology, 1861–1865*. 6 vols. Washington, DC: GPO, 1971.

Newton, Steven H. *The Battle of Seven Pines, May 31–June 1, 1862*. Lynchburg, VA: H. E. Howard, 1991.

————. "The Engagement at Eltham's Landing. *Civil War* (May/June 1995): 42.

————. "Johnston and Davis at Seven Pines: The Uncertainty Principle in Action." *The Peninsula Campaign of 1862: Yorktown to Seven Days*. Edited by William J. Miller. Vol. 3. Campbell, CA: Savas, 1997.

————. "Joseph E. Johnston and the Defense of Richmond, January–May 1862." Ph.D. diss., College of William and Mary, 1989.

————. "Seven Pines." *Civil War* (May/June 1995): 49.

Nichols, James L. *Confederate Engineers*. Tuscaloosa, AL: Confederate Publishing, 1957.

Osborne, Charles C. *Jubal: The Life and Times of General Jubal A. Early, CSA, Defender of the Lost Cause*. Baton Rouge: Louisiana State University Press, 1992.

Owsley, Frank L. "Local Defense and the Overthrow of the Confederacy." *Mississippi Valley Historical Review* 11, no. 4 (March 1925): 462–504.

————. *State Rights in the Confederacy*. Chicago: University of Chicago Press, 1925.

Parish, Peter J. *The American Civil War*. New York: Holmes and Meier, 1975.

Patrick, Rembert. *Jefferson Davis and His Cabinet*. Baton Rouge: Louisiana State University Press, 1944.

Piston, William Garrett. *Lee's Tarnished Lieutenant: James Longstreet and His Place in Southern History*. Athens: University of Georgia Press, 1987.

Rankin, Thomas M. *Twenty-third Virginia Infantry*. Lynchburg, VA: H. E. Howard, 1985.

Riggs, David F. *Seventh Virginia Infantry*. Lynchburg, VA: H. E. Howard, 1982.

Robertson, James I. *Eighteenth Virginia Infantry*. Lynchburg, VA: H. E. Howard, 1984.

————. *Fourth Virginia Infantry*. Lynchburg, VA: H. E. Howard, 1982.

————. *General A. P. Hill: The Story of a Confederate Warrior*. New York: Random House, 1987.

Roland, Charles. *Albert Sidney Johnston: Soldier of Three Republics*. Austin: University of Texas Press, 1964.

Sanger, Donald B., and Thomas Robson Hay. *James Longstreet*. Baton Rouge: Louisiana State University Press, 1952.

Scharf, J. Thomas. *History of the Confederate States Navy from Its Organization to the Surrender of Its Last Vessel*. New York, 1887.

Schwab, John C. *The Confederate States of America, 1861–1865: A Financial and Industrial History of the South During the Civil War*. New Haven: Yale University Press, 1913.

Sears, Stephen W. *George B. McClellan: The Young Napoleon*. New York: Ticknor and Fields, 1988.

————. *To the Gates of Richmond: The Peninsula Campaign*. New York: Ticknor and Fields, 1992.

Sifakis, Stewart. *Who Was Who in the Civil War*. New York: Facts on File, 1988.

Stark, Richard B. "Surgeons and Surgical Care of the Confederate States Army." *Virginia Medical Monthly* 88, no. 10 (1973): 605–9.

Starr, Stephen Z. *The Union Cavalry in the Civil War*. 3 vols. Baton Rouge: Louisiana State University Press, 1979.

Stiles, Kenneth L. *Fourth Virginia Cavalry*. Lynchburg, VA: H. E. Howard, 1985.

Stohlman, Robert F. Jr. *The Powerless Position: The Commanding General of the Army of the United States, 1864–1903*. Manhattan: Kansas State University Press, 1975.

Stover, John F. *Iron Road to the West: American Railroads in the 1850s*. New York: Columbia University Press, 1987.

Sublett, Charles W. *Fifty-seventh Virginia Infantry*. Lynchburg, VA: H. E. Howard, 1985.

Summers, Lewis P. *History of Southwest Virginia, 1746–1786; Washington County, 1777–1780*. Richmond: J. L. Hill, 1903.

Swinton, William. *Campaigns of the Army of the Potomac: A Critical History of Operations in Virginia, Maryland, and Pennsylvania from the Commencement to the Close of the War, 1861–1865*. Revised edition. New York: University Publishing, 1881.

Symonds, Craig L. *Joseph E. Johnston: A Civil War Biography*. New York: W. W. Norton, 1992.

Tanner, Robert G. *Stonewall in the Valley: Thomas J. "Stonewall" Jackson's Shenandoah Valley Campaign of 1862*. Garden City: Doubleday, 1976.

Thomas, Emory. *Bold Dragoon: The Life of J. E. B. Stuart*. New York: Harper and Row, 1986.

————. *The Confederate State of Richmond*. Austin: University of Texas Press, 1971.

————. *Robert E. Lee: A Biography*. New York: W. W. Norton, 1995.

Trask, Benjamin H. *Ninth Virginia Infantry*. Lynchburg, VA: H. E. Howard, 1984.

Turner, Charles W. "The Virginia Central Railroad at War, 1861–1865." *Journal of Southern History* 12, no. 4 (November 1946): 510–33.

U.S. Navy Department. *Official Records of the Union and Confederate Navies in the War of the Rebellion*. 30 vols. Washington, DC: GPO, 1896–1922.

U.S. War Department. *The War of the Rebellion: A Compilation of the Official Records of the Union and Confederate Armies*. 128 vols. Washington, DC: GPO, 1880–1901.

Utley, Robert M. *Frontiersmen in Blue: The United States Army and the Indian, 1848–1865*. Lincoln: University of Nebraska Press, 1967.

Wakelyn, Jon L. *Biographical Dictionary of the Confederacy*. Westport, CT: Greenwood Press, 1977.

Wallace, Lee A. Jr. *First Virginia Infantry*. Lynchburg, VA: H. E. Howard, 1985.

———. *A Guide to Virginia Military Organizations, 1861–1865*. 2d ed., rev. Lynchburg, VA: H. E. Howard, 1986.

———. *Third Virginia Infantry*. Lynchburg, VA: H. E. Howard, 1986.

Warner, Ezra. *Generals in Gray: Lives of the Confederate Commanders*. Baton Rouge: Louisiana State University Press, 1959.

Weigley, Russell F. *History of the United States Army*. Enlarged edition. Bloomington: Indiana University Press, 1984.

Wellman, Manly Wade. *Giant in Gray: A Biography of Wade Hampton of South Carolina*. New York: Charles Scribner's, 1949.

Wert, Jeffrey. *General James Longstreet, the Confederacy's Most Controversial Soldier: A Biography*. New York: Simon and Schuster, 1993.

———. "I Am so Unlike Other Folks." *Civil War Times Illustrated* 28, no. 2 (April 1989): 14–21.

———. "Lee's First Year of the War." *Civil War Times Illustrated* 12, no. 8 (December 1974): 4–9.

White, Laura. *Robert Barnwell Rhett: Father of Secession*. New York: Century, 1931.

Wiatt, Alex L. *Twenty-sixth Virginia Infantry*. Lynchburg, VA: H. E. Howard, 1984.

Wiley, Bell I. *The Life of Johny Reb, the Common Soldier of the Confederacy*. 1943. Reprint, Baton Rouge: Louisiana State University Press, 1978.

Williams, T. Harry. "Freeman, Historian of the Civil War: An Appraisal." *Journal of Southern History* 21, no. 1 (February 1955): 45–54.

Wise, George. *History of the Seventeenth Virginia Infantry, C.S.A.* Baltimore, 1870.

Wise, Jennings C. *The Long Arm of Lee, or the History of the Artillery of the Army of Northern Virginia*. 1915. Reprint, New York: Oxford University Press, 1959, 1 vol. edition.

Wise, Stephen R. *Lifeline of the Confederacy: Blockade Running During the Civil War*. Columbia: University of South Carolina Press, 1988.

Woodworth, Steven E. "Dark Portents: Confederate Command at Williamsburg," In *The Peninsula Campaign of 1862: Yorktown to Seven Days*. Edited by William J. Miller. Vol. 3. Campbell, CA: Savas, 1997.

———. *Davis and Lee at War*. Lawrence: University Press of Kansas, 1995.

Wright, Marcus J. *List of Staff Officers of the Confederate Army, 1861–1865*. Washington, DC, 1891.

Yearns, Wilfred Buck. *The Confederate Congress*. Athens: University of Georgia Press, 1960.

INDEX